The Thrill Makers

The publisher gratefully acknowledges the generous support of the Humanities Endowment Fund of the University of California Press Foundation.

The Thrill Makers

Celebrity, Masculinity, and Stunt Performance

Jacob Smith

UNIVERSITY OF CALIFORNIA PRESS
Berkeley · Los Angeles · London

University of California Press, one of the most distinguished university presses in the United States, enriches
lives around the world by advancing scholarship in the
humanities, social sciences, and natural sciences. Its activities are supported by the UC Press Foundation and by
philanthropic contributions from individuals and institutions. For more information, visit www.ucpress.edu.

University of California Press
Berkeley and Los Angeles, California

University of California Press, Ltd.
London, England

Library of Congress Cataloging-in-Publication Data

Smith, Jacob, 1970–
    The thrill makers : celebrity, masculinity, and stunt
performance / Jacob Smith.
        p.   cm.
    Includes bibliographical references and index.
    ISBN 978-0-520-27088-6 (cloth : alk. paper)
    ISBN 978-0-520-27089-3 (pbk. : alk. paper)
    1. Stunt performers—United States—History.
2. Daredevils—United States—History.   I. Title.
    PN1995.9.S7S65   2012
    791.4302'8092—dc23
                                    2011045472

21 20 19 18 17 16 15 14 13 12

10 9 8 7 6 5 4 3 2 1

Contents

Illustrations

Acknowledgments

Many people helped me to gather research materials for this book, and I would like to thank the staff at the Robert L. Parkinson Library and Research Center in Baraboo, Wisconsin; the National Fairgrounds Archive at the University of Sheffield; the Buffalo and Erie County Public Library; Tim Tindall and the Archives Reference Team at the Smithsonian National Air and Space Museum; the British Film Institute; the Indiana University Herman B. Wells Library; Jenny Romero at the Special Collections Department of the Margaret Herrick Library in Los Angeles; and Lutz Bacher.

Several portions of *The Thrill Makers* have appeared elsewhere in an earlier form. Parts of chapter 1 appeared in "The Adventures of the Bridge Jumper," *Celebrity Studies* 1, no. 1 (Spring 2010). Parts of chapter 2 appeared in "The Adventures of the Human Fly, 1830–1930," *Early Popular Visual Culture* 6, no. 1 (April 2008), and in *Journal of Film and Video* 56, no. 3 (Fall 2004) © 2004 by the Board of Trustees of the University of Illinois. Used with permission of the University of Illinois Press.

Various colleagues and friends have inspired and encouraged this work. My interest in stunt work began after Dale Lawrence shared with me his appreciation for early Burt Reynolds movies. Bob Rehak, Barb Klinger, Jim Naremore, Richard Bauman, Paula Amad, and Chris Anderson were all crucial to the early stages of the project during my studies at Indiana University. Greg Waller offered guidance and friendship in the book's later stages. Matthew Solomon was a key advisor every step of the way, and I am profoundly grateful for all of his insight and friendship.

The transatlantic component of the book owes much to my time at the University of Nottingham, and thanks are due to colleagues there, especially Roberta Pearson, Paul Grainge, Mark Gallagher, Dave Murray, Peter Messent, Vivien Miller, Matthew Pethers, Tony Hutchison, and Ian Brookes. Vanessa Toulmin was extremely generous with her time and resources, and I learned much from the participants at conferences in Exeter and Sheffield. Michael Eaton kindly listened to some of my ideas and shared my enthusiasm for cat burglars. Northwestern colleagues have been supportive during the final stages of the book: Scott Curtis, Lynn Spigel, Jeff Sconce, Max Dawson, Jacqueline Stewart, Mimi White, Dave and Deb Tolchinsky, Eric Patrick, John Haas, Aldis Kaza, and Michele Yamada.

I am particularly grateful to everyone at the University of California Press, where it continues to be my great pleasure to be able to publish my work. Sharron Wood and Jacqueline Volin did much to polish the manuscript in its final stages. I could not ask for a better editor than Mary Francis, who guided this project with her usual grace and wisdom. I was given the gift of two readers' reports that were truly remarkable for their careful engagement and breadth of knowledge. Their suggestions did much to improve the book.

My family continues to make my work possible through their love and support. Freda has always played an essential role in my research, but it was a real pleasure to draw upon her insights as a writer in our mutual fascination with some of the colorful biographies I uncovered. The book, however, is dedicated to the two most important stuntmen in my life, Jonah and Henry, who have taught me more than all the research in the world.

Introduction

In December 1916 the *New York Tribune* published an article about a group of "anonymous heroes" who were appearing daily on cinema screens across the country. These heroes, the "understudies of the great actors in the movie thrillers," were those who did "stunts" in the movies. The "Stunt Men's Club" was said to include "fallers," who jumped from high places; swimmers and divers; lion and tiger fighters; and steeplejacks who specialized in scaling walls and chimneys.[1] Notably, the article was framed as the revelation of a secret: these stunt performers were "unheralded, unknown," and "unsung"; their names never appeared on film programs, nor were their pictures featured in theater lobbies or in film magazines. Though readers of the *New York Tribune* may not have known the members of the Stunt Men's Club by name, they were certainly aware of "fallers" like Steve Brodie, "swimmers" like Paul Boyton, lion tamers like Jack Bonavita, and steeplejacks like Rodman Law. Thrilling celebrities such as these may have been relegated to the role of understudy to "great actors" in 1916, but there was nothing "unheralded" or "unsung" about bridge jumpers, human flies, lion tamers, and aeronauts in the decades before cinema. Some rose from obscurity to entertain Queen Victoria; some were pioneers of modern media publicity, appearing on the front pages of national newspapers and in early motion picture newsreels; and some performed before thousands of awestruck fans at state fairgrounds and aviation meets. These "thrill makers," as they were sometimes called in the press, were part of a largely forgotten cast of media celebrities who developed the performances that became the stock-in-trade of the Stunt Men's Club.

This book explores the history of American stunt performance both *in* the cinema and *before* the cinema, and it demonstrates the key role played by a cohort of popular stunt entertainers in the construction of modern media spectacle and celebrity. Stunt performers from diverse traditions became a crucial component of Hollywood production, taking the place of star actors during the filming of dangerous scenes and providing thrilling action sequences for the cinema audience. For example, circus lion tamers were celebrities of the nineteenth-century entertainment world and later doubled for Hollywood stars in scenes featuring wild animals; Harold Lloyd's famous antics on skyscrapers in films such as *Safety Last* (1923) drew upon the iconography of "human flies" who generated thrills and publicity by climbing public buildings; and the skills of fairground stunt pilots were a key ingredient in a cycle of Hollywood aviation films. The film industry repackaged the spectacle of these nineteenth- and early twentieth-century popular entertainments, even as the modern media did much to push their original sites of performance at circuses, variety theaters, dime museums, and fairgrounds to the cultural periphery.

The Thrill Makers describes the process by which nineteenth-century popular entertainments were incorporated into the cinema, and in so doing it explores the ways in which a new medium drew on earlier and adjacent expressive forms. Jay David Bolter and Richard Grusin describe this as the process of "remediation," in which one medium is represented in another. André Gaudreault refers to the "intermedial status" of the cinema and writes that it is "essential for anyone interested in understanding how the cinema came to be" to take this "alternate route through the intermedial relationships of cinema at its conception."[2] Film scholars have explored dynamics of remediation and intermediality in the cinema in terms of entertainments such as the panorama, the legitimate stage, melodrama, museums, vaudeville, and magic shows. Stunt performance offers a new approach to the intermedial status of the cinema, a less well traveled "alternate route" that illuminates hitherto unexplored tensions and synergies between film and adjacent entertainments.

Raymond Williams asserts that new cultural forms and practices always encounter existing ones, and, though some become dominant, they coexist with the remains of previous "residual" social formations still on the cultural scene.[3] *The Thrill Makers* tracks a set of entertainment traditions and celebrity performers as they emerged during the nineteenth century, achieved varying degrees of cultural visibility, and then were displaced by a new set of media forms and celebrities, most significantly by the cinema and film stars. Williams notes the potential for residual forms to have an alternative relation to the dominant culture, and one of the goals of this book is to make readers "see double," that is, to draw attention to the unheralded labor of stunt doubles and, by extension, to an alternative history of popular entertainment. Stuart Hall writes that popular culture is a field upon which different social groups struggle over cultural meaning such that some forms and practices become central while others are actively marginalized. That the performers described in this book came to be actively marginalized in the era of the modern media is indicated by their relegation to the unsung domain of the Stunt Men's Club, but their history casts an illuminating sidelight on what became the dominant mode of media celebrity and helps us to understand a broader range of popular entertainment during a critical period in the development of the modern media.[4]

One story that this book tells involves the struggle between adjacent forms of popular entertainment, the incorporation of popular performance traditions into the modern media, and the power dynamics that exist between residual and dominant forms of culture, but stunt performance could seem "alternative" even before its integration into Hollywood film production. In fact, the thrill makers were remarkably adept at developing performance forms that spoke to a wide range of class constituencies and sustained multiple interpretations. In other words, their acts were "multiply accented." Marxist literary theorist V. N. Volosinov wrote that since the members of different social classes use the same language, cultural signs become "an arena of the class struggle" open to a variety of inflection and meanings, what Volosinov terms the "multi-accentuality of the ideological sign."[5] Historian Michael Denning took Volosinov's concept of multiaccentuality as a theoretical framework for his analysis of the conflicting accents found in nineteenth-century dime novels.[6] Following Denning, I understand the acts of the thrill makers as a "contested terrain, a field of cultural conflict where signs with wide appeal and resonance take on contradictory accents."[7] Though the bridge jumpers, human flies, lion tamers, and aeronauts described in the following chapters enacted public performances that were open to multiple meanings, the alternative, and frequently working-class, accents of their acts were strong: some embodied a culture of working-class sporting men at odds with those who sought to maintain Victorian models of fame; some were skilled construction workers or "mechanics" who went against the grain of trends in American industry; and some interacted with wild animals in a way that was anathema to middle-class reformers. All of these performers were purveyors of "body techniques" that recalled a kind of skilled artisanal labor that was disappearing in an era of mass consumption, the deskilling of factory work, and the rise of white-collar office work, and all of them came to play an integral but unpublicized role in the promotion of the film industry's star players.

One benefit of taking the body techniques of stunt performance as an alternate route through the cinema is that it heeds Rick Altman's call for a "performer-oriented" approach to film history. Altman reminds us that nineteenth-century American entertainment was heavily dominated by performers and organized around acts and the people who performed them as opposed to around media products. Altman suggests that scholars must put aside a "firmly entrenched film-oriented approach to cinema in favor of a performer-oriented position."[8] The study of stunt performers enables a fresh perspective on cinematic spectacle, one based not on the analysis of editing techniques or special effects, but on the performers who embodied and created cinematic thrills and therefore on the permeable boundaries that existed between film technology and body technique. As an example of how the study of cinema spectacle has tended to privilege the cinematic apparatus at the expense of performance, consider film theorist Francesco Casetti's discussion of cinema's "excited gaze."[9] Casetti gives examples primarily in terms of film editing: the parallel editing in D.W. Griffith's *Intolerance* (1916), the montage in Sergei Eisenstein's *Old and New* (1929), and contrasting musical numbers in *Gold Diggers of 1933* (1933). Casetti also compares the cinema to amusement park attractions like the roller coaster and to instruments of scientific observation. Sometimes the cinema is a merry-go-round, he writes; "sometimes it is a telescope, sometimes it is an experimental painting, sometimes a self-reflexive novel. It is each of these things, in forms that are often extreme, and it is a place in which the opposites meet, until they are finally fit."[10] What is missing from this coverage of cinema's excited gaze is performance. Casetti's focus is so squarely on the sensory experience of cinema technique and the mechanisms of mass amusement that one might forget that the amusement parks, circuses, fairgrounds, and cinema screens of this era were also the sites of embodied performances that were part of rich historical traditions of popular entertainment. *The Thrill Makers* brings genealogies of these performance traditions to the history of cinema.[11]

Besides taking up Rick Altman's call for a performer-oriented approach, the analysis of stuntwork expands what has typically counted as performance in film and television studies. Stuntwork involves the display of the body, but it differs from the exhibition of "physical peculiarities" in venues like the turn-of-the-century freak show, where the bodies on display were remarkable for what they were rather than what they did.[12] *The Thrill Makers* is concerned with performers who were remarkable for what they did but who were not engaged in the most commonly discussed modes of cinematic "doing": singing, dancing, and acting. The bridge jumpers, lion tamers, human flies, and aeronauts that populate this book specialized in dangerous activities whose vehicle was the body and whose acts had a visceral effect on audiences. Turn-of-the-century observers typically referred to the product created by such stuntwork as "thrills." In 1904 the *Atlanta Constitution* described a class of "thrill makers" who "trifle with death in feats that make the spectators hold their breath and the women in the crowd turn pale and hide their eyes."[13] This mode of entertainment can be understood as action that has been framed as performance. Richard Bauman defines *performance* as a mode of communication that formally sets itself off from everyday interaction, presenting itself to an audience for an evaluation of the performer's skill. Performers are accountable to and evaluated by their audiences and so must typically display a certain degree of communicative mastery.[14] By *action* I refer to Erving Goffman's notion of activities in which "chance-taking and resolution" are brought into "the same heated moment of experience." (I will discuss Goffman's notion of action in more detail in chapter 1.)[15] "Action" is among several of Goffman's concepts that guide this book. Goffman's work is well suited to the analysis of media performance because it offers a framework for discussing the social dimension of embodied behavior. Goffman was concerned with how the self is a product of "performances that individuals put on in social situations," and his fine-grained ethnographies of everyday interaction provide an invaluable theoretical vocabulary for understanding the nuances of social performances both on and off the screen.[16] In other words, Goffman's theories on the nature of social interaction help us to talk about the interpenetration of media texts and contexts, and to take seriously the dense social meanings to be found in the particular accents and gestures of media performance.

The four chapters that follow are archaeologies of stunt performance that explore both the cinema and the era before the cinema, and so I have faced the challenge of writing about embodied actions that can be experienced only through written historical documents. Historian Rhys Isaac notes that although direct observation cannot be applied to "social worlds long vanished," a large proportion of historical data consists of "accounts of the doings of particular people in particular circumstances": in documents from the past, Isaac writes, the historian can occasionally find vivid glimpses "of *people doing things.*" Isaac holds that, with patient attention to "the processes of reporting," it is possible to collect "action-statements" and set about interpreting them.[17] *The Thrill Makers* investigates four interrelated genres of action-statements using evidence from historical documents and media texts. The physical settings in which these action-statements took place were a vital part of their cultural meaning. Joseph Roach refers to places like the marketplace, theater district, city square, or burial ground as "vortices of behavior," sites that provide "the crux in the semiotext" of the cityscape, where "the gravitational pull of social necessity brings audiences together and produces performers . . . from their midst."[18] The acts of the thrill makers coevolved with vortices in the modern city, convening audiences around "action as performance" on modern steel suspension bridges, the sides of skyscrapers, in steel circus cages, and at fairgrounds and aerodromes.[19] Film scholars and cultural historians have frequently described the experience of "shock" caused by the sensory environment of the modern city. The thrill makers developed stunts that went beyond absorbing that shock to enact a vital response to the scale of modern experience.

Urban vortices of behavior drew crowds, and performing on or around them could make one famous. For Goffman, action was a heightened mode in the performance of self since social maneuvering took place in moments of accelerated consequence. The "peculiar appeal" of action, Goffman writes, is that it provides a means for displaying character, and so the self "can be voluntarily subjected to re-creation."[20] Stunt performers were adept at re-creating themselves in their displays of spectacular action, and *The Thrill Makers* provides a new perspective on media celebrity in the nineteenth and early twentieth centuries. Historians of celebrity culture have described how a number of social and technological innovations surrounding the medium of print greatly enhanced the "scope and intensity" of renown by the mid-1800s.[21] The thrill makers have much to tell us about the ways in which those new media forms could be mobilized in order to create renown in the decades around the turn of the twentieth century. Modern celebrity has often been understood in terms of the increasingly intimate depiction of the individual faces and voices of actors or politicians made possible by technological developments in media representation. Historian Warren Susman famously described this as a shift from a culture of "character" to a culture of "personality."[22] The thrill makers operated by a related yet distinct logic of media celebrity by which accounts and images of spectacular bodily performances seen from a distance were circulated in newspapers, newsreels, and narrative films.

Moreover, the thrill makers' embodiment of working-class subcultural styles and artisanal skills complicates a tendency to view early twentieth-century celebrity in terms of a binary between "idols of production," such as politicians and captains of industry, and "idols of consumption" from the realm of popular entertainment. The quintessential "idols of consumption" were those Hollywood workers whose names and faces *did* appear on film programs, marquees, and magazines: movie stars. In his seminal work on early American film stardom, Richard deCordova traced the emergence of the film star in popular discourse.[23] If, as I argued above, the analysis of cinematic spectacle has privileged the apparatus and filmic techniques, then deCordova's work privileges dramatic acting as the model for screen performance at the expense of other traditions. The thrill makers were a vivid embodiment of what Jennifer M. Bean has called a "competing logic" of early film stardom at the same time that they became an essential component of the Hollywood star system. As actors became increasingly important as economic commodities for film companies, they had to be protected from the potentially dangerous work of stunts. The fallers, lion fighters, and steeplejacks who became stunt performers played a crucial, yet often invisible, role in structuring film stardom. Hollywood stars—the paradigmatic example of the modern media celebrity—thus coevolved with and relied upon specialized stunt performers whose role it was to "double" the actors. *The Thrill Makers* gives names, faces, and histories to those doubles, and in doing so it offers a new perspective on the Hollywood star system and the dynamics of screen labor.

The 1916 *New York Tribune* article described above made passing reference to a handful of female wire walkers, swimmers, and "devil-may-care motorists" who provided thrills for the movies, but its language and emphasis made clear that this was understood as a men's club. The performers in the traditions under examination here were overwhelmingly male, and their acts spoke to audiences about shifting conceptions of masculinity. I agree with Gail Bederman that manhood is best seen as a "continual, dynamic process," and that at every point in history multiple and often contradictory ideas about manhood are available to "explain what men are, how they ought to behave, and what sorts of powers and authorities they may claim, as men."[24] Goffman argues that gender, like all social roles, is something achieved through socially and historically determined interaction, and he defines conventionalized appearances and behaviors meant to indicate a gendered self as "gender displays."[25] Goffman also claimed that "action" in Western cultures seemed to belong to "the cult of masculinity."[26] The thrill makers were specialists in action framed as gender display, and their acts reflected and refracted tensions and ambiguities in the ideologies of American manhood. Lion tamers, bridge jumpers, human flies, and stunt aviators all created dramatic forms in which notions of male heroism could be enacted, experienced, and discussed. To borrow a phrase from Clifford Geertz, the thrill makers provided a "sentimental education" in turn-of-the-century Western masculinity, the form of their acts serving as a powerful nexus for the affective exploration of the various interconnected cultural discourses of modern manhood.[27]

My analysis of the gender displays enacted by the thrill makers supplements the scholarly work done on film actors and so broadens our understanding of the multiple and often contradictory ideas about manhood that were in circulation during the decades around the turn of the twentieth century. In his examination of Eugen Sandow, Harry Houdini, and Edgar Rice Burroughs, John Kasson wrote that white male bodies became powerful symbols of modernity at the same time that they revealed "the degree to which thinking about masculinity in this period meant thinking about sexual and racial dominance as well."[28] As we shall see, the thrill makers' displays of white masculinity were similarly entangled with discourses about class, race, and femininity. Ironically, though the acts of the thrill makers were frequently understood to be the province of an exclusively male prowess, these same supposedly male performance forms became a resource for female performers who intervened in them and so called into question conventional definitions of gender.

My goal, then, is for the history of the thrill makers to bring with it a surplus of additional insights into the dynamics of Hollywood film production and the place of cinema in the larger history of American popular entertainment. There are many benefits to an analysis of Hollywood stunt performance and the nineteenth-century traditions from which it emerged: it offers a performance-centered approach to film history that explores the nature of labor in the modern cultural industries; it helps us to grasp the intermedial links between cinema and other forms of entertainment; and it illuminates cinema stardom by juxtaposing it with competing models of male celebrity.

With this overview of my larger goals in mind, I will now turn to the structure of the book. Each of the first four chapters tracks a different genealogy of nineteenth-century stunt performance up to and across the threshold of American cinema. In all of these cases the historical frame begins in the nineteenth century and ends in the first three decades of Hollywood film: chapter 1 ends just before the birth of Hollywood cinema; chapter 2 culminates in the birth of the Hollywood star system and an analysis of Harold Lloyd's *Safety Last* (1923) and Dorothy Devore's *Hold Your Breath* (1924); chapter 3 focuses on a cycle of films of the early 1930s that made use of wild animals and circus performers; and chapter 4 looks at airplane stuntwork in films of the 1920s and 1930s.

The author of the 1916 article in the *New York Tribune* sought to illustrate the novelty of the Stunt Men's Club by comparing it to an earlier performer whose name had become synonymous with dangerous stunts: "Steve Brodie has been out-brodied," the article claimed, since "falls from the Brooklyn Bridge and jumps from the decks of ocean steamers are now commonplace." Brodie is the subject of the central case study of chapter 1, which is concerned with a tradition of spectacular popular performance that developed in a close symbiotic relationship with the canals, rivers, docks, and waterfalls that drove the commerce of nineteenth-century industrial mill towns and shipping ports. The career of Steve Brodie, who claimed to have jumped from the Brooklyn Bridge in 1886, illustrates the dynamics of an incipient modern celebrity and its relationship to the mass media. Brodie achieved a particularly modern fame, one that was circulated by newspaper coverage and the popular stage. Brodie appropriated both modern architecture and the modern media to his own ends, creating a celebrity that combined the attractions of a workingmen's entertainment culture, the techniques of public relations, the spectacle of the modern cityscape, and a montage of real and prosthetic bodies. I will argue that Brodie's "art" not only encompassed a variety of nineteenth-century entertainment traditions but also prefigured the film star and the cinematic stuntman.

In chapter 2 I bring to light the tradition of traveling performers who billed themselves as the "Human Fly" and consider them in connection to early American cinema. Human flies developed a performance of spectacular male heroism in the first decades of the twentieth century, a period when a new type of urban architecture, modern modes of advertising and publicity, the motion picture newsreel, and film stardom were all emerging, all of which played a role in shaping the meaning of the human fly performance. Human flies appropriated tall buildings for their thrilling acts, and so, like the bridge jumpers described in chapter 1, their acts developed in tandem with changes taking place in the lived environment. Human flies explored vernacular techniques of promotion and publicity in feats of "action as performance" that found a place in the production of fiction films and motion picture newsreels. Rodman Law, whose spectacular performances included the scaling of tall buildings, serves as a key case study for the chapter. Law appeared in newspapers across the nation, as well as in early newsreels and action films. The chapter is framed by a discussion of the production and promotion of Harold Lloyd's *Safety Last* (1923), which reveals how Hollywood and its emerging star system both absorbed and obscured a rich tradition of spectacular entertainment that had run parallel to the American cinema. The history of that tradition also demonstrates the process whereby genealogies of performance are gendered: male human flies had to distinguish their labor from earlier, and primarily female, "ceiling walkers"; and the Dorothy Devore film *Hold Your Breath* (1924) reveals the discursive work required subsequently to frame the act for a female performer.

The filming of wild animal sequences has traditionally fallen to stunt performers, and legendary Hollywood stuntmen have devoted entire chapters of their memoirs to "animal adventures."[29] Like bridge jumpers and human flies, the lion tamers that I discuss in chapter 3 were popular celebrities before the development of the Hollywood star system. Lion tamers made their entrance on the cultural stage at the same time as modern zoos and circuses, and, like those institutions, they dramatized shifting notions of the natural world and Western colonialism. Lion tamers were frequently described as the embodiment of white male ideals, yet their acts betray the extent to which those ideals were bound up with anxieties about nonwhite bodies, and their status as paradigms of masculinity was complicated by the presence of death-defying female animal trainers. The film industry sought to repackage the spectacle of wild animal acts, and during the same years that Los Angeles became the center of American film production, that city also became a home for many zoos, circuses, and wild animal farms that provided animal performers for the cinema. Big cat acts posed certain problems for filmmakers, however, and the early 1930s mark a moment when the professionalization of stuntwork and developments in film technology facilitated the depiction of a new kind of interaction between human actors and wild animals. The MGM Tarzan films and lion tamer Clyde Beatty's star vehicle *The Big Cage* (1933) illustrate how Hollywood remediated the lion tamer act, and they also provide another example of how nineteenth-century performance traditions became part of Hollywood second unit production and the labor of uncredited stunt doubles.

In addition to falls from high places, dangerous tasks done on tall buildings, and work with wild animals, cinematic stuntwork also frequently involved "mechanical" stunts.[30] This form of stunt performance articulated a link between the motion picture and another quintessentially modern technology: the airplane. Note that 1903 saw both the release of Edwin S. Porter's landmark narrative film *The Great Train Robbery* and the Wright brothers' first successful flight in a heavier-than-air, motor-powered flying machine. At early public demonstrations and aviation meets, stunt flyers explored the entertainment function of the airplane and forged connections with filmmakers who were eager to exploit public interest in aviation. World War I increased the extent to which aviation was culturally coded as a masculine domain, as the glamorous image of the male combat pilot played an important role in wartime public relations campaigns. The prewar "birdman" and wartime flying ace emerged as prominent new forms of male celebrity. After the war, flyers traveled the country as itinerant barnstormers and applied their skills to Hollywood filmmaking as stunt performers who crashed their planes while the cameras rolled. Stunt flyers played a key role in a cycle of Hollywood air pictures, and they even produced a crossover film star in the person of wing walker Ormer Locklear, who starred in two feature films before his untimely death. Hollywood flyers provide a new perspective on the history of Hollywood labor and the economics of film performance, and the work of the stunt flyer even became the subject of RKO's *The Lost Squadron* (1932), which made a social critique by linking Hollywood production to the experience of warfare, with the stuntman as the metaphorical stand-in for the soldier.

These chapters describe a constellation of popular performance traditions that spoke to wide audiences about the nature of modern identity, work, and the lived environment, and that found an integral place in the most powerful and influential entertainment industry in the world: the Hollywood cinema. The fact that the performers who carried those traditions into the era of the modern media were something of an open secret paradoxically suggests their cultural importance: they were essential to, and yet potentially disruptive of, emerging structures of Hollywood spectacle, labor, stardom, publicity, and gender display. Stunt performers embodied a continuity of thrills during the decades that saw the rise of the media industries, and thus they can serve as cultural barometers for dynamics of intermediality, performance, celebrity, and masculinity in the modern era. Situating the performances of the thrill makers in a history of popular entertainment, celebrity, work, and male spectacle deepens our understanding of the affective experience of American cinema at the same time that it reminds us that Hollywood was not the only game in town.

CHAPTER I

The Adventures
of the Bridge Jumper

On July 22, 1886, a figure was seen falling from near the center of the Brooklyn Bridge. The body was in the air for about three seconds as it traversed the 135 feet from the bridge to the water, and after striking the East River it disappeared from sight for nearly half a minute. A man was soon pulled from the water into a tugboat and brought to shore, where he was promptly arrested for attempted suicide. By the time the jumper, named Steve Brodie, emerged after a brief stint in a police court cell, he had become an instant celebrity. Brodie was shown newspaper illustrations of his jump and signed a contract to appear in dime museums across the country. Newspapers around the United States published accounts of Brodie's leap, and tourists were soon crowding into Brodie's New York saloon in order to catch a glimpse of him. Within a decade he was a traveling performer on the stage, serving drinks in a stage replica of his Bowery Street saloon and reenacting his famous jump from the bridge.

Brodie's career has much to tell us about the emergence of modern media celebrity and the kinds of spectacular stunt performances that could be mobilized to create it in the years just before the cinema. Bridge jumpers like Brodie took the modern urban landscape as their stage and in so doing reinterpreted the city and reinvented themselves. During the same years that stunt performers like Brodie were transforming the cityscape into a backdrop for their own entertainments, representations of the urban environment became attractions on the spectacular melodramatic stage. Brodie's jumps from both actual steel suspension bridges and stage representations of them collapsed distinctions between indoor and outdoor entertainment, just as the cinema would soon bring images of the world into theatrical spaces. Though I will argue that Brodie and the cast of stunt celebrities with whom he was associated point toward a distinctly cinematic entertainment and stardom, they also continued two older traditions: a workingmen's entertainment subculture whose center was the saloon, and a tradition of popular spectacle that took place along the canals, rivers, docks, and waterfalls that drove the commerce of nineteenth-century industrial mill towns and shipping ports.[1] In regard to the latter, stunt jumping as a mode of American popular performance began earlier in the nineteenth century with another man who used dangerous stunts as a vehicle for a new kind of celebrity. We begin then, sixty years before Brodie's leap from the Brooklyn Bridge, at the construction site of a bridge that was being built thirty miles to the northwest of New York City.

THE ART OF THE JUMP

In 1827, a builder and sawmill owner named Timothy B. Crane was overseeing the completion of Forest Garden, an elite resort on the north bank of the Passaic Falls in Paterson, New Jersey. Paul E. Johnson describes the class tensions surrounding this project: Crane's Forest Garden was built on what had once been a "public playground," and his upscale developments had aroused the anger of many of the working people of the area.[2] Conflicting emotions therefore existed amid the crowd that gathered to watch as the bridge to Forest Garden was moved into place. Suddenly, a log that was being used in the operation fell into the water and the bridge lurched precariously. At that moment a young man named Sam Patch, dressed in the parade uniform of the local mill spinners, appeared on a ledge high above the falls.[3] He told the crowd that "Crane had done a great thing," and now *he* meant to do another. He then jumped into the water below, a spectacular feat that effectively stole the thunder from Crane's celebration.[4]

The geography of industrial labor provided the setting for Patch's jump and charged it with class tensions. Johnson reminds us that waterfalls like the one in Paterson were an integral part of the emerging American industrial economy: the falls were the engines that drove the factory mills where Patch was a mule spinner.[5] Patch's occupation is significant: as a mule spinner he was a skilled and respected manual laborer in a "craftsmen's empire" that "limited the power of employers," a holdout of autonomous work in an era that saw the "initial proletarianization" of American factory work.[6] Indeed, Patch's distinctive jumping technique was a direct outgrowth of the context of factory labor, having been invented by young mill workers who gathered at the falls and then developed a style whereby they jumped "feet first, breathing as they fell," and stayed under water "long enough to frighten spectators" before shooting triumphantly to the surface.[7] Patch's leap was thus "a kind of occupational skill," and class conflict continued to be a factor in his subsequent high-profile jumps: one was meant as an alternative to a private fireworks display at Crane's Forest Garden, and another coincided with a factory walkout.

In order to describe the subtleties of social meaning conveyed by the events at Passaic Falls, Johnson distinguishes between two types of artistry that were put on display there. Sam Patch stated in newspaper accounts that his act was "an art" that he had practiced from his youth. For Johnson, Patch's use of the term *art* is suggestive:

> In Patch's world a man's art was his identity-defining skill . . . the whole range of combined mental and manual performances by means of which trained men provided for the wants and needs of their communities. The word "art" affirmed the intelligence, learning, and dexterity that went into building a house, making a shoe, or raising a field of wheat. . . . [It] called up the yeoman-artisan republic and the ideals of manhood and individual worth that it sustained—ideals that Sam Patch and other workingmen had reformulated and extended into the industrial world of the nineteenth century.[8]

We might say that Patch's art was a self-forming activity whose vehicle was his body, akin to what Michel Foucault calls a "technology of the self" or Marcel Mauss a "body technique."[9] Johnson contrasts this definition of *art* with one represented by industrialists like Timothy Crane, for whom art was embodied in "works of technology and entrepreneurial vision," such as canals and bridges, that transformed nature and put it to human use. Notably, such industrial projects had "little to do with the skills practiced by ordinary men."[10] Whereas Patch's art was based in manual skill, bodily action, and physical performance, Crane's was made manifest through engineering and the rationalized labor of capitalist mass production. Patch's was a body technique, Crane's an industrial technology.

To better understand the distinction between the "arts" of Patch and Crane, note that Patch's jump is an example of what Erving Goffman calls "action": "activities that are consequential, problematic, and undertaken for what is felt to be their own sake." As noted in the introduction, Goffman uses the term *action* to refer to tasks in which the consequences of one's decisions are felt immediately, and events inundate "the momentary now with their implications for the life that follows."[11] Action is to be found in occupations where one's activity is "a practical gamble voluntarily taken," such as high construction work, test piloting, and soldiering.[12] Following Goffman, we can see that the risks and consequences of Sam Patch's dangerous jumps were made manifest in the "same heated moment of experience." By contrast, the "art" of Crane's bridge was the result of a long period of planning, the labor of many workers, and a considerable passage of time between the project's undertaking and its completion. Compared to the immediacy of action, the bridge was the site of frozen time and petrified labor. We might understand Patch's jump, then, as an act that unleashed or reconfigured the frozen cultural meaning embedded in the bridge, redirecting it through individual action. To put it another way, a single working-class person could not design, fund, and build the bridge, but he or she could jump from its span, and in that moment appropriate and redirect some of its cultural power.

Goffman notes that social maneuvering takes place during moments of accelerated consequence, making action a powerful mode for the performance of self. In other words, action constructs character. It is during moments of action that the individual has the opportunity to display his or her "style of conduct when the chips are down," Goffman writes. "Character is gambled; a single good showing can be taken as representative, and a bad showing cannot be easily excused or reattempted. To display or express character, weak or strong, is to generate character. The self, in brief, can be voluntarily subjected to re-creation."[13] Patch's jump re-created the self in a dramatic way. Patch soon remade himself as a traveling showman and entertainer: he exhibited himself at a Buffalo museum; he made appearances in silk scarves and a sailor's jacket, accompanied by a pet black bear; and his jumping career reached its zenith with a well-publicized leap at Niagara Falls in 1829.[14] For Johnson, Patch was a pioneer of modern celebrity whose fame went against the grain of a social world governed by "inheritance, fixed social rank, and ordained life courses." Patch was "born into obscurity," Johnson writes, "and he did nothing that classicists considered worthy of renown. Yet he *wanted* to be famous and he succeeded."[15] The famous jumper thus represented a new kind of celebrity, one who departed from the model of a hero who embodied the ideals of duty, order, and social obligation, and indexed modern conceptions of the individual that resulted from the freedom from feudal obligations, kinship customs, and vocational ties.[16] In this sense, we might say that the thundering chasm into which Sam Patch leaped was modernity as much as the mists of a New Jersey waterfall.

The notoriety created by Patch's "art" was still resonant fifty years after his death, at least among young working-class Americans like Steve Brodie. After his 1886 leap from the Brooklyn Bridge, Brodie indicated his debt to Patch with a number of direct references to Patch's career. Brodie visited Genesee Falls, in Rochester, New York, where Patch had died in November 1829.[17] In May 1889, Brodie jumped into the basin below the Passaic Falls in Paterson, where Patch had begun his public career. Three months later Brodie took what the *New York Times* called a "leap for sentiment," at Pawtucket Falls, Rhode Island, his "chief motive" being that Sam Patch had jumped there. But Brodie sought to outdo Patch as well as pay tribute to him, announcing that his drop was from a point thirty feet higher than Patch's had been.[18]

Brodie may have become familiar with the highlights of Sam Patch's career by reading about them in newspapers, which were an important part of what Johnson calls the "new apparatus of publicity" that packaged Patch's feats for a mass audience.[19] Patch's entrance on the public scene had been timed fortuitously in this regard, as it coincided with a revolution in the "penny presses" in the 1830s, when newspapers began to reflect "not the affairs of an elite in a small trading society, but the activities of an increasingly varied, urban, and middle-class society," and whose focus increasingly became news items that were actively sought out by reporters.[20] Sensational stunts like Patch's provided the kind of content that reporters needed and that appealed to a broad readership. Brodie would have had plenty of opportunities to become familiar with Patch's career, which was still a topic of newspaper coverage decades after his death, since he had worked as a newsboy. In fact, Brodie's career is closely tied to both the tactics of publicity in newspapers and the culture of the boys who distributed them.

THE LIFE-SAVERS AND THE CAPTAIN

Steve Brodie was one of seven boys raised by his single mother. Brodie never knew his father, who was killed in a gang-related street fight three weeks before his birth.[21] By one account, his father died in a battle between iconic New York gangs, the Bowery Boys and the Dead Rabbits.[22] Like many other urban working-class boys, Brodie grew up "in the shadow of the great newspaper buildings" and made money selling their afternoon editions along Park Row and the Bowery.[23] Brodie was part of a generation of "newsies" who helped to facilitate a boom in afternoon newspaper circulation during the 1880s.[24] The culture of the newsies overlapped with another working-class boys' social club, one that received extensive coverage in the same papers Brodie was selling: the New York Amateur Life-saving Association.[25] The group was initially composed of four boys who patrolled the wharves along the East River at night. The group's leader was named William O'Neill, but he was known as "Nan, the Newsboy." Nan was, in fact, twenty-three years old when he achieved fame as a Life-saver, but he was described as "an over-grown boy in appearance," and he sold newspapers and blackened boots on the Sylvan Line of Harlem steamers in order to support his widowed mother. Other Life-savers included Gilbert Long, age twenty, who was a tinker; Edward Kelly, age sixteen, who worked in a leather manufactory; and Patrick Marr, age ten, also known as "little Patsey" and by trade an apprentice painter. The boys were credited with saving numerous lives and were hoping to upgrade their operation through the purchase of a life buoy, rubber capes for rainy nights, and perhaps a boat.[26]

Nan and company's lifesaving work was an outgrowth of a working-class boys' culture along the New York City docks. In 1879, the children's magazine *St. Nicholas* described the boys' Cherry Street neighborhood as a place of "tenements, sailor boarding-houses and drinking saloons," where "idle urchins" found a "hundred ways to amuse themselves among the boxes and bales":

> The fish-dock and the old "dirt" dock in Peck Slip on summer evenings are white with the figures of bathers. Often, too, even when the law was more stringent against it than now they found means to swim in the day-time. They wrestle and tumble over one another, remain in the water for hours, swim across the swift stream to Brooklyn and back, and dive to the muddy bottom for coins thrown to them by spectators. This was the training-school of our life-savers. Accidents were very frequent here, and the boys made many rescues without thinking much of them.[27]

Steve Brodie took part in pursuits such as these: his first rudimentary lessons in bridge jumping came from "diving for silver quarters from the piers along South street."[28] Brodie and his fellow newsboys also enjoyed jumping into the water from the vessels docked along the wharves. Brodie worked his way up the ships, culminating in leaps from "the third cross-bar," an eighty-foot drop that attracted the attention of commuters riding the ferry.[29] As in Sam Patch's era, practices associated with working-class boys' culture and the spaces of industry were becoming spectacular public entertainment.

Nan and the Life-savers emerged from this culture to achieve a degree of notoriety that must have astonished their working-class peers, a notoriety circulated by newspapers, national magazines, and even the melodramatic stage. *St. Nicholas* reported that the Life-savers had the "odd experience of seeing themselves and their work represented on the stage": "They went to see, at one of the cheap down-town theaters, a sensational piece entitled, 'Nan, the Newsboy,' which was acted to the satisfaction of quite a large audience." The boys spoke with "great disgust" of the melodramatic flourishes of the play: "There was river pirates and a milliner. A girl she comes singin' down the docks about twelve o'clock at night. There aint no girls comes singin' around us. The river pirates they stabbed the girl and throwed her in. Then there was another one throwed in. We had all three of 'em out in five minutes." Perhaps most galling of all, however, was the fact that the actor playing Nan was "about thirty years old," and the one playing Kelly had a mustache.[30] Steve Brodie thus had Nan as well as Sam Patch as a model for modern media celebrity. There was, however, another important influence on Brodie's career, another person who helped to shape his notions of performance, publicity, and celebrity. Indeed, the Life-savers gained a considerable amount of their own renown through an association with another public figure who was adept at his own novel body technique, a technique that was intimately connected to the nation's waterways.

On December 29, 1878, the *New York Times* reported that Nan and the Life-savers ate "high pie" at the Fifth-Avenue Hotel with Captain Paul Boyton, who publicly promised to aid the boys and in return was made an honorary member of their "society."[31] Who was this Captain Boyton? Born in 1846 in Allegheny City, Pennsylvania, Boyton told one interviewer that ever since he could walk, he had felt an "irresistible desire to be in the water." Like the New York City dock boys, Boyton had spent much of his childhood in the water, diving not for quarters but for flat stones used in paving streets.[32] He recounted how, at the age of eleven, he had saved a boy from drowning under a newly built suspension bridge on the Allegheny River, after which a crowd had gathered and filled his cap with money. "I was afraid to accept it," he said, "for I knew if it was discovered in my possession at home the fact that I had been playing truant and swimming in the river would surely be betrayed." After briefly attending college and then accompanying his father on trading expeditions among the Native American population, he joined the navy and fought in the Civil War.[33] Water takes on an almost mystical, Melvillian quality in Boyton's description of sailing to

FIGURE 1. Paul Boyton. Courtesy of the British Library.

the West Indies, where he was a pearl diver after the war: "I have seen in the deep water of the West Indies many peculiar things, and landscapes as beautiful as ever human eye rested upon. The coral banks, in the perfectly clear element, with the tropical sun shining down upon them, present a most wonderful sight."[34]

When he returned to the United States in the early 1870s, Boyton went to Atlantic City, where he served as a "submarine diver" and volunteer lifesaver on the New Jersey coast.[35] In 1874, Boyton was hired to give public demonstrations of a newly invented "life-preserving apparatus." The centerpiece of this apparatus was a watertight rubber suit that covered one's entire body except the face. The suit, which had been patented by C.S. Merriman in 1872, contained air chambers behind the head, along the sides of the body, and under both legs, making the wearer float on the surface of the water.[36] Wearing this suit, Boyton would recline on his back in the water and, equipped with a paddle, become a kind of human kayak, impervious to the cold in nearly frozen water and able

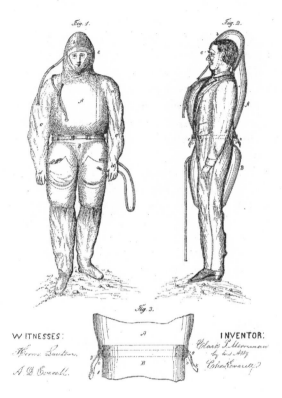

FIGURE 2. C.S. Merriman's patented "life-preserving apparatus," which Paul Boyton made famous in the 1870s and 1880s.

to cover remarkably long distances. Reporters who encountered Boyton in the water referred to his uncanny, even semihuman, appearance; one writer noted that the captain took on "the aspect of some fabled amphibious monster."[37] Along with his suit, Boyton's apparatus consisted of an array of remarkable accessories. Around his neck hung a shark knife, a horn, and a bottle of brandy, and on his aquatic excursions Boyton took with him a small floating craft that he dubbed the "Baby Mine," which contained an assortment of items that he might need in the water: rockets, fireworks, torpedoes, and creature comforts such as a pipe, food, and beverages.[38] Dressed in his modern rubber suit and equipped with its various accessories, Boyton presented a picture of manly independence in a performance that combined the arts of Sam Patch and Timothy Crane, being both body technique and industrial technology.

By the end of the 1870s, Boyton and his remarkable suit had become known throughout the United States and Europe. His international fame began when, in the autumn of 1874, he donned his suit and jumped from the transatlantic steamship that had carried him from New York, swimming the last leg of the journey to the Irish coast.[39] Thousands of curious spectators gathered to see him demonstrate his suit in a public park in Dublin, and that night he appeared on stage at a local theater to narrate his adventures off the coast.[40] In January 1875, Boyton traveled down the Thames River in London, where thousands are said to have "looked on open-mouthed" at "the gentleman who, encasing himself in an armour of indiarubber, walked into and along the river without touching the bottom."[41] A stunning indication of how Boyton's act appealed across social classes, in April of that year the captain was invited to perform for Queen Victoria, who watched him from the deck of the royal yacht. Boyton received the queen's congratulations, as well as an order for one of his suits, which was to be made an "essential feature" of the royal yacht's equipment.[42] One month after meeting the queen, Boyton became the first man to swim cross the English Channel. After spending twenty-three hours in the water, the captain received congratulatory telegrams from Queen Victoria, the Prince of Wales, the lord mayor of London, and President Ulysses S. Grant, who wired, "America is proud of you!"[43]

The following year Boyton toured Europe demonstrating his lifesaving apparatus, and the Russian government was said to be so impressed that it was considering making his suit a mandatory piece of equipment for its coast guard.[44] At the end of the 1870s, Boyton was back in the United States, where he made a variety of appearances to promote himself and his suit. In January 1876, he gave an exhibition in New York City's East River before a large crowd that "cheered lustily" in response to blasts from his horn.[45] In Washington, D.C., Boyton floated on his back while a young boy sat on his chest, handing out glasses of wine to passing boating parties.[46] The various resources in his "Baby Mine" became a central component of his act: "Among the captain's maneuvers in the water were cooking and preparing his meals on a raft constructed by himself, fishing, smoking, shooting, writing and signaling with flags and rockets. He also liberated two carrier pigeons, which never returned to him, and concluded his entertainment by blowing up

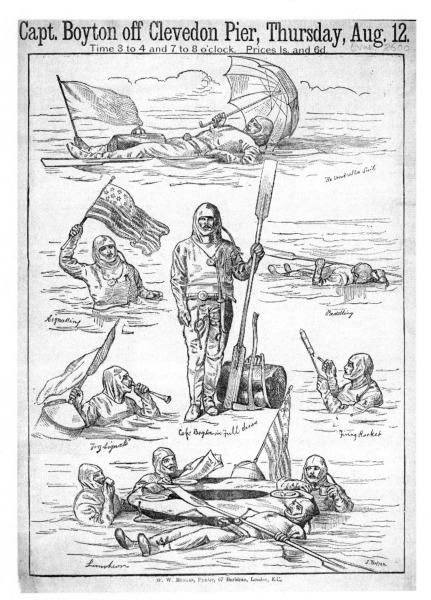

FIGURE 3. Flyer announcing one of Paul Boyton's performances in Merriman's remarkable suit. Courtesy of the British Library.

with a torpedo a miniature sailing vessel. The torpedo did its work in good style, for after it was fired there was little to be seen of the sailing craft. The exhibition was greatly enjoyed by the children."[47] Boyton also embarked on several well-publicized long-distance swims. In February 1879, he went down the freezing Allegheny River from Oil City to Pittsburg accompanied by a "sleighing party, largely composed of members of the press."[48] That same March, he swam down the Ohio River to Cincinnati. In later years Boyton traveled to the Western states, in 1882 taking a trip down the Arkansas River and in June 1886 drawing 3,500 spectators to view his performance on Palmer Lake in Colorado.[49]

By the end of the 1870s Boyton was an international celebrity who fired the imagination of the public through personal appearances and sensational coverage in the popular press that detailed his encounters with sharks, his engagement in naval battles, and his epic voyages down icy rivers. It was this Captain Boyton who suddenly appeared in the lives of the Cherry Street Life-savers, took them out for an expensive meal, and promised them jobs and equipment. It is clear that Boyton had big plans for remaking Nan's organization and saw himself as more than an "honorary" member of the Life-savers. First, Boyton compelled the boys to quit their day jobs and become regular employees of the city earning fixed wages.[50] Boyton also promised to "devote all his spare time" to instructing the boys in lifesaving methods and to oversee the construction of several floating rescue stations that were to be fitted with lifelines, a lifeboat, a stretcher, and "every description of restorative, including galvanic batteries."[51]

Despite these optimistic prospects, the Life-savers disbanded in a flurry of recriminations only a few months after their "high pie" with Boyton. Nan claimed that the boys had not been "properly encouraged" by those who promised to support them, nor had they been kindly treated, and he traced their trouble to Boyton. Though Boyton had claimed in a newspaper interview that he had found the boys "ragged and starving," Nan said that they had been better off before they met him. The dinner at the Fifth-Avenue Hotel had been the only time he had fed them, and even that, claimed Nan, was only "to advertise himself."[52] One small life station had indeed been built, but it was far from the elaborately outfitted one that had been promised: "The front door of the establishment, as it might be called, is through a hole in a dilapidated fence; then down a ladder, and perhaps across a canal-boat or two to where it lies wedged in the crowded basin. They have a row-boat, and a life-saving raft of the catamaran pattern. Inside, the station has three bunks, some lockers to hold miscellaneous articles, a small stove in a corner, and a small case of books."[53] With the loss of their day jobs and paltry new salaries, the boys claimed that they had to spend long hours at the station which, being anchored near a sewer, was "hot as an oven" and filled with poisonous sewer gas.[54] Boyton, the boys reported, had been aloof and unresponsive to their complaints.

Faced with this blast of negative publicity from the unhappy Life-savers, Boyton fired back in the newspapers, claiming that he had "worked hard for weeks" getting the boys established and procuring them clothing with two hundred dollars of his own money. As to his alleged neglect of the Life-savers, Boyton said he had been "compelled to leave the City on business before the life-saving station was built." To counter Nan's complaint about their low salaries, Boyton stated that he had intended to give Nan a fourteen-dollar-a-week position in his own organization but would no longer consider it after hearing the Life-savers' "ungrateful and untrue story."[55] The dispute came to a head when the two parties faced each other at a July 1879 meeting of the executive committee of the New York Volunteer Life-saving Society, where the issue of celebrity and self-promotion came to the fore. Nan said that Boyton's sole object in approaching the boys had been "to advertise himself," to which Boyton replied that "he didn't want advertising; that he had 'written his name across the face of Europe,' in swimming the Rhine, crossing the Straits of Gibraltar, and other feats, before 'Nan' was even heard of." Nan and the boys maintained that Boyton had merely been using them as a way to publicize a swim down the Mississippi River. "Would you ever have taken us to dinner at the Fifth-Avenue Hotel," asked Life-saver Gil Long, "if it hadn't been for the reports in the newspapers next day?"[56] Boyton "angrily retorted" that "this was his reward for what he had done," adding that he couldn't expect any more from "a bunch of wharf rats," who, when he had found them, "had not known enough to complain of the sewer-gas which rose into the life-saving station from the river," a gas that was, Boyton added, "far superior to the obnoxious odors that permeated the tenements in which they lived." The Life-savers, "with flashing eyes," denied that they had ever been "wharf rats."[57]

Boyton's bad press with the Life-savers did not slow his rise to fame, and over the course of the 1880s he gradually transformed himself from lifesaver, adventurer, and military man to popular entertainer. That process was complete in 1887, when he traveled with P.T. Barnum's Circus.[58] In a review of his act with Barnum, we are told that he walked to a water tank "with all the frisky grace of a young hippopotamus and disported himself in its waters with the joyful levity of a light-hearted sea lion." He then gave a ten-minute demonstration of the "wonderful things" that could be accomplished with his lifesaving suit: "He paddled about, set sail, fished, shot, signaled a supposititious steamer in the imaginary distance, cooked and ate supper, rescued from drowning a small boy who fell into the water, and finally lit his cigar and went to sleep."[59] After his acrimonious parting of ways with Boyton, Nan did not fare as well. He told the press that he and the other boys would continue with lifesaving as before and recruit new members to the corps. By 1880, however, Nan had given up lifesaving to become a policeman in the Fourth Ward. He was dismissed for drunkenness not long afterward and could later be found giving testimonials titled "The Evils of Drink." In subsequent press accounts Nan's life was offered up as a cautionary tale about the dangers of undeserved fame: "The newspapers made him," wrote the *St. Louis Globe-Democrat* in 1883, "and rum unmade him."[60]

The well-publicized dispute between Boyton and the Life-savers surely must have left lingering feelings of animosity and resentment among the boys and their supporters, as well as conveyed a lesson in the use of newspapers to shape public opinion and the utility of stunt performance as a mode of self-promotion. We should note that Steve Brodie was a lieutenant Life-saver himself, and he is also said to have appeared in a stage production of *Nan, the Newsboy.*[61] It is safe to assume that Brodie, who was a part of Nan's milieu, felt a certain antagonism towards Boyton, and indeed it is hard to resist the temptation to see much of Brodie's subsequent career as either an oedipal conflict with Boyton (a stand-in for the father he never knew), or as a drama of class resentment, with aquatic arts the terrain of a struggle between "wharf rats" and a sporting man with aristocratic pretensions.[62] What is certain is that Boyton was the motivation for many of Brodie's actions after his 1886 jump from the Brooklyn Bridge. Once on the public stage, Brodie quickly sought to make a name for himself as a long-distance swimmer utilizing a Boyton-style rubber suit: in the words of his biographer, Brodie resolved to win from Paul Boyton the "swimming championship of the world."[63] The same year that Boyton was touring the country with Barnum's circus, Brodie was in Cincinnati, making a ten-mile swim up the Ohio River dressed in "a Boyton suit." Not only that, but he arrived equipped with a "little boat" from which he produced fireworks, a small gun, and an oil stove that he used to make himself a cup of coffee.[64] In June 1888, Brodie swam down the Hudson River from Albany to New York wearing "a Boyton rubber suit," with the explicit purpose of besting Boyton's previous time on a similar swim.[65] In fact, even Brodie's career-defining leap from the Brooklyn Bridge can be understood as a riposte to Boyton. It is quite possible that Brodie made that jump in order to take advantage of another public relations disaster that beset the captain soon after his run-in with Nan and the Life-savers.

A BRIDGE TO THE TEMPLE OF FAME

Brodie may have grown up in the shadow of New York's newspaper buildings, but another feature of the urban landscape cast an even more dramatic shadow over his childhood: the Brooklyn Bridge, a work of technological and entrepreneurial art that made Sam Patch's old nemesis Timothy Crane look like an amateur.[66] Designed by John Augustus Roebling and his son Washington, the bridge was a stunning feat of America's emerging engineering and entrepreneurial prowess. In 1870 construction began on the two 276-foot-high towers that would support a bridge spanning the East River from Brooklyn to New York. The building of the bridge, like the skyscrapers described in the next chapter, was a public spectacle, and huge crowds gathered to watch the first steel wire being hung in 1876. Thousands cheered when an engineer crossed the East River on a wire three hundred feet above the river.[67] The grand opening of the bridge, at the time the longest suspension bridge in the world, took place on May 24, 1883. The Brooklyn Bridge was a steel monument to the triumph of American technology. For historian T.J. Jackson Lears, the bridge was also a sign that the nation's "technical expertise" was increasingly being "placed in the service of big business," marking a shift from "the disorganized entrepreneurial capitalism of the earlier nineteenth century to the organized corporate capitalism of our own time."[68] The Brooklyn Bridge was thus a technological "art" that dwarfed Timothy Crane's, and perhaps it is not surprising that a modern-day Sam Patch would arrive on the scene to steal the limelight from the engineers and corporate industrialists. Brodie was a representative of the same class as the laborers who had built the bridge, and he had grown up in the bridge's literal and figurative shadow. Drawing on the reservoir of embodied skills that he had acquired along the wharves, Brodie found a way to unleash and reconfigure the frozen cultural meaning embedded in the bridge and to use it as a prop for character-defining action.

The first to try such a stunt, however, was not Steve Brodie but a man named Robert Odlum—a man, it should be noted, who was closely associated with Captain Paul Boyton. On May 13, 1885, the *Syracuse Daily Standard* wrote that Odlum, a "Washington professional swimmer," was in negotiation with Boyton to make a jump from the Brooklyn Bridge.[69] Odlum jumped exactly a week later, a feat that the *National Police Gazette* claimed was enacted "under the auspices" of Boyton.[70] On the day of the jump Odlum, Boyton, and a number of "sporting and theatrical men" met at Paddy Ryan's liquor store, where "wine was being opened freely, and a cluster of newspaper men hung around the bar room taking notes." The same crew of sporting men and reporters was soon waiting beneath the Brooklyn Bridge in a tugboat.[71] The *National Police Gazette* provided a detailed account of the moments leading up to Odlum's jump:

> As [Odlum] stood there alone the crowd surged with one common impulse in that direction and scanned every feature of the man. He seemed to be about thirty-six years old and looked not less than 5 feet 10 in his bare feet. His features were sharp: a jet black mustache, closely cropped, adorned his face; his lips were compressed and determined-looking. He seemed calm, and as he looked down into the placid water 140 feet below there came a shiver over the crowd, followed by the involuntary burst of admiration at the calm courage of the man. A Fulton ferry-boat passed from the New York side with a great crowd. The people all looked up tremblingly and some of the women felt faint. It was now 3:30 o'clock. Capt. Boyton and his friends looked up from the tug-boat and met the eyes of the professor, who smiled as calmly as though 140-feet jumps were trifling matters. Then he softly stroked his hair, which was combed over his forehead toward the right, braced his legs close together, planted his left arm down along his side as though responding to an order on parade. For a moment he steadied himself, stretched his right hand to his utmost limit above his head, took a deep and prolonged breath and sprang into the air. At the moment he jumped a cry broke from the great crowds on the bridge and those aboard vessels in the river. Capt. Boyton, on the tug-boat, was about the only man in the thousands who remained calm. He surveyed the descent of his reckless friend with the cool precision of a professional man.[72]

The description here suggests that Odlum had a body technique that was just as distinctive as that of the Paterson mill boys during Sam Patch's era: legs braced close together and left arm planted down along his side. Odlum's technique, however, was not a match for the sheer scale of Roebling's technological art, and the jump did not end well: "Three seconds after he left the bridge Odlum touched the water. His position had been changed as he shot through the 140 feet of space, and he struck the water almost horizontally." Boyton jumped into the water with a life preserver and brought Odlum on board the tugboat. Odlum briefly regained consciousness and asked, "Did I make a good jump?" Before long, "blood oozed from his ears and mouth" and he was taken to Bellevue Hospital, where he died of internal injuries.[73] According to a report in *Scientific American,* Odlum's injuries were "such as would be found in a man crushed to death by the caving in of a sand bank." "Odlum was simply mangled to death."[74]

Some held Boyton responsible for this grisly event. The *New York Times* published a letter written by the captain to Odlum's mother, who apparently had been blaming Boyton publicly for the death of her son: "The great God who knows all knows that I did everything in my power to prevent the jump, and the same God knows that I am not his murderer you accuse me of being," Boyton wrote. "I would not have gone to the river to witness his leap but for the thought that I might be of assistance to him. In answer to my entreaties that he should abandon his idea, he said: 'This feat will give me fame and a reputation that will survive me . . . and thus enable me to help my mother and myself, as I would wish to do and, as I have not been able to do for a couple of years.'"[75] It is difficult to know what Mrs. Odlum made of Boyton's rather improbable and melodramatic account of the event. What is certain is that Odlum's jump made an impression on Steve Brodie, who is said to have known the former and set himself the task of succeeding where Odlum—and Boyton—had failed.[76]

Brodie's famous jump from the Brooklyn Bridge took place a year after Odlum's death. Brodie later claimed that he had prepared for the feat by making a trial jump at night, using a large umbrella from a brewer's wagon that was braced with steel wire: "It was like flying," he said.[77] The leap itself was front-page news for the *New York Times,* which described how Brodie had hid himself in a lumber wagon in order to sneak past the New York tollgate. Leaving the wagon, he quickly removed his coat and hat, under which he wore an "electric belt," a layer of protective bandages, and trousers that had been tied around the ankles with strong twine so that they wouldn't flap in the wind during his descent.[78] Brodie promptly headed for the railing of the bridge, and onlookers assumed that he intended to commit suicide. As a crowd stood powerless to stop him, he climbed down to the lower girders and from there dropped into the water below. The doctor who examined Brodie at the police station after the jump reported that he had "shrieked as if suffering agony," although it was unclear whether his discomfort was real or simulated, and it might have had something to do with the fact that Brodie was "more than half drunk."[79] Regardless of whether Brodie's agony was real or simulated, in the realm of public opinion Brodie had bested Odlum and Boyton, and he subsequently achieved a level of fame that eclipsed Nan's and rivaled the globetrotting captain's.

Like Sam Patch sixty years earlier, Brodie became a pioneer of a new kind of celebrity. "As Minerva sprang fully equipped from the brain of Jupiter," wrote the *New York Tribune,* "so Brodie sprang into popular recognition from the waves of the East River."[80] The *New York Herald* described how, on the morning after his jump, he awoke in a prison cell and immediately asked to see the morning papers. When his "twinkling eyes swept down the columns containing the story of the jump," he exclaimed, "That settles it. I'm famous as [President Grover] Cleveland. . . . I'm the biggest man on earth today."[81] After his bail was paid, he left the station, but when he reached the street he was "paralyzed": "Fame was there waiting for him. The managers of all the dime museums in the country were ready to gobble him up. . . . A hundred boys, blasé with dime novel reading, shook hands with their 'hero,' and actually impeded his way. . . . [T]he street was almost blockaded with enthusiastic Fourth Warders."[82]

Writers in the popular press struggled to understand Brodie—and the jumpers who were soon imitating him—in relation to a classical model of fame.[83] For one thing, Brodie seemed to have gained his fame too easily. "The temple of Fame was formerly believed to top a most austere, stony peak," *Peterson Magazine* wrote in 1895. Brodie was "a latter-day Marco Polo" who had discovered a new "air line" route to the summit: "Previous seekers after fame have trusted to Genius. Mr. Brodie gave himself into the hands of Gravity. He pushed himself; it did the rest."[84] Not only did Brodie rely on gravity instead of genius to make his leap to fame, but his jump had not demonstrated a skill that was recognizable to many writers: "There is no more skill required to jump from the middle of the Poughkeepsie or the Brooklyn Bridge into the river than to jump from a pier ten feet or less above the surface of the water. . . . It is the risk alone that constitutes the attraction."[85] To those used to the notion of fame as the accident of effort and not its end, Brodie's leap to notoriety seemed far too calculated. Brodie was, as the *Brooklyn Daily Eagle* put it in 1887, a "newsboy" who had "thirsted for celebrity": "The artist, the inventor, the poet, the statesman are not concerning themselves with what the world will think or say of their actions; they see an opportunity to do the world a service and they do it; fame is the concomitant of their deed."[86] Unlike the inventor, poet, or statesman, Brodie had achieved a notoriety that seemed to some pundits to render no public service: "If the achievements of Brodie and his imitators were a source of benefit to the human race the extravagance of their performances might be overlooked," wrote one critic in 1889. "There is, however, absolutely no excuse for their existence."[87] The *New York Times* argued in 1895 that "a man might be pardoned and even praised for risking his life to demonstrate that by means of some mechanical appliance a leap from a high place might be made without injury, but this is not at all the object of the bridge jumper. He jumps either to win somebody's money or to acquire . . . notoriety."[88] The ability to "leap from perilous heights" may require "a certain form of brute courage," concluded the *Brooklyn Daily Eagle,* but not the bravery that "carries men through great crises or stimulates them to sacrifices for the good of humanity."[89]

One way to understand Brodie's critics is in relation to Thomas Baker's observations on a "fear of ill-deserved and capricious popularity" in the nineteenth century: "That the 'people' were sovereign was certainly a nineteenth-century republican commonplace, but they also frequently fell prey to puffery and manufactured sensation . . . hence the era's abiding concern to sort out enduring fame from mere fleeting celebrity."[90] Taking a cue from Warren Susman, we can also see Brodie's leap to fame as a harbinger of a dawning "culture of personality" that was repugnant to critics still invested in a residual "culture of character" that prized self-control, sacrifice to a higher law, and the ideals of duty, honor, and integrity.[91] As a third point of reference, note that the writers who resisted Brodie's fame put forth arguments that resemble Daniel J. Boorstin's well-known discussion of celebrity in his 1961 book *The Image.* Like Brodie's critics, Boorstin contrasted an earlier, more authentic hero to the celebrity, whom he defined as a person known for their "well-knownness."[92] Boorstin connected this sea change in public notoriety to the modern media, referring to a "Graphic Revolution" made possible by the ability "to make, preserve, transmit, and disseminate precise images."[93] The key effect wrought by the Graphic Revolution, according to Boorstin, was that it changed the temporality of fame: the hero had been "born of time" through the circulation of "folklore, sacred texts, and history books," but the celebrity was "the creature of gossip, of public opinion," and of the modern media. "The celebrity is born in the daily papers," Boorstin wrote, "and never loses the mark of his fleeting origin."[94] In addition to his claims about media influence, Boorstin's argument relied on Romantic notions of "folk" as opposed to mass culture: he wrote that the "usually illiterate" and "unselfconscious" folk was "creative," while the mass was inherently passive, "the target and not the arrow . . . the ear and not the voice." "While the folk created heroes," Boorstin concluded, "the mass can only look and listen for them."[95] Like Brodie's critics, Boorstin dismissed modern media celebrity as an inauthentic, fleeting, and degraded version of a previous heroism that arose organically from, and served the needs of, society.

If we adopt this perspective on media celebrity, we are left with a limited, and in the end elitist, perspective on public figures such as Brodie. More recent scholars of media notoriety have made more focused claims about the protocols of various media industries, and they have stressed the democratic potential of celebrity culture.[96] P. David Marshall, for example, argues that celebrity invokes "the message of possibility of a democratic age," suggesting that "the restrictions of a former hierarchy are no longer valid in the new order that is determined by merit and/or the acquisition of wealth."[97] Steve Brodie tested that "message of possibility" through dangerous acts that had the potential to create and project character on a national level, thus upsetting established social hierarchies that ratified only certain kinds of fame. Brodie's celebrity was certainly "born in the daily papers," but his fame was remarkably intertextual, and Brodie's career on the stage allows us to test assumptions about the social function and democratic potential of modern celebrity.

"THIS AIN'T ART. IT'S ON THE BOWERY."

For proof that Brodie was lacking in the "moral force" required of authentic fame, the *Brooklyn Daily Eagle* pointed to the "unsavory reputation" that he had acquired since his entrance onto the public stage: "His jumping eccentricities may serve to attract attention to his grog shop, but they excite no sympathy from lovers of manly sports and provoke nothing but contempt in the minds of thoughtful people."[98] The "grog shop" mentioned here was a saloon that was owned and operated by Brodie at 114 Bowery Street and that became a key component of his public image. Saloons such as Brodie's had a central place in nineteenth-century urban working-class culture. Kathy Peiss writes that most tenement neighborhoods were dominated by saloons and estimates that there were more than ten thousand in operation in greater New York City around 1900. Saloons were "at the heart of working-class life," according to Elliott Gorn, creating "informal but stable brotherhoods" for working men, and the tavern keeper was "the caretaker of a cultural style that emphasized camaraderie and reciprocity among peers." In his 1931 history *Old Bowery Days,* Alvin Harlow describes the Bowery saloon as a "poor man's club" and refers to the saloon keeper as the workingman's "business adviser, his political mentor, his agreeable gossip, sometimes his banker." Drinking occupied an important portion of workingmen's leisure hours in the mid- to late 1800s, with the saloon standing as a place of leisure separated from both work and home.[99] For historians like Peiss, Gorn, and Roy Rosenzweig, workingmen's saloon subculture was an alternative to a dominant capitalist, middle-class culture.[100] Peiss writes that "workers who sold their time and labor and submitted to bosses' control could daily assert a sense of independence" in the public spaces of the saloon or lodge, which became "a refuge from the dominant value system of competitive individualism."[101]

Of all the ten thousand saloons in New York, Brodie's Bowery grog shop took on iconic status in the decades around the turn of the twentieth century. In 1908 one newspaper wrote that Brodie's saloon, with its "marvelous gallery of prize fighters' portraits," had been one of the leading attractions of the Bowery for more than a quarter of a century.[102] No visit to the Bowery was complete, claimed one 1901 article, without seeing the "distinctly tough" clientele at Brodie's, as well as its collection of "photographs of the celebrated pugilists of the past and present" and mementos of "famous fistic encounters."[103] With its iconography of roughneck male entertainments, Brodie's bar was firmly situated in urban workingman's culture, and it even served as the site of well-publicized donations of free bread, coffee, and umbrellas to needy locals.[104] Recall the claims made by Brodie's critics that his fame served no social service. Such claims beg the question, service to what part of society? Brodie's notoriety allowed him to situate himself as a "caretaker" of a workingmen's cultural style, and he used his saloon as a kind of community center. Brodie's fame, particularly as manifested in the saloon, thus articulated a connection to, and expression of, an urban workingmen's culture. As such, Brodie illustrates Marshall's claim that, compared with the classical model of fame, modern celebrity was "touchable by the multitude," that "the greatness of the celebrity is something that can be shared and, in essence, celebrated loudly and with a touch of vulgar pride."[105] Brodie's saloon anchored his notoriety to a place and a social milieu, and in doing so it kept his fame "touchable."

The saloon at 114 Bowery was clearly marked as a working-class space, but it also attracted wide-eyed middle-class tourists keen on "slumming" in the Bowery, a fact of which Brodie was keenly aware. During an interview in his saloon Brodie told a reporter, "Look at these people in here. What do they come in for? To get something to drink? Not much. They're mostly strangers and curiosity hunters; fellows that patronize the dime museums. They come in to look at me. And I'm just smart enough . . . to be here when they come in, so that they can take a good look at me and shake hands."[106] Brodie was even said to enlist his compatriots at the bar to impersonate well-known "sporting characters" so as not to disappoint sightseers.[107] Brodie's saloon was thus a setting for performances that were doubly legible as both enactments

TYPES THAT ASSEMBLE IN BRODIE'S SALOON.

FIGURE 4. "Types that assemble in Brodie's saloon," an illustration of the "sporting characters" who patronized Steve Brodie's Bowery saloon. Collection of the New York Historical Society.

of workingmen's camaraderie and as displays of colorful and authentic street life for middle-class visitors. Brodie's reference to the dime museum audience is telling. His Bowery saloon provides a vivid illustration of Barbara Kirshenblatt-Gimblett's notion of the "museum effect," whereby "the museum experience itself becomes a model for experiencing life outside its walls."[108] Kirshenblatt-Gimblett points to a common mid-nineteenth-century trope of "the city as dark continent" and the journalist and social reformer as "ethnographer." When experiencing the city in this manner, "an ethnographic bell jar drops over the terrain," such that "a neighborhood, village, or region becomes for all intents and purposes a living museum in situ."[109] The Bowery became this kind of "extended ethnographic theme park" for tourists and middle-class visitors, and Steve Brodie's saloon, with its mementos of past "fistic encounters," was explicitly referred to as a "curiosity shop," with the famous bridge jumper as the perennial main attraction.

Visitors flocked to his saloon on the Bowery, but Brodie also took his urban ethnographic show on the road, appearing in dime museums from the first days after his 1886 jump. The American dime museum had "reached its apex" during the 1880s and 1890s, and New York—and the Bowery in particular—became America's "dime museum capitol."[110] Luc Santé characterizes Bowery museums as "the true underworld of entertainment," since they featured "anything too shoddy, too risqué, too vile, too sad, too marginal, too disgusting, too pointless to be displayed elsewhere."[111] Santé notes that Brodie was exhibited at Alexander's Museum at 317 Bowery—one of the best-known museums in the city—but the bridge jumper appeared well beyond the confines of the Bowery in this capacity. In the year after his leap he embarked on a brief career as a traveling dime museum "curiosity," during which time he appeared in Providence, Boston, Cincinnati, Chicago, St. Paul, and Milwaukee.[112] In February 1887 he was arrested in Pittsburg for attempting to jump from the top of a dime museum into a net in order to publicize his appearance at the establishment.[113]

Brodie's stint as dime museum curiosity was soon followed by other kinds of stage work, including nonspeaking roles as a stunt performer on the melodramatic stage. In 1886 and 1887 Brodie appeared in a play called *Blackmail,* in which he made a leap from "a high tower into the sea," achieved by jumping through a trap door in the stage.[114] He made a similar jump from a bridge in Steele MacKaye's 1890 play *Money Mad* at the New York Standard Theatre.[115] This association with MacKaye is significant, since it indicates a point of convergence between Brodie's outdoor stunt performances and developments on the melodramatic stage. MacKaye was an influential late nineteenth-century playwright, director, and actor who had studied the Delsartean approach to "naturalistic" acting.[116] Along with Henry Irving and David Belasco, MacKaye is credited with a turn to protocinematic spectacular realism or "pictorial illusionism" on the late nineteenth-century melodramatic stage.[117] Ben Singer describes how stage melodrama of this period often featured a display of realistic scenic effects made possible by new technologies of "mechanical-electrical stagecraft."[118] MacKaye was a key figure in the development of these technologies, but it is important to remember that the display of mechanical stagecraft was typically accompanied by perilous stuntwork that heightened popular melodrama's visceral effect: "Characters swung by ropes from ledge to ledge, tightrope-walked across telegraph wires, dove off cliffs into the ocean, moved inches away from real buzz saws or pile drivers, and so on."[119] The vogue for such stuntwork enabled Brodie to transfer his skill at outdoor bridge jumping to the indoor world of the stage.

Singer finds at the heart of popular melodrama of this era an effort to portray "situations and environments that challenged the physical and spatiotemporal boundaries of the indoor stage."[120] Modern suspension bridges and bridge jumping became a key part of that project. Steele MacKaye's *Money Mad,* which featured a jump by Brodie, had a drawbridge as its most striking stage set.[121] The bridge opened over the orchestra to let a steamboat pass, a moment that one reviewer claimed "brought forth the mightiest cheers and applause of the evening."[122] A *Chicago Tribune* review of MacKaye's 1888 play *A Noble Rogue* described the production's "wonderful bridge": "It swings towards the audience and lets a big steamer through. Smoke rises from the vessel's funnel. Whistles blow. Bells ring. Stars glitter in the midnight sky. The cry of the tender is heard. The machinery of the bridge creaks. And the black hull passes. Realism could no further go."[123] In Joseph Roach's terms, the modern suspension bridge—like the mill waterfalls of Sam Patch's era—became a "vortex of behavior," a site in the lived environment where "the gravitational pull of social necessity brings audiences together and produces performers . . . from their midst."[124] Bridges offered dynamic set pieces in realistic melodramas, and the bridge jump was a logical bit of action custom-made for that environment. *A Noble Rogue* was even called a "a triumph of Boytonism" because MacKaye, who not only wrote but also starred in the play, made a "heroic plunge" from the bridge: "Having succeeded as a dramatist," the *Tribune* wrote, MacKaye was now "anxious to excel as a diver" and so had become "the Boyton of the boards."[125] Though the review compared the actor to Paul Boyton, it was Steve Brodie who was making similar leaps on the melodramatic stage.[126]

Bridge jumping and representations of suspension bridges were key selling points in Thomas H. Davis's 1893 stage production *On the Bowery.* The play's plot involves "a betrayed young woman" who hunts down her betrayer in hopes of revenge. The villain hires two thugs to kill her by throwing her from the Brooklyn Bridge, but a "heroic young saloon keeper" saves her just in time.[127] The name of that heroic young saloon keeper was, of course, Steve Brodie, and the part was played by none other than Brodie himself in an early example of an actor employed "as a consequence of non-theatrical celebrity."[128] As had been the case with MacKaye's *Money Mad, On the Bowery* was frequently singled out by critics for the stunning realism of its bridge set: "The scenery is the most artistic feature of the performance," wrote one reviewer. "The perspective view of Brooklyn Bridge is the most striking optical delusion [sic] ever seen on the stage and is so perfect as to give the impression of looking off in the distance."[129] Reprising his earlier stuntwork, Brodie enacted his famous jump from the bridge by leaping through a trapdoor

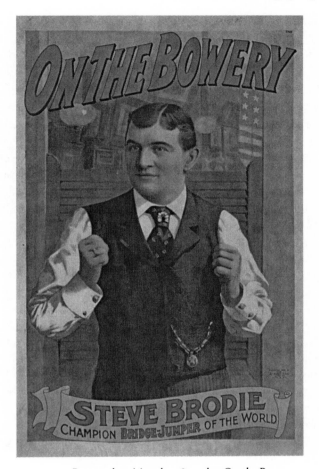

FIGURE 5. Poster advertising the 1893 play *On the Bowery*, starring Steve Brodie as himself. Courtesy of the Library of Congress.

in the stage as handfuls of rock salt were thrown into the air to simulate the splash.[130] Like Steele MacKaye's spectacular melodramas, *On the Bowery* illustrates the importance of the bridge as setting and the bridge jumper as thrill maker for dramatic entertainments of this time, but the show also exploited Brodie's iconic status as a Bowery type.

The second act of the play was set in a detailed representation of Brodie's Bowery saloon, where the bridge jumper sang a song entitled "My Pearl Is a Bowery Girl" in what was described as "a round, but slightly husky, tone" that came out of one corner of his mouth.[131] Just as Brodie's bridge jumping lacked a clear display of "skill," so his performance on the stage seemed to some to be little more than a glorified dime museum exhibition. A critic in the *Decatur Bulletin-Sentinel* wrote that Brodie "freely admits that he is no actor and does not try to be. He is there merely to be seen, and as the public is willing to pay for it, that suits Brodie."[132] The "Steve Brodie" of the play was "exactly the Steve Brodie of real life," wrote his biographer, who quoted him as saying, "When I'm on the stage in the saloon scene . . . I feel just as if I was in my place on the Bowery."[133] "I don't want people to think they are coming to see [Edwin] Booth or [Lawrence] Barrett when they come to see me tonight," he told a Portland reporter in 1896. "I want them to come and see the first man on the American stage who ever appeared representing himself, as he is, in everyday life in his business, see?"[134] "I thought there was some strange trick in acting that everyday people didn't have," Brodie told a Buffalo newspaper. "I didn't know it was simply a matter of going on the stage and talking and behaving as natural as possible. I never had any trouble in being myself, no matter how many people were looking on. So, as I have only to be myself in this play, I found it dead easy. . . . I don't think I could play [stage actor] Henry Irving's part as well as he can, but I'm dead sure he couldn't play my part [in] 'On the Bowery' as well as I do."[135] One of Brodie's lines in the play slyly asserted his seeming lack of artifice: "This ain't art," Brodie said, "It's on the Bowery."[136] It should be noted that enacting one's offstage public persona in this manner, though perhaps notable on the turn-of-the-century stage, soon became the modus operandi of film players. Richard deCordova argues that during the early 1910s public discourses about "picture personalities" outside their appearances in film narratives emerged such that "the illusion that was operative was that the player's real personality . . . preceded and caused the representation of personality on the screen." Joshua Gamson claims that later, during the Hollywood studio era, "the merging of screen roles and offscreen personality was central to studio star making," and that studio publicity departments worked to "match the star's personal life with the traits of the screen character." Many film stars thus came to specialize in what Barry King calls "personification," in which the actor is "limited to parts consonant with his or her personality."[137] With its realistic sets, spectacular stuntwork, and Brodie's style of nonacting, *On the Bowery* begins to look like a dry run for the cinema.

Ironically, Brodie could "be himself" on the stage in part because he was seen to powerfully represent a social type. In a review of *On the Bowery*, the *San Francisco Chronicle* claimed that "Brodie may be an ideal bridge jumper and he certainly tends bar with neatness and dispatch, but he can neither act, sing nor make speeches. But what difference does that make? One can see a play any night, but a genuine Bowery lad: nit."[138] Another review claimed that Brodie did not try to "act anything but himself" and instead was presented as "a typical Bowery boy, which he is in many respects."[139] The Bowery boy was one of a number of social types prevalent on the late nineteenth-century American popular stage. Unlike the stage "Dutch," "Hebrew," "Italian," or "minstrel" types, however, the Bowery boy was not based on descent from a particular ethnic group. Instead, Bowery boys were an updated version of "the youthful working-class dandy."[140] The social identity of the Bowery boy depended upon his presence in commercial culture. Elliott Gorn characterizes the Bowery boy type not only in terms of work (they were "young single males, wage earners who earned their livings with their muscles"), but also their "rough and exuberant" leisure pursuits: "After hours, free from masters and bosses, they gravitated toward places like the Bowery, where they took back a sense of control over their lives that the workplace denied."[141] Christine Stansell writes that the Bowery boy "did not spin out his associations with his fellows on the basis of common membership in a trade union or an ethnic group or even an organized gang; rather, he defined himself through his use of his leisure time. In an after-hours world, he created commonalities through dressing, speaking, and acting in certain ways." The Bowery boy was "a member of youth culture, a milieu characterized by a symbiotic relationship to its own symbolic elaboration."

In fact, workingmen had long defined their perceptions of how to be a Bowery boy through watching "delightfully recognizable characterizations acted out on the stage."[142] Such characterizations began with popular plays in the 1840s that featured the actor Francis S. Chanfrau in the role of Bowery fireman Mose. For folklorist Richard Dorson, the Mose plays "sounded a popular, realistic note in the American theater that did not appeal to certain custodians of the drama." Dorson quotes a drama critic of the period who decried both the "vulgarity and illiteracy" of the Mose plays and the working-class audiences that they drew to the theater: "The boxes no longer shone with the elite of the city; the character of the audiences was entirely changed," and, instead of simply appearing on the stage, Mose "was in the pit, the boxes, and the gallery."[143] A similar complaint was echoed fifty years later in a *New York Times* review of *On the Bowery* that described how Brodie's "own kind" had "flocked to see him": "There was a house full of underdeveloped Brodies in the gallery" who "applauded everything that Brodie, the actor, did, but it was easy to do that; it was because it was Brodie, the bridge jumper."[144] At the Boston Theatre in 1894, Brodie appeared before "two galleries full of street arabs, who yelled, whistled, stamped and commented with courageous and seldom erroneous discrimination."[145] In Denver, Colorado, a newspaper treated its 325 newsboys to tickets to see *On the Bowery*. After parading through town and giving Brodie an ovation in front of his hotel, the newsboys are said to have gone "wild" at the performance, "cheering and applauding the athletic barkeeper."[146] Similarly, when *On the Bowery* came to Buffalo in 1895, a great crowd of "men and boys" lined the street "like a political procession." Brodie took the stage at the Lyceum Theater in front of "one of the biggest crowds ever assembled in any theater in Buffalo." "Not a seat in the house was empty," and every time Brodie "drew a glass of foamy lager, every time he raised his eye brows or opened his lips to say 'See?' the gallery gods became hysterical. Mr. Brodie had to ask them to keep quiet several times in order that some of the lines of the actors could be heard."[147] When the play returned to Buffalo four years later, Brodie still had a hold on "the hearts of the people and especially the boys. . . . [I]f there was one of that class of boys that Brodie helps so often, who was not there, it was because there wasn't room for him."[148] "I never forget my newsboy days, and every newsboy on the streets has my sympathy," Brodie told the local paper, and he talked about a Thanksgiving dinner that he had provided for five hundred newsboys in Detroit. The boys were so grateful that they sent Brodie a gold-headed cane, and his wife Gert a diamond locket.[149] Brodie thus embodied and individuated the Bowery boy social type and continued a vibrant tradition of nineteenth-century popular drama that had a powerful connection to young working-class audiences.

If spectators from around the country came to Brodie's saloon on the Bowery as an ethnographic "curiosity shop," the stage saloon in *On the Bowery* brought that ethnographic display to paying audiences around the country. The desire for an "authentic" experience in a workingman's saloon could pose certain dangers, however, even in the form of a theatrical reenactment. One of these dangers had to do with the fact that Brodie's stage saloon served actual alcoholic drinks. The *San Francisco Chronicle* called *On the Bowery* the "wettest play ever put on the San Francisco boards." "Rounds of drinks were served every few seconds and if there had been any more than one act of it the players couldn't have wobbled to the culmination."[150] A Portland newspaper wrote that the amount of beer that the players drank "raised the question how much more they could stand and maintain their equilibriums."[151]

Not only could audiences witness authentic inebriation, but some of the cast were genuinely "tough" characters prone to violence and, by some accounts, crime. At a Boston performance of the play in February 1896, some local college students were hired to play nonspeaking roles as patrons in the saloon scene. Trouble began when the students drank Brodie's beer "with a gusto," ordering it faster than the bridge jumper could serve it. Tensions increased when Brodie launched into his song. As Brodie "struggled through the first verse," the rowdy extras "banged the beer glasses down on the tables until they were smashed." At this point Brodie attacked the "apparent leader" of the students. Soon the other members of the cast, made up largely of Brodie's "sporting" friends, lent the bridge jumper a hand in giving "the would-be 'toughs' the worst drubbing they had ever received in their lives, and . . . ejecting them bodily from the stage." "That's the way I always serve guys who can't behave in my saloon," Brodie told the appreciative crowd.[152] In Idaho, two members of Brodie's company who had played the roles of safe-crackers in the show gave "a genuine exhibition of their Bowery proclivities" by picking the locks of a door at the theater during a dispute with the management.[153] Brodie's traveling ethnographic display thus held some of the same dangers as well as the same appeals as the experience of slumming on the Bowery—"real" drunken barroom violence and the encounter of "authentic" and potentially dangerous Bowery characters.

The cultural life of *On the Bowery* and Brodie's embodiment of the Bowery boy social type reveals the fluidity between "folk" and "mass" culture in late nineteenth-century popular entertainment and celebrity. The Bowery boy's "symbiotic relationship with its own symbolic elaboration" was a process that encompassed both an urban "folk" culture and an incipient mass culture, and illustrates that the latter could be "creative" of its own heroes; it could be the arrow as well as the target, the voice as well as the ear. The stage Bowery boy—like the outlaws, tramps, and mechanics found in nineteenth-century dime novels—was a multiply accented hero who could entertain a middle-class audience as an exotic and "genuine" lad and at the same time inspire a "yell of recognition" from working-class audiences. Brodie fused a variety of nineteenth-century stage traditions, combining museum attraction, stuntwork, and acting to create a mongrel art than anticipated both film stardom and cinematic stunt performance. Though Brodie found a niche inside the theater, his fame was still ostensibly based on his leaping ability outside of it. However, the closer we look at the distinctions between his technique in the theater and out of it, the more those distinctions begin to collapse in a manner that, like his stage performances, points to the cinema.

THE PRIZE FAKER OF THE WESTERN HEMISPHERE

"When I see that trade is getting dull and customers ain't standing two deep in front of my bar," Brodie told an interviewer, "I go off somewhere and make a jump."[154] Business must have been slow in the autumn of 1889, when Brodie, once more following in Sam Patch's footsteps, left his saloon and headed for Niagara Falls. Niagara had become a travel destination for the wealthy during the 1820s, when the genteel American elite began to "cultivate an appreciation of natural beauty and a consuming interest in scenic tourism."[155] Beginning with Sam Patch's 1829 jump, Niagara also drew daredevils like a magnet, and with them a less "genteel" class of tourists.[156] After Patch, the most famous of these was Chevalier Blondin (Jean François Gravelet), a ropewalker who crossed the falls in August 1859. Blondin astounded onlookers first by making the perilous crossing, and then by proceeding to sit down on the tightrope, lie on his back, and stand on one foot. During subsequent performances he crossed the chasm with a sack over his head, dressed as a monkey, pushing a wheelbarrow, carrying his manager on his back, and with baskets on his feet. Captain Matthew Webb, who was the second man to swim across the English Channel, after Paul Boyton, died while trying to swim the rapids above Niagara Falls in 1883. By the turn of the century, the first successful trips over the falls in a barrel were being made.[157]

Like the stunt performers who preceded him, Brodie was drawn to the falls, with its guarantee of large crowds and promise of glory on a truly massive scale. The *New York Times* reported that on an afternoon in early September, Brodie had donned a Boyton rubber suit and paddled himself out into the river about six hundred feet above Niagara Falls with the intention of going over. He was soon in police custody charged with attempted suicide, but despite Brodie's claims, the police magistrate did not believe that he had navigated the falls at all. Brodie was told that if he would admit to a hoax, he would be discharged. "Well, then," Brodie replied, "I did not go over, and I am off." The *Times* reporter noted that Brodie "seemed very nervous and frightened throughout the proceedings."[158] The following day Brodie was said to be "very indignant" that people doubted his claims and stated that he had witnesses of "undoubted integrity" who would make affidavits to the truth of his story.[159] Three men who had been with Brodie at Niagara did indeed sign affidavits before a magistrate to the truthfulness of Brodie's account of the feat.[160] The *Washington Post* quipped that two or three affidavits would serve Brodie's purpose "a great deal better than an actual trip."[161] The issue was not settled, however, and the same day as news of the affidavits was published, the *Chicago Tribune* quoted two crew members on the steamer that sailed in the gorge beneath the falls to the effect that it was unlikely that either Brodie or his party had gotten "even a whiff of Niagara spray."[162]

The Niagara controversy prompts us to reconsider earlier episodes in Brodie's career, such as the strange occurrence a year earlier when word spread that he would be making a jump from the Poughkeepsie Bridge. The figure of a man was indeed seen falling from the top of the bridge, but it turned out to be a human effigy whose trouser legs were filled with stones.[163] Perhaps eager to quell any suggestions of trickery and maintain his public status, Brodie did in fact jump from the bridge a few months later, but on this occasion he did not emerge unscathed as he had so often done before, instead sustaining severe internal injuries and breaking three ribs.[164] Niagara and Poughkeepsie took a toll on Brodie's profile in the press, and soon thereafter the possibility that even the Brooklyn Bridge leap of 1886 had been a hoax was being openly discussed. According to one informant, a tugboat captain had been paid two hundred dollars to participate in Brodie's "rescue" from the East River and then confirm every detail of his story.[165] "There are reliable newspaper men in New York," wrote the *Washington Post* in 1901, who said that a weighted dummy and not Brodie had hit the water and that the dummy had sunk to the bottom of the river while Brodie climbed into the boat and "panted realistically for a while" before answering the questions of reporters as he had been rehearsed by a New York press agent.[166]

If such accounts are true, Brodie's real "art" had much in common with the incipient field of public relations (a topic to which I will return in the next chapter), and the hoax ratifies his status as a working-class trickster and master media manipulator. In fact, on one occasion Brodie took advantage of his media publicity in a manner that is almost as stunning and prescient as his possibly phony bridge jump. Several prominent newspapers carried stories on March 31, 1898, that Brodie had died on a Lake Shore train in Chicago.[167] On the previous night, a large lithograph picture of Brodie draped with crepe had been placed in the center of the stage at the Alhambra Theater, where Brodie had been scheduled to appear. A hush fell over the audience, and the theater manager announced that Brodie had died. The following afternoon crepe was hung on the door of his Bowery saloon.[168] It was soon discovered that Brodie was quite alive and had only fallen ill on the train and passed out after an injection of morphine.[169] When Brodie arrived back home in New York at Grand Central Station, he was greeted by a crowd of supporters and a hearse. He told the crowd, "I'm not dead, though it's no fault of yours." As was the case with his occasional bridge jumping expeditions, the press coverage generated by this event translated into big business for Brodie's saloon, where patrons were said to be "three deep," with hundreds more waiting in the street outside.[170]

Besides bolstering his image as a mass culture confidence man, the open question of the authenticity of his jumps made Brodie resemble a film star all the more. Film producer Carl Laemmle's well-known 1909 publicity stunt, his claim that his newly signed actor Florence Lawrence had been killed by a streetcar, is often cited as the birth of the modern film star. Seen in the context of the reporting of Brodie's "death" a decade earlier, Laemmle's stunt looks like a page taken from the bridge jumper's playbook.[171] Furthermore, Richard deCordova claims that a crucial distinguishing characteristic of the movie star was the enigma of the star's "true" self, thought to reside behind their various film roles and studio publicity. DeCordova argued that during the growth of cinema, "all discourse about those who appeared in films emerged in a secretive context. The fascination over the players' identities was a fascination with a concealed truth, one that resided behind or beyond the surface of the film." DeCordova finds this discourse of secrecy at each stage in the early development of the film star: during what he calls the "discourse on acting," when the film player became the site of discourse about labor in the cinema; in the early 1910s, around the revelation of the names and personalities of the players; and later in the decade, with the increased circulation of information about the private lives of film stars.[172] Brodie's stardom is a historical point of reference for deCordova's argument that broadens the scope of the discussion beyond dramatic acting. Like the film player, Brodie's celebrity rested on a compelling secret: did he jump or not?

The possibility of a hoax behind Brodie's public image points to practices that would become common in the film industry, as well as the technique he is said to have used to pull it off: using a dummy as a body double. Indeed, several landmarks of early cinema made prominent use of a dummy to create the illusion of a thrilling stunt. The Edison Company's *The Execution of Mary Queen of Scots* (1895), which has often been described as the first special effects film, relied upon the strategic substitution of a live actor with a dummy.[173] Edwin S. Porter's *The Great Train Robbery* (1903) features a fight during which a man is thrown from the roof of a moving train, an illusion achieved by a match on action edit that substitutes a dummy for the body of an actor. In Walter Haggar's *The Life of Charles Peace* (1905), what Noel Burch calls "one of the true masterpieces of primitive cinema," the celebrated English criminal attempts to escape from the police by leaping from a moving train, and the actor is again replaced by a dummy.[174] Both *The Great Train Robbery* and *The Life of Charles Peace* combine location shooting with studio sets, and they rely on stuntwork, editing, and the use of a dummy to create seemingly impossible or dangerous stunts. These cinematic thrills can be understood as a continuation of the trends displayed on MacKaye's melodramatic stage, early examples of an incipient tradition of cinematic special effects, or, just as easily, as a professionalization of performances and promotional techniques explored by Brodie.

Brodie's use of a dummy was a novel innovation in the ongoing dialectic between the rival "arts" of Sam Patch and Timothy Crane, between body technique and industrial technology. Robert Odlum's death had demonstrated that body techniques suited to a previous industrial landscape could not easily be applied to the vast scale of industrial technologies represented by the Brooklyn Bridge. The "craftsman's empire" that had given skilled workers like Sam Patch pride of place in factory production had, by Brodie's era, been eroded due to the systematic deskilling of labor. The techniques of the mule spinner had been made irrelevant by new factory technologies, but the "art of the jump" developed by mill boys could still be employed to reawaken the body memory of a previous era.[175] Brodie restored that body memory in a display of nineteenth-century art that combined workingmen's subculture, the spectacle of the modern cityscape, and a montage of real and prosthetic bodies—an art, it should be noted, that looks a lot like the cinema. Porter and Haggar's landmark films were made just a few years after Brodie died—for real this time. Just before his death, Brodie moved to the drier climate of San Antonio, Texas, in an attempt to slow the tuberculosis that eventually killed him in 1900 at the age of thirty-eight. It seems strangely incongruous that Brodie, the iconic embodiment of the Bowery, should die in Texas, and yet it is fitting that he moved West just before the film industry, which relocated from New York to Hollywood

FIGURE 6. Paul Boyton's Shoot the Chutes ride at Coney Island. Courtesy of the Library of Congress.

in the 1910s. In the decades after the bridge jumper's death, the constellation of working-class Bowery entertainments that included saloons, dime museums, and spectacular melodrama would be eclipsed by the products of the Hollywood film companies.

Brodie's old nemesis Captain Paul Boyton lived to take part in the transition to a new world of modern mechanized amusements. Boyton attempted to establish a saloon along the lines of Brodie's grog shop, and when that endeavor failed he found a permanent home for his traveling "water circus" by establishing Sea Lion Park, the first enclosed amusement park at Coney Island.[176] In addition to trained sea lions, water races, and swimming displays, Sea Lion Park's main attraction was the captain's own invention: the Shoot the Chutes ride, in which a mechanized boat sent passengers down a steep incline and across an artificial lake. Boyton also patented a "pleasure canal" ride in which sightseers rode on boats along a waterway bordered by artificial scenery that provided a panoramic view of a river journey.[177] Boyton's Shoot the Chutes and pleasure canal were modern commercial amusements that commodified elements of the aquatic action-packed spectacle that had previously been experienced through exhibitions like his own. We might note that in his discussion of action, Goffman referred to "commercialized places of action" like the rides at fairs and amusement parks, which he claimed resolved the dilemma of action by providing danger that was guaranteed to be safe.[178] Goffman goes on to claim that the "manufacture and distribution of vicarious experience through the mass media" provided audiences with the opportunity to participate vicariously in action, and so allowed for "excitement without cost."[179] As we shall see in subsequent chapters, Hollywood stunt performers also manufactured vicarious action for a mass audience, but they did so through the development of body techniques, not industrial technologies such as Boyton's aquatic thrill rides.

Boyton's move to entertainment machines after the failure of his saloon proved to be a prescient one. Working-class audiences were shifting their leisure time from neighborhood taverns to amusement parks such as Coney Island and, later, to the new cheap nickelodeon movie theaters. At the same time, middle-class patrons found the "thrilling mechanical devices" at Coney Island to be an exhilarating liberation from the "normative demands of conventional bourgeois society."[180] Coney Island and the cinema also exemplified the rise of a heterosocial culture that was more receptive to female participation than the world of homosocial male entertainment typified by the saloon.[181] Stunt performers such as Brodie and Boyton figured in that process in that they, to paraphrase Tom Gunning, carved out a popular receptivity to certain types of media celebrity and thrilling performance "into which the film experience crept like a hermit crab."[182] It is hard to miss the significance, then, of the fact that before Steve Brodie moved to Texas, he lived for a short time in Buffalo, where he purchased a saloon at 475 Main Street, which he outfitted it in a manner similar to his grog shop on the Bowery. After his death, the location was taken over by Mitchell and Moe Mark.[183] The Mark brothers converted Brodie's saloon first to the Edisonia Penny Arcade and then, in 1908, to the Theatre Comique, a ten-cent movie theater.

CHAPTER 2

The Adventures
of the Human Fly

Few images from Hollywood cinema are more famous than Harold Lloyd hanging from the clock hands of a high-rise building in *Safety Last* (1923). The resonance of that iconic image is due not only to its stunning visual composition, but also to the fact that it refers to aspects of American cultural life that have become lost to popular memory. Indeed, Lloyd's death-defying climb in that film resonates with a whole culture of early twentieth-century spectacular performance wherein men climbed public buildings without the help of any mechanical or safety devices: human flies. Lloyd's biographies describe how he struck upon the idea of using a human fly in his film when he saw one in action at the Brockman Building on Seventh Street in Los Angeles in July 1922: "I watched him scale this whole building . . . until he finally reached the top. Well, it made such a terrific impression on me, and stirred my emotions to such a degree that I thought, 'My, if it can possibly do that to an audience—if I can capture that on the screen—I think I've got something that's never been done before.'"[1] Lloyd returned to the building and introduced himself to the fly, a steelworker named Bill Strothers, whom Hal Roach placed under contract to appear in Lloyd's new film.[2] That *Safety Last* owes a debt to the human fly performance is clear enough, but the film has further connections to that public spectacle. Consider an aspect of the film's publicity not typically mentioned in Lloyd biographies: a human fly named Harry Young plummeted to his death as he scaled a building in New York City in order to promote Lloyd's film.

"Human Fly" Plunges to Death in New York

While his bride looked on, Harry S. Young (inset), famous "Human Fly," fell ten stories from the wall of the Martinique Hotel to his death in Broadway, New York. Young was engaged in a publicity stunt when he met his death. On the right, Young is shown midway in his climb. The photo above was taken as the body struck the side- walk and shows the police rushing to hold back the crowd.

FIGURE 7. News article reporting "human fly" Harry Young's death during a publicity stunt. Courtesy of NewspaperARCHIVE.com.

Lloyd biographer Tom Dardis makes reference to this event, but only obliquely: "Human flies soon became the rage. One of these, named Harry Young, fell to his death while climbing the façade of the Hotel Martinique in New York; Pathé had paid him fifty dollars for the climb."[3] This statement seems to imply that the film sparked the development of the human fly performance, which I will show was already well known a decade before *Safety Last* was made. Also, although Dardis makes the connection between Lloyd and Pathé, he ignores the startling aspect of the incident, which was that Harry Young had been hired specifically to promote Lloyd's film: "Young was scaling the Broadway side of the Martinique as a publicity stunt for Harold Lloyd's latest screen comedy, 'Safety Last,' and Greely Square was jammed with thousands of men and women tense in the anticipation of a successful climb. Young began his climb during the noon hour, when the Thirty-fourth Street shopping district was most crowded, for the Pathé Exchange, which releases Lloyd's pictures, wanted the greatest possible number of persons in the picture."[4] The irony that Young had the words *Safety Last* painted in large letters on the back of his shirt makes clear that this was a publicity stunt to promote Lloyd's film. Notably, the tragic event was captured by newsreel cameramen: "Three camera men were on the fourteenth floor, and a motion picture cameraman was on the roof. The machine clicked repeatedly as he went higher and higher."[5]

In fact, Lloyd's well-known climb in *Safety Last* is just one point in a larger cultural loop in which spectacular thrills were produced for motion picture cameras and packaged as "news," a practice that helped to popularize the human fly performance that Lloyd was then inspired to reproduce in narrative film. At the heart of this chapter, then, is a genealogy of the traveling performers who billed themselves as human flies and an examination of their place in American cinema. Between 1830 and 1930 the term *human fly* in American discourse shifted from describing a type of theater and circus act that was frequently performed by a woman to the kind of performance typified by Harry Young and featured in Lloyd's film. In the course of this shift, human flies developed a performance of spectacular male heroism during the first decades of the twentieth century. This was a period when a new type of urban architecture, modern modes of advertising and publicity, the motion picture newsreel, and film stardom were all emerging, and all of these played a role in shaping how human flies were understood. The human fly act in turn addressed, and in some cases helped to shape, those various cultural forces. As was the case with the heroic jumpers whose acts were seen against the backdrop of waterfalls and suspension bridges, human flies developed behaviors shaped by the gravitational pull of imposing constructions in the lived environment. That is, human flies appropriated tall buildings for their death-defying performances, and, like the bridge jumpers described in the previous chapter, they should be understood as a form of street performance that took place within the "total space" of the city, what Barbara Kirshenblatt-Gimblett calls the "folk imprint on the built environment."[6] At the same time that they enacted a vernacular response to changes taking place in the urban environment, human flies were quintessentially modern in their association with skyscrapers and in their ability to attract urban crowds and generate publicity.

Though Steve Brodie died just before the boom in nickelodeon theaters and the rise of the Hollywood film star, human flies played a tangible role in the early film industry as representatives of what Jennifer M. Bean has called a "competing logic" of early film stardom and as featured content of the motion picture newsreel. That the newsreel changed the status of truth claims about thrilling stunts is demonstrated by Daniel Carone's 1921 jump from the Brooklyn Bridge. Waiting in the water beneath the bridge was not a boat full of "sporting men," as had been the case in Brodie's day, but a boat full of motion picture camera crews contacted by Carone so that "his feat might be imperishable throughout the ages." Brodie's alleged substitutions with prosthetic dummies would have been more difficult to pull off in an era of newsreel cameras, and twentieth-century thrill makers would have to learn to exploit those cameras both to ratify their claims and spread their renown. Indeed, a press account of Carone's jump reported that there were, by that time, few who believed that Brodie had accomplished his jump "in any other place except in a warm Bowery barroom where the rum was flowing freely."[7] The history of the thrill makers thus intersects with the motion picture industry and early film stardom, but in order to understand what was distinctively modern about the human fly, it is necessary first to look at some of his precursors, who can be found performing in circus and variety shows of the nineteenth century.

CEILING WALKER

The use of the term "human fly" to describe a mode of American popular entertainment had two sources in nineteenth-century circus and stage performance. The first was the act of "walking on the ceiling," which, according to Ricky Jay, had its earliest incarnation in an English performer named Sanches. Billed as "The Wonderful Antipodean" in 1806, Sanches performed a stage act in which his "iron shoes" were "fitted in grooves [slots] in a board fastened to the top of the stage."[8] Jay also describes a female performer in Nuremberg as one of the first to duplicate this stunt, in May 1828. This Spanish performer was described at the time as having walked a beam with flags in her hands, "free like a fly," and "danced a polonaise to the beat of the music."[9] Circus historian John Turner documents a number of nineteenth-century ceiling walkers working in Britain, including Madame Retza, Richard Sands, Madame D'Antrelo, and Professor Potter.[10] Ceiling walking remained a popular attraction throughout the nineteenth century and into the twentieth, judging by the issue of patents such as an "Electrical Device to Enable Showmen to Walk on the Ceiling" (1885), Victor Waid's vacuum shoe "theatrical device" (1905), and a 1909 "Electric Aerial Ambulating System."

Evidence from the 1880s and 1890s suggests that ceiling walkers in America were frequently female. An 1885 story in the *Ohio Democrat* described how "much excitement was caused" in a New Haven museum by a female performer who was called the human fly because "she walks on the ceiling head downward."[11] Perhaps most telling was an 1890 article in the *Daily Northwestern,* which described how "considerable scientific interest" had been produced by the human fly act. Note how the writer assumes that the performer is female:

> The performer, who is known as the human fly, is equipped with pneumatic attachments to the soles of her shoes. Sitting in the trapeze with her face to the audience, she draws herself upward by the arms and raises her feet until they press against the board. They adhere by atmospheric pressure. She leaves the trapeze, and hangs head downward. . . . Taking very short steps, not over eight inches in length, she gradually walks the length of the board backward. She then slowly turns round, taking very short steps while turning, and eventually returns, still walking backward. This closes the performance.[12]

A female ceiling walker named Mademoiselle Aimee received significant press coverage in the United States in the mid-1880s. Born in London in 1870, Aimee traveled across Europe as part of the Austin family of acrobats, appearing before royalty and heads of state before signing a contract to travel with W. W. Cole's Circus in the United States between 1883 and 1886.[13] A Louisiana newspaper described Aimee's appearance with Cole's Circus in 1883. Billed as "The Human Fly" and described as "a young lady, beautiful in face and figure, and with the glaring flush of early life on her cheeks and the bright prospects of womanhood before her," she was said to shock audiences by risking her life in a feat, the sight of which made "the blood to run cold and heart to stop beating." Taking the end of a rope in her teeth and spreading her arms, she was raised to a trapeze fifty feet in the air. Over her head was the end of a forty-foot-long polished board. Taking hold of the trapeze, she swung her feet up against the board and let go of the rope as the crowd held its breath: "Many such exclamations as 'My God!' 'Oh My!' and so on follow, and as she puts one foot before the other, walking in a forward direction, the situation is most thrilling. Often ladies have fainted at the sight of the almost child's peril, and men have trembled while looking up at her. Many refuse to look up at all and those who do continue to look are in constant apprehension of a terrible accident. There is no question in the world but that the feat is without parallel in the matter of tempting fate."[14]

Evidence such as this suggests that the big top human fly act was absorbed into a tradition of nineteenth-century "lady thrill acts" that combined dangerous stunts with the exhibition of the female body.[15] Female circus performers inspired considerable controversy, as indicated by the debate caused by the 1863 death of the wire walker Madame Blondin (Selina Powell) when she was eight months pregnant.[16] Though there was public resistance to female performers placing themselves in harm's way for the entertainment of paying audiences, teenage girls seem to have dominated this type of human fly act, perhaps because of the physical limitations of suction-cup shoes, which became less reliable the heavier the wearer and could only be counted on to hold a maximum of 240 pounds.[17] As an example of how this circus performance continued to be largely identified with women, the 1939 Marx Brothers film *At the Circus* features Peerless Pauline (Eve Arden), who leads Attorney Loophole (Groucho Marx) in a lesson on the use of suction-cup shoes.

Female ceiling walkers like Aimee Austin, however, were not the only human flies of nineteenth-century American popular performance. Perhaps the most closely related ancestor to the modern human fly was Harvey Leach, whose stage names included Hervio Nano and "The Gnome Fly." To use Jay's words, Leach "defied conventional taxonomy": "Neither dwarf nor midget, he was sometimes billed as the shortest man in the world." One of his legs was eighteen inches long and the other twenty-four, and his arms "easily touched the ground when he walked. He appeared like a head and trunk, moving about on castors."[18] Born in Westchester County, New York, in March 1804, Leach became a circus attraction in England. Leach, however, was not displayed only for his "remarkable physical peculiarities," but also for the stunning acts he was able to perform. At a May 1829 performance in England the playbill described the act that became his trademark: "Miraculous Feat of Running up the Roof of the Circus, Like a Fly, Back Downwards!!" The London *Times* provided a description of his act in 1838:

Signor Hervio Nano performs some of the most astonishing feats ever exhibited within the walls of a theatre. He appears to fly from the stage to a lofty tower with the celerity of an insect; he runs up places perfectly perpendicular; he climbs, without any apparent exertion, along the side of the theatre, gets into the upper circle in a moment, catches hold of the projection of the ornaments of the ceiling of the theatre, crosses to the opposite side, and descends along the vertical boarding of the proscenium. It is a most extraordinary performance, and if it creates a rather nervous sensation during its actual process, it affords a commensurate admiration at its termination.[19]

Unlike female ceiling walkers, Leach accomplished his feats without the aid of suction devices.[20] The insectlike nature of his climbing was emphasized by Leach's roles and costumes. Advertisements and reviews in England and America described how, in a show entitled *The Gnome Fly,* Leach first appeared as "Alnain, King of the Gnomes in his palace in the center of the Earth," and then as "Sapajou, the Baboon to the Prince of Tartary," before metamorphosing into "an enormous fly, covered with silver and green, and supplied with larger glittering eyes; in this capacity he flies to the rear of the stage, releases an imprisoned princess, and escapes the guard by crawling up the side of the proscenium, across the ceiling in front, as a fly, with his back to the floor, and descends on the other side."[21] In another advertisement Leach is billed as the "King of the Honey Hive," who would "Fly from the Top of the Ceiling! Crossing the Gallery—the Pit—the Orchestra—the Stage and Alight on a Village Spire! A Distance of 200 feet!" This is described as "an Act of Volition peculiar to himself, and never attempted by any other Artiste."

As was the case with the ceiling walkers, Leach demonstrates that one of the origins of the term "human fly" in American performance can be found in stage and circus traditions that involved fantastic feats of acrobatics and climbing in the indoor space of the theater or circus big top. Leach is a particularly notable precursor to the human flies of the twentieth century in that he made his climbs without the use of suction devices. Further, by taking his act to the ceiling, Leach broke the boundaries of typical stage performance space in what would become the hallmark of a new type of human fly that emerged in America during the first decades of the twentieth century. Where Harvey Leach had transgressed performance space by crawling on the ceiling of the theater, these new flies eschewed conventional performance spaces altogether. Instead, they performed outdoors, on public places not typically associated with entertainment: urban skyscrapers. This instantiation of the human fly was the result of the fusion of popular entertainment with a type of labor done in connection with tall buildings in England and America.

STEEPLEJACK

In William Hogarth's 1733 print *The Humours of a Fair,* we see a number of performers, including actors, musicians, and jugglers.[22] High above the crowd two figures can be seen on ropes. One of these is the tightrope walker Violante, a precursor to Chevalier Blondin, the "Hero of Niagara" described in the previous chapter. It is the other figure, however, that is most pertinent here. That performer was Robert Cadman, well known at the time for what was called "rope flying" or "steeple flying."[23] In Joseph Strutt's 1801 *The Sports and Pastimes of the People of England,* we read that Cadman and other steeple flyers would attach one end of a rope to the top of cathedral steeples and the other end to the ground. Placing a flat board on their chests, they would slide down the rope headfirst, adding to the spectacle by firing pistols or blowing a trumpet. According to Strutt, Cadman traveled so quickly along the rope during his "airy journey" that he "raised a fire by friction, and a bold stream of smoke followed him."[24] Cadman died while attempting such a performance in Shrewsbury in 1740, and a tombstone commemorating his death can still be seen there.[25] The act crossed the Atlantic not long after Cadman's death, as indicated by the 1757 performance of John Childs in Boston. Childs, who was billed as "The Flying Man," made a well-publicized "flight" from the 190-foot spire of Boston's Christ Church along a rope stretched to the ground seven hundred feet away.[26]

Cadman, Childs, and other steeple flyers indicate that the appropriation of tall public buildings—in this case, cathedrals—as props for spectacular performance has a long history. Some modern descendants of Cadman were not professional entertainers per se, but instead nineteenth- and early twentieth-century laborers who repaired church steeples, factory smokestacks, and other tall public monuments: steeplejacks. In England, opportunities for this work had proliferated with the growth of modern industry in the north.

In 1896 the *Chamber's Journal* claimed that "in Lancashire and Yorkshire, and the other great centres of the factory system in the north of England, there is naturally constant work for steeple-jacks, and a number of men ply that hazardous trade on the high chimneys which cover some of those districts like a forest."[27] Indeed, for some commentators the heroic feats of the steeplejack were an antidote to the dehumanization of modern industrial life. The author of a 1926 article on the history of steeplejacks argued that the ultimate goal of "mechanical civilization" was "the man who feeds, clothes, houses and moves himself by pressure of a button," and mourned the loss of "the old crafts," which were being altered by the changing world. He claimed that even sailors were no longer "a breed apart with their own songs, speeches and traditions." The steeplejack, however, "goes on pitting his limbs and nerves against the altitudes": "We build giant chimneys for our machines, but our machines cannot mend the chimneys. It needs plain human pluck and muscular agility to keep the mechanical Leviathan bound with the necessary hooks. The pillar-swarming steeplejack, the craftsman who is still greater than any machine, is more than a romantic figure, he is a social necessity."[28] Like the jumping mill boys described in chapter 1, steeplejacks displayed a performance of body technique associated with the spaces of modern industry. For some observers, steeplejacks provided an assurance that there was still a place for skilled labor and manly independence in an era of industrial work, although that place was outside the factory, not inside it.

England's most famous turn-of-the-twentieth-century steeplejack was William Larkins, who his 1925 memoirs wrote that whereas earlier, "medieval" jacks such as Robert Cadman had been showmen as well as workmen, there was nothing of "romance or adventure" to his occupation: he had simply taken up the family profession.[29] Nonetheless, Larkins's "greatest climb" had been a public spectacle: in 1905 he repaired and decorated Nelson's Column in London's Trafalgar Square as part of a celebration to commemorate the centenary of the famous admiral's death.[30] Despite downplaying the notion that he was a showman, Larkins described the excitement caused by his work on the famous landmark: "An immense crowd watched us start our climb. Every office window in the vicinity was opened wide and dark forms hung out of them, while the doors of shops and hotels were black with men and women, and in the Square a sea of upturned faces watched our every movement."[31] Though such high-profile jobs brought him a degree of media notoriety, his more routine work on church steeples and factory smokestacks was not accompanied by the kind of discourse of popular entertainment or self-promotion that surrounded steeplejacks in America. Indeed, Larkins wrote that his brother George had moved to America, and that steeplejacking in the two countries were "things apart."[32] Larkins claimed that his American counterparts had more in common with the "early steeplejacks," since they mixed showmanship and workmanship, and he noted that the American descendants of Cadman had begun to call themselves "human flies."[33] American human flies were not primarily climbing cathedral steeples or industrial smokestacks but instead plied their "hazardous trade" on another kind of tall public edifice that was beginning to cover many American cities "like a forest": the skyscraper.

The last decades of the nineteenth century saw the development of a new type of particularly American urban building: the modern steel-and-glass office tower, as typified by Chicago's sixteen-story Monadnock Building, competed in 1893; the Flatiron Building in New York, completed in 1902; and the Woolworth Building, which was begun in December 1910 and finished in 1913.[34] Skyscraper construction continued at a rapid pace through the 1920s, right up to the Depression era, with the Empire State Building—what Carol Willis refers to as "the quintessential monument" of the golden age of skyscraper design and construction—completed in March 1931.[35] The construction of these stunning buildings involved the labor of steeplejacks and construction workers, who, along with theater-based ceiling walkers, were precursors to the twentieth-century human fly. Newspaper coverage from the first decade of the twentieth century makes clear that the labor of the steeplejack could function as public entertainment. Consider this 1910 *New York Times* article: "Almost every one who passed through Times Square yesterday afternoon paused for a minute or two to watch a steeple jack who had swung out of one of the upper stories of the Knickerbocker Hotel."[36] Indeed, Donald L. Miller writes that the construction of a skyscraper was "a technological show that took place—like the building of a medieval cathedral—out in the open, in the heart of town."[37] The American steeplejack was the star of that technological show.

The career of F.S. Sutherland can illustrate the process whereby the labor of the steeplejack morphed into popular entertainment, a shift that is signaled by the use of the moniker "Human Fly." Sutherland was born in San Jose, California, and became a sailor in the U.S. Navy in 1876.[38] By the 1890s he had embarked on a new career, repairing the tops of tall buildings. A 1901 article referred to Sutherland as "the champion climber of the world" and stated that he was known "throughout the United States and in Europe" as the "Human Fly": "It was he who put up the pole and halyards and raised the American flag on the Eiffel tower in Paris, worked on the spires of the cathedral in Cologne, Germany, and climbed up the outside of the chemical stack in Glasgow, Scotland, one of the tallest chimneys in the world. He has climbed the steeples of St. Patrick's Cathedral and Trinity church in

New York and St. Paul's in London."[39] Although a steeplejack by trade, Sutherland was connected to the tradition of ceiling walking via his use of suction-cup shoes. One account claimed that Sutherland had been searching for a way to improve his methods of ascending smokestacks and steeples when his attention was attracted by a fly crawling up the wall of his room. He was then "seized with the idea of duplicating the methods of the fly": "He found out that the fly was enabled to crawl up a vertical surface . . . by the use of little suction pads or cups on its feet, and he set himself to the task of duplicating these." After many "experiments and trials" he succeeded in perfecting shoes that allowed him to climb "up a steeple at an angle of 60 degrees or less."[40] This origin story provided an explanation for the moniker "Human Fly" at the same time that it worked to elide any connection to the obvious cultural reference point for Sutherland's suction-cup shoes: the largely female entertainment tradition of ceiling walking.

Whatever his unacknowledged debt to stage ceiling walkers, Sutherland took their climbing technology out of the theater and into public spaces. He is described as, in one demonstration, donning "an odd-looking pair of shoes and a still more peculiar looking pair of gloves" and calmly walking up a wall until "his head touched the ceiling with as much ease and facility as if he were climbing a ladder."[41] He is even said to have had an audience with President William McKinley, during which he "demonstrated his ability as a climber by going up the walls of the room and walking out on the ceiling where he hung head downward."[42] Considering the fact that the circus and theater traditions of the human fly performance were often associated with female performers, it is notable how Sutherland's labor was made explicitly male: "Sutherland, who is built like a gladiator, laughed in a deep chested basso and waved his hand scornfully. 'Ropes, scaffolds—I don't use them. They are for amateurs. I walk up. That is where I got the name of the Human Fly.'"[43]

Though Sutherland was not primarily a professional entertainer, some of his high-profile jobs sounded like publicity stunts. In 1898 Sutherland scaled the Trinity Methodist Church spire in Denver as part of a church fair, and he set up a telephone wire so that, for a charge of ten cents, visitors could speak to him or hear him sing a song. Sutherland stated that he had received $1,000 for a similar stunt in Louisville, Kentucky, where a church had wanted "something sensational."[44] In a 1903 issue of the *Decatur Review*, one can read of Sutherland's plans to climb the "550 feet of sheer ascent" by means of "his wonderful suction pads" to do repairs on the top of the Washington Monument.[45] Sutherland was certainly versed in self-promotion, judging by accounts that described how he traveled on a bicycle that was decorated with the names of the high buildings he had climbed.[46] That Sutherland kept a close eye on how the media covered him is made clear by a 1909 New Mexico newspaper account, which described how Sutherland owned a "bulky scrapbook" that contained newspaper clippings about his work around the world, as well as pictures of himself "climbing like an insect far up on lofty steeples and flag poles, smoke pipes and cornices in every corner of the globe."[47] Sutherland is a transitional figure in the life of the human fly, as he emerged from the labor of the steeplejack, used the technique of the ceiling walker, framed the act in masculine terms, and began to exploit the publicity potential of this new type of outdoor spectacle.

A 1905 article in the *Cumberland (Md.) Evening Times* provides another example of a transitional fly. Headlined "The Human Fly," the article describes "a man who climbs the outer walls of the highest buildings and who uses neither rope, tackle or scaling ladder." The man, named John Garrick, was hired to hang and remove awnings, and we are told that he "perform[ed] this work in view of gaping multitudes who cheer and shudder as this man goes up sheer walls."[48] As was the case with F. S. Sutherland, Garrick's labor was made explicitly masculine, in part through an emphasis that, like Sutherland, he had come to this work via experience as a merchant seaman: "He followed the sea from boyhood to manhood, and during his service on deep-sea sailing ships he learned to climb and cultivated his nerve."[49] These comparisons to the traditionally masculine pursuit of merchant sailing, which made modern skyscrapers symbolically analogous to ships, had implications for Garrick's married life. The article stated that Garrick had been married five years earlier, but that "naturally his wife wished him to quit sea-faring." As a result, he found a job as an awning hanger and so was able to make "his climbing skill pay."[50] Steeplejacking is seen here as a social role that resolves certain tensions in modern urban living: it is both work and entertainment; both nostalgically romantic and socially useful; both traditionally masculine and compatible with modern married life.

In the cultural alchemy that christened the labor and growing celebrity of the steeplejack with the name of a circus and theater tradition, the human fly appears to have became an almost entirely male performance: I have not found a single account of a female human fly scaling public buildings in America during the 1910s or 1920s.[51] We might account for the lack of female flies by recalling that the act is essentially a form of street performance, a form in which the vast majority of performers are male, since female street performers are all too frequently "harassed, physically as well as verbally, by men who view them as 'fair game' on the streets."[52]

Men may also have been particularly predisposed to participate in and respond to a form of spectacle that seemed to represent a modern continuation of traditionally male occupations such as the merchant seaman. Historians have described the expansion of white-collar clerical work during the last decades of the nineteenth century. Michael Kimmel, for example, notes that by 1910 about 20 percent of adult men were working in "white-collar jobs in large companies, banks, and retail firms."[53] Kimmel places the growth of white-collar labor in the context of "rapid industrialization, technological transformation, capital concentration, urbanization, and immigration," all of which created "a new sense of an oppressively crowded, depersonalized, and often emasculated life. Manhood had meant autonomy and self-control, but now fewer and fewer American men owned their own shops, controlled their own labor, owned their own farms."[54]

A significant proportion of the new nonmanual labor was located in urban skyscrapers. Mona Domosh writes that by end of the 1800s, New York's economy had experienced a shift in its workforce from "the productive to the nonproductive sectors," and that the "large white-collar class occupied the offices of the speculative, new tall buildings." Many of these middle-class white men were drawn to activities that were believed to embody a connection to a "primitive" and revitalizing masculinity that was feared lost in modern life.[55] We will return to these dynamics of atavistic masculinity in the following chapter, but for now simply note that the human fly represented an urban variation on this theme. John Kasson's description of the appeal of escape artist Harry Houdini, perhaps the biggest male celebrity of this era, could also apply to the human fly: "He appealed to a desire for momentousness and risk felt by those caught up in predictable urban routines."[56] There was thus a strong affective connection between the male white-collar laborers inside tall American office buildings and the male performers climbing the exterior.

In the previous chapter I argued that bridge jumpers appropriated the cultural prestige of modern suspension bridges from the engineers and industrialists who had built them. In a similar way, the human fly performance brought the gigantic skyscrapers springing up in American cities down to human scale. Georges Bataille argues that great public monuments were erected "like dikes" against "all disturbing elements": "It is in the form of cathedral or palace that Church or State speaks to the multitudes and imposes silence upon them."[57] One could certainly read American skyscrapers as a modern corporate twist on this kind of architectural alienation, and architectural critic Anthony Vidler has noted a trend in modern architecture toward a progressive distancing of the human body from building design.[58] Seen in this regard, the human fly worked to redefine the skyscraper, measuring a gigantic industrial structure in terms of body technique. The "scaling" of the skyscraper by the human fly is thus a kind of measurement, recasting the building in human dimensions and allowing audiences to experience the urban landscape in relation to their own bodies. As with such phenomena as the gigantic inflated figures maneuvered through Macy's Thanksgiving Day parade route, the human fly act was a playful exercise in urban scale, a mapping of the body onto the city.[59]

Though it humanized the skyscraper, the human fly performance simultaneously dehumanized the climber. Susan Stewart describes how the category of the "gigantic" has the potential to transform the human body into miniature, especially pointing to "the body's 'toylike' and 'insignificant' aspects."[60] The human fly act could make apparent the human body's insectlike relation to tall buildings, a dynamic that is revealed in accounts of the human fly's unsettling effect on spectators. In the newspaper accounts of John Garrick cited above, for example, we are told of the reaction of his wife (whose name is not given) to seeing her husband in action: "I grew dizzy and wanted to turn away. Something held me fascinated though, and I watched him coming down in a sort of criss-cross fashion as quickly as a man would run down a ladder." This description is typical in accounts of human flies, whose audiences apparently were both fascinated and troubled by the movements of the tiny figures above, often describing them with terms such as "criss-cross," or "pendulum-like."

Again, we might notice the performer's symbolic designation as an insect: Garrick's wife went on to say that her husband "looked like a little black fly against the white stone." In fact, the designation of these performers as *flies*—a powerful symbol of dirt and decay—can tell us something about how audiences experienced the act. Mary Douglas famously defined "dirt" as "matter out of place," suggesting that "dirt is the by-product of a systematic ordering and classification of matter."[61] What is considered "dirty" in any particular culture varies and will point to larger systems of cultural classification. Because it exists in the margins of cultural categories and can even call those categories into question, that which is "dirty" is both reviled and capable of wielding a certain cultural power. Leach's performances could be described in terms of Douglas's notion of dirt since they transgressed accepted spaces of performance. The "out of place–ness" of Leach's act might help to explain the blend of astonishment, nervousness, and admiration we find in reviews of his appearances. It is fitting, then, that Leach's stage name, "The Gnome Fly," indexed a kind of symbolic vermin or pest: recall that he had emphasized the insectlike aspects of his act through his stage names and costume. Sutherland and Garrick's performances on the face of skyscrapers were similarly "out of place," and it is fitting that they, too, should be known as "human flies," a name that suggests the confounding of cultural categories.

Of course, the most obvious explanation for the allure of this performance was the very real potential for the audience to witness a spectacular and horrifying death, a key ingredient in all of the acts of turn-of-the-century "thrill makers," and a topic to which I will return in chapter 4. Human flies were heroic figures that "humanized" a potentially alienating new landscape at the same time that the buildings that were their stage could make them seem less than human, nothing more than little black flies against the white stone. Either way, this performance allowed audiences to experience the sublimity of the urban landscape as well as its relation to their own bodies. Whether the effect produced by human flies on their audiences was primarily disturbing or reassuring, one thing is certain: they drew crowds wherever they went.

PR MAN

Though the human fly act was born in conjunction with the rise of the vertical city in metropolitan centers of the United States, its coverage in the mass media and the exploits of traveling human flies spread the performance throughout the country. To get a sense of the excitement and interest that could surround a human fly's appearance at this time, consider that on the evening of December 2, 1916, a crowd of around forty-five thousand people gathered in Fort Wayne, Indiana, to see Harry Gardiner climb the Allen County Courthouse. The *Fort Wayne News*, the local newspaper that had sponsored Gardiner's appearance, described the unprecedented size and sheer spectacle of the crowd that had gathered to watch him:

For blocks in every direction the streets were literally packed with humans. Every window within a radius of three blocks from the court house was filled with people while the roofs of adjoining buildings were crowded to the danger point . . . street car traffic was simply impossible. Several cars were caught in the human jam and unable to proceed in either direction waiting until [Gardiner's performance] should be over and the crowd should disperse. The space occupied by the cars was not wasted however, as within a twinkling of an eye the tops of the cars were crowded with young men and boys who watched [Gardiner] from there. . . . [I]t was the greatest crowd ever gathered together in Fort Wayne for any sort of event.[62]

Throughout the mid-1910s and into the 1920s, men such as Gardiner, Jack Williams, and George Polley performed as professional human flies in cities throughout the country, climbing three-story banks or capitol buildings and drawing enormous crowds. To focus only on metropolitan centers such as New York City, then, would be to miss the fuller resonance of the human fly in the 1910s and 1920s.

As had the bridge jumpers described in the previous chapter, human flies put the mode of activity that Goffman calls "action" on public display. A press account of Gardiner's 1920 climb of the First National Bank in Gettysburg, Pennsylvania, reveals the spectators' engagement with the moment-to-moment action created when a human fly wagered "his future estate on what transpires precariously in the seconds to come." A "silent multitude" of more than six thousand watched as Gardiner, illuminated by a searchlight, climbed the side of the building:

Now he had reached the top story. Below him was a drop to death; on either side, sheer wall; above a cornice. A moment's hesitation, then—He leaned backward and stood upward in the same movement, gripped the edge of the cornice and let his body hang down straight. The crowd gasped. Now the limp body began to swing, back and forth, back and forth, like a pendulum, rising higher, higher at each sweep. Suddenly its motion seemed strangely accelerated, a second time it swung, and then—the feet shot straight out, the heels reached up to and rested on the cornice and held tight. A moment's wait and then the body seemed shaken with short quick convulsions—as if it were shot through and through with a powerful electric current. But at each convulsion the heels moved farther from the point where the fingertips gripped hard until, in another moment, the body was almost straight. The head and shoulders rose, pulled up by the powerful arms, the trunk of the body rolled onward and over, the left hand shot still higher up and gripped a crevice in the wall. And there was Harry Gardiner standing upright on the cornice.[63]

Here is a vivid example of "chance-taking and resolution" brought into the "same heated moment of experience," and the heightened meaning invested in even the smallest movements when the "momentary now" has such immediate implications for the life (or death) that follows.[64]

As already noted, action constructs character, and Gardiner's climbs allowed him to reinvent himself through his dangerous performances. Indeed, just as gigantic buildings could make climbers seem insectlike and thus *less than* human, their demonstration of "action" could make them appear to be *super*human. "Every one of the vast crowd were satisfied that they had seen a super-man in action," wrote the Gettysburg reporter.[65] Indeed, terms like "superman" were a recurring trope in press accounts of human flies. Jack Williams's fingers were described as "more like steel claws than bone and flesh, as they clung and hung to the tiniest of crevices," and one reporter stated that Williams was "superhuman."[66] Note that these press accounts were published almost two decades before the debut of the comic book character Superman. Scott Bukatman draws our attention to the connection between superheroes and the modern city, arguing that fictional heroes such as Superman and Spiderman allowed readers a vicarious "freedom of movement not constrained by the ground-level order imposed by the urban grid."[67] Bukatman mentions the workers who built the Empire State Building in the 1930s as precedents for the comic book superhero, but stunt performers such as Gardiner and Williams were equally important precursors, since they shaped the public understanding of spectacular male heroism and enacted feats of fantastic movement in the modern American city.

Unlike fictional superheroes who fought crime, traveling human flies like Williams and Gardener were flesh-and-blood professionals with business managers and press kits, and they used their stunts to exploit the crowds they attracted. Their modus operandi typically involved advanced publicity in a local newspaper, followed by the climb of a tall building while assistants moved through the crowd and took donations. The earnings would be split between the sponsors and the fly after the climb was completed. Some flies would also stop halfway through their ascent to make speeches and to plug their sponsors. For example, on August 10, 1918, Harry Gardiner could be found on top of a column of the Hall of Records shouting to the crowd below "to contribute liberally to the Knights of Columbus War Fund," while collectors passed through the crowd.[68]

Human flies, then, should be placed in the context of developments in modern advertising and public relations at this period in history. In fact, the modern skyscrapers that were integral to the fly's act have been understood as a corporate advertising strategy. Writers on the history of skyscrapers have argued that one of their central functions was as advertising, what Miller calls "billboard architecture." Fenske and Holdsworth state that skyscrapers were made to be seen and were built "primarily for the purpose of image." Robert Jones notes that the Woolworth Building proclaimed to the world "the thriving existence of the F. W. Woolworth Company," and Woolworth himself is said to have enjoyed pointing out that its height made it "the world's largest billboard."[69] There were certainly other explanations for the development of the vertical city, not the least of which was the economics of real estate development in densely packed urban areas. Still, when seen in relation to the skyscrapers on which their performances took place, human flies must be understood as a rival mode of advertising. Human flies made tactical use of the skyscraper, hijacking these monolithic corporate billboards to their own ends.[70] But "billboard architecture" was only one aspect of modern advertising, and the human fly's tactics become more striking when placed in the context of larger developments in corporate promotion taking shape at that time.

Before its twentieth-century modernization, American advertising was closely linked to what T. J. Jackson Lears has called a "carnivalesque tradition" that combined entertainment with moneymaking and was embodied by a "subculture of itinerants" consisting of circus performers, traveling medicine show salesmen, freak show impresarios, and peddlers.[71] In the 1910s and 1920s, modern ad agencies sought to define themselves in contrast to that tradition of Barnum-esque ballyhoo, presenting themselves as "engaged in informing the public, educating the mass of people to higher and better things."[72] Human flies more closely conformed to the older mode of advertising in their combination of itinerant entertainment and salesmanship. In this, flies had something else in common with the cast of characters described in the previous chapter. Recall how Steve Brodie's jumps were meant to publicize his grog shop. Captain Paul Boyton also exploited the synergies between salesmanship and stuntwork. In fact, Boyton worked closely with the makers of a patent medicine called St. Jacob's Oil. When Boyton traveled down the Arkansas River in his rubber suit in 1882, he was accompanied by a steamer named *The St. Jacob's Oil.*[73] Boyton worked plugs for the company into his newspaper interviews, as can be seen in this 1880 example:

> Of late I carry a stock of St. Jacobs Oil in my little boat. Before starting out, I rub myself thoroughly with the article, and its action on the muscles is wonderful. From constant exposure I am somewhat subject to rheumatic pains, and nothing would ever benefit me, until I got hold of this Great German

Remedy. Why, on my travels I have met people who had been suffering with Rheumatism for years; by my advice they tried the Oil, and it cured them. I would sooner do without food for days than be without this remedy for one hour. In fact, I would not attempt a trip without it.

The article concluded by observing how Boyton "became very enthusiastic on the subject of St. Jacobs Oil," and that when the reporter had left him, he was still "citing instances of the curative qualities of the Great German Remedy to a party around him."[74] There is a good chance that this interview was sent to the newspaper by the makers of the "Great German Remedy." In fact, a Kansas newspaper complained that they had been sent a "ready-printed interview with Paul Boyton" from "the patent medicine house with which he is connected," but that they had declined to publish it since it had "already appeared in substance in all the up-river papers."[75]

Like Boyton, human flies learned to combine dangerous stuntwork and self-promotion, and in the process they appropriated not only modern architecture but also the modern media. A 1927 article described how the inhabitants of "a small New England town" had been startled by the appearance of a car on whose front seat sat a man with a megaphone. As the car passed slowly through the streets of the town, a "slow and meticulously enunciated bulletin" issued from the megaphone, stating that the human fly would "scale the perilous face of the Masonic Temple, otherwise known as the opera house." The man behind the megaphone was the human fly himself, who was said to repeat this program day after day, culminating with "the daring performance."[76] Also consider an account of a Missouri human fly in 1921. A man is said to have "eased into town" and begun to circulate his handbills announcing that "the human fly would scale the New Leeper Hotel building promptly at 7:30 o'clock." When a crowd of two thousand people showed up, they saw "a squatty, slightly bald, silver tongued human fly" appear "on top of a transfer bus in front of the hotel." "In his best professional voice" he informed the spectators that he was about to perform the "feat of climbing to the very top of the building bare-footed, bare-fisted and bare-headed, holding no one save himself responsible should the worst come to the worst." A "free will collection" was passed: "A hundred berries was his usual price but he was flying here under special dispensation and would be satisfied with fifty dollars." The act, once it began, was less than heroic: "Three bell hops, two porters and the elevator boy of the hotel held a window secure until the fly was well astride it, and then by combined effort they raised it until the fly could hop gingerly up to the window of the next story, where the same process was again employed, sending the human fluke to the 3rd story window from where he climbed safely to the roof by aid of a rope dropped conveniently from the top by an assistant."[77]

A final example makes clear a connection between the human fly and commercial promotion. In 1926 the *New York Times* described how Johnny Meyer, who called himself "the human fly of America," was planning to sail for Europe to begin a "two-year campaign against the tallest steeples and most difficult buildings there." Having already conquered the "best-known buildings in the United States," Meyer announced that he was "determined to seek world-wide fame." Fame was not the only goal of his climbing, though, as he was also going to sell nerve tonic: "I will return to New York, I will climb the Woolworth Building again, and everywhere I go people will point me out. I can sell nerve tonic and my picture then for the rest of my life and I will tell people, 'See, I used this nerve tonic and I wasn't afraid of anything.'"[78] We see, then, how human flies after F. S. Sutherland used a style of vernacular promotion to sell both products and themselves in a manner that resembled the "subculture of itinerants" described by Lears, and that represented a residual form of advertising from which professional advertising agencies were working hard to distance themselves.

Although he went against the grain of modern advertising, the fly prefigured some of the strategies of public relations, a field that was taking shape during the same period. One such strategy involved the exploitation of the mass media in order to create news: "The public relations counsel," wrote public relations pioneer Edward Bernays, "must lift startling facts from his whole subject and present them as news. He must isolate ideas and develop them into events so that they can be more readily understood and so that they may claim attention as news."[79] Boyton's discussions of St. Jacob's Oil in newspaper stories, as well as commercial plugs given by human flies in the press and on the sides of buildings, demonstrate how thrill makers of this era employed some of Bernays's strategies.

At this point let us return to *Safety Last* and consider the narrative context in which the human fly's climb takes place. Lloyd plays an unnamed "boy" working at a department store who overhears his boss complain, "Something is wrong with our exploitation! We simply are not getting the publicity that our position in the commercial world calls for." Lloyd suggests they hire a friend of his—played by Bill Strothers, the fly Lloyd had seen in Los Angeles—to perform as a human fly and draw a crowd to the store. Bill is a steeplejack by trade, and we see him working on steel girders high above the city. The front page of the next day's newspaper features an article about a "mystery man" who will make the dangerous climb. Lloyd's film thus demonstrates how useful human flies could be as a tactic of the emerging field of public relations. In fact, human flies were widely used during World War I Liberty Loan drives, thus playing a role in George Creel's Committee on Public Information, which is often cited as the fountainhead of modern public relations. Under the influence of men such as Bernays, public relations was born in a tight symbiotic relationship with the mass media. Bridge jumpers and human flies created vernacular forms that explored that symbiosis and subsequently became important "content providers" for both newspapers and, later, a new media outlet that survived largely on the depiction of fabricated news events: the motion picture newsreel. The links between human fly and film production will become clearer through an examination of one notable human fly by the name of Rodman Law.

STUNTMAN

A 1919 article in the *New York Times* stated that Law got his start doing stunts in 1910, taking pictures of New York "seen from the gilded globes on the top of skyscraper flagpoles." "To do it he climbed the poles, leaned over the globes, pointed the camera down—and clicked. It was a remarkable trick of steeple-jacking in those pre-war and pre-modern airplane days."[80] A wandering and varied career that included stints as a sailor, a steeplejack, a detective, an ironworker, and a circus rider came into focus around stuntwork.[81] Most pertinent to the topic of this chapter, Law was one of the earliest, and certainly most widely publicized, examples of a person scaling tall buildings as a public performance and being referred to as a "human fly." Law stated that he had started his career in 1909, when he climbed the Flatiron Building in New York in order to win a bet with a fellow steeplejack.[82] Notably, Law developed his stuntwork in close collaboration with the film industry. He claimed that in 1912 he suggested to the film production company Pathé that "it would be a good little stunt to jump off the top of the Statue of Liberty." Law's account is backed up by interviews in the 1930s with Pathé executive Leon Franconi. Becoming "frantic"

FIGURE 8. Rodman Law, human fly and "Unkillable Actor" for the movies. Courtesy of Corbis.

because "there didn't happen to be any good news happening," Franconi described how "a young fellow walked into my office in Jersey City and said that he had a spectacular stunt in mind. His name was Rodman Law, the greatest daredevil that ever lived."[83]

Law's jump from the Statue of Liberty with a parachute on February 2, 1912, was featured in New York newspapers and shown across the nation's cinema screens as the subject of an early Pathé newsreel. Law told the *New York World* that his jump was meant to demonstrate the utility of the parachute, which he claimed would "enable steeplejacks to land safely should ropes give way."[84] Law arrived at the base of the statue accompanied by his assistant, five cameramen, and a dozen reporters and photographers. He and his assistant climbed to the top of the arm of the statue, 345 feet above the ground. After checking that his parachute was ready, Law noticed that his assistant was crying:

> I lighted a cigarette, took a few puffs, and then climbed outside the rail and looked down. . . . I must admit that just then I didn't enjoy the prospect of dropping three hundred and forty-five feet. I pulled myself together, however, made positive that my gear was in proper shape and, with no more

preliminaries, jumped backward in the air as far as I could. This was my first leap in a parachute, and it seemed as though I traveled five times the distance to the ground, when the 'chute opened with a jerk which nearly broke my grip on the bar. A few seconds later—it seemed minutes—I landed hard on the frozen ground, unhurt except for a few scratches and bruises. The next day the New York papers gave columns of space to what they then called a great exploit.[85]

Stunt performers such as Law were a perfect fit for an early newsreel industry in which, according to Raymond Fielding, more than 50 percent of the scenes were fake or manufactured.[86] In Albert E. Smith's account of his career with the Vitagraph Company, he wrote that each edition of the monthly newsreel carried "one sensational feature" in addition to the news. As examples, Smith offered "The Man Who Went over Niagara Falls in a Barrel" and the film of early aviator Frank Coffyn, who flew "over and under the bridges on the East River in one continuous journey."[87] The human fly was one of an array of thrill-making performances that fit with the imperatives of newsreel production, and so flies such as Law could find their way onto movie screens across the nation. Recall that Steve Brodie had been shown newspaper images of himself jumping from the Brooklyn Bridge within hours of his arrest, an indication of how his act exploited the particular "temporality of circulation" of late nineteenth-century newspapers.[88] Likewise, Law made prescient use of the newsreel's immediacy: "I thought that I should like to jump off of Brooklyn Bridge three weeks ago, and I did," Law told the *Washington Post* in May 1912. "I visited the moving picture shows a week later and there I saw the picture of my jump."[89] Law's spectacular performances, which included the scaling of tall buildings, became a key source of content for the nascent motion picture newsreel, and they even attained a kind of iconic status decades later for the men who worked in that field.

Law's collaboration with the film industry expanded from newsreel appearances to narrative films. A few months after his Statue of Liberty jump, Law leaped into the East River from the highest point of the Queensboro Bridge, while below a tugboat waited with "a battery of moving picture machines."[90] In 1913, Law dislocated his neck during a jump from an airplane flown by his sister, the well-known aviator Ruth Law (to whom I will return in chapter 4). The stunt had been made for the Ryno Film Company.[91] Law worked on a feature film for the International Film Company entitled *At the Risk of His Life,* in which he jumped into the Hudson River with a parachute from a balloon that was in the process of being blown to pieces with 120 pounds of dynamite. He rode a motorcycle off an open drawbridge as part of an Imp film entitled *A Daredevil Mountaineer.*[92] The same year, the *Boston Daily Globe* reported that Law had been shot out of a rocket to descend in a parachute "for the benefit of the movies." The film was to have been entitled *From New York to Paris in 160 Minutes,* but that title did not end up fitting the stunt's outcome: he descended through a "25-foot sheet of flame which burned his face and arms terribly."[93]

Despite this setback, an article published the following year, "Movies Responsible for New Brand, the Unkillable Actor," declared that "when the film producers want to achieve the impossible, they send for Rodman Law, and it is done forthwith."[94] That same year, Law's film *Fighting Death* was called "the most thrilling photo-drama ever made."[95] The film seems to have been a series of Law's stunts made to fit into a narrative: Law is described riding a horse off a sixty-foot cliff into a half-frozen river; climbing across a ravine on a 250-foot steel cable; and, in an homage to Steve Brodie, jumping from the Brooklyn Bridge.[96] An advertisement in *Motion Picture News* indicates that the film was sold on the basis of Law's renown: "You've heard of Rodman Law . . . the man who was shot from a huge gun high into the air—the man who stood on his head on the ball which tips the flag pole of the Singer Building—the man who climbed the side of the Flatiron building with his bare hands . . . the man who has defied death a hundred times. . . . Rodman Law, the calculating daredevil, who has thrilled millions by his mad recklessness in performing seemingly impossible stunts." This same Rodman Law, the copy declared, was featured in *Fighting Death.*[97] Law's fame as a film performer can be gauged by a 1914 article that stated that a young man who was "anxious to outdo the exploits in high jumping which have made Rodman Law well known in the moving-picture world" had jumped from the span of High Bridge into the Harlem River.[98] Law's career thus demonstrates the interrelationships between certain modes of stunt performance, newsreel production, and film stardom.[99]

As a preferred subject of newsreels and early action films, flies found their way onto cinema screens across the country, but the symbiotic relationship between film industry and fly extended beyond film production. For example, human flies were sometimes hired to promote films. In the September 25, 1920, edition of *The Moving Picture World* one finds a description of how the Paramount exchange in Omaha, Nebraska, had hired Jack Williams, "one of the human flies who were prevalent in Liberty Loan times." According to the article, "Williams would swarm up the side of the Rialto with a Paramount banner in his pocket and seven or eight thousand persons would gather to cheer him on his way."[100] While flies promoted films, they also promoted themselves in movie theaters. In September of 1928 the *Daily Northwestern* reported that Johnny Woods would appear at the Oshkosh Theater "in a ten minute demonstration of muscle control and balancing . . . immediately after climbing the 10-story Raulf Hotel Building."[101] George Polley appeared at the Fort Wayne, Indiana, Lyric Theater in April of 1918 to deliver a lecture on "how he became the Human Fly" in conjunction with motion pictures of his "daring climbs."[102] While Harold Lloyd's *Safety Last* was playing at Miller's Theatre in Los Angeles in July 1923, Bill Strothers—billed as the man "who did Harold Lloyd's climbing"— appeared at the L.A. Motion Picture Exposition in order to scale a fire tower. I have been arguing that the performances of thrill makers such as bridge jumpers, steeplejacks, and human flies gained a significant portion of their affective charge from an association with cultural signs that could register as an alternative to middle-class notions of fame, work, and masculinity. Appearances on, in, and adjacent to movie theaters reveal the human fly to be an alternative mode of male celebrity, albeit one not so much in competition with inventors, poets, artists, and statesmen as with Hollywood film stars.

Stunt performers such as human flies were, in fact, part of what Jennifer M. Bean describes as a "constellation of figures associated with thrilling modern film genres" that represented an alternative model of stardom, "one favoring the affective sensation of realistic thrills and grounded in the practice of on-location shooting."[103] Human flies seen in newsreels, action films, and on the sides of cinema theaters represented part of that competing logic of film stardom. Indeed, the appearances of human flies were always "on location," dependent as they were upon the modern built environment. Bean is among many film historians who have located the rise of film stardom in the "transitional period" of Hollywood cinema, roughly the same years that human flies were scrambling up buildings across America: 1907–15.[104] With a growing number of regularly employed actors and the standardization of production schedules, film companies began to draw upon stars as an "advertising ploy," marketing their films based on featured players and not company brand names. By 1910, film stars such as Florence Lawrence (the "Biograph Girl") and Florence Turner (the "Vitagraph Girl") were making personal appearances and garnering significant press coverage, and by the end of the decade the star system had become institutionalized with the establishment of studio publicity departments.[105]

One way in which we might see flies and film stars as competing forms of popular celebrity during the 1910s is by noting how both were mobilized to take part in fundraising during World War I. Hollywood film stars such as Charlie Chaplin, Douglas Fairbanks, and Mary Pickford made appearances to raise funds for the Liberty Loan drive and the Red Cross in 1918. Twenty thousand people gathered in the financial district of New York City on April 8 to hear Chaplin and Fairbanks give speeches in support of the Liberty Loans, and then they saw Fairbanks raise Chaplin over his head.[106] Human flies such as Harry Gardiner and Bill Strothers made similar appearances throughout the country and drew comparable crowds. In May 1918, for example, a crowd of fifty thousand saw Harry Gardiner climb a twenty-nine-story Park Row building while dressed in a white suit with a Red Cross emblem on the back. As he passed each story he received a round of cheers, and he paused now and then to send "a thrill over the watchers with some antic of his feet and hands." As he made his climb, several hundred "Red Cross girls," soldiers, and sailors moved through the crowd making collections for the Red Cross. When Gardiner returned to the street, his coat, trousers, hat, and shoes were auctioned off, and then he addressed the assemblage on behalf of "the mercy fund."[107]

Although film players and human flies shared the public stage at these outdoor events, in the Hollywood film production system, actors and stunt performers came to occupy very different positions. Indeed, there is one aspect of the early growth of the star system that film historians have tended to overlook: the rise of the star system was accompanied by, and to some degree relied upon, the professionalization of stunt performance. In the chapters that follow, I will examine the rise of Southern California as the center of American film production from several perspectives. For now, note that one important reason that East Coast and Midwestern film companies chose to relocate to Los Angeles was the promise of cheap labor. In order to be economically competitive with cities such as San Francisco, the Los Angeles chamber of commerce made it a policy to hold down wages and discourage union organization, and in so doing it encouraged businesses to move into the area.[108] One result of this labor policy was that work in the early motion picture industry was "irregular and in no way guaranteed" and relied upon a large pool of extras who were available on short notice.[109] Most of these extras were denied full-time employment, leading to two distinct types of workers:

those inside the studio gates, who worked every day, and those outside, who "lined up outside the studio gates every morning in the hopes of securing a job for that day."[110] Here we find the Hollywood version of larger trends in American labor, whereby skilled and deskilled workers were segmented from each other, as were white- and blue-collar workers.

Stunt performers at this time were a specialized category of extra. Early stunt performer Harvey Parry described how extras would sit outside the Paramount studios, shooting craps and playing cards: "A casting director would come out and say 'Anybody wanna make ten bucks?' The guy would go up there and maybe jump off [a] building."[111] Film historian Kevin Brownlow writes that "an extra or bit player would be paid more for stunt work and this proved a great incentive." For example, one stunt performer active in the mid-1910s recalled that "If I did stunts, like jumping off a moving train, I got an extra five dollars, and when you get fifteen dollars a week, five is very important."[112] As the film players "inside the gates" became one of the film companies' key economic commodities, they had to be protected from potentially dangerous stuntwork. As early as 1916, a New York newspaper wrote of how the film star "gets the credit" while "the stunter takes the risk": "A motion picture company cannot afford to have a high-priced star exposed to any danger. So when the four-figure-per-week favorite mounts a prancing steed or takes the steering wheel of a racing car he or she usually rides a few feet, then gets out. A stunter, dressed exactly like her or him, takes the place and goes through the risky part of the performance. At the finish, the star again resumes the role, and the audiences have marveled over the daring of the leading actor."[113] Stuntman Yakima Canutt echoed the close connection between stunt performance and the economics of the star system: "Should a star break a leg, an arm, or even get his face skinned a little, the overhead goes up while the actor recuperates."[114]

It is notable that the systematic doubling of the star actor was kept a secret. Stunt performers worked mostly anonymously and without credit, and although "the public had some vague idea of their existence, the industry would not permit stunt people to be publicized."[115] Film historian John Baxter claims that the film industry tended not to acknowledge the "existence or importance of stunt men."[116] An anonymous stuntman told a *Saturday Evening Post* writer in 1936 that "for a double to let it be known publicly what he does, and whom he does it for, is an unforgivable sin." He described how, when he entered the film industry, it was "gently but firmly" impressed upon him that "under no circumstances was I to be seen in the proximity of the star I was doubling for. . . . [M]y domain is strictly under cover. I must never seek the sunshine of publicity or the glow of glory. Pay checks alone must brighten my solitude."[117] The industry's refusal to publicize stunt performers is notable, given that they clearly had personality as well as talent. The author of an article published in the popular press in 1945 claimed that "although they are by far the most colorful guys in the business, stunt men are the least publicized, which is the way the studios want it."[118]

The veil of secrecy surrounding stunt work was maintained because it was felt to be imperative to the maintenance of the unity of the star image: "There was a widespread belief that it could only be harmful to the industry were the public to learn that screen stars did not perform their own heroics. When a stunt person was doubling for a star, the set would be closed to the press. More than a few stars objected to giving their 'doubles' public credit."[119] Stuntman Dick Grace described how stunt performers were obliged to keep their roles in film production a secret in order to corroborate the claims of film actors:

> I have heard stars sit around right here in Hollywood and tell some great fish stories. . . . One in particular used to delight in telling of a narrow escape he had in making a fire dive from a burning building, and he would turn to me for verification. I got to be quite a proficient liar backing him up. Well, I guess it's expected of us. When we sign a contract we have to do more than earn our money risking our health. It's better that we tell how brave some of our stars are; otherwise we couldn't work for them.[120]

Baxter asserts that stuntmen were used "promiscuously" as early as the action serials of the 1910s and adds that it was always done "without credit and often in the face of flat statements from the producers that the star took all his or her own risks."[121] The unnamed stuntman from the 1936 *Saturday Evening Post* article cited above summed up his situation this way:

> I'm the mystery man of the movies—the skeleton in the star's closet. Though I've performed under the aliases of thirty different stars, you've never read my name as a cast credit. Socially, I'm poison and stars resent the suggestion that they even know me. Yet they can't get along without me. I wear their clothes, I ride their horses, I sail their boats, I fly their planes; for I am the man they are supposed to be. . . . I'm the one individual Hollywood can't take as a joke, the one embarrassing relation it can't laugh off; that unpopular stepbrother of the stars, the double.[122]

One way to understand the air of secrecy around the "mystery man of the movies" is to return to the work of Richard deCordova, who argued that during the growth of cinema between 1909 and 1915, "the truth of the human labor involved in film" was constituted as a secret. For deCordova, the featured actor, or "picture personality," became "the site of this truth" in film discourse, and consequently "the biggest secret of all."[123] In this process, the unified image of the actor across screen roles and extratextual materials such as articles in fan magazines took on particular importance. The persona of the star actor as it circulated through films and publicity became the recognized site of labor in films.[124] The system of Hollywood publicity was thus built around actors, and the visibility of the stunt performer's labor threatened to prevent the establishment of and control over the unified public image of a star. In order to prevent the fragmentation and destabilization of the star image, stunt performers' faces and identities would need to be hidden and their performing bodies sutured to the film stars' faces, producing a literal embodiment of a multiply accented performance.

Recall the use of the moniker the "Stunt Men's Club" in the 1916 *New York Tribune* article described in this book's introductory chapter. The gendering of that term is one indication of the long-standing assumption that the majority of stunt performers were men, even those that doubled female stars. Baxter links a number of male stunt performers (including Rodman Law) to the production of films starring "serial queens" such as Pearl White and Ruth Roland.[125] Stuntmen would often wear wigs and dresses to double for female players. Dick Grace described an unnamed female star who "was known as a daring girl on the screen" and who made public appearances during which she told of "the great perils she went through to give the public thrills: how much punishment she subjected herself to to produce dramatic moments, how she loved to do it. . . . Then she showed flashes of the various stunts she had done for ten or fifteen years. Ye gods! Every one of them was the work of her stunt man, who is down and out and broke at present."[126] The point I want to make is not that more men than women performed certain stunts. There is evidence of female stunt performers working in film production from the 1910s, and, Grace's complaints notwithstanding, some female stars certainly did some of their own stunts, just as some male stars did. What I want to stress is the establishment of a greater segmentation of labor between stars and stunt performers regardless of the star's gender, such that the actors who were said to perform some of their own stunts—Tom Mix, Buster Keaton, Pearl White, Douglas Fairbanks, and, of course, Harold Lloyd—became notable exceptions.[127]

Perhaps now we are better able to appreciate the tangle of performance and publicity that surrounded Harold Lloyd's *Safety Last.*

Despite the widely held belief that Lloyd did all of his own stunts, the climbing in the film was inspired and partially enacted by Bill Strothers, and many of his "riskiest scenes" were performed by stuntman Harvey Parry, with Lloyd stepping in "for the closer and relatively safer shots." Parry stated that he never mentioned this fact until Lloyd died in 1971: "The only thing I couldn't have was publicity, which was alright with me, I didn't care."[128] The same techniques of film editing that substituted Parry for Lloyd could be used for a female star, allowing a woman to perform a human fly act that had come to be associated with men. The labor of the stunt double should be seen, then, as a crucial component of the "technologies" of early film stardom that Jennifer M. Bean describes in relation to the stars of the action serials of the 1910s. Bean notes that public attention was drawn to the "unusual fact" that many of these action heroes were female.[129] As we have seen, the thrill-making stunts that serial stars enacted had a cultural life outside the cinema, and the genealogies of those performances helps us to understand the gendered discourses that made the participation of women notable and therefore marketable.[130]

Despite the fact that there had been few if any female human flies scaling public buildings in the style of Jack Williams or Rodman Law, the novelty of a female fly became the basis for the 1924 Al Christie comedy *Hold Your Breath,* starring Dorothy Devore. Devore's gender was a means to promote and differentiate the film, as is made clear by ad copy that billed her as "The Girl Who Outstunts Lloyd" and "A Harold Lloyd in Skirts."[131] Prerelease hype in the *Los Angeles Times* stated that "theater audiences have grown used to seeing a male star do daredevil stunts," but that Harold Lloyd now had a rival in "this petite young actress, who climbs about on tall buildings, with all the courage, ease and abandon of the spectacled comedian."[132] The transposition of the human fly act to a female player resulted in some notable shifts in the narrative logic of the film. Devore plays Mabel, who is being courted by the corpulent Freddie (Walter Hiers). When Mabel's brother Jack (Jimmy Harrison) collapses from ill health while at work at the local newspaper, she steps in as family breadwinner. Hired as a reporter, Mabel hopes to get an interview from the millionaire curio collector Blake (Tully Marshall), who has arrived in town with a priceless bracelet and a rabid hatred of newspaper reporters. Mabel pays a bellboy at Blake's hotel for the use of his uniform and strolls into Blake's office to announce the arrival of a reporter. As Blake angrily tears up the reporter's card, Mabel reappears in her own dress. Blake is confused and asks, "Where's the bellboy?" Mabel coquettishly raises her skirt to reveal the bellboy's trousers underneath. Blake is impressed and agrees to give Mabel her interview. Unfortunately, an organ-grinder's monkey steals the priceless bracelet as they talk, and Blake assumes that Mabel has stolen it. Desperate to clear her name as the hotel police arrive, Mabel climbs out the window onto the side of the building in order to find the monkey. What follows is a mad chase along the lines of *Safety Last,* with comic business involving the hotel's neon sign, an affectionate dog, a guest playing a trombone by an open window, and a fire hose. When Freddie discovers Mabel's predicament, he arranges for hay and mattresses to be thrown onto the sidewalk beneath her. Eventually Mabel succeeds in capturing the monkey and returning the bracelet to Blake. When she is reunited with Freddie, we learn that the family has struck it rich, prompting Mabel to exclaim, "I guess I'll let him do the reporting—and I'll do the wife-ing!"

The producers of *Hold Your Breath* clearly intended to stick closely to the formula that had been so successful in *Safety Last,* but the star's gender has some notable consequences. First, the narrative frame must work to motivate the performance of stunts set in a public sphere traditionally restricted to men.[133] Mabel's empowerment in that sphere is tempered by the narrative's comic register and an ending that reestablishes gender norms ("I guess I'll let him do the reporting—and I'll do the wife-ing"). Second, publicity for the film suggests that it was to be read as a comic failure of masculinity as much as a tribute to feminine ingenuity: one newspaper ad proclaimed, "He was too fat to climb up to rescue his sweetheart from a high building so he bought a load of hay and a ton of mattresses for her to fall on."[134]

Finally, what are we to make of the emphasis placed on the bellboy's trousers in both the film and its publicity? Newspaper advertisements for the film featured images of Devore hanging from a flagpole, trousers prominently shown, or hiking her dress to reveal the trousers beneath.[135] The prevalence of the trousers is ostensibly motivated by their significance as a plot device for gaining access to Blake, but that reason alone cannot explain their heavy emphasis. In fact, the trousers seem to have been meant to ensure the propriety of a film that depicts a female star performing in public space high above an ogling crowd. Devore's trousers are thus reminiscent of the long dresses that would sometimes be drawn on female trapeze artists in circus promotional images.[136] Brenda Assael argues that the performances of female circus acrobats were controversial not only because of the danger of their acts but also because of their "perceived lewdness," and she adds that the acrobat's success depended upon the performer's ability to negotiate tensions caused by "the public's approval of her 'ladylike' athletic exhibitions, on the one hand, and the controversy surrounding her sexually provocative poses and costumes, on the other."[137] Devore's trousers are thus a reminder of the complex negotiations that female stunt performers often had to make when their erotic objectification could produce a different kind of thrill in audiences.[138] Despite their narrative differences, *Hold Your Breath* bears a striking similarity to *Safety Last* in terms of the film form used in the stunt sequences: we see primarily medium shots of the star on the ledge, framed in such a way that any nearby safety precautions cannot be seen, along with a few brief long shots of what are most likely stunt doubles on the side of the building.[139] Here may be another reason for Devore's trousers: to facilitate continuity in sequences containing shots of what was most likely a male stunt double.[140]

We begin to see, then, that *Hold Your Breath* and *Safety Last,* as well as the iconic images of Harold Lloyd scaling a high-rise building, absorb and obscure a rich tradition of spectacular entertainment that had run parallel to the American cinema. Indeed, I find it hard to resist the urge to see the rise of Lloyd's celebrity from this, his most famous film, and the tragic fall of human fly Harry Young as reflective of larger historical currents in American popular entertainment. In fact, Young's death is a convenient marker for the end of the human fly tradition: Young's death sparked legislation that outlawed human flies in New York City. On April 11, 1923, the *New York Times* reported that human flies would be prohibited from "climbing the sides of buildings in the city": human flies were classed as "reckless individuals who for advertising purposes climb up the sides of large buildings, endangering their own lives and the lives of others and block traffic." Referring to the recent death of Young, it was decided that violation of the ordinance banning human flies would result in a fine of ten dollars, ten days imprisonment, or both.[141] News accounts after this time sometimes describe human flies being thwarted in their attempts to climb, like Jack Bettinger, who appeared in Brooklyn on January 8, 1927, ready to climb, but was "confronted by a policeman armed with a copy of the city ordinance prohibiting such exhibitions."[142] While that legislation certainly saved lives, the prohibition of human flies should also be considered in terms of a struggle between rival approaches to advertising and the cultural meaning of public monuments. The skyscrapers themselves would, of course, continue to provide twenty-four-hour advertising for their corporate owners, but their public facades could no longer be legally appropriated for promotion by freelance operators.[143]

I have argued that human flies were one of several competing types of male media celebrities at this time, but the cards were stacked against them. Their mode of self-promotion was closer to the "carnivalesque tradition" of the traveling peddler than to the clout of either Hollywood studio promotion or the professional sports organizations that provided the news media with a more predicable and reliable source of action heroes.[144] Human flies of this era were part of a mode of male stunt performance that achieved a degree of public visibility through the film industry before being subsumed by the economics of the star system and the professionalization of stuntwork, both of which led to a mode of production whereby thrills were performed by uncredited stunt workers, whose bodies were sutured to the faces of film stars.[145] Though now merely a footnote, human flies were an important part of the landscape of American popular entertainment in the first decades of the twentieth century, and in their heyday they enacted powerfully affective modern performances. In fact, to call to mind that December evening in 1916, when forty-five thousand people gathered in Fort Wayne, Indiana, to watch Harry Gardiner climb the Allen County Courthouse is to catch a glimpse of how a parallel history of American popular performance might have developed. The stunt sequences in *Safety Last,* then, are best seen as one instance of a much larger discourse about the lived environment, the nature of public persuasion, and the modern media, forgotten aspects of which can be glimpsed in the long shots of Lloyd and his stunt doubles.

CHAPTER 3

The Adventures
of the Lion Tamer

A steel cage is cloaked in darkness. Inside can be seen the dim out-
lines of a chaotic, shifting mass of snarling animals. Overhead lights
illuminate the cage and a man enters firing a pistol loaded with blank
cartridges. The agitation of the lions and tigers gives the impression of
savage violence precariously held in check by the man's kitchen chair
and whip. The man is lion tamer Clyde Beatty, and this is the climactic
scene of the 1933 film *The Big Cage*. At one point in Beatty's act a lion
named Nero is brought into the cage. Beatty moves within a few feet of
the lion and their gazes meet. The moment is prolonged and accentuated
by close-up shots of their eyes. After this tense standoff, Nero backs
away and takes his place on the platform with the other lions. At first
glance, this might appear to be simply the most spectacular episode in a
throwaway novelty film made to cash in on the recent success of Beatty's published memoirs. But why those excessive shots of Beatty and
the lion's eyes? What exactly was the audience meant to see from this
perspective? What occurs between Beatty and the lion in that moment?
Unpacking the cultural meaning of that exchange of glances will serve
as a starting point for an examination of lion taming as a mode of modern stunt performance and the lion tamer as a form of nineteenth- and
twentieth-century celebrity. Big cage lion tamer acts gave dramatic form
to cultural discourses having to do with celebrity, masculinity, and the
human relationship to the natural world, and tracking the history of the
cultural meaning that accrued to acts such as the one seen in *The Big*

FIGURE 9. A reciprocal look between Clyde Beatty and a lion.

Cage sheds light on the process by which nineteenth-century thrill makers were incorporated into Hollywood cinema.

Like bridge jumpers and human flies, lion tamers were popular celebrities before Hollywood. The display of wild animals as popular entertainment has a long history, indicating a powerful fascination with both exotic animals and the heroic men and women who performed with them. The form of wild animal acts, however, is shaped by culture and history, a fact that an examination of nineteenth- and early twentieth-century lion tamers will illustrate. Lion tamers rose to cultural prominence at the same time as did modern zoos and circuses, and, like those institutions, their acts dramatized the changing ways in which Westerners understood their relationship to the natural world. In the process, lion tamers embodied the ideals and paradoxes of Victorian masculinity for many who saw them perform. The wide appeal of the lion tamer act, like the interest in bridge jumpers and human flies, relied upon the act's ability to sustain multiple and often contradictory interpretations: lion tamers enacted manly self-restraint for some middle-class observers, and, at the same time, their violent and frequently bloody acts bore a family resemblance to an alternative culture of plebian entertainments such as dogfighting. In either case, the lion tamer act placed the interaction between trainer and animals on display as a form of popular entertainment. One of my goals is to explore the "unnatural history" of wild exotic animals on the stages and screens of nineteenth- and twentieth-century

America. By "unnatural histories" I refer to Nigel Rothfels's notion of accounts made of animals that live not in their "native haunts" but in "human environments" such as museums, circuses, and zoos.[1] I agree with Rothfels's assertion that such unnatural histories are as worth telling as natural ones, and big cage acts provide a case study in the lives of wild animals performing in the human environment.

Displays of human interaction with exotic animals held a powerful appeal for audiences at nineteenth-century circuses, fairgrounds, and variety stages, but they also posed certain problems for filmmakers during the first decades of the twentieth century. Despite those challenges, the film industry found ways to repackage the spectacle of wild animal acts as part of Hollywood cinema's "excited gaze," and one could argue that production facilities at Selig and Universal during the 1910s were zoos as much as they were film studios. During the early 1930s, the establishment of an infrastructure supplying trained animals to filmmakers coincided with developments in filmmaking technology to facilitate a new depiction of action with wild animals in Hollywood. This led to what the *Los Angeles Times* referred to in 1932 as an "animal trend" that was sweeping the American cinema: "All Hollywood will soon be one vast menagerie," claimed the *Times* upon observing the number of pictures that demanded the performances of caged animals.[2] The MGM Tarzan films and Clyde Beatty's *The Big Cage*, which were among the cinematic animal trend of the early 1930s, illustrate Hollywood's remediation of the lion tamer act. Though the chapter will culminate in an analysis of these Hollywood films and the exchange of looks between Beatty and Nero in *The Big Cage*, we must first establish the formal and cultural parameters of the modern lion tamer performance, which began one hundred years earlier.

THE KING OF CREATION

In November 1826 a giraffe was sent from the viceroy of Egypt to France. Initially housed in Marseilles, the giraffe drew crowds of curious onlookers during its daily walks. In May 1827 the giraffe began a trek to Paris that became a public sensation: the press followed its progress, and crowds gathered to catch a glimpse of the animal as it headed for the capitol. Once installed in Paris's Jardin des Plantes, the animal drew six hundred thousand visitors over the course of a year and inspired the creation of giraffe-related stage plays, songs, clothing, and dances.[3] France's "giraffe-mania" reveals the powerful fascination that exotic animals held for European and American audiences during the middle of the nineteenth century, a fascination that popular entertainments such as circuses and zoological gardens began to rationalize. Histories of the modern zoo often begin with seventeenth-century private menageries, where wild animals demonstrated the wealth and power of their aristocratic owners.[4] Eric Baratay and Elisabeth Hardouin-Fugier describe how, in the wake of the French Revolution, such princely menageries were converted into establishments intended to "serve the entire nation rather than the select few."[5] For example, admission to Regent's Park Zoo in London was restricted when it opened in 1828, but economic pressures led to the acceptance of a broader audience in 1846.[6] Zoological gardens spread rapidly throughout European and American cities in the middle of the nineteenth century. In the United States, New York's Central Park Zoo and Chicago's Lincoln Park Zoo were opened in the 1860s.[7] By the mid-1860s, Carl Hagenbeck, a trader in wild animals and influential animal trainer, could write that the demand for wild animals was growing, with zoos "springing up on all sides."[8]

Hagenbeck noted that public interest in exotic animals was being stimulated in part by the growing number of traveling menageries in Europe and America.[9] Itinerant wild animal shows had been a common source of entertainment in New England since the 1720s and 1730s.[10] John Culhane writes that by the early 1820s there were thirty or more such traveling menageries, or "rolling shows," touring the eastern United States. As animal exhibits expanded to include equestrians and clowns performing in center rings and under large tents, modern circuses were born.[11] During the mid-1830s, a number of traveling enterprises based in the New York area formed the Zoological Institute, which managed properties, rationalized the allocation of animals, and organized show routes.[12]

It was at this moment, when the "static menagerie exhibition began to reflect more of the performance orientation of the circus show," that the lion tamer first emerged as a popular figure.[13] The performer often credited with originating the modern lion tamer act in America was Isaac Van Amburgh.[14] Born in 1808 in Fishkill, New York, Van Amburgh was reportedly descended from "one of the original Dutch settlers" of the state. When he was fifteen years old, Van Amburgh took a job in New York City, working as a clerk in the warehouse of a relative. That kind of office life did not suit his "enterprising spirit," so he "packed up, and set out on his travels." Van Amburgh was connected with a traveling menagerie by the time he was twenty, and he made

FIGURE 10. Illustration of Isaac Van Amburgh and his menagerie of wild animals.
Courtesy of the Bodleian Library.

his first performances with the Zoological Institute in New York in the
early 1830s.[15] Evidence suggests, then, that despite a fairly prosperous
background, Van Amburgh rejected the comfortable life of urban office
work for a form of manual labor that, like steeplejacking, could draw
crowds of fascinated spectators and become an entertainment spectacle.
An 1847 newspaper article stated that Van Amburgh had been working in a traveling caravan of wild animals when he made his first public appearance in a lion's cage. When the keeper who typically fed the
animals was absent, "He took a cane, entered the cage, and walked up
to the lion, talked to him, and in a few seconds they became quite intimate."[16] This anecdote presents the lion tamer act as an outgrowth of
work in traveling menageries, where the workers who fed or handled
wild animals could become full-fledged entertainers.[17]

According to an 1836 advertisement for a Van Amburgh appearance
in Philadelphia, spectators were "completely surprised and astounded"
by his "perfect control and power over the brute creation." We can get a
sense of Van Amburgh's act in the following description:

> The leopards would spring upon their master's shoulders, or, spreading
> themselves on the ground, form pillows for his head. Now he would box

at them, growling, snarling, and snapping at him with their fangs; now he would knock their heads together and cuff them, when, if they shewed the slightest signs of displeasure, a hint from their master would bring them groveling and prostrate at his feet. He would distend the jaws of a lion while it roared, and by shutting and opening them rapidly, break the roar into a succession of sounds that mingled the ludicrous with the horrible. When the lioness snapped and struck at him, he coolly put his face down to her head, and gazing into her eyes until she shrunk back ashamed, brought down the house with applause.[18]

Van Amburgh's act seems to have been characterized by a rough-and-tumble, agonistic interaction with a relatively small number of animals in a small cage, and it culminated in his trademark routine: putting his head inside a lion's mouth.[19] Why did this type of intimate interaction with wild animals become a popular entertainment that appealed across social classes? How did this small-time operator rise to became an international celebrity? To address these questions we need to explore the cultural meaning of the nineteenth-century lion tamer act.

Van Amburgh's performances demonstrate how that act synthesized the semiotics of the circus and the zoo. For Paul Bouissac, the modern zoo presented a "pedagogical discourse" in that it provided a "general system for interpreting the animal world."[20] The basic feature of the zoological taxonomy was a "strict separation between privileged species (homo sapiens) and all others."[21] By contrast, the circus was geared toward "creating confusion between the animal species" by promoting "unnatural" behavior on the part of animals, who were made to behave in ways typically understood as human.[22] Bouissac sees these two semiotic systems as complementary: the zoo organized the natural world into "a network of discontinuous categories," while the circus compensated for the inadequacies of such a system through a display of performing animals that restored a sense of "biological continuity."[23] The lion tamer act had a foot in both of these semiotic camps. The act lacked a strict taxonomic separation of species since "cat men" and animals shared the stage as coperformers.[24] At the same time, lion tamers asserted mastery over the animals under their control. Though humans and animals were performing together, the act often established clear and discontinuous categories of human and beast in a manner similar to Bouissac's reading of the zoo.

The blending of the codes of circus and menagerie was certainly part of what "surprised and astounded" spectators, but lion taming evoked a range of cultural associations.[25] For example, a pamphlet made to accompany Van Amburgh's 1860 performances at the New York Palace Gardens claimed that the trainer's goal was to demonstrate "that man, in accordance with the decree of God, was and should be the monarch of the universe."[26] What this and other documents make clear is that Van Amburgh's performance was typically framed as a biblical allegory. Van Amburgh enacted the story in the sixth chapter of the book of Daniel, wherein the faith of the eponymous hero is proven by surviving a night in a den of lions. In fact, the 1860 pamphlet claimed that the story of Daniel had convinced Van Amburgh that "the age of miracles had not expired" and induced him to "contemplate the possibility of subduing the whole animal kingdom."[27] Another biblical reference for Van Amburgh can be found in the book of Isaiah: "The wolf shall dwell with the lamb, and the leopard shall lie down with the kid, and the calf and the lion and the fatling together, and a little child shall lead them. The cow and the bear shall feed; their young shall lie down together; and the lion shall eat straw like the ox."[28] Van Amburgh enacted this famous passage by placing a lamb in the cage with his lions, which an advertisement claimed would be "literally fulfilling the prophecy of the Holy Writ, viz: That the Lion shall lie down with the Lamb."

The biblical orientation of Van Amburgh's act was also manifested in the way in which it indexed the common Christian belief that, before the Fall of man in the Garden of Eden, humans had not eaten meat, animals were tame, and the two had lived together peacefully. It was widely believed that only after the Fall had wild animals become fierce.[29] The book of Genesis ratifies the post-Edenic dominance of humans over nature: "The fear of you and the dread of you shall be upon every beast of the earth."[30] An 1838 magazine article declared that Van Amburgh was "a very religious man" who had decided to tame lions after reading the first chapter of the Bible. Inspired by the book of Genesis, Van Amburgh declared that "whenever he heard of a man flying from a tiger, or having been devoured by a lion," he said to himself, "this ought not to be: it was the man's own fault."[31] Not only was Van Amburgh a modern-day Daniel whose spiritual purity was tested in the den of lions, but his power over animals was an enactment of the ultimate reality of the pre-Fall world. This belief helps to explain why the effect of Van Amburgh's power over the big cats was said to have been "instantaneous":

> The Lion halted and stood transfixed—the Tiger crouched—the Panther, with a suppressed growl of rage and fear sprang back, while the Leopard receded gradually from its master. . . . By degrees [Van Amburgh] drew his

subjects around him. The Lion licked the hand that overcame him, and knelt at his conqueror's feet; the Leopard fondled as playful as a domestic tabby; the Tiger rolled on his sides, while Van Amburgh placed his foot on his neck, and laid the now docile Panther between his paws. Then came the most effective tableaux of all. Van Amburgh with his strong will, bade them come to him, and he reclined upon the back of the cage—the proud king of the animal creation.[32]

A similar sentiment can be found in an 1839 newspaper report that described how Van Amburgh had entered the cage of a new lion in his menagerie. Although it was the first time he had been with the creature, "he lay down by the side of the lion, who licked his face and hands, and he took the animal by the jaws and made him roar and bark in the same fashion with those which are nightly exhibited, to the astonishment and almost consternation of every one present. There can now be no doubt but that this extraordinary person has some power over animals which is as inexplicable as it is astonishing."[33] Instead of being described as the result of a slow, methodical course of training, the act here is framed as a demonstration of Van Amburgh's quasi-supernatural power of will, and so is not understood as animal "training" at all. The obedience of the animals represents the removal of layers of corruption brought about by human sin. The lion tamer is not "adding" conditioned performances to the animals' instinctive behavior but is making them "more natural" by returning them to their original pre-Fall condition. The instantaneous power of the lion tamer makes sense in this context: since human sin had made wild beasts ferocious, human purity and power of will could "convert" them in an instant. Van Amburgh's performance was thus a powerful affirmation of an array of biblical attitudes toward nature.

On a more pragmatic level, Van Amburgh's references to the Bible could both counter the attacks of those Victorians who opposed popular entertainments and facilitate his appeal to bourgeois audiences. John Culhane has suggested that circus promoters had to make their entertainments seem both moral and educational since such performances were frequently seen as a source of moral ruin.[34] A history of the American circus published in 1905 claimed that the "most serious obstacle" faced by traveling shows of Van Amburgh's era was "the puritanical hostility to all forms of amusement so characteristic of Americans of the first half of the nineteenth century."[35] In fact, the menagerie itself helped to circumvent that hostility, providing as it did an educational rationale for parents to take their children to see the animals. To promote their attractions, showmen "searched the Scriptures" for "texts that might be tortured into a reference to objects under the canvas." For example, a hippopotamus could be advertised as "the Behemoth of Holy Writ, spoken of by the Book of Job," and a showman would have considered it "an omen of ill luck to have painted on the sides of the 'lion's den' any scene other than that of Daniel."[36] The opening statements of Van Amburgh's 1860 promotional pamphlet certainly stress the act's earnest moral instruction: "There is no study that is more important to the youth of a rising generation, or to adult age, than that of Natural History. It teaches man his superiority over the brute creation, and creates in his bosom a knowledge of wisdom and goodness, and omnipresence of a supreme and All-wise Creator. It also teaches him how entirely dependent he is on the providence of God: it elevates his character, and fits him for the discharge of the nobler duties of life."[37] These are weighty claims for a circus act, but Van Amburgh's instructional rhetoric was clearly effective, and in 1908 the *Washington Post* could look back on Van Amburgh's menagerie as "a great moral show," one "uncontaminated by fair equestriennes in abbreviated fluffy skirts." Even the clergy were said to have patronized it.[38]

The reference here to "fluffy skirts" signals that the bodies of circus performers provided a potent appeal above and beyond moral education. Indeed, despite all the biblical platitudes, there were aspects of Van Amburgh's act that were perhaps not so far from those denigrated equestriennes. Van Amburgh performed in Roman gladiator attire, a style that became the standard uniform for lion tamers in the nineteenth century. We might note here a similarity to the body builder Eugen Sandow, who frequently appeared dressed as a gladiator in order to present himself as a modern embodiment of "ancient ideals."[39] That such a costume offered the lion tamer's body as a spectacle can be suggested by the frequency with which Van Amburgh's physique was described in the popular press. A personal account of meeting the "Lion King" in 1838 stated that "in personal appearance Van Amburgh was, even off the stage, rather remarkable": "He stood about 5 ft. 10 in. in height, walked extremely upright, studiously so, and very slowly: a sort of theatrical strut, which would have drawn your attention to him had you not known he was the great brute-tamer direct from New York and London. He had immensely broad shoulders, small hips, and very straight legs, small in proportion to his 'uppers.' He features were long and narrow, quite the American type: an exceedingly pleasing expression, a frank, good-natured manner."[40] An 1847 article described Van

Amburgh as having "a fine figure, iron frame, and Herculean strength, which admirably suited his development of peculiar faculties": "He is singularly made, and one of the most athletic of his size in the world. His body is nearly round, but greater in thickness than in breadth. His bones are large and firmly set, and his flesh almost muscle. Nevertheless, from his singular conformation, he is remarkable for the lightness and grace of his movements."[41] Framing the act in biblical terms served to sanitize its more visceral and sensational appeals and so override concerns about the morality of popular entertainments, at the same time that it facilitated an address to middle-class patrons.

It is difficult to gauge the reception of Van Amburgh's moral rhetoric, but what is certain is that his act made him an international celebrity. In the words of his promotional pamphlet, "His star of popularity arose immediately; crowds rushed to see him, and Van Amburgh's fame spread through civilization, and is now contemporaneous and extensive with the universe itself."[42] Such hyperbole can be justified when one considers that the cage boy from Fishkill achieved a fame that spread across the social universe of the time. That is, Van Amburgh's success extended to an aristocratic audience as well as a popular one. Most notable were his experiences in 1839 touring England, where he found a particularly devoted fan in the recently crowned Queen Victoria. Not only did the queen return to see Van Amburgh's act at the Royal Theatre in Drury Lane multiple times, but she even paid him a high and, by contemporary accounts, "unprecedented" compliment by going onto the stage in order to get a closer look. This was the first time that a queen of England had ever appeared on "the public stage."[43] The queen remained after one Van Amburgh performance in order to see the animals being fed, and "when all the ladies of the Court shrank back in terror" at the roars that accompanied the first piece of meat being thrown to the animals, the queen is said to have "remained unmoved and perfectly calm and collected." The twenty-year-old unmarried queen's enthusiasm for the "singularly made" lion tamer raised a few eyebrows. "There is a growing disposition to find fault with her Majesty for patronizing such exhibitions," wrote the *Observer,* though the paper concluded that her actions were "perfectly natural, and not in the smallest degree derogatory."[44] The queen commissioned Edwin Landseer to paint Van Amburgh's portrait in 1839, and the resulting work presented him reclining in the cage while his carnivores lay down with a lamb. Eight years later Landseer accepted a commission from the Duke of Wellington, Arthur Wellesley, to paint

FIGURE 11. Edwin Landseer's painting *Van Amburgh and His Lions* (1847). Courtesy of Corbis.

the lion tamer again. In *Van Amburgh and His Lions* (1847) we see the performer in the cage subduing various big cats. The "Iron Duke" is said to have hung the painting in his library at Aspley House, surmounted with a text from the first chapter of Genesis, "where it is recorded that the Creator gave man dominion over 'every living thing that moveth upon the earth.'"[45]

Thanks to this royal patronage, Van Amburgh enjoyed the approval of the English aristocracy, helping to lend cultural prestige to the circus in general and lion taming in particular. As a result, he became what Culhane calls "a figure that even the American upper crust could admit to appreciating."[46] Van Amburgh's career demonstrates that by the 1840s lion taming was a well-known mode of spectacular male performance, one that appealed to a remarkably wide audience that crossed age, class, and gender lines. Evidence suggests that Van Amburgh inspired many imitators, some of whom continued to frame their act in biblical terms.[47] Van Amburgh was a pioneering figure in a transatlantic entertainment tradition that was still going strong decades later, though by that time key elements of the act, as well as the popular understanding of the animals that were its main attraction, had undergone significant change.

THE BIG CAGE

Van Amburgh was an influential pioneer in the field, but by 1894 a renowned animal trainer could regard him as part of a bygone era: "If you are old enough to remember," he wrote, "the days when Van Amberg [sic] and his confreres used to go into a lion's cage, make them leap over each other and put their heads in the mouths of the lions, you will remember that the cages in which their wild beasts were kept were small ones, and that the lion tamer rarely moved from a certain spot, and this was just in front of a sliding door, behind which stood an attendant ready to open it quickly in case of emergency."[48] Because these early acts were performed in small cages, the lion tamer could always keep the animals in front of him. Landseer's 1847 portrait of Van Amburgh illustrates the dimensions of such a performance space.[49] The large cages in use by the 1890s, however, fundamentally changed the dynamics and dangers of the act: "The animals, feeling themselves in a larger space, are more likely to feel their power," the above-mentioned trainer stated, "and, were they so inclined, could make a rush at a trainer that it would be next to impossible for him to withstand."[50] The man who made these statements was Edward Deyerling, chief trainer at Frank Bostock's animal show at the 1893 World's Columbian Exposition in Chicago. World's fairs such as the Chicago Columbian Exposition were, along with American rail-driven circuses and amusement parks, one of the key sites where the lion tamer act took on its modern "big cage" form in the 1880s and early 1890s.

Circus historians have described the mid- to late 1800s as a time when the American circus was transformed into a truly modern "big business" through improved management, railroad travel, the rationalization of labor, and modern advertising methods. W. C. Coup and P. T. Barnum converted the traditional horse-drawn wagon show to a "moving army of thirty wagons mounted on railroad flatcars."[51] With increases in available capital, circuses expanded acts that made use of expensive wild animals. Brenda Assael demarcates a phase of circus development between 1880 and 1900 when wild animals became a star feature of those circuses that had "the money necessary to make large investments in lions, tigers, and elephants from the far corners of the globe."[52] Changes in the scale of the American circus resulted in the lion tamer's "big cage" act, which featured a large number of animals. Culhane asserts that the Adam Forepaugh Show of 1891 was the first wild animal act presented in a large steel arena.[53] We should note that the lion tamer's steel cage was—like the bridge jumper's steel suspension bridge and the human fly's steel, glass, and concrete skyscraper—a quintessentially modern performance space, part of a turn-of-the-twentieth-century entertainment environment that included world's fairs and amusement parks. The acts that took place within the big cage took on a form that was also quintessentially modern in that they articulated social and cultural discourses of the late Victorian and Edwardian eras.

The performances of Captain Jack Bonavita provide a means to gauge the formal dimensions of the big cage act. Bonavita was a celebrated lion tamer at Frank Bostock's Great Animal Arena at the 1901 Pan-American Exposition in Buffalo, and later at Dreamland in Coney Island.[54] Bonavita was the featured performer in Bostock's show at the expo in Buffalo, during which he entered the steel cage dressed not in tights and spangles but in military garb: "The gates at the back of the arena opened, and slowly and majestically out walked twenty-seven kings of the forest, and at the unspoken order of one man, for he never speaks to them when performing, each one took his special place on a certain pedestal." "The sight of this one man moving quietly about among all the lions," Bostock wrote of his star trainer, "made a deep impression upon many people." Among those impressed was Vice President Theodore Roosevelt, who attended Bonavita's 1901 show and later claimed that he had "never seen or heard of anything" like it, that he admired the lion tamer's "pluck," and that he considered him "a hero."[55] As Bonavita's act indicates, the late nineteenth-century big cage allowed for a greater number of animals and new forms of visual spectacle compared to Van Amburgh's day, and it also enabled new kinds of interactions between big cats and trainer.

Despite the fact that Bostock's animal arena was described in advertising material as a "Sermon in Living Characters" and a "Pulpit of Biblical Explanations," we should note the lack of overt biblical imagery in Bonavita's act.[56] Perhaps by the turn of the century circus performers no longer felt the need to justify the morality of their entertainments to the same degree their predecessors did.[57] Nonetheless, a subtle biblical rhetoric can be found in the discourse related to the act of one of Bonavita's contemporaries, Carl Hagenbeck. Like the showmen who came before him, Hagenbeck used the Bible to frame his act, although he cast his show not as an illustration of the cruel dominion over nature, but as a demonstration of the efficacy of his humane system of training. In an article previewing the Chicago World's Fair, we read that under Hagenbeck's tutelage, "the lion and the tiger, the leopard and the hyena lie down like lambs together or play like schoolboys." The astounded reporter described how he had seen three lions, two leopards, a Bengal tiger, a panther, a hyena, a polar bear, a black bear, and five monkeys all in one cage: "They all trotted about in that cage as peacefully as a flock of sheep until Hagenbeck threw into the arena a large rubber ball. Then the fun commenced. That rubber sphere was knocked and tossed about the cage as if a crowd of schoolboys were at play rather than a dozen of the fiercest beasts of prey."[58] Hagenbeck's "happy family" animal acts were presented as a biblical utopia, except here it was the kindness of the trainer, not his cruelly enforced dominance, that was to re-create the Edenic brotherhood of creation. In this regard, big cage animal acts served as a sensitive cultural barometer whose dramatic shape registered shifting attitudes toward the natural world.

Traditional Western thought about the animal world had been shaped largely by Christian doctrine and the mechanistic worldview of René Descartes, whose seventeenth-century writings had presented the view that "animals were mere machines or automata, like clocks, capable of complex behavior, but wholly incapable of speech, reasoning, or, on some interpretations, even sensation."[59] James Turner describes the early nineteenth century as a time when those models broke down, when a pattern of attitudes toward animals was shattered.[60] Turner argues that "the majestic isolation" of human beings from animals had begun to corrode by the end of the eighteenth century, but it was Charles Darwin's arguments about evolution that "undermined the foundations of human mental uniqueness."[61] In addition to these seismic shifts in scientific and philosophical discourse, another important factor in the shattering of a pattern of attitudes toward animals was the spread of urbanization. The shift from an agrarian to an industrial society resulted in a change in the nature of day-to-day interaction with animals. Ironically, it was precisely people's distance from animals that facilitated a new concern for them: Harriet Ritvo writes that once nature "ceased to be a constant antagonist, it could be viewed with affection."[62] Indeed, the rise of the anticruelty movement in England and the United States in the nineteenth century was spurred by the experience of the modern city as much as by the post-Darwinian recognition of kinship with animals. The British Parliament passed a bill to prevent cruel and improper treatment of cattle in 1822, and the Society for the Prevention of Cruelty to Animals was formed two years later.[63] In 1840, just a year after she had attended the performances of Isaac Van Amburgh, Queen Victoria became the society's patron, granting permission for the prefix "Royal" to be attached to the organization's name.[64] In America, Henry Bergh founded the American Society for the Prevention of Cruelty to Animals (ASPCA) in 1866.[65]

The first anticruelty legislation protected work animals in the modern city.[66] Another early concern of anticruelty reformers had to do with entertainments involving animals that were popular with the urban working class. Just as Steve Brodie's Bowery saloon was part of an alternative workingman's culture, so too were agonistic displays of animals, such as cockfighting, dogfighting, and bull- and bearbaiting, as well as traveling circuses and menageries.[67] Isaac Van Amburgh's Great Black Horse Menagerie, which appeared at the Bowery Amphitheater in 1842, no doubt featured the showman's rough style of knocking leopards' heads together.[68] In his history of the ASPCA, Sydney Coleman claimed that the "lowest parts" of New York City were "infested" with "dog and cock fights, ratbaiting and other equally bloody and degrading sports," and that Henry Bergh had opened a "vigorous fight upon these cruelties, often exposing himself to great physical danger in the raids that he led against them."[69] Reformers such as Bergh tended to perceive the crowds who gathered around the animal pits not only as "rowdy laborers of easy morals," but as "a dark, barbaric, primitive horde."[70] Indeed, Kathleen Kete argues that kindness to animals came to stand as an index of civilization in the nineteenth century: "The barbarian others—the urban working classes, continental peasants, southern Europeans, Irish Catholics, Russians, Asians, and Turks—were defined in part by their brutality to beasts."[71] In a sense, then, it was the working class who were the real target of anticruelty laws.[72] What is certain is that the experience of the modern city encouraged a new middle-class concern for animals that was articulated by the anticruelty movement. This same constellation of historical factors shaped the aesthetics of the big cage lion tamer act.

Traveling menageries and lion tamers might well have benefited from animal protection legislation since their attractions provided a legal alternative to working-class entertainments such as dogfighting. Nonetheless, "cat men" now had to inoculate themselves against charges of animal cruelty in order to avoid prosecution. Carl Hagenbeck was a key proponent of a more humane approach to animal training and sought to distance himself from a past in which animal trainers were thought of as cruel taskmasters. Hagenbeck demonstrated his "gentle" methods of training at Paris's Nouveau Cirque in 1889, London's Crystal Palace in 1891, and the Chicago World's Fair in 1893.[73] In his memoirs, Hagenbeck argued that lion taming was not at odds with the anticruelty movement:

> There is probably no sphere in which the growth of humanitarian sentiment has been more striking than in the treatment and training of performing animals. Obedience which in former days was due to fear is now willingly paid by the animal from motives of affection. The period when unfortunate animals were driven to jump over a bar from dread of a whip or a red-hot iron—a disgrace to the humanity of man!—is gone by. Sympathy with the animal, patience with its deficiencies, has brought about a perfection of education which cruelty altogether failed to secure. And at the same time relations between trainer and beast have improved too. The trainer is no longer a taskmaster, or the beast a slave. There subsists between them the wholesome and happy relation of teacher and pupil.[74]

Hagenbeck wrote passionately about treating animals as individuals and recognizing their intelligence. "Brutes," he wrote, were "beings akin to ourselves," and their minds were "formed on the same plan as our minds; the differences are differences of degree only, not of kind."[75] There is a painful irony to Hagenbeck's earnest concern for animals and his rhetoric of brotherhood since he was also famous for his "anthropological-zoological exhibitions," in which groups of "exotic" non-Western people were put on public display for profit.[76] Nonetheless, Hagenbeck helped to crystallize what came to be called the "European" or "soft dressage" approach to animal training.[77] Notably, some of the most prominent exponents of this gentler style in the big cage were women.

Adgie Costillo, who was described as a pupil of Hagenbeck, entered the cage to the strains of Bizet's *Carmen* before dancing with her lions.[78] Claire Heliot was another renowned female performer who was said to use "sentimental" techniques to train lions. In a 1901 article titled "She Controls Lions by Kindness," a writer described Heliot's "marvelous display of the power of kindness to tame animals," which was "a great contrast to the old type of lion tamers, who fired revolvers, burnt red fire, made hideous noises, and scared the audience as much as they did the poor animals, who were kept huddled in a corner of a caravan cage." Heliot entered the cage dressed in an ordinary evening gown, calling the lions by "pet names" and then "patting and caressing them as if they were a number of cats."[79] One account described how Heliot had rebuffed a disobedient lion in a particularly feminine manner: "She turned upon the lion, put her face towards him, and laughed in a deliciously musical way, and gave the discomfited monarch of the forest a love tap on the nose with her shapely hand. 'Naughty boy!' she said, and the lion actually seemed ashamed of his temper."[80]

FIGURE 12. Adgie Costillo and her lions. Courtesy of the Library of Congress.

These successful female wild animal trainers implicitly challenged cultural definitions of gender, as can be seen by the varied response that they provoked in both the popular press and rival performers. At one extreme, a bear trainer named Albers declared that "no woman has any business in the animal cage. The animals know she hasn't the strength to hurt them."[81] A 1905 article in the *New York Times* took a slightly more subtle tack, declaring that Heliot represented a "new problem" in lion taming. Although the male lion tamer was thought to control wild cats through self-control, willpower, and a show of strength, Heliot, "being intrinsically, not artificially feminine," was assumed to be unable to control "the brutes by force." Instead, her success was based on the misguided belief that "not one of her fourteen lions would have the heart to kill her," and so she controlled them "as the best of women govern the human brute, by trusting them blindly."[82] Heliot's act, then, was characterized as a performance not of manly self-control but of female self-deception.[83]

The "new problem" of female lion tamers was also negotiated by describing their acts in terms of domestic life. In the article "Why It Is

Harder to Tame a Husband Than a Lion," Heliot was asked, "Would not the taming of a dashing husband be more an accomplishment than the taming of a mere lion?"[84] Although press discourse such as this domesticated the act by framing it in terms of courtship, the dangerous interaction between female animal trainers and their animals was also domesticated by a discourse of bourgeois pet ownership. Harriet Ritvo describes how pet owning became a widespread practice in the early nineteenth century and, like the anticruelty movement, relied upon a modern perception of the nonhuman world as relatively nonthreatening.[85] Whereas male lion tamers were described as "Kings of Creation," female lion tamers such as Heliot were described as giving lions "love taps" and calling them "pet names," as in the article cited above. The *New York Times* described how Heliot patted her lions on the head "like ponies, hug[ged] them like kittens, romp[ed] about with them as no mere woman could possibly do if they were not as safe as house cats."[86] Heliot's act seems to have been designed to invite such comparisons, and it even included a "dinner-party scene" in which her animals seated themselves at a table and were fed by their mistress.[87] Framing the act in such terms rankled other performers, and Heliot's claims that her animals were "as tame as cats" was said to have been greeted with "courteous incredulity" by other, presumably male, lion tamers, who asserted that "a lion may be subdued, but never really tamed."[88]

Female lion tamers clearly faced a certain amount of skepticism, but they were also praised for entering what was considered to be a male sphere of dangerous activity. As was the case for their male counterparts, part of the spectacle of their performances had to do with the ever-present possibility of their being horribly maimed, and, in the face of questions about the authenticity of their acts, they had the scars to prove that they faced real danger. In 1907 a reporter described how "many people" had been dismissing Miss Essie Fay, a lion tamer with "Big Otto's animal show," by suggesting that her lion was "old and tame as a canary bird."[89] Miss Fay's scars, however, served as visible proof of the authenticity of her act: "Her neck and face still showed the wounds inflicted when the lion she was exhibiting two weeks ago became angry and closed his mouth on Miss Fay's head." This provided the evidence, the writer concluded, that "after all there is real danger in trifling with lions and leopards, and Miss Fay can be truly regarded by her sex as being one of those who have vindicated the reputation of women for bravery."[90] Similarly, although Adgie Costillo danced the tango with her lions, she was described as a "battle-scarred heroine," her body "covered with the marks of wounds inflicted by the pitiless brutes."[91]

I will discuss lion taming and the cinema at length at the end of this chapter, but for now I want to suggest that these early twentieth-century female lion tamers should be placed alongside the serial queens of early film melodrama. For Ben Singer, the serial-queen melodrama reflected cultural conflicts surrounding the "New Woman"—a figure who broke with Victorian norms of femininity—and presented a "mythology of female power" that was both a "utopian fantasy reaction" to the sexist ideology of the period and a regressive display of the "lurid victimization of the heroine by male villains."[92] Jennifer M. Bean claims that the careers of serial stars such as Kathlyn Williams, Juanita Hansen, and Marie Walcamp were "built on the backs of ungainly elephants and leveraged through climactic encounters" with tigers, leopards, and lions.[93] More so than did film stars who were frequently doubled by stunt performers, female wild animal trainers risked life and limb in spectacular, immediate, and public ways, and they enacted performances in which female power and "lurid victimization" existed side by side.[94]

In the larger history of the lion tamer act, female performers such as Heliot and Costillo indicate the influence of Hagenbeck's "soft dressage" and suggest the range of new forms of interaction between trainers and animals made possible by the big cage. The same shifts in attitude toward animals that had stimulated the anticruelty movement opened the door for the soft dressage school of trainers, who pioneered a more playful, gentle approach to their interaction with animals. As was the case with Dorothy Devore's enactment of the human fly act described in the previous chapter and the female stunt flyers I will discuss in the next chapter, female wild animal trainers had to overcome resistance in order to participate in forms of stunt performance assumed to be the domain of men. In the process they prompted discourses that sought to reconcile assumptions about gender with their dangerous line of work. Female wild animal trainers such as Adgie Costillo and Claire Heliot were notable exceptions that proved the rule that lion taming was a predominantly male endeavor.[95] In fact, lion tamers were often described as the pinnacle of a certain kind of masculine identity.[96] As we shall see, such notions of the lion tamer's ideal masculinity were inseparable from turn-of-the-century discourses concerning race and empire.

A SOUL-STIRRING ANACHRONISM

If evolutionary theory, urbanization, and the anticruelty movement made lion taming a resonant cultural performance at the turn of the twentieth century, colonialism and related dynamics of race and gender were certainly another factor. Ritvo writes that European menageries symbolized conquest, acquisition, and influence over "remote exotic territories," and she characterizes the London Zoo as an "emblem of British domination over its colonial empire."[97] Baratay and Hardouin-Fugier agree, noting that zoos satisfied a "craving for exoticism and escape" that had intensified with the advent of "Romanticism and colonial adventure."[98] Lions and tigers held a particular fascination as some of the most dangerous exotic animals from colonial Africa and India. Assael writes that circus acts in the second half of the nineteenth century narrated a version of imperial conflicts that worked to draw clear boundaries between "a savage East and a civilized West."[99] As we have seen, lion taming developed in tandem with Western zoos and circuses, and it dramatized a similar set of shifting anxieties and desires.

One way to understand the lion tamer's engagement with empire is by reference to Shelley Streeby's description of a "double axis of city and empire" in mid-nineteenth-century popular culture that balanced a vision of American cities on the one hand and scenes of U.S. empire building on the other.[100] An undercurrent of that "double axis" can be found in the careers of some of the thrill makers described in previous chapters: recall, for example, the allusions to colonial adventure made by writers who compared steeplejacks to merchant seamen, or consider the fact that both Paul Boyton and Steve Brodie took part in a culture of filibustering. Robert E. May has shown how, prior to 1900, the term "filibuster" referred to American adventurers who participated in private military forces that invaded foreign countries with which the United States was formally at peace.[101] The most famous filibuster of this era was William Walker, who invaded Mexico in the early 1850s. Notably, May points to connections between filibusters and workingmen's culture: "Just as some youths sought identity in a fluid social environment by joining volunteer militia and fire companies or by frequenting taverns or illegal boxing matches, others cast their fate with filibuster companies."[102] Steve Brodie and his brother were reportedly involved in organizing a mission of Fourth Ward filibusters to assassinate the president of Honduras in March 1886.[103] We might chalk this up as one more case in which Brodie was emulating Paul Boyton, since the captain had garnered considerable press coverage five years earlier for his adventures in South American waters, where he was employed by the Peruvian army under Nicolás de Piérola to fire torpedoes at the Chilean fleet that was blockading the port of Lima.[104] Of all the thrill makers, however, it is the lion tamer who most vividly combined city and empire, appearing in a big cage where the spaces of the northern metropolis overlapped with the habitats of exotic animals from colonial lands.

Lion taming was also bound up in the experience of empire as part of a constellation of turn-of-the-century American leisure activities prized for enacting a "primitive" masculinity. Gail Bederman describes how a generation of white, middle-class American men were eager to prove that civilization had not undermined their "primal masculinity."[105] Many turn-of-the-century men were drawn to a variety of "savage" activities such as prizefighting, camping, hunting, and fishing due to a belief in the connection between "powerful manhood" and the supposed primitive vitality of "dark-skinned races."[106] In order to situate lion taming in this context, we might note the particular conflation of race, "primal" masculinity, and exotic animals found in accounts of Theodore Roosevelt's 1909 hunting trip to Africa.[107] Bederman describes how Roosevelt's encounter with Nandi warriors proved to be a challenge to his "fantasy of himself as the masculine hunter."[108] Roosevelt asked the warriors to accompany him on a lion hunt, but they would only concede if they were allowed to kill the lion themselves. Roosevelt reluctantly agreed and later waxed poetic about the spectacle of these "splendid savages" trapping and killing the "grim lord of slaughter," a procedure that culminated in a "savage dance of triumph" that Roosevelt described as "a scene of as fierce interest and excitement as I ever hope to see."[109] Despite Roosevelt's purple prose, the "splendid savages" who so professionally dispatched the "grim lord of slaughter" threatened to make the great white hunter, with his many accoutrements of civilization, look decidedly unmanly. Along these lines, consider a passage from animal trainer Carl Hagenbeck's memoir: "For the European, armed with weapons both accurate and deadly, big-game hunting is attended with little danger. . . . But for the natives, big-game hunting is a very different matter. Then the fray is far from one-sided; the weapons of the man are little, if at all, superior to those of the brute; and the 'hunting' is more of the nature of a hand-to-hand encounter, requiring the utmost skill and courage on the part of the human combatant."[110]

Hagenbeck's comments suggest that big game hunting, although certainly a sign of colonial privilege, could call into question as much as solidify Western masculine supremacy. Returning to the work of Erving Goffman, we might say that for action to create character it must involve (or at least be seen to involve) real fatefulness and real consequences. The acts of lion tamers, who met the "grim lords of slaughter" armed only with a kitchen chair and whip, seemed to provide that genuine action, and so they demonstrated that, despite modern civilization, the white man could still enact his superiority over the African "king of the beasts." In fact, the lion tamer was a powerful embodiment of white masculine ideals at this time. One reporter writing in 1925 breathlessly recalled seeing the lion tamer George Conklin: "A soul-stirring anachronism! That nineteenth century audience beholding George Conklin defend himself against the king of beasts as man defended himself before the Stone Age!"[111] Another male writer had vivid memories of seeing Captain Bonavita's act: "People were calling him 'the perfect man.' I'll never forget the thrill of watching him stride into the steel arena and put twenty-four big-maned, snarling lions through their paces. I took deep breaths, and felt the blood rush up to my head. 'That's what I want to do,' I said to myself."[112] We find a similar dynamic in popular fiction of the time. An 1897 short story published in *Harper's Monthly* describes a young man named Theodore who is miffed to find that the object of his desire, a woman named Alma, is enamored with a lion tamer at the Chicago World's Fair. Alma declares that she admires the lion tamer "because he is a type of true manhood." They go to see the lion tamer's show, which is described as follows: "Dressed in spangled tights . . . his dark eyes [shooting] out rapid glances . . . as with imperious gesture, snap of whip, or sharp word of command he put the fierce beasts through their round of tricks." Theodore turned and looked at Alma: "Her eyes were glistening, her cheeks were burning, her breath was coming in quick gasps. He had never seen her look so beautiful, and never had she seemed so far away from him."[113]

Lion tamers seemed to be "perfect men" and embodiments of "true manhood" in part because their acts managed certain contradictions in Victorian norms of masculinity. Anthony Rotundo describes how middle-class American men were confronted by "two ethics of sexual conduct, one urging the 'natural' expression of aggressive impulses and the other demanding stringent self control." On the one hand, men had to display a sense of self-mastery and restraint, learning to suppress their sexual desires, and so become "athletes of continence" who constantly tested their manliness in "the fire of self-denial."[114] But while men were to be "athletes of continence," there was also a widespread assumption that it was necessary and natural for them to express their "urgent sexual passions."[115] Notably, those passions were associated with animals: "Men spoke of their animal nature in phrases like 'animal instincts' and 'animal energy.'"[116] Peter Filene writes that Victorian manliness was achieved only by "earnest, often desperate suppression of instincts": "Without control, his sexual appetites would make a beast of him, abusing the delicate spirit and body of a woman while also abusing his own." Marriage and the family might provide an "institution for civilizing his animal nature," but at the same time that control must not go so far as to "tame his manhood away," and nineteenth-century men "commonly believed that they would injure their health unless they satisfied, at least partly, their sexual drive."[117] "Purity and wild oats," Filene concludes, "formed a contradictory masculine mythology."[118] These two contradictory ethics found dramatic expression in the lion tamer act, which featured the human trainer as paradigm of control and the big cats as a living embodiment of dangerous but compelling animal passions.

Manly self-control was frequently described as the key to the lion tamer's ability to hold wild animals at bay. In a 1913 *Washington Post* article, one reads that an animal trainer is first required to have "complete control over himself, and must possess a placid disposition. A man who gets excited is worthless as a trainer."[119] Also note that turn-of-the-century big cage acts tended to involve the representation of "a state of balance" by the arrangement of the animals in symmetrical ensembles. For example, Captain Bonavita had his lions arrange themselves into a pyramid, presenting "a living picture that outrivals all attempts at reproduction by the artist's hand," and during Hagenbeck's act at the 1893 World's Columbian Exposition in Chicago, the animals were made to form a "Great Zoological Pyramid."[120] Such geometrical forms were well suited to the steel arenas in which large audiences encountered circus acts at the end of the nineteenth century, but they could also signify Western culture formed from the raw materials of colonial wildlife, or animal passions controlled by the male trainer.

That control, however, was always tenuous, and the lion tamer act was prone to failure of the most spectacular kind. In press coverage of the countless gruesome accidents that took place in the big cage, there was often discussion of a trainer's momentary hesitation and his resulting perilous "fall." Many accounts offer a variation on one lion tamer's succinct advice to those interested in trying their hand at his profession: "A lion tamer must never fall."[121] In the popular imagination, the lion

FIGURE 13. Jack Bonavita surrounded by his extraordinary pyramid of lions. Courtesy of Corbis.

tamer's fall could be emotional as well as physical. Consider a 1903
narrative titled "The Romance of the Lion Tamer." Vallens, an aloof lion
tamer, falls in love with a "pretty, sprightly little" aerialist but is tricked
by a rival into thinking that she has died. Crushed by the news, Vallens
nevertheless tries to go on with his act. Once in the cage, however, "the
sense of his bitter loss seemed to rush upon him with overwhelming
force, utterly and completely unnerving him. I saw him give in, saw him
slip to his knees and slap his hands to his head, while a groan came from
him that was heard throughout the whole tent. . . . As if by common
instinct the four brutes sprang upon the kneeling man."[122]

In a 1913 short story, a lion tamer named Mario holds his lions in
check with his piercing gaze. If his eyes were removed from his animals
for even a moment, we read, his life "would be snapped as swiftly, as
easily as one severs a cob-web." On one fateful occasion, the woman
whom Mario loves flirts with another man during his act. When Mario
hears her "shrill laugh," he forgets his danger and raises his eyes from
the lions: "Before he had time to even dimly realize the incident that
flashed before his gaze, a lithe, tawny body darted through the air, a

mighty paw rested momentarily on his shoulder—with a groan Mario fell and lay prone upon the ground."[123] In narratives such as these, a momentary lapse of will instantly triggers a ferocious attack by animals previously held in check by the performance of the masculine ideal. Recall Goffman's notion of action as tasks in which the consequences of one's decisions were felt immediately, in which "chance-taking and resolution" were brought "into the same heated moment of experience."[124] The big cage was the site of dangerous action that tested manliness and displayed character. Though character was created during such fateful moments, Goffman noted the belief that it could just as easily be lost. In a single bad showing, nerve could be lost, moral fiber destroyed: "Once an individual has failed in a particular way he becomes essentially different from that moment on and might just as well give up." The narrative of the lion tamer's fall gave shape to, and served as confirmation of, a belief in the "losability of nerve."[125]

As Mario's fate indicates, the precarious quality of lion taming often found expression in the commonly held belief that the trainer's eyes were the key to his hypnotic powers of animal magnetism. German therapist Franz Mesmer's theory of animal magnetism enjoyed a certain vogue in America during the same decades as the rise of lion taming, and by the early 1840s it could even be said to be "a popular movement."[126] Writers and audiences frequently made a connection between lion taming and magnetism. Many articles described Van Amburgh's enigmatic eyes: "His power lay in his iron will, the strength of his nerves, and the magic of his eye, by which he fascinated, humbled, subdued, and rendered obedient the most ferocious of wild beasts"; the Lion King was "afflicted with the most mysterious, profound, and unintelligible squint of the left eye that ever revolved in the head of a human being. . . . By some his complete dominion over his animals was attributed to this peculiarity of vision."[127] The belief in the lion tamer's magnetic eyes continued into the early twentieth century. "Some say it was magnetism, some say it was will power, and some say it was the devilish handsomeness of the man," one reads of Signor Morello, a lion tamer in a short narrative published in 1907, "but whatever it was, he had a power over animals I have never seen before or since."[128]

The lion tamer's purported magnetic power over animals could blur into erotic power over the opposite sex. In popular representations, the lion tamer's big cage became the site of courtship, marriage, or lovemaking. In 1902 the Bostock Animal Show in New York had several takers when it offered couples $500 to get married in the lion den. Similarly, newspapers and magazines at this time published narratives with titles such as "Love among the Lions," "Married in a Lion's Den," "They Did Their Courting in a Den of Lions," and "Herma, the Lion-Tamer," the last of which is a darkly sexual and oneiric story written by Leopold von Sacher-Masoch, the man after whom "masochism" was named.[129] The lion tamer act was evidently a dramatic form that gained much of its affective charge through the interweaving of cultural discourses about sexuality, masculine performance, and the wild animals of colonial lands.[130]

In the end, references to personal magnetism worked to mystify the lion tamer performance: it ratified the white lion tamer's power and so implicitly supported fantasies of racial supremacy, and it submerged the brutality and sheer drudgery of animal training during an era of incipient anticruelty legislation. Though magnetism affirmed white male power, it also revealed the manly ideal to be fragile and unstable, full as the papers were of accounts of lion tamers being horribly mauled and killed. In fact, press coverage sometimes made explicit the performative nature of the masculinity put on display in the big cage. Consider a *New York Times* article from 1909, which stated that the lion tamer's only hope of "gaining mastery" over the animals lay in convincing them that he was "a ferocious aggressor . . . more terrible than they themselves." This was, however, only a "shallow pretense," a "monumental bluff" that enabled "man to 'conquer' wild beasts." "Like all pretenses," the article continued, "the time comes, only too often, when this one collapses": "The least unusual excitement happens, a fire engine clangs and screeches through a neighboring street, and in an instant the dense, one-idea creatures become aroused, and, forgetting all fear of the human, burst through the film of authority that has held them in check and throw themselves upon their trainer."[131]

Was the lion tamer the victorious king of creation, or was he a con artist whose display of control was but the thinnest film of authority? That troubling ambiguity extended even to the "perfect man," Captain Jack Bonavita, who suffered numerous debilitating injuries from his trained lions, culminating in a brutal and very public attack—one that resulted in the amputation of his right arm—before a crowd of three thousand spectators at Dreamland in 1904.[132] As an embodiment of white male ideals, the lion tamer in the end seems to have raised as many questions as he answered. Lion tamers were turn-of-the-century celebrities who managed ideological contradictions concerning the ethics of male conduct, with the big cage as a cultural furnace of dangerous action that forged masculine character. Raymond Corbey argues that nineteenth-century zoos, circuses, and botanical gardens served to create "an illusion of cognitive control over a colonial experience that might otherwise have been disturbingly chaotic."[133] The lion tamer's creation of orderly geometric arrangements of exotic animals can be seen as a similar reassurance of "the orderliness of empire." Corbey is quick to add that these attempts to harmonize are "ultimately bound to fail."[134] The all-too-common spectacle of the violent disintegration of the geometric "living pictures" in the big cage, and the proliferation of narratives about the lion tamer's "fall," reveal the precariousness of male ideals at this time, as well as the texture of anxieties felt by white men at the turn of the century, tenuously holding on to a dominant position in the face of "social rivals" such as the New Woman, immigrants, and ethnic and colonial Others. To paraphrase Clifford Geertz, the big cage lion tamer act was a sentimental education in turn-of-the-century Western masculinity, its form serving as a powerful nexus for the affective exploration of shifting discourses concerning the natural world, colonial power, and masculinity.[135]

In sum, lion tamers were captivating popular celebrities that were often held to embody late nineteenth- and early twentieth-century masculine ideals, and whose performances resonated across class and gender lines. The lion tamer would seem, then, to have been a natural subject for a film industry that was emerging during the same decades as the big cage act, but he did not cross over from circus and fairground to film stardom. Exploring why surprisingly few films of "cat men" were made in the first decades of cinema, and why the display of interaction between humans and wild animals came to the screen in large numbers during the early 1930s, can tell us more about the history of nineteenth-century thrill makers in the era of the modern media.

BOTH SIDES OF THE SCREEN

Early American filmmakers turned to animal spectacle for subject matter, as can be seen in Edison Company films such as *Trained Bears, Cock Fight, Rat Killing,* and *Sommersault Dog,* all from 1894. Like the boxing films of this era, some of these titles showcased working-class entertainments that had been marginalized by reformers.[136] Though Edison filmed circus performers such as contortionists, dancers, and strongmen as well as O'Brien's Trained Horses and trained elephants from the Barnum and Bailey Circus, he made no early films of lion tamers. The lion tamer act certainly would have presented difficulties for film producers of this era. How could the "grim lords of slaughter" be safely packed into Edison's Black Maria, a small indoor production facility? Yet the act could not be approached as a purely outdoor or panoramic film either. Vanessa Toulin claims that cinematograph filming in the early twentieth century was "restricted to outdoor activities or those staged in an outdoor studio. As circus performances took place in an indoor venue such as a tent or specially constructed building, films capturing the full spectacle of the late Victorian and early Edwardian circus were rarely attempted."[137] Captain Bonavita's Great Zoological Pyramid was perfectly suited to the big cage and open arena, but its sheer scale and potential hazards militated against its easy transfer to film production.

Despite the logistical difficulties, filmmakers were drawn to wild animals as a practical means of creating cinematic spectacle. In fact, during the same years that Los Angeles became the geographical center of the American film industry, it also became the national center for wild animals and their trainers. Circuses that had traditionally spent the winter in Florida or the Midwest moved their winter quarters to Southern California.[138] By 1916 the *Los Angeles Times* could write that the city had become "the wild animal center of the world. Nowhere is there such a great variety and such numbers of rare and expensive animals."[139] The convergence of zoos and cinema in Hollywood at this time is perhaps best illustrated by the Selig Company, which in 1908 became both one of the first major film companies in Los Angeles and the proprietor of the city's Selig Zoo.[140] In 1917, *Moving Picture World* described how the Selig Polyscope Company film studio was located on one end of the Eastlake Park Zoo.[141] Indeed, Selig's first serial, *The Adventures of Kathlyn* (1913–14), was said to have been conceived principally to give Selig's zoo animals "something to do."[142] Universal first opened a production facility in Los Angeles in 1912, and when the operation was expanded to become Universal City in 1915, the studio boasted a "huge zoo containing several hundred wild animals and a specially patented cage with big runways and shutoffs for the protection of actors and cameramen in the taking of wild-animal pictures."[143] By the early 1920s, Hollywood film companies could draw on specialized animal farms around Los Angeles, such as Goebel's Lion Farm and Gay's Lion Farm. Lions were prominently featured in slapstick comedies such as Henry Lehrman's Sunshine Comedies, which had titles such as *Roaring Lions and Wedding Bells* (1917), *Hungry Lions in the Hospital* (1918), *Roaring Lions on the Midnight Express* (1918), and *Wild Women and Tame Lions*

(1918). The most famous alumni of Gay's Lion Farm were Numa, who appeared in Charles Chaplin's *The Circus* (1928), and Slats, the roaring lion of the MGM trademark.[144] Indeed, the MGM logo is a succinct testament to the importance of zoo and circus iconography to the young Hollywood studios.

Despite a burgeoning infrastructure to provide trained animals to film producers, Hollywood companies still faced problems integrating wild creatures into their films. First, animals had trouble interacting with large film crews. By contrast, animal performers in vaudeville had only to grow accustomed to the audience and their keepers. Several articles in the popular press described the dangers of making photographs of lion tamers, since it often took hours to get the animals in position, and the glare of the lights and sudden flashes had the potential to disorient and agitate them.[145] There was also the issue of the space restrictions of many indoor moving picture studios, which by one account were "not much larger than an ordinary bedroom." Finally, there was greater pressure on animal performers to complete tricks on the first attempt in the film studio. According to a 1914 newspaper article, "On the vaudeville stage when an animal is refractory and takes a little time to do what is expected of him, the audience is amused and will applaud all the louder, because the feat appears extra difficult when more than one trial is necessary, but in the 'movies' when an animal fails to take the proper cue at the proper time, the whole scene is utterly destroyed, and an expensive film wasted."[146]

There was also a long-standing belief that animal training and dramatic acting were inherently incompatible. Since the days of Van Amburgh lion tamers had been contrasted with stage actors as models of authentic male heroism. Consider a much reprinted anecdote concerning an encounter between lion tamer Jacob Driesbach—a contemporary of Van Amburgh—and the famous stage actor Edwin Forrest. We read that Forrest had a reputation as a "tyrant" and "bully," but he "met his match" when he shared a bill with Driesbach. Forrest had a habit of claiming that he had never been afraid in all his life and could not even imagine the emotion. Overhearing this remark, Driesbach invited Forrest home with him after the show. Forrest entered Driesbach's house and "walked a long distance through many devious passages—all dark—until finally Driesbach, opening a door, said. 'This way, Mr. Forrest.'" Forrest entered, immediately heard the door slam, and soon "felt something soft rubbing against his leg, and putting out his hand, touched what felt like a cat's back. A rasping growl saluted the motion, and he saw two fiery, glaring eyeballs looking up at him. 'Are you afraid, Mr. Forrest?' asked Driesbach, invisible in the darkness. 'Not a bit.'" After several tense minutes, Forrest "owned up in as many words that he was afraid." Driesbach let him out, but only after Forrest had promised him a champagne supper.[147] Regardless of the veracity of this anecdote, it illustrates a prevalent sentiment that the thrill maker and the actor were competing modes of male stardom, with the former's authentic courage revealing the latter's empty bluster.

An antagonism between lion taming and acting can also be seen in an anecdote concerning Captain Jack Bonavita's experience working on a film in 1913. Recall that Bonavita was the much-celebrated big cage lion tamer featured at Bostock's arena at the Pan-American Exposition in 1901. Bonavita went on to become a transitional figure in the cultural life of animal acts as they moved from the big cage to the silver screen, making a series of films in the 1910s after Dreamland was destroyed by fire in 1911. In a film titled *The Child of the Jungle* (1913), Bonavita played a man shipwrecked on a jungle island who had been trained in his childhood as a lion tamer.[148] In one scene Bonavita's character encounters a lion and is forced to recall his character's childhood skill. The camera operator filmed the scene from just outside the cage, with the lens of his camera poking through the bars. When shooting began, the lion did not respond to Bonavita's commands, and when Bonavita stumbled it suddenly sprang forward, savagely attacking him. The fact that Bonavita had been acting was said to have been the cause of the attack: "Every animal trainer holds mastery over his charges by sheer power of personality. Bonavita in adding to the realism of the picture was compelled for a moment to abandon his own personality and assume that of another. He did it too well. The lion was deceived."[149] By this logic, lion taming is fundamentally at odds with the kind of role-playing required of the actor: if the trainer breaks character or outwardly changes his persona for even a moment, the animals might not recognize or obey him.[150] For lion tamers, the actorly play with the performance of the self could have life-and-death consequences.[151]

Despite such risks, Bonavita took part in a series of films made by Centaur Features in 1915 and 1916. *Billboard* magazine wrote that Bonavita had been engaged to "break" his animals from their "arenic performances to the more hazardous task of film production" and claimed that he accomplished "almost super-human effects in teaching animals to attack him in order to acquire the extreme of realism in the film dramas."[152] In *The Rajah's Sacrifice* (1915), Bonavita played the eponymous role of a rajah who entered a lion's den and sacrificed his life for the heroine's safety: "The lions leap upon the Rajah from all parts of the den. . . . [T]he effect that such a scene carries can readily be imagined."[153] As with the planned airplane crashes described in the next chapter, filmmakers who remediated the acts of the thrill makers were often drawn to enactments of an act's failure, to the moments when the thrilling performance broke down, providing audiences with a sense of immediacy and excitement.[154] The producers of the Centaur film series sought to trade on Bonavita's circus celebrity. An advertisement in a May 1916 issue of *Moving Picture World* informed film exhibitors that Bonavita and his Bostock animals would be appearing at Luna Park, Coney Island, over the summer: "Animal pictures will be produced there which the public (your customers) will be permitted to witness," thereby increasing their interest in the films.[155] A series of photographs published in the *New York Tribune* in July 1916 invited the public to watch "animal rehearsals for the movies" at Bostock's Arena at Luna Park.[156] The abrupt end of Bonavita's film career underlines the dangers inherent in the combination of acting and animal training: in 1917 Bonavita was killed by a polar bear while shooting a film at the David Horsley film studio in Los Angeles.[157]

If limited in their role as actors, lion tamers could and did work behind the scenes as stunt doubles. As we saw in the last chapter, Bonavita's short film career coincided with the years during which stuntwork became professionalized as part of the larger Hollywood star system. Work with dangerous animals became a key component of second unit production, and circus performers worked as uncredited stunt doubles for Hollywood stars. Bonavita did stuntwork in films such as Graphic Features' *The Woman and the Beast* (1917) and *A Kaffir's Gratitude* (1916), the latter being, to my knowledge, the only film featuring Bonavita or his animals to survive. The narrative concerns John Melbourne (William Clifford), the son of a "prominent English family" working on a South African ranch. He sends for the "girl he left behind," Margaret Carlyle (Margaret Gibson), and they are married. Soon afterward an African servant leads them through the bush as they ride horses together. The guide comes upon a lion, and, through strategic editing, we are shown the lion attacking the servant and Melbourne jumping off his horse to rescue him with a shot from his rifle. In one brief shot the lion shares the frame with a figure whose face is obscured behind the bush. Next we see the lion briefly tussling with a prone figure before moving offscreen. The man twitches as if to verify that this is a living performer and not a prosthetic dummy. Is this figure Captain Bonavita interacting with one of his trained lions?

If the stunt double here is in fact Bonavita, then there are several ironies to his brief appearance. First, he is enacting not the "perfect picture" of balance typically displayed in his big cage act but instead its collapse. Second, Bonavita would have had to "black up" in order to double for the Kaffir servant. Such racial crossing on the part of stunt doubles was required by the colonial narratives in which lions would likely appear. Consider, for example, the personal narrative of another stunt performer, who described shooting a similar scene twenty years later. The scene called for the hero to leap out of a tree in front of a crouching lion. The lion was to jump on his back and bring him to the ground. Preparation for the scene had gone well during rehearsal with a lion named Topsy, but the animal's disposition changed when he prepared for the actual shoot: "The makeup man stripped me down to a loin cloth and painted me a dark ochre color. When I went near Topsy's cage she glared at me from the back—she didn't recognize me at all, though she knew my voice. . . . In order to retake the scene I dressed again and let Topsy see me being made up once more. When she was sure of my identity under the grease paint the scene clicked."[158] That stuntman was Bert "Suicide" Nelson, a lion tamer and stunt double on the MGM Tarzan films.

Edgar Rice Burroughs's Tarzan stories are certainly rich texts for the consideration of Western notions of race, empire, modernity, and masculinity, and have been discussed as such elsewhere.[159] Tarzan is the story of a white aristocrat who is raised from childhood among wild animals. In the racial logic of the time, he then becomes a superhuman "king of the jungle." That is, when Tarzan's white, aristocratic genes are combined with a strenuous, "primitive" upbringing unfettered by the emasculating influence of modern life, he becomes a paragon of the masculine ideals of the time. Note that Tarzan's ideal masculinity is enacted by controlling and subduing the dangerous wild animals around him: he is a "soul-stirring anachronism" along the lines of the nineteenth-century lion tamer. Indeed, Tarzan might be seen as an update of Isaac Van Amburgh's enactment of the white "monarch of the universe" who wields his God-given power over caged animals. Van Amburgh had even been referred to as "the Lord of the Forest."[160] Tarzan's famous call demonstrates his uncanny ability to control wild animals, just as Van Amburgh was thought to be able to cow his animals instantaneously. The fact that native Africans are both Tarzan's enemies and his inferiors in controlling the wild animals that live around them is, of course, white wish fulfillment, an anxious revision of Theodore Roosevelt and the Nandi hunters. We might place the Tarzan narrative, then, in a shared tradition with the lion tamer since both reaffirmed white male supremacy through the control of wild animals.[161]

Film versions of Burroughs's narrative had been made since 1918, but when MGM began a new Tarzan franchise in the early 1930s, the studio made use of a crucial development that helped to make possible the animal trend of the 1930s: the rear projection process, whereby "a previously filmed background scene is projected in the studio onto a large translucent screen from behind, while the actors are filmed in front of it to give the combined image directly on the film in the camera."[162] The first screens used for this procedure were of a limited size, so the process was typically restricted to showing such things as the passing street through the back window of a car. The year 1932 marked the introduction of new cellulose screen material, as well as the redesign of background projectors, both of which made it possible to project on much larger screens. Rear projection technology was clearly an area of interest and development in the late 1920s and early 1930s, as indicated by a spate of patents at this time.[163] A 1932 article in *American Cinematographer* stated that rear projection was one of the motion picture industry's "most recent developments" and was being used by "practically all of the studios."[164] As an illustration of the new possibilities of rear projection, Barry Salt points to *King Kong* (1933), which used the new large screens to combine animated models with live action.[165] Animal trend films like the MGM Tarzan series are equally impressive in their inventive application of rear projection to a range of visual thrills and reveal how this new technology was mobilized to articulate long-standing discourses about human interaction with wild animals.

Rear projection is first seen in *Tarzan the Ape Man* as a means to display the native African people who come to the trading post where Jane Parker (Maureen O'Sullivan) is visiting her father, James Parker (C. Aubrey Smith). Though the use of rear projection here was certainly a pragmatic production decision, a means to enable the combination of second unit footage with footage of actors in the studio, it also creates two visual planes that correspond to a colonial worldview defined by "two states of mankind," and so perpetuates the aesthetics of nineteenth-century anthropological-zoological exhibitions by showmen like Carl Hagenbeck.[166] More often, rear screens in the Tarzan films depicted a tantalizing sense of proximity between performers and wild animals. Such a depiction of human and animal interaction was, of course, an illusion created by the rear screen that allowed for a cinematic update on the zoological taxonomy that separated the "privileged species" from all others. In the rear projection sequences in the Tarzan films, we typically see shots of Tarzan (Johnny Weissmuller) tussling with the stuffed effigy of a wild animal, intercut with shots of him reacting to images of wild animals on a rear screen and shots of a stunt double engaged in hands-on interaction with live animals. One of the most striking of these sequences can be found in *Tarzan and His Mate* (1934), in which Jane and Tarzan come face to face with a charging rhino. The scene is composed of shots of Weismuller in the studio riding on a manufactured rhino, a double riding on an actual live rhino, and rear projection shots of O'Sullivan and Weissmuller reacting in the studio to second unit footage of the rhino. Rear projection is used here to depict humans in close quarters with wild animals, a spectacle hitherto reserved to the circus or zoo. Similar scenes can be found in other animal trend films of this era: Paramount's *Murders in the Zoo* (1933) depicts the villain pursued by lions projected on a rear screen, and *Zoo in Budapest* (1933), promoted as "Tarzan of the Zoo," used rear projection to show the players among escaped zoo animals.[167]

Though rear projection visualized a certain discontinuity between humans and animals along the lines of the semiotics of the zoo, the stunt doubles working on these films embodied a circuslike confusion of categories. As stated above, Johnny Weismuller's double in the Tarzan films was lion tamer Bert Nelson, who worked at the E&R Jungle Film Company and Selig Zoo in Los Angeles in the early and mid-1920s, and at the Al G. Barnes Circus and Keith-Albee vaudeville circuit with his costar, "Princess Pat, the Original Wrestling Lion," between 1926 and 1932.[168] Nelson was known for his intimate contact work with lions and would dance with Princess Pat in a manner that resembled the "soft dressage" of female lion tamers such as Adgie Costillo and Claire Heliot.[169] A review in *Billboard* magazine described how Nelson's act began with a film showing the trainer and Princess Pat at their Hollywood home before the two appeared on stage. Princess Pat's attitude was said to be calm and playful, like "a big house cat," and Nelson wrestled with her, teased and hugged her, and chased her around the cage before sticking his head in her mouth. "Every once in a while in her 'playing' with Nelson," the review noted, the lion "looks out at the audience as if to get its reaction. Its demeanor is never vicious."[170] Nelson described how this playful approach to his stage work with Princess

Pat had caused "a storm of protest" from his colleagues in the animal training community: "They didn't object to my wrestling with the king of beasts, but they did resent the fact that I dealt a body blow to the traditional hurrah with which animal acts heretofore had been staged. Instead of coming out before the footlights adorned in the conventional glittering uniform, shiny leather boots, revolver, snake whip and chair, I made my entrance in evening clothes, top hat and all! 'You are making our racket look like a job for Little Lord Fauntleroy,' one outraged trainer wrote me. 'You're spoiling your own game.'"[171] Nelson's top hat was a tacit admission that the act was a performance, and thus threatened to undermine the lion tamer's role as a paradigm of authentic white masculinity. The meaning of Nelson's interactions with animals was radically altered, however, when they were sutured to the Tarzan narrative: instead of dancing with lions he was killing them. It is ironic that Tarzan's heroic acts of primal white masculinity relied upon Nelson's intimate and playful contact with lions. It is the potential for just this kind of double or ironic reading of stunt performances in relation to the film narrative or the star's image that necessitated their erasure in studio promotional discourse.

The "conventional" shiny leather boots, revolver, chair, and whip mentioned by Nelson were the trademarks of a distinctly American form of "hard dressage" animal training. American trainers in this tradition traded in the tights and spangles of an earlier era for khaki jodhpurs, a white button-up shirt, and leather boots in a more casual, American version of a safari getup. This style was popularized by the most famous lion tamer of the 1930s, Clyde Beatty. We return, then, to where this chapter began—Beatty's *The Big Cage*. Beatty began his career with the Hagenbeck-Wallace Circus, and national press coverage of his struggle to recover from a lion bite in 1932 elevated him to a new level of fame.[172] Culhane argues that at the height of the Depression Beatty came to represent "the national longing for recovery, and the belief that an American boy could overcome the 'Law of the Jungle.'"[173] What is certain is that by 1933 Beatty was famous enough to publish his memoirs and have them made into a Hollywood film. Press discourse around the production of the film contrasted the lion tamer with Hollywood business as usual. According to one writer, Beatty had "the spark to awaken Hollywood from its lethargy of parlor dramas, sex plays and make-believe gangster stories. He came, stayed ten weeks and departed a few days ago, leaving a trail of open-mouthed professionals who marveled at his courage and daring."[174] During several trips to Los Angeles around this time, Beatty

FIGURE 14. Clyde Beatty, the most famous lion tamer of the 1930s.

acted as an advisor to MGM during the filming of the first Tarzan film, and he later shot *The Big Cage,* the success of which helped him to achieve a remarkable degree of celebrity: he graced the cover of *Time Magazine* in March 1937 and formed his own organization, the Cole Bros.–Clyde Beatty Circus, which opened the 1937 season at Madison Square Garden, something that the Ringling Bros. and Barnum & Bailey Circus had done every year since 1909. Even during the declining years of the American circus, Beatty maintained a long career that straddled the circus and the modern media: he appeared in feature films (*Africa Screams* [1949], *Ring of Fear* [1954]), film serials (*The Lost Jungle* [1934]), and a radio drama series (*The Clyde Beatty Show* [1949–50]).[175]

Beatty's celebrity did much to define an explicitly American style of lion taming. Beatty's act was a suspenseful struggle between man and beast, featuring snarling animals, cracking whips, and pistols ablaze with blank cartridges. Unlike Bert Nelson's appearances with Princess Pat or Hagenbeck's "happy family" acts, Beatty's act could not easily be associated with female performers or "Little Lord Fauntleroy."[176] In fact, Beatty encouraged eruptions of violence between the animals in his show and stated that the principal reason for the success of his act was the mixing of lions and tigers on a larger scale than ever attempted before, something that amounted to a "virtual guarantee of a fighting act." Beatty claimed simply to be giving the American public what it wanted: "Circus-goers have decreed that animal acts be fighting acts, and the only way to meet the demand is to mix warring species, and to complicate matters further by mixing the sexes."[177] *The Big Cage* emphasizes this aspect of Beatty's act from the opening title: "For the first time in history, lions and tigers are worked together in THE BIG CAGE. These jungle-born animals are noted for the ferocity of their mutual hatred and it is due to the unequaled courage and fearlessness of Clyde Beatty[,] the youngest living trainer of wild beasts[,] that the thrilling scenes you will witness have been made possible." The film does not disappoint, featuring multiple scenes of big cats fighting: two tigers skirmish in their cage and must be separated with a hose; later a lion and tiger battle in the big cage; and, near the end of the film, chaotic fighting breaks out among the big cats during a storm.

Beatty's act was decidedly agonistic, unlike the dancing or dinner parties that might be seen in a "soft dressage" act, and thus also conventionally "masculine." Note, for example, how Beatty stressed the fact that his act featured only animals who had been bred in the jungle. Lions born in captivity, according to Beatty, were "ruined": "Give me animals fresh from the veldt or the jungle. Give 'em to me every time. Nine times out of ten they are more formidable than their cage-born brethren—stronger, more ferocious, and better supplied with primitive passion."[178] There were pragmatic reasons for this view, tied to the process of training wild cats, but despite such justifications, one can't help but hear in these comments the echoes of the crisis in masculinity that had sent white middle-class men out fishing and camping during the first decades of the twentieth century.[179] Beatty made the gendered aspects of his preferences clear when he added that animals bred in captivity were inferior largely because of contact with "the women who visit circus menageries," who had taught the animals that "man is a softy."[180] That

Beatty's celebrity was closely connected to the performance of a certain kind of masculinity is indicated by the narrative of *The Big Cage,* which largely concerns the achievement of male social roles.

The film has two secondary male characters that contrast with Beatty: his friend Russ Perry (Wallace Ford) and a washed-up lion tamer named Tim O'Hara (Raymond Hatton). O'Hara's son Jimmie (played by a very young Mickey Rooney) arrives unexpectedly at the circus's winter quarters. Beatty and the other trainers try to prevent Jimmie from discovering that his father is no longer the successful lion tamer that he used to be and is now a barely functioning alcoholic. When he learns about the presence of his son, O'Hara puts on his old lion-taming costume, which consists of a pair of tights and an ornate military-style jacket. In order to impress Jimmie, O'Hara affects a brutal, authoritative tone with his fellow circus workers, in marked contrast to Beatty's unassuming conversational manner. Jimmie sees through this ruse, though, when O'Hara staggers and falls. "I'm just tired," O'Hara says. "My work is just too much for me." The camera follows Jimmie's eyes as he examines his father's costume and lingers on holes in his tights. O'Hara's costume signifies that he is stuck in an earlier era of masculine display: the tights are dated and worn, in contrast to Beatty's immaculate boots and jodhpurs. More than simply embodying an antiquated style of performance, however, O'Hara's crime is to make visible the fact that the lion tamer's enactment of ideal masculinity was a performance at all, to reveal that there were styles and fashions of masculine performance. His narrative punishment soon follows. That night, Jimmie sneaks into O'Hara's room, where he finds his father in the throes of a drunken delirium: his dependency on alcohol is a final sin against the cult of manly independence, which saw intemperance as an "especially insidious threat" since it "installed the 'monster' of dependency within the individual himself."[181] Despite Jimmie's pleas, O'Hara enters the big cage, where he—or, more precisely, a prosthetic dummy—is brutally torn to pieces by tigers. When Beatty tries to console Jimmie, the boy asks if he can stay and live with him. Beatty agrees, and for the rest of the film he assumes the role of Jimmie's surrogate father.[182] The accumulation of these plot points indicate that the lion tamer was still functioning as "sentimental education" in male roles in the 1930s.

The Big Cage was not the only animal trend film to make such overt connections between lion taming and male social identity. *O'Shaughnessy's Boy* (1935) was part of a cycle of films that paired

Wallace Beery and Jackie Cooper in narratives concerning father/son dynamics. Beery plays an animal trainer named Michael O'Shaughnessy, whose son, Stubby (played first by *Our Gang* star Spanky McFarland and then by Cooper), is taken from him by the boy's Aunt Martha, who has a passionate hatred of the circus. Soon after losing his son, O'Shaughnessy loses his nerve in the cage with a tiger, and as a result he loses his right arm in a vicious attack.[183] O'Shaughnessy's ability to function as a father, as an able-bodied man, and as an animal trainer are thus all explicitly linked in the film: when O'Shaughnessy learns that he will get custody of Stubby for a few months, he declares, "I lost my nerve when I lost the kid, now I'm getting my right arm . . . with him, I've got my nerve." At one point O'Shaughnessy sneaks into the animal tent at night in order to confront the tiger for the first time since his attack. James Wong Howe's photography in this scene is striking, beginning with a disorienting handheld shot as O'Shaughnessy approaches the cage. When the trainer hesitates before the tiger's cage, the wild animals in the tent erupt in a wild frenzy, depicted with canted angles and expressive lighting that suggests the precarious nature of controlling both wild animals and male animal passions. O'Shaughnessy's boss, Dan Hastings (Willard Robertson), appears in the tent, scolds him ("Wrap your fist around that whip, you're going in there"), and makes clear that "it's the boy you're letting down, you've got to whip this for his sake." The film's narrative closure involves O'Shaughnessy finally earning the full respect and love of his son and regaining his place in the big cage, achievements that are linked by a shot of Stubby polishing his father's shiny black boots.

In addition to offering parables of patriarchy, the 1930s animal trend films continued the tendency of turn-of-the-century popular literature to use the trope of lion taming to explore the affective texture of romance and sexuality. No less than the nation's most erotically charged female performer of the late 1920s and early 1930s, Mae West, wrote a script for herself, *I'm No Angel* (1933), in which she played a lion tamer in a traveling circus.[184] That same year, *Zoo in Budapest* updated the "married in a lion's den" motif with its depiction of an agile animal keeper and young woman named Eve (Loretta Young) who share an Edenic love nest in a zoo enclosure. Returning to *The Big Cage*, Beatty's friend Russ Perry is an up-and-coming lion tamer who has a problematic relationship with an aerialist named Lillian Langley (Anita Page). Russ is unable to enact his role as a dominant breadwinning male. Lillian pleads with Russ to give up animal training and get married on her income: "I'm making good money, why can't we get married?" "Say," an incredulous Russ replies, "what kind of a guy do you think I am?" Russ is also struggling to regain his nerve in the big cage after being attacked by a lion: "I'm washed up," he tells Beatty, "the old nerve is gone."[185] Like *O'Shaughnessy's Boy*, the narrative links the nerve required to control the big cats to the attainment of an authentic male role. In this case, Russ must learn to tame the lions before he is able to tame Lillian. *The Big Cage* demonstrates that the male lion tamer's performances continued to be a useful resource for the exploration of male anxieties about sexuality and courtship.

The attainment of male social roles in *The Big Cage* is worth noting, but the narrative is not the primary attraction of the film. Indeed, in many ways it simply provides a framework for Beatty's circus act, which is certainly stunning. The long-standing incompatibility of acting and animal training is overcome here, since an actual lion tamer is in the leading role and the narrative is set in a circus's winter quarters. In fact, Beatty's animal action is shown without the aid of rear projection, although that technology *is* used when other characters need to be depicted near the animals, for example, when an escaped tiger creeps up behind Jimmie, or when Russ has to rescue Lillian from lions. In both of these instances we see Beatty himself appear on the rear projection screen interacting with the animals: he crosses over, you might say, from one realm of screen reality to the other. Capable of appearing in both the world of the actor and the world of the stunt double, he is a cinematic circus performer who confuses established visual taxonomies.

As a dramatic actor Beatty is stiff and one-dimensional, and as a movie star he is short of stature and unspectacular, but as a performer in the big cage he has a wordless electric intensity that is *mesmerizing* in the literal sense of the word. In the cage with forty lions and tigers arranged on pedestals, Beatty bobs his head back and forth, locked in what appears to be a dangerous dance with the fierce animals around him.[186] Under a single spotlight he whistles to a tiger, which slowly descends the pedestal to stand before him, looking ready to spring at any minute. Beatty moves his hand in jerky movements to signal the tiger to lie down and roll over. Much of this is shot through the bars of the cage, or in long shot from a camera high above the enclosure. It is as part of this performance that we see the confrontation between Beatty and the lion, Nero, that I described at the beginning of this chapter. Recall that we are shown Beatty moving close to a lion, and when their gazes meet we see close-up shots of their eyes. Over the course of this chapter we have encountered several possible explanations for the cut-in to Beatty and the lion's eyes. This stylistic technique might be an example of residual biblical meaning accruing to the lion tamer performance. After all, here is a moment where the lion tamer subdues the animal not through whips, pistols, or chairs but through an almost supernatural power, perhaps enacting the biblical worldview. Or this shot could be a stunning example of the belief in the hypnotic power of the lion tamer's eyes, still alive and well in the 1930s. Beatty vociferously debunked the still-prevalent theory of the lion tamer's hypnotic eye, but he admitted that he made staring into the eyes of his animals part of his act as "an effective trick of showmanship."[187]

The reciprocal look between Beatty and the lion holds a certain power that goes beyond mere showmanship. Alison Griffiths describes the "return gaze" of ethnographic cinema, wherein the ethnographic subjects of a film look back at the camera as a "provocative and potentially disruptive" act, capable of triggering audience discomfort.[188] *The Big Cage* cut-ins might be read as a disruptive entrance of the lion's point of view, as if to say, "I see you looking at me and I don't like it."[189] They might also be read as the disruptive entrance of the *stunt double's* point of view in the person of Beatty, the stunt double being, after all, typically both faceless and gazeless.[190] But more than seeing simply the lion or Beatty looking, we see an exchange between human and wild animal, an exchange that has become increasingly rare in modern times. In an often-cited essay, John Berger writes that animals in the zoo are always "the observed," and the fact that they can, in return, observe us has "lost all significance."[191] "Nowhere in a zoo," Berger writes, "can a stranger encounter the look of an animal." The reciprocal look between human and animal had, according to Berger, been prevalent in previous centuries, but it had been extinguished for most Westerners in the modern era.[192] Berger's notion of a lost reciprocity of looking between human and animal provides a final way to read the shot of Beatty's eyes, and indeed the lion tamer act more generally.

In the wake of the anticruelty movement and the knowledge of the undeniable brutality that has accompanied many animal acts, it is easy to dismiss or condemn lion tamers like Beatty. In fact, although the first anticruelty legislation had focused on urban work animals and dogfights, a central objective of subsequent animal rights activists has been to end the mistreatment of circus animals. We have seen, however, how complex and multivalent the performances of lion tamers could be. The act accommodated changing views of the natural world, making it a stage on which performers could enact, and audiences could encounter, the fluid relationship between culture and nature, and a host of secondary associations that such a relationship could signify. The big cage became a resonant vortex of spectacular behavior that could align a Russian doll of nested spaces that included the modern city, circus fairground, zoological exhibition, global empire, and the wilds of nature.

The act could certainly be an index of human power and domination, but another possible relationship between human and animal was always present as well. In this regard, Vicki Hearne, an English professor and professional animal trainer, has offered an insightful perspective on the kind of communication possible between trainers and animals. In one essay, Hearne takes as her point of departure Wittgenstein's assertion that if a lion could talk, we wouldn't be able to understand him. "There is a minor mistake of fact here," Hearne writes, "since lions do talk to some people, and are understood."[193] As evidence, she describes trainer Hubert Wells as he works with a lion named Sudan on a film shoot: "If the scene calls for the lion to be run over by a truck, the lion must hold a Sit-Stay in the road while a semi bears down on him, as fast and as close as negotiations and arguments between the lion trainer and the director and producer will allow. So the lion trainer is riding on the front bumper of the truck, the camera cunningly placed so as to show lion and truck but not lion trainer. The trainer is saying, 'Stay, Sudan, Stay!'"[194]

Hearne argues that in moments such as these Wells and Sudan are engaged in a kind of exchange that involves an "overlap between his consciousness and the lion's."[195] In light of this, Hearne regrets that Wells's intimate communication with lions does not receive more attention from scholars, including animal rights philosophers, "who have even less interest in finding out what the lion and Wells might be saying to each other than the ordinary run of philosophers."[196] In a world where wild habitats are rapidly disappearing, and more tigers live as pets in America than in the wilds of Asia, we might heed Hearne's suggestion that the relationship between trainers and animals "may contain clues to imaginative and enlightened ways to take up the burden of responsibility toward animals."[197] I would like to open the possibility that the look between Clyde Beatty and Nero included such an "overlap of consciousness" and might indeed contain clues to a "new way of thinking about and living with animals," what Erica Fudge calls an "interspecies competence."[198] In the larger context of this book, we should note that it is in these easily overlooked moments of Hollywood film—in the residual traces of older traditions of performance, in the "unnatural histories" of wild animals and their human coperformers, and in the faceless bodies of stunt doubles half seen in rapid-fire montage sequences—that one might catch a glimpse of a quiet but profound communication, one that has, like the cinema itself, gone beyond words.

CHAPTER 4

The Adventures of the Aeronaut

The *Oxford English Dictionary* defines the verb *to thrill* in two ways: as an action of "material bodies" and as an action of "non-material forces." In the first case, *to thrill* means to pierce, bore, or penetrate, as by a piercing weapon such as a lance or dart. As an action of nonmaterial forces, *to thrill* implies another kind of penetration: "to affect or move with a sudden wave of emotion." The material and nonmaterial are intertwined in the noun form of *thrill,* which refers to "a subtle nervous tremor" of the body caused by "intense emotion or excitement." Thus far I have examined the performances of professional entertainers who were adept at creating such subtle nervous tremors. One type of thrill maker neatly combined the multiple senses of *thrill* by flying through the air like a dart in order to excite audiences: the pilots of airships and airplanes. Michael Balint points out that the word *acrobat* literally means "he who walks on his toes, i.e. away from the safe earth," and he argues that the thrills caused by professional entertainers increase with the distance of the performer from "some firm structure." If Balint is correct, then stunt pilots were aerial acrobats par excellence, performing farther from the safety of the earth than anyone had ever done before, thereby multiplying the thrills that they produced in audiences.[1]

Like lion tamers, the pilots of modern aircraft were seen as paradigms of a certain kind of masculine control, but whereas the former subdued the iconic representatives of the natural world, the aviator tamed the most awe-inspiring of modern technologies. In both of these cases, we are concerned with the performance of "stunts," as Erving Goffman defines the term: "the maintenance of guidance and control by some willed agency under what are seen as nearly impossible conditions." As examples, Goffman lists jugglers, tightrope walkers, knife throwers, high divers, daredevil drivers, and animal acts.[2] For Goffman, the "guided doings" done by such performers pointed to fundamental distinctions between what were understood as social or natural frameworks. We see an occurrence as either an undirected, unguided natural event or as a willfully guided social act. Happenings that trouble that distinction can produce an "astounding complex," as in reports of communication with the dead, UFO or monster sightings, encounters at the circus sideshow, and seemingly impossible stunts. The aeronauts in this chapter astounded the public through the control of modern flying machines under what seemed to be impossibly perilous conditions. As had been the case with the bridge jumpers, human flies, and "cat men" of previous chapters, the thrilling performances of the "birdmen" became a means of forging character and generating media celebrity.

A history of the aeronaut must engage with a chapter of early-twentieth-century experience that stands as a vivid nexus of many of the topics with which this book is concerned, such as modernity, technology, and male heroism. Indeed, the traces of that experience are inscribed in the word "stunt," which the *Oxford English Dictionary* links to the talk of soldiers during World War I, where it was applied specifically to aerial warfare. In the case studies in this book, I have moved across a time period ranging from the Gilded Age to the 1930s. The Great War of 1914–18 slices through that era like a jagged scar and must be taken into account in any study of the cultural life of modern masculinity, publicity, public heroism, and the film industry. The same anxieties about modern "overcivilization" that had helped to create a cultural niche for human flies and lion tamers also fostered a "martial ideal" that shaped the reception of aviation technology. Many men saw World War I as a solution to the "crisis of their sex role," with the battlefield envisioned as "a proving ground where they could enact and repossess the manliness that modern American society had baffled."[3] When the twentieth-century battlefield confounded those expectations, the image of the military pilot became useful, both for governmental propaganda and a civilian population desperate to make sense of modern combat. After the war, many American flyers embarked on careers as freelance itinerant entertainers before flocking to the nation's new center of aviation in Southern California. The proximity of the incipient aviation and filmmaking industries helped to facilitate a cycle of air films in the late 1920s and early 1930s, a cycle that was reliant upon the performances of stunt flyers.

One of the goals of this chapter, then, is to explore the articulations between aviation and the cinema. As several historians have noted, 1903 was the year of both Edwin S. Porter's iconic narrative film *The Great Train Robbery* and Wilbur and Orville Wright's first flight in a motor-powered, heavier-than-air flying machine. In what follows I will provide evidence to back up Paul Virilio's claim that cinema and aviation formed "a single moment" at the turn of the twentieth century.[4] The interpenetration of these two modern industries was most vividly embodied by the stunt pilots who helped to create the cinematic conventions for representing flight during the classical Hollywood era. Hollywood stunt flyers were part of a lineage of spectacular aeronautic performance that took place in the modern entertainment environment.[5] We have already seen how thrill-making bridge jumpers, human flies, and lion tamers appropriated modern spaces for their entertainments, and in the process juxtaposed the scale of the human body to gigantic urban structures such as steel suspension bridges, skyscrapers, and arenas housing the largest and most imposing living representatives of vast empires and the natural world. Susan Stewart argues that the archetypical example of the "gigantic" is the sky, "a vast, undifferentiated space marked only by the constant movement of clouds with their amorphous forms."[6] It was precisely this vast, undifferentiated space that became the backdrop for performances at fairground balloon ascensions, aviation meets, and airplane demonstrations over urban centers. These events cast individual performers against the sublime space of the sky in a modern act of technological augury in which the heavens were given new kinds of social meaning. Aviation displays were a thoroughly modern form of performance that drew tens of thousands of spectators and posed unique challenges to filmmakers who sought to repackage their thrills.

Like the other thrill makers, aeronauts were often considered to be male ideals, and their manly independence above the clouds was understood in terms of both science and chivalry. T.J. Jackson Lears writes that the airplane epitomized a number of turn-of-the-century "technological marvels" that seemed to embody a "regenerative force" that could satisfy middle-class cravings for intense, authentic experience.[7] At the same time, aviators embodied the skilled labor of the working-class "mechanic." In his discussion of Buster Keaton's *The General* (1926), Noel Carroll observes that the film's central character is an engineer and argues that such a skilled worker had a double appeal: for the white-collar clerical sector, the labor of such a hero could be "compensatory," since it reflected the values of another work culture; for the blue-collar factory sector, it could "gratify audiences by rehearsing a lost dimension of their work experience" in an era when labor was being increasingly deskilled.[8] Carroll concludes that Keaton was "a cine-poet of industrialism" who presented a type of artisanal hero that enabled diverse audiences to recall the kind of "concrete intelligence" that was disappearing from their work experience.[9] Keaton, of course, is one of the early film stars best known for enacting his own stunts, and we can take the logic of Carroll's argument a step further by applying it to a class of screen laborers even more closely aligned with the kind of concrete intelligence Carroll describes: stunt performers, and in particular the stunt pilots who operated modern flying machines.

Though often called "conquerors of the sky," aeronauts were privy to a unique view of the earth from great heights, a view that cast human society in miniature. This aerial view was first distributed to a mass audience via newspaper publicity, and we can best understand the interaction of aeronaut and cinema if we first examine the nineteenth-century discourses and practices that set the stage for it. I will thus begin with the type of entertainer that a 1904 newspaper article referred to as the founders of the guild of the "thrill makers," since they were the first to "ply the trade of risking life for the amusement of the public": "those who went up in flimsy balloons."[10]

AERONAUTIC GYMNASTICS

In June 1873, two well-known American "aeronauts" secured financing from the New York newspaper the *Daily Graphic* in order to embark on a balloon flight across the Atlantic Ocean. The flight of Washington Donaldson and John Wise in what became known as the "Graphic balloon" generated immense interest and discussion across the country, with one newspaper writing that, if successful, it would "contribute immensely in giving prestige to American enterprise in all parts of the world."[11] The endeavor relied upon the partnership of the two aeronauts Donaldson and Wise, an unlikely partnership in several respects. First, it was a contrast in terms of age: Wise was sixty-five years old and Donaldson only thirty-three. The two men also embodied very different attitudes toward their occupation. Wise was the grand old man of American ballooning, having made his first ascensions in the 1830s. Over the course of his long career, Wise had gained a reputation for a scientific approach to the balloon, having published numerous articles in *Scientific American* as well as a book titled *A System of Aeronautics* (1850). For Wise, the voyage across the Atlantic in the Graphic balloon was to be a scientific experiment to test his theory that there was a wind current flowing from west to east that corresponded to the Gulf Stream in the ocean. This "easterly current" was believed to make possible quick and easy balloon travel to England and the rest of Europe. Wise wrote that, in addition to proving his theories, the trip would show the "feasibility of transmarine ballooning," as well as elucidate the balloon's "commercial value" and "civilizing tendencies."[12] Determined to raise the standing of his craft, Wise wrote that the voyage would "open the eyes of scientific men" to the fact that ballooning was not "the merest bauble of a toy" or a "simple, spectacular foolhardy amusement," but instead had a "niche in the Arcanum of meteorological science."[13] Wise's quest for scientific legitimacy led him to criticize those aeronauts who used ballooning merely for the sake of entertainment. In 1870 he wrote that "it is a deplorable truth that many, if not most, persons who use balloons are not scientific. And yet, this class have generally the most marvelous stories of blood oozing from their finger ends, and the balloon turning topsy-turvy and the miraculous escapes they have made."[14]

Those words could well describe Wise's partner in the voyage in the Graphic balloon, Washington Harrison Donaldson. Born in Philadelphia, Pennsylvania, in 1840, Donaldson's father had been one of the earliest photographers in the city. Donaldson learned the family business and was employed in a photographic studio in 1860.[15] Just as a young Isaac Van Amburgh had rejected his position as a clerk in the family business in order to become a lion tamer, so did Donaldson find himself unsuited to shop work, and his health failed under the confinement of those pursuits. Donaldson described what he saw as a "class of people who were only half alive" and who spent "hours in a place which they call their office": "They sit themselves in a dark corner, hidden from the sun's rays, and in one position remain for hours, inhaling the poisonous air with the room full of carbonic acid gas, which is as poisonous to man as arsenic is to rats; and in addition to this, will fill their lungs with tobacco smoke, and to steady their nerves require a stimulation of perhaps eight or ten brandies a day."[16] Leaving the "dark corner" of his father's office in 1861, Donaldson became a teacher of "muscular development" and gymnastics.[17] Donaldson's career trajectory illustrates what T. J. Jackson Lears has described as a middle-class

WASHINGTON H. DONALDSON,
AERONAUT.

FIGURE 15. The aerial gymnast Washington Harrison
Donaldson.

longing for intense physical and emotional experience at this time, the
result of the "diffuse fatigue produced by a day of office work or social
calls" that had, for many Americans, come to replace the "bodily testing
provided by rural life."[18]

In addition to gymnastics, Donaldson also took up tightrope walking, making his first public appearance in that capacity in 1862. Emulating Chevalier Blondin, Donaldson walked across a rope twelve hundred
feet above the Schuylkill River in Philadelphia. Adding a little bit of
Sam Patch for good measure, Donaldson finished the act by leaping
from the rope into the river. Two years later he made a similar crossing
at Sam Patch's old venue, the Genesee Falls in Rochester, New York.[19]
After spending several years as a traveling tightrope walker, ventrilo-
quist, and magician, Donaldson debuted a new kind of performance

in August 1871 in Reading, Pennsylvania. Donaldson wrote that his first experience of this new act was "so glorious" that he "resolved to abandon the tightrope forever."[20] One spectator described Donaldson's show as "one of the most extraordinary and almost incredible exhibitions of human intrepidity and daring" that had ever been seen, and one that equaled or surpassed in "thrilling and painful interest anything ever attempted by Sam Patch or Blondin in their wildest effort."[21] This incredible exhibition began with an ascent in an untethered gas balloon that was equipped not with the usual passenger basket but only a trapeze. With his "glittering dress" sparkling in the sun, Donaldson waved his handkerchief to the crowd as the balloon began to rise, and he then gracefully took his seat on the trapeze. He then performed a variety of hair-raising maneuvers above the heads of the spectators, with no net should he fall, and no means to steer the free-floating balloon. He lay down on the bar with hands and feet outstretched, stood on the bar, and hung by one hand, by one foot, and then by the back of his head.[22]

The most shocking part of the act was a bit of business that Donaldson referred to as his "drop act": lying extended on his back on the bar, he dropped headfirst, as though falling, only to catch himself at the last moment by his toes. Then, hanging head downward, he would ascend still higher into the air, waving his handkerchief to "the horror-stricken multitude below." Reports attest to the fact that the drop act did indeed produce thrills: it was said to send "a sudden thrill" through the crowd, until "the blood ceased to curdle" in their veins and they "gave vent to their feelings in cheer after cheer."[23] In some cases, the reactions of the crowd were just as fascinating to reporters as the act itself: "Some were thrilled with admiration of the courage of the daring man, and kept their eyes riveted on him," wrote a Massachusetts reporter, while "others shuddering with horror turned away with pallid faces and beating hearts and covered their eyes with their hands to shut out the dreadful sight. Faint shrieks were heard from the ladies, and some turned to leave the spot. . . . [Others] concluded to take one more look, and looking once, looked again."[24] Another account described how "a thrill and a low murmur of horror passed through the immense multitude," who watched Donaldson "with intensest interest," though many hurried away from the sight "giddy and faint."[25] These reports demonstrate Donaldson's mastery of a performance that could convene and captivate a large copresent audience. As compared to lion tamers confined to animal cages, or bridge jumpers and human flies reliant upon specific features of the built environment, the great benefit of Donaldson's act was that it was eminently portable, and thus capable of transforming any well-populated area into a performance space. Descriptions of Donaldson's act also suggest an addition to our working definition of "thrill": though experienced as a subjective bodily tremor, it is something that happens in crowds. It is an intersubjective affective wave that passes through groups of copresent people in a manner similar to contagious laughter.

Donaldson was clearly a gifted showman, and, like human flies, he used his elevated performance position for marketing and publicity. Some reports have him throwing advertising circulars from the air, which appeared like "twinkling stars surrounding the balloon, producing a most novel and pleasing effect."[26] He told one reporter that he had begun his aerial gymnastics simply as a means to advertise his magic act but had then hit upon a system whereby his ascensions were followed by paid appearances in local halls where he would describe his "aerial journey."[27] All evidence thus supports a conclusion that Donaldson was exactly the "deplorable" class of balloonist about whom John Wise had complained. Nevertheless, the two men pooled their resources and renown in order to attain backing for the transatlantic voyage of 1873, and so for a time they became somewhat reluctant partners. Press coverage of the enterprise often played up the contrast between the two aeronauts. The *New York Tribune* wrote that Wise had "studied the scientific points of the problem with care and intelligence," and so gave reason to expect "something of permanent scientific value, and not the mere amusement of an idle curiosity." Donaldson, on the other had, was simply a gymnast "whose courage and agility may perhaps be found of use in the course of the trip." Another article referred to Donaldson as a "reckless fellow, who would jump at the prospect of being shot out of a mortar up to the moon, if he could depend upon the presence of half a million spectators at such an experiment." "Science and civilization" meant little to Donaldson, wrote an Arkansas paper: "If he is successful in having his name conspicuous for twenty-four hours in the newspapers, his highest ambition will be abundantly gratified."[28]

Despite the crew's differing motivations for making the voyage, the inflation of the balloon began in Brooklyn on September 10, 1873. Wise became increasingly critical of the enterprise during the final preparations and claimed that the *Daily Graphic* organization had refused to act on his recommendations. For example, Wise had insisted on having a balloon made of silk, but instead the owners of the *Daily Graphic* had cut costs on materials in order to spend more on advertising. On the day of the ascension, Wise announced that the cloth balloon was unsafe and left the grounds. Wise's fears were soon justified when the balloon ripped before the inflation was complete. Donaldson spoke dismissively of Wise, suggesting that the older man had lost his nerve: "He is like a child, and wants a silk balloon," he said, "but I guess we will make a bigger sensation with the one we have."[29] Wise angrily parted company with the project, and after several postponements and false starts the inflation of a smaller balloon was completed. Donaldson and a small crew ascended before a paying crowd on October 6. This time the balloon remained intact, but a storm forced an emergency landing in Connecticut, a disappointing end to the dream of the transatlantic current.

The press lambasted the endeavor as a "pure advertising dodge." The owners of the *Daily Graphic* had been the only winners, wrote one commentator, since "all publicity spurs trade." The voyage would take a place in "the annals of humbug," wrote another critic, besting even "the numerous contributions of Mr. Barnum to the history of fraud."[30] In fact, P.T. Barnum himself had taken a keen interest in ballooning that same month. No doubt recognizing a good publicity scheme when he saw one, Barnum in September 1873 met with several "noted aeronauts," including John Wise, who gave Barnum a copy of his book.[31] But it was Donaldson, not Wise, who was working with Barnum soon after the debacle: the great showman hired the aerial gymnast to perform balloon ascensions as part of his traveling Great Roman Hippodrome shows of 1874 and 1875. Donaldson's ascensions in the Barnum balloon worked brilliantly to generate publicity for the shows. A system was devised whereby local newspaper reporters were invited to go aloft and then write about their experiences. Besides providing the shows with free publicity, these press accounts are notable as documents of early aerial vision. In France, the photographer and caricaturist Nadar (Félix Tournachon) had taken the first aerial photographs from a balloon in the 1850s. Newspaper accounts of the Barnum balloon ascensions offer an American, commercial variant on the nineteenth-century aerial view. Not surprisingly, a recurring theme in these accounts is the reporter's description of the social world as seen in miniature.

Susan Stewart describes how the space of the miniature in narrative fiction is typically managed through the use of similes that establish an equivalence between nature and the body. Scale is thus established by means of a set of correspondences to the familiar and the domestic, such that the natural landscape is transformed into a cultural one.[32] Similar techniques can be found in reports of the view from the Barnum balloon. For a writer from the *Brooklyn Daily Eagle*, New York's city blocks appeared "like the squares of tessellated pavement," while the immense dome of a bank seem to be "a mere toy structure." A reporter in Indiana wrote that the crowd below was like "an army of ants," and the earth "looked like an immense garden laid off into beautiful squares and blocks. The forests were orchards, and the fields of moving grain, flower gardens."[33] We should note that aeronauts were not the only nineteenth-century thrill makers to have access to such views. In an 1852 interview a steeplejack described "the small houses, the narrow streets, the little creatures creeping along them, and the feeble sounds they send up," all of which made him "feel grand."[34] Both aeronaut and steeplejack enacted a social role that allowed the public to play with the scale of the modern lived environment: miniaturized by their performances, both gave spectators a vicarious experience of a gigantic perspective. Reports of these tantalizing perspectives sold newspapers, and in Donaldson's case sold tickets to Barnum's traveling show as well.[35]

In addition to taking reporters aloft, Barnum also perfected the balloon wedding as a form of ballyhoo. In October 1874, the city of Cincinnati, Ohio, was said to be "in a state of excitement" as thirty thousand people, including Barnum and his wife, saw the Rev. H. B. Jeffries marry Miss Mary E. Walsh and Mr. Charles M. Colton in a "bridal basket" covered with flowers and guided by Washington Donaldson.[36] Anticipating the vogue for marriages "in the lion's den" described in the previous chapter, balloon weddings were a popular fairground attraction that drew tens of thousands of spectators for the rest of the century.[37] It was in the hopes of grabbing newspaper headlines that an agent of Barnum's organization encouraged Donaldson to make a voyage over Lake Michigan when the Hippodrome was camped in Chicago during the summer of 1875. Donaldson took the challenge, but one witness recalled that on the day of the ascension he seemed nervous, vacantly whistling to himself as he observed the sky. At one point he swung himself to a platform of wire netting just under the balloon, where he could be plainly seen and described: "He looked short and very square shouldered, with a gymnast's breadth of chest and big jointedness." His collar was turned up to shield his neck from the sun, he wore a silk hat drawn down over his face, and he sported "hair cropped short, a thick dyed mustache twisted up in an inquisitive point at each end, and a pair of dark bright eyes which roved hither and thither." Someone in the crowd called out, "Donaldson, you'd better get out." The aeronaut was silent for a minute and then replied, "I wish to Christ I could!"[38] The original plan had been to take two reporters on the ascension, but at

Balloon Wedding.—98th Ascension.

FIGURE 16. An 1874 balloon wedding with Washington
Donaldson guiding the "bridal basket."

the last minute Donaldson announced that the weather was such that
it was unwise to take more than one. The two reporters drew lots, and
the winner was Newton Grimwood of the *Chicago Evening Journal.*
Donaldson and Grimwood ascended early that evening, and the wind
carried them out over Lake Michigan. A few hours later a tugboat saw
the balloon thirty miles offshore, with its basket skimming along the
surface of the lake. The boat changed course to assist the balloon, but
a gust of wind lifted it into the air and it disappeared from sight. Soon
thereafter a violent thunderstorm broke over the lake.

With no reports of the aeronauts, public curiosity and fascination
became intense. One newspaper wrote that the whole country was
waiting with "deep concern" for news, and that Donaldson's name had

become "known from one end of the land to the other."[39] In Chicago, people stood on street corners to gaze into the sky for a sign of the missing balloon. Some gathered at the Hippodrome tents on the beach, lingering for words of hope: "There were men who left their counting-rooms and talked of the last mariner of the winds. Women . . . came down and stood under their umbrellas with anxious faces and drabbled skirts, and grew bold to ask strangers as they hurried by if anything had been heard of Donaldson." Despite growing fears about Donaldson's fate, the Hippodrome tried to return to business as usual. Donaldson's press agent took the aeronaut's place in the Barnum balloon for a short ascension. He waved his hat to the audience, but "not a single cheer went up to tell him that he was missed from the face of the earth. It was probably the first and only balloon ascension ever made in silence."[40]

For weeks, the uncertainty that surrounded the missing Barnum balloon turned to widespread speculation and even hysteria. There were reports that Donaldson was alive in Michigan, but in disguise. In Cincinnati, a man who registered at a hotel under the name of Donaldson raved about taking a balloon trip around the world. There were stories that a note from Donaldson had washed ashore in a bottle.[41] Some writers believed that the whole thing had been arranged by Barnum in order to garner publicity and pointed to the fact that, only a few months previously, a dispatch had been sent to the manager of the Hippodrome from a "J.M. Spencer" stating that the Barnum balloon had crashed and Donaldson's dead body had been found in the basket. After a flurry of newspaper reports, Donaldson was found to be alive and well, and the mysterious "Spencer" was never identified. "The mythical character of Dr. Spencer looks very much like a prearranged programme," wrote a New Jersey paper, and "Barnum's tricky ear marks stick out all over it." The publicity potential of such a hoax was clear: "The possibility of such a dreadful accident being brought so vividly before the public will attract thousands of morbidly curious people to see the balloon ascend hereafter. It is a ghastly way of making money."[42]

This kind of speculation was brought to an abrupt and tragic end when, on August 17, the body of the reporter Grimwood was found on the shore of Lake Michigan. Though the aeronaut's body was never found, Donaldson was almost certainly dead. The widespread discussion of Donaldson's death was marked by the same rhetorical contrast between science and entertainment that had surrounded the *Daily Graphic* voyage. There was no cause to mourn over the tragedy, wrote the *Brooklyn Daily Eagle,* since Donaldson had only gone "because

Mr. Barnum paid him to go" and was merely "an advertisement for the circus": "He was not a man of science and never pretended to take the slightest interest in the problems that have wooed the scientific enthusiasts of the past to destruction." In an article titled "Foolhardiness," a pundit wrote that Donaldson had "risked his life in the most reckless and objectless manner, and claimed the applause of mankind for his achievements." "Haven't we had enough of ballooning?" asked the *Hartford Daily Current.* "It is practically good for nothing," and the accounts of aeronauts like Donaldson being killed were "an imposition of sympathetic suffering upon a public who have enough to worry over without having to be fretted by flighty fools and the results of their folly."[43] The sentiments expressed here are similar to those of Steve Brodie's critics a decade later. In both cases, commentators in the popular press offered themselves as cultural gatekeepers policing the attribution of a celebrity status that seemed to be deviating from classical models of fame. The primary criterion in that gatekeeping was whether or not an individual's renown was judged to be in the service of dominant social interests, in this case "science."

But just as Brodie's critics had defined social service from a particular class perspective, so Donaldson's detractors based their judgments on a narrow view of what counted as science. Historians of both popular entertainment and science have described the importance of showmanship for eighteenth- and nineteenth-century "natural philosophers," scientists, and inventors, as well as a host of magicians, electrical healers, mesmerists, and mind readers who cast their acts in scientific terms.[44] Furthermore, the American public had long had an inclination to see the aesthetic qualities of modern technology.[45] During an era characterized by "show inventors," "wonder showmen," and the "technological sublime," the condemnation of Donaldson for his particular blend of science and showmanship says more about the social position of his critics than about any inherently "scientific" uses of balloon technology. In fact, the champion of scientific ballooning and Donaldson's one-time collaborator, John Wise, met his end four years later under remarkably similar circumstances. After ascending from St. Louis in September 1879, Wise was lost over Lake Michigan. As was the case for Donaldson's flight, the body of a passenger washed up on the shore, but Wise's remains were never found. For some critics, Wise, too, had betrayed science: "It would be gratifying to learn that Professor Wise perished in a scientific attempt. The fact that he left all his instruments behind him, and took a companion who paid for a seat in his car, divests the voyage of that scientific romance which would give his fate a luster, and reduces the ascension to the circus level."[46] In press coverage such as this, Wise's long dedication to "science" was swept aside in a more general disillusionment with ballooning. By 1881 the *Brooklyn Daily Eagle* could write that "no invention that promised so well at the outset" had proved more disappointing, or had been responsible for as many deaths, as the balloon, which had "degenerated into a circus property."[47] The *Chicago Tribune* agreed, writing in 1900 that although there had once been a time when ballooning "carried a dignity with it" and "learned men used it in establishing scientific observations of the upper air," it had since become "a sort of museum attraction."[48]

The discourses around the Graphic balloon and the careers of its two famous aeronauts reveal what might be called an "aeronautic structure of feeling" in the late nineteenth century.[49] The nineteenth-century aeronautic structure of feeling was characterized by an internal tension between what were considered scientific and entertainment uses of balloons. Though denigrated at their death for seeming to fall too far on the entertainment side of the spectrum, Donaldson and Wise can be seen as two of the founders of a tradition wherein aeronauts astounded audiences through their precarious control of balloons, a form of display well suited to the modern entertainment environment of fairground or city center, and a powerful vehicle of multimedia publicity and celebrity. An internal tension between science and thrills continued to define the aeronautic structure of feeling during the next phase of airship technology, but in the early twentieth century the view from the skies would be publicized not only through newspaper accounts, but on cinema screens as well.

BIRDMAN

In June 1907, a dirigible (steerable) balloon, or "airship," appeared in the skies over Boston, "dipping and gliding, soaring and circling" around the city's skyscrapers and spires with "all the easy grace of some huge bird," as thousands of people watched from the streets below. Later that summer the same airship was in New York City, where crowds watched it from the Brooklyn Bridge and the windows of tall office buildings. In July, the airship circled the Washington Monument, and the roofs of "every available building in the business section" were converted into a grandstand.[50] At the controls of this airship was Lincoln Beachey, the twenty-year-old "boy aeronaut." Beachey had made his first dirigible balloon flight in 1905, at the age of eighteen. At the Lewis and Clark

FIGURE 17. The aviator Lincoln Beachey, one of a cohort of celebrity "birdmen."
Courtesy of the Library of Congress.

Exposition in Portland, Oregon, Beachey flew from the exposition grounds to the city and back, stopping to deliver letters at the chamber of commerce building and the offices of two newspapers.[51] Two years later, his flights on the East Coast established his national fame, such that in 1908 he was hired to be the "supreme, up-to-date touch" for Philadelphia's Founder's Week celebration.[52] Though promoted as quintessentially "up-to-date," Beachey's airship would, by the end of the year, be made somewhat outmoded by public demonstrations of a new kind of flying machine. Indeed, 1908 was a watershed year for aviation, since it was then that Orville and Wilbur Wright made their wildly successful public demonstrations in America and Europe of the airplane they had invented in 1903.[53] Beachey was well aware of this sea change in aviation technology and had switched from his dirigible airship to an airplane by 1911. Beachey's fame in this new realm of aviation was established when he won the first cross-country airplane race in the United States in August 1911. Beachey was soon a prominent member of a small fraternity of male aviators, or "birdmen," who captured the imagination of the American public through appearances at sponsored races, demonstrations, and aviation meets.

In the years after the Wright brothers' 1908 demonstrations, aviation meets were held across the country at fairgrounds, racetracks, and aerodromes. The first American aviation meet was held in Los Angeles, California, in January 1910, when fifteen thousand people filled the grandstand and an equal number watched from cars and carriages. The performances of the aviators had a powerful effect on the multitudes: "Women gave vent to hysterical laughs that changed into sobs and in the eyes of many men were tears of excitement."[54] We can get a sense of the atmosphere at aviation meets of this era from a 1912 account in the *Los Angeles Times,* which described crowds making their way to the grandstand past hawkers selling ten-cent photographs of "the greatest living aviators," a "pretty girl" singing "Oh, please take me up in your airship" through a megaphone, and a man who instructed the crowd on how to avoid being beheaded by the airplanes during the show. All in all, the author concluded that an aviation meet was "a kind of salad of the old-fashioned county fair, the circus, and an unexpurgated Coney Island."[55] Besides the possibility of being beheaded, this new form of entertainment posed certain challenges for the spectators: the airplanes were often far away; the most exciting action sometimes happened out of sight or behind clouds; and looking into the sky for long periods of time could be uncomfortable. A cartoon in a Colorado paper depicted spectators at an aviation meet with their necks bent painfully backward to look into the sky. Next to the caption, "The Day After," we see a man with a bandage around his neck and a bottle of arnica liniment. Similarly, a Boston paper noted that the thirty-five thousand people who had attended a 1910 aviation meet would wake up with "cricks" in their necks, reaching for a liniment bottle.[56]

Despite the sore necks, aviation meets became a popular mode of entertainment between 1910 and 1914. In 1911, *Billboard* magazine proclaimed that aviation was "the youngest member of the open-air amusement family, but it's a very lusty child, and its growth promises to be sure and rapid." The magazine bragged that it was the first paper to recognize aviation as an amusement, just as it had been the first to recognize the carnival and the motion picture.[57] The same issue devoted several articles to aviation as a form of amusement, in one case stating that the airplane held more "spectacular interest" than any other entertainment and was "easily one of the most important factors in the amusement world." Another article called the airplane "the greatest of all scientific machines in its ability to amuse, instruct, and to advance the interests of the people."[58] The following year, predictions about the growth of the "lusty child" were coming true, with a report stating that the airplane was unquestionably "the chief feature of attraction at the various fairs and expositions to be held in this country during the coming season," and that in every case in which airplane flights were billed as scheduled events, record-breaking attendance was reported.[59]

Public displays of aviation became the site of a jurisdictional dispute over the nature of this new form of entertainment.[60] Updating the tension between scientific and circus ballooning, displays of aviation technology were variously framed as either scientific demonstration or thrill-making entertainment. Many pundits, members of the elite Aero Club of America, and aviation supporters strongly favored the former and saw an incipient mode of "circus flying" as a dangerous fall from grace.[61] In 1911, the *Philadelphia Inquirer* bemoaned the fact that the leading exponents of aviation were failing to discriminate between "scientific, sportsmanlike flying and foolhardy, valueless, death-on-a-hairspring feats of bravado." The paper warned of a "dangerous tendency to drift from scientific flying to aerial circus performing": "An aeroplane is not a circus accessory. An aerial acrobat is not an aviator. The science of aviation is not properly a get-rich-quick scheme." The *Inquirer* drew a sharp distinction between the earliest aviators and inventors, who were decidedly not in "the showman's class," and more recent commercial flyers, who were "of an entirely different class, physically and temperamentally, from the aeroplane inventors." The latter had become "a curse to the science, a blot upon the sport."[62] The article was accompanied by a cartoon that depicted the new generation of airmen as moths circling a flame that bore a dollar sign. By contrast, some commercial flyers were happy to promote themselves as popular entertainers. A 1912 California aviation meet was advertised as "an aerial three-ring circus, one mile high and three miles wide." The promoters proudly announced that there would be "none of the so-called scientific demonstrations. The spectators demand sensational flying, and real nerve racking thrills."[63] The same year another Los Angeles meet was billed as "a three-ring aerial circus" made up of "sky vaudeville" acts with "all scientific and educational features eliminated. A premium is placed on daring rather than science, and 'stunts' calculated to thrill will replace the barograph tests of the earlier days."[64]

The jurisdictional dispute over the cultural meaning of aviation spectacle might best be understood as a debate over whose labor was on display at aviation meets. Should the public applaud the machine itself, and by extension the scientific prowess of engineers and inventors, or should they applaud the daring operators who guided the machines? One way to understand this distinction is by reference to Erving Goffman's subdivision of the term "speaker" into an "animator" (the physical body engaged in utterance production), an "author" (who crafts the words spoken), and a "principal" (in whose name the words are spoken).[65] Participants in a speech event could be directed to attend primarily to one or another of these categories. For example, at a government press conference our attention might be directed not so much to the press secretary who animates a statement, nor to the speechwriter who authored it, but to the president in whose name the utterance is made. Aviators were the "animators" of the thrilling flights at aviation meets, while the inventors could be read as the "authors" of their machinery, and their flights an expression of the larger "principal" of American science and technology. Putting it another way, Richard deCordova uses the linguistic concept of enunciation (the act of producing a statement) to track how the film actor, instead of the production company or the technology itself, became the recognized site of labor in the cinema.[66] The debates around early aviation meets can be understood as a dispute over the designation of the site of enunciation in aeronautic display.

As a final analogy, consider Iwan Rhys Morus's study of early nineteenth-century British scientific exhibitions, in which he describes two distinct and conflicting visions of proper scientific practice that were rooted to some degree in class distinctions. One approach to scientific experimentation and display was embodied by "elite, largely middle-class gentlemen centered at institutions such as the Royal Society," whose aim was "to articulate a highly abstracted view of nature, divorced from instruments and apparatus," and who tended to draw a strict distinction between private laboratory experimentation and the public presentation of their productions to elite audiences. A contrasting approach was embodied by popular lecturers, instrument makers, and mechanics, who were closely connected to their instruments and who made a far less clear-cut distinction between private laboratory practice and public presentation. Morus sees these antagonistic trends as part of a larger conflict between "artisanal and middle-class definitions of work and skill in terms of their ownership, status, and relationship to machinery."[67] A similar tension can be found in the debates over aviation display, with the wealthy, science-minded Aero Club members that sponsored the meets at odds with the "mechanics" who operated the planes.[68] In this struggle to establish the interpretive frame of aviation spectacle, Lincoln Beachey was one of a host of celebrity birdmen

FIGURE 18. Lincoln Beachey's 1911 flight under a bridge spanning the Niagara River. Courtesy of the Library of Congress.

who keyed popular attention to the labor of the operators. It is in this light that we should recognize the significance of Beachey's much publicized June 1911 flight over Niagara Falls and under a steel arch bridge spanning the river below in front of 150,000 spectators.[69] Beachey's act placed the airplane squarely in the iconic domain of thrill makers from Sam Patch and Blondin to Steve Brodie.

The tension between aeronautic science and thrills was also manifested in the acts of the birdmen, as can be seen in a discourse that framed airplane stunts as practical instruction. For example, there was much discussion of the practical merits of the French aviator Adolphe Pégoud's thrilling loop-the-loops and upside-down flying. One article in the popular press referred to "Pégoud's reassuring feats"—reassuring in that they demonstrated the "safety of the present day aeroplane under any condition."[70] Another magazine described Pégoud as "a pioneer with a great lesson to teach" and claimed that his acrobatic feats were "of the utmost value to pilots throughout the world" since they showed the capabilities of the modern flying machine.[71] In rhetoric such as this, stunt flyers such as Pégoud and Beachey married the public images of Washington Donaldson and John Wise, becoming public figures that resolved long-standing tensions in the aeronautic structure of feeling. The *Hartford Courant* even wrote that Beachey possessed "two entirely different personalities," one the "scientific, ambitious, non-mercenary, careful Dr. Jekyll Beachey," the other the "danger-calloused, money-loving, death-inviting and scientific-hating" Mr. Hyde Beachey.[72] Beachey became famous for loops like those performed by Pégoud, but his trademark stunt was the "death dip," which involved turning off his engine while high over the crowd and plunging downward so that the audience thought he had lost control. At the last moment Beachey would straighten out and sail over the heads of the crowd just as they had begun to "shiver and grow faint."[73] The "death dip" was an update of Washington Donaldson's "drop act," but note that Beachey framed his shtick in terms of its practical instructional value: "I was furthering the interests of science, in that I was showing airmen that it was possible to cheat death when your motor stalled above."[74]

There was, however, clearly more to the appeal of aerial stunts than the rational demonstration of aviation technique for an audience of fellow flyers and engineers. The performances of flyers such as Beachey and Pégoud were powerful enactments of human mastery over new technology in a bid to "conquer the air." When Beachey appeared at the 1914 Texas State Fair, a reporter described how he performed his loops against "the dome of the great heavens," so that his miraculous "contrivance of wood and wire and canvas" seemed to represent an "uncanny defiance and awesome disregard of the very law that holds the universe itself in check."[75] In 1911 the San Francisco Chronicle published this description of a recent aviation meet:

> The birdman, master of his delicate craft, is the last touch of magic that lifts man into the dominion of his birthright above the brute creation. When he leaves the ground . . . he gives the most inspiring and thrilling manifestation of exquisite beauty, detached and independent power, personal mastery and light, undaunted courage that it is possible for a human being to give, or we of the mundane multitude to gaze upon delightedly. Suspended in the impalpable atmosphere, doing as he wills, willing what he does, he is, for once, man stripped of all sordidness—a vision to make your heart beat high at being a human being.[76]

In accounts such as these, the birdman's ultimate success involved transcending the mechanical qualities of the airplane. "I can't call it a machine, for the very word seems too heavy and cumbrous for it," commented the San Francisco Chronicle writer. In the hands of the birdmen, the airplane was instead "like a realized, visual flight of the imagination."[77] In 1912 the Washington Post compared Beachey's flights to "a giant kingfisher" plunging into the water after his prey and described his airplane's awe-inspiring "snake-like movement toward the earth," as well as "a series of serpentine movements, dipping first one wing of his machine and then the other."[78] These reports indicate how the bird-men developed techniques to key the "technological sublime," but at the same time focused audience interest not just on the machines but on the aviator's skill at making the machines come to life. Where big cage lion tamers had rationalized the living representatives of wild nature, the concrete intelligence of the birdmen made modern technology organic.

The spectacular flights of early stunt pilots were resonant cultural performances that cued a diverse audience to channel its fascination with aviation technology toward the skilled labor of the pilots, who soon became media celebrities and masculine ideals. A writer in 1910 noted a pervasive fear that modern life, with its "many comforts and luxuries" and "numerous incitements to ease," had resulted in the loss of "the spirit of daring and the love of adventure." Aviators gave the best proof that such a spirit was still as keen as in "the days of old romance and chivalry": "The flying men of our own day are taking their life in their hands with as buoyant a grace as ever distinguished the explorers or warriors or crusaders in the most epic days of the world." These new heroes, however, could come in an unexpected physical form. The article gave the example of airman Charles K. Hamilton, who was "no matinee idol": he was "small and freckled and red-headed," with an awkward gait and a figure and features that were "no symphony." Though he did not make "a graceful appearance on the surface of the earth," he was perfectly built for flying: he weighed only 110 pounds, had an "instinctive sense of balance," and nerves that were "always on edge."[79] Some writers took the notion that airmen were a new type of man quite literally. By one account, aviators were in the process of becoming birds through "doing as birds do." This included acquiring a "distinct birdlike look," with thin bodies, large, beaklike noses, and "alert, sharp, firmly set" eyes.[80] A Kentucky newspaper announced the scientific discovery that flyers were "developing the instincts of birds." As signs of an "evolution birdward," the article pointed to flyers' unnaturally quick reflexes, their "more than human sense of equilibrium," and a certain "strange, arresting, magnetic flash" in the eye that was the "visible sign of a new sense." In a gathering of famous pilots, one could see the beginning of a "new type of man."[81] Beachey played up his reputation as a man-bird hybrid, sometimes taking his hands off the controls and spreading his arms out "full length like the wings of an eagle" while flying over the crowd.[82]

That the popular press tended to describe the "birdman" as a male type was one example of the considerable resistance faced by women hoping to enter the field of aviation. The Wright brothers refused to train female flyers, claiming that women lacked "coolness and judgment."[83] Claude Grahame-White, a prominent early aviator, stated that "women lack qualities which make for safety in aviation. They are temperamentally unfitted for the sport."[84] Nonetheless, women were strongly attracted to flight, in part because, according to Joseph Corn, it symbolized "the freedom and power" that was lacking in their daily lives: "As pilots, women experienced feelings of strength, mastery, and confidence which, particularly at a time when Victorian norms still rendered all strenuous effort and most public activity by women suspect, seemed delicious indeed."[85] Despite barriers to their entry, female flyers such as Harriet Quimby, Blanche Scott, and Ruth Law were a notable presence in the decades after Kitty Hawk. Quimby, who became the first licensed female pilot in the United States in 1911, wrote that no other sport "affords the same amount of excitement and enjoyment, and exacts in return so little muscular strength," as aviation: "Flying is a fine, dignified sport for women," she continued, "healthful and stimulating to the mind, and there is no reason to be afraid so long as one is careful."[86] Quimby received international press coverage when she became the first woman to fly across the English Channel on April 16, 1912, but her career came to a tragic end less than two months later when she fell from her airplane to her death at an aviation meet in Boston.[87]

One of the thousands of spectators at the Boston event where Quimby lost her life was Ruth Law, the younger sister of human fly Rodman Law, whose career was described in chapter 2.[88] Law provides a useful case study for gauging the opportunities open to talented female flyers and their reception in the popular press. Inspired by Quimby, Law attempted to enroll in the Wright School of Aviation, but Orville Wright refused to teach her, convinced that women had "no mechanical ability." Wright conceded, however, to sell her an airplane on installment.[89] Law learned quickly, and during the summers of 1913 and 1914 she made stunt flights at Newport Beach, Rhode Island, sometimes with electric lights adorning her airplane. In August 1914 she made appearances with her brother Rodman during which they ascended together in Ruth's airplane, and then he leaped out with a parachute. By 1915 she was a featured performer on the same state fair circuit as male flyers such as Lincoln Beachey, performing loops and dives, and in April of that year she even graced the cover of *Billboard* magazine.[90]

Law's fame shot into the stratosphere when, on November 19, 1916, she broke the record for the longest nonstop airplane flight, traveling

FIGURE 19. Ruth Law, who broke the record for the longest nonstop airplane flight in 1916. Courtesy of the Library of Congress.

590 miles from Chicago to Hornell, New York.[91] As had been the case with the stunts performed by her brother Rodman, Law's feat made her front-page news in newspapers across the country, as well as the subject of newsreels such as the Selig-Tribune Semi-Weekly News film titled "New Air Queen."[92] The press coverage of her flight, however, tended to minimize her achievement by emphasizing her small stature, the outdated nature of her machine, and her supposedly feminine concern with her appearance. The *Baltimore Sun* was among the newspapers that accompanied the announcement of her flight from Chicago to New York with headlines such as "Powder for her nose first thought on reaching New York."[93] The *New York Times* described Law as "a hundred and twenty pounds of pluck" who flew a "little old 100 horse power 'pusher' aeroplane." The first thing one noticed about Law, the article stated, were her "blue eyes looking through the goggles," and the author claimed that her first act on landing was to reach for her "blue serge skirt" and ask to borrow a powder puff. She was reportedly greeted in New York by an official who declared, "Little girl, you beat them all!"[94] Law spoke back to coverage like this by carefully but firmly making clear her feminist sentiments. For one thing, she explained the practical utility of a female pilot packing a skirt for a flight across the country: "Women fliers ought to remember that a skirt is a fine thing to have along, and it does not take

up much room. I did not like the idea of coming down in a strange town, among a lot of strange people, without a skirt."[95] Facing newspapermen on the morning after her November 19 flight, she was asked, "You have made the longest flight a woman ever made, haven't you?" "I have made the longest flight an *American* ever made," she replied.[96] She concluded her published account of the flight by stating, "I suppose I ought to say that I am in favor of suffrage—but what has that got to do with it?"[97]

Law, like other early aviators, attained celebrity status and was a hero to young people. The *New York Times* published excerpts from letters that Law had received from the pupils of Grade 8-A Public School in Brooklyn. Virginia Mead wrote that "it makes all girls proud" to think of her nonstop flight: "The boys thought we girls are cowards. But not now; we point to you. Everywhere you go, you hear of Ruth Law and her flight." Esther Silverman described how, when she saw Law's picture on her classroom bulletin board, she had wondered why "a girl's picture" was "where men usually showed their faces. Now, I am glad I am a girl, because girls can do just as wonderful things as men. I am dreaming of a day when I may come to see you fly." Boys were also enthusiastic. Dominic Salerno wrote, "I think you are about the most courageous girl I ever read about. . . . [S]ome girls do not believe in such things, as they do not like machinery, but you are the first I've ever heard that took to it kindly." Fred Lahn confessed that "to tell the truth, we children talk of nothing else" but her achievement.[98]

Riding high on this crest of fame, Law was the featured attraction at the ceremony to light the Statue of Liberty on December 2, 1916. Hundreds of thousands of people lined the shores of New York harbor as President Woodrow Wilson gave a signal by wireless to throw electric lights on the statue. The "most spectacular feature of the ceremonies," according to the *New York Times,* was Law's "unusual flight" around the top of the statue, her wings aglow with electric lights that spelled the word *Liberty.*[99] Law's career up to 1916 indicates how a handful of female pilots found a place in the field of early aviation but could do so only by struggling against industry resistance and condescending press coverage that assumed aviation to be a masculine endeavor. As an indication that Law pushed gender conventions in the popular imagination, we might note reports circulating a few years after her Statue of Liberty flight that she was, in fact, a man disguised as a woman, and perhaps even a German spy.[100]

While female pilots such as Law had to struggle against gendered notions about aviation, those same assumptions worked to reinforce the masculinity of male flyers. One newspaper described Lincoln Beachey as having a commendably "simple, straightforward" manner that was unquestionably masculine: "I am sure he never wore velvet suits or Fauntleroy collars, and that no boy on the block ever threw a brick at him and got away with it." The article even delved into Beachey's personal life, as the author asked him about romance and marriage. At this point the birdman is said to have "turned his very pleasing eyes upon his desk and declined to be interviewed on quite such a personal question."[101] That birdmen such as Beachey had a certain sex appeal might be gauged by the fact that, when Beachey's wife was granted a divorce in 1912, she publicly declared that her husband had been "as assiduous and as successful in his conquest of feminine hearts as he has been in the conquest of the air," and claimed that during his public career, he had been "emulating the sailor, who is noted for his tendency to have a sweetheart in every port."[102]

As had been the case with nineteenth-century aeronauts, part of the public fascination with birdmen had to do with their privileged aerial view of human society. In 1911, the French aviator André Beaumont wrote of how, when seen from the sky, "houses look like dice thrown on a billiard table; the largest cities seem like Liliputian [sic] towns, the bas-relief melts away, roads, rivers and railways appear to wind their way in a child's model landscape toy."[103] By this time, the view of the aeronaut and the spectacle of flying machines had become the content of media forms other than the fairground and newspaper report. James Montgomery's stage play "The Aviator" toured across the country in 1910–11 and was referred to as "the first aeroplane play produced on the American stage." Interest in the play was centered on the third act, when a full-size monoplane was shown onstage. The hero climbed into the cockpit and started the engine, and the plane was seen to rise into the air as the curtain fell.[104] In September 1910, the B.F. Keith vaudeville theater in Boston featured an exhibition of aviator Glenn Curtiss's biplane, and eager audiences went onstage to get a closer look at the flying machine.[105] The birdman Harry Atwood accepted a $50,000 offer from the Orpheum Circuit of vaudeville houses for a 1911 tour, during which he gave twenty-minute talks about his adventures in the air and displayed his machines.[106] The logistics of the stage limited the use of airplanes in drama, and newspapers struggled to convey the spine-chilling moves of the birdmen with intricate diagrams and dotted lines drawn over still photographs. There was thus a niche for moving images of the birdmen, and it is not surprising that Lincoln Beachey collaborated with the traveling film exhibitor Lyman Howe to create what were called the world's first "aerographs."[107]

While flying over Wilkes-Barre, Pennsylvania, Beachey tried a new aerial stunt: operating a motion picture camera. Beachey's film became a major part of Lyman Howe's 1911 publicity campaign. "Do You Want to Ride With Lincoln Beachey?" asked an Iowa newspaper headline, which concluded, "Here's Your Opportunity." The film opened with shots of the camera being attached to Beachey's airplane followed by images of the airplane taking off, both of which had a visual appeal not unlike what could be offered on the stage. But what followed was truly novel: views from the camera operated by Beachey himself. Beachey's ride over Wilkes-Barre was deemed an "important and historic" flight, since it gave millions of people an opportunity to "feel all the thrills and pleasure of participating in a real aeroplane ride, yet without any of the attendant dangers to life and limb."[108] Cinema audiences could now experience firsthand the social world as seen from above: a Wilkes-Barre newspaper wrote of how the film took the viewer "over the city, across a river, over the tops of trees and high above undulating fields and farms. . . . Now it dips low and boats and tiny men and women are perceptible as the plane trembles above a wide river. Up she goes once more until the composite treetops of a forest look like a bunch of ferns on a dining room table." As the result of images such as these, the Beachey aerographs were said to be "one of the most remarkable in all the history of moving pictures or any other sort of theatrical entertainment."[109] For film historian Charles Musser, Howe's films meant that "the new, dynamic technology of airplanes" was synthesized with motion pictures.[110]

Lyman Howe was not alone in attempting such a synthesis at this time. In November 1911, a Pathé film shown in Macon, Georgia, depicted the fatal crash of birdman Eugene Ely, who had died at the Georgia State Fair a few weeks earlier.[111] A month later, the Champion Film Company sent a cameraman aloft with aviator Robert Fowler, claiming that "to see what mother earth looks like from the birdman's point of view is bound to be an opportunity few people would want to miss."[112] That same year, a crowded house in Olympia, Washington, watched moving pictures taken by "Mr. Harbeck of the Western State Illustrating company" that showed a birdman named Wiseman in flight, as well as views from the air.[113] In February 1912, aviator Frank Coffyn made a flight above the skyscrapers of New York City and then flew under the bridges along the East River, all performed with one knee on the controls while he used his hands to operate a moving-picture machine lashed to the front of his craft.[114] Several narrative films were also made at this time to capitalize on public interest in the birdmen. In September 1911 the Imp Company released *Through the Air,* which featured a "thrilling race" between an airship and an automobile. The film would "prove a winner," assured the trade press, due to "interest taken in all things pertaining to air navigation."[115] That same year, employees of the Thanhouser Company were given training by professional aeronauts to assist in the making of *The Higher the Fewer,* which featured an "aeroplane elopement."[116]

Lincoln Beachey explored his own synthesis of aviation and stage entertainment, giving talks on flying and showing "views of his many perilous flights" in vaudeville houses during a short retirement from stunt flying in 1913.[117] Beachey announced that his retirement was due to remorse over the deaths of aviators who had tried to emulate him, as well as a growing unease with the appeal of "circus flying." "I was never egotistical enough to think that the crowds came to witness my skill in putting a biplane through all the trick-dog stunts. There was only one thing that drew them to my exhibitions," he stated. "They paid to see me die."[118] That's what they got on March 14, 1915. After coming out of retirement, Beachey appeared at the opening ceremonies of the Panama-Pacific International Exposition. Beachey did loops over the Jewel City exposition, wrote his initials in the sky with smoke, and then fifty thousand spectators watched as the wings on his new monoplane fell apart and he plunged into the ocean.[119]

In the wake of Beachey's death there was a fresh round of newspaper coverage bemoaning how stunt flying was holding back the science of aviation, making clear that the birdmen inhabited an aeronautic structure of feeling still characterized by a tension between science and thrilling entertainment. There was, however, another quiet but persistent theme emerging in the aeronautic structure of feeling of this era, a third center of gravity into whose orbit the image of the aeronaut could be pulled. Note that when he retired, Beachey announced that the only circumstance under which he would fly again was if the United States were forced to enter a war.[120] Indeed, there was a steady crescendo of military rhetoric surrounding the airplane throughout the first decades of the century. There had long been a military tinge to even the scientific side of aviation, most clearly articulated in the notion of the "conquest of the air." For example, in 1912 the *Philadelphia Inquirer* wrote that those who died in the cause of aerial science were "soldiers fighting for a cause. Their antagonist is Nature—conservative, hide-bound, merciless old Nature, which has stood through all the ages as a barrier between men and progress, surrendering ditch by ditch and fortress after fortress only as man has fought his own way to a finality, against the accepted traditions of his fathers."[121] That same year Beachey performed mock battles and dropped bombs on imitation fortresses in order to demonstrate the capabilities of a wartime aerial fleet.[122] In 1914 Beachey returned to the skies over the nation's capital, where he had first gained national acclaim in his airship seven years earlier. Crowds of people watched his flight from downtown streets, the tops of buildings, and the Capitol steps, but Beachey was also watched by President Wilson, the cabinet, and members of Congress. When he landed, he was met by Army and Navy officers, and he announced to the press that he was ready to offer his services to the government in order to "bring America first in things aeronautic."[123] "If I made a good impression upon the men who can make it possible for our army and navy to have a properly equipped aviation corps," he told the press, "I am well pleased with my effort."[124] Beachey represented an American variation on an international trend, an emergent aeronautic structure of feeling in which aviation was increasingly bound up with military nationalism.[125] As Peter Fritzsche put it, aviation became a "measure of nations at the beginning of the twentieth century."[126] When those nations clashed in all-out modern warfare, the public image of the flyer and the future of the aviation industry were remade, with repercussions for notions of male heroism and the Hollywood cinema.

KNIGHTS OF THE AIR

The Great War of 1914–18 represented the dawn of a new era of modern warfare in which the individual combatant seemed to disappear into the anonymous mass, and soldiers became ancillaries to deadly new technologies of war in a grisly parallel to the homogenization of factory labor. In the face of this harrowing new form of combat, military aviators came to play an important role in the public experience of the war. Conversely, the furnace of the war forged a new public image for the aeronaut. There were many reasons why the fighter pilot dominated the popular imagination during the war. First, the same longstanding myth of flight that had loaned a heroic aura to the birdmen still surrounded the wartime aviator.[127] Second, the view from the air that had been exploited for publicity by Barnum and captured on film by Lyman Howe became a crucial component of military strategy. Balloons had been used for military observation since the American Civil War, but during World War I aviation became crucial to mapping the vast conflict. Aviation thus became "the eyes of high command," illuminating a terrain that was "constantly being turned upside down by high explosives."[128]

Much of the cultural meaning of the flying ace, however, was defined in opposition to the horrors of the ground war, and it is significant that the two most iconic representations of the soldiers who took part in World War I were the Unknown Soldier and the fighter pilot.[129] The view from the air was in stark contrast to the inability to see of the soldiers in the trenches, where "the enemy was more or less invisible save for the flash" of his guns.[130] A key aspect of the public perception of the wartime aviator was his individual agency, despite the fact that military planes typically flew in group formation.[131] "In the patch of sky visible from the trenches," writes Peter Fritzsche, "pilots seemed to retain the mobility and regain the perspective the infantry had lost."[132] For John H. Morrow, airmen gave the impression of being able to "rise above the anonymity of mass society and modern warfare to wage a clean and individual struggle," and so the image of the fighter pilot allowed for the preservation of ideals of sportsmanship and individual combat in the context of a kind of modern warfare that had rendered such ideals "obsolete and ludicrous."[133]

For those stuck in the trenches, the experience of being a soldier was a "military version of the factory worker, doing his coglike part in the military machine."[134] The war was thus a cruel disappointment for men hoping to prove their masculinity through displays of dynamic heroism. But unlike trench warfare, air battle was thought to retain a measure of manly skill and daring, and some even claimed that the air war had replaced lion hunting as the gentleman's "finest sport."[135] Even more than being compared to the sportsman, however, the flyer was compared to the medieval knight, what T. J. Jackson Lears describes as the most prominent "avatar of martial virtue" in the late Victorian imagination.[136] The flying ace thus recast the reckless birdman of the past decade as a noble fighter on a metal steed. As a modern embodiment of chivalry, military flying articulated a longing for the preindustrial age.[137] At the same time, however, aviators were thought to harmonize man and modern machinery. Soldiers on the ground experienced what Leo Braudy calls "the pulverizing power of industrial war" and found the battlefield to be less "a proving ground for manly courage" than a site for "the technological ferocity of military machinery."[138] But the pilots again seemed to be an exception, with air combat the ideal coexistence of machine and man. Gone were the birdman's flimsy "contrivances of wood and wire and canvas." During the war, airplanes became more streamlined and formidable, with forward-firing, synchronized machine guns that shot through the propeller, thus fusing gun and airplane into a single mechanism. The fact that a physically small man might operate this deadly machine only heightened the sense that airplanes were an extension of the pilot's body.[139] The prewar birdmen had seemed to be curiosities of modern evolution, but flying aces were heroic "New Men" who offered the hope that man and the modern war machine could be melded successfully.[140]

All of this meant that wartime flyers became powerfully resonant international celebrities. To paraphrase Richard Dyer, aces managed prevailing ideological contradictions of their society, magically synthesizing opposites such as modern and premodern, and the labor of the mechanic and the aura of the aristocratic duelist.[141] This was in no small part the result of government information policy on both sides of the war. In Germany, the kaiser lavished attention on flyers, and aces such as Oswald Boelcke and Manfred von Richthofen signed autographs, answered fan letters, and went on promotional tours.[142] In France, the press singled out aces for attention and praise, and wealthy French women offered their furs for flight apparel.[143] In the United States, the glamorization of pilots gave the impression that the war could be understood in terms of individual heroism and helped to elicit public support for the war. The combat pilot became, according to historian Linda Robertson, "standard fare for publicity campaigns, newsreel footage, and newspaper copy."[144] The American "ace of aces" was Captain Eddie Rickenbacker, and the press provided details of his career as an automobile racer, his inclination to feats of daring, the death of his father when he was fourteen and his subsequent need to support his mother and sisters, his rise from serving as General Pershing's chauffeur to being the nation's top ace, and even his rumored engagement to movie star Priscilla Dean.[145] Press coverage of aces such as Rickenbacker occurred during the same years that there was, according to Richard deCordova, a shift in the promotion of Hollywood film players to a form of stardom that depended on the circulation of knowledge about the players' private lives.[146] We have seen that the private lives of prewar birdmen were sometimes discussed in the press, but wartime aces were backed by the national government rather than a fairground promoter, and as a result they had a cultural reach that could truly rival that of the Hollywood film star.

The war also solidified the cultural association of aviation with masculinity by making clear that the opportunities available to female flyers in the military were extremely limited. Recall that Ruth Law was a record-setting aviation hero and much sought-after attraction at government events and fairground entertainments in 1916. When America entered the war, Law publicly declared her ambition to fly on the Western Front. In an article titled "If the President Said to Me, 'Go Get the Kaiser,'" she described how she would go about bombing the German lines and assured readers that she could "drive an airplane into battle and perform the destructive work of bombing without any feeling of remorse." While conceding that "the average woman" was not prepared for the "intense nervous strain of flying and fighting," Law stressed that there was a place for women in supply and messenger flying, as well as the teaching of aeronautics. She drew the line at "dueling in the air," however, stating that it required a degree of "skill and mental repose" that made "the average woman's place in its midst impossible."[147] Despite her lowered ambitions, demonstrable skill, and public stature, Law was refused a military commission by the secretary of war, who warned that to employ her would "let down the bars to women in the United States to seek commissions in the army."[148] Like Hollywood stars and human flies, Law took part in the Liberty Loan drives, but she spoke of the double standard by which the government accepted her services in that capacity while denying her the chance to be "of greater service" in the war effort because of her gender.[149] Law's experience thus demonstrates how the war helped to ratify a sense that crucial aspects of aviation were the domain of men, and it underlines the rhetorical importance of "dueling in the air" in that process.

In sum, the Great War dramatically altered the shape of the aeronautic structure of feeling as well as the public profile of the flyer, who came to be seen as a predominantly male bastion of Old World character as well as the herald of a technological future that avoided the worst aspects of the war. Fritzsche writes that although before the war, flyers had been "regarded as Bohemians and acrobats on the edges of bourgeois respectability, the war gave them the proportions of supermen."[150] The war, as has often been noted, provoked a widespread crisis of European culture, particularly in relation to masculinity and technology. Michael Adas writes that the war resulted in a pervasive sense of "humanity betrayed and consumed by the technology that Europeans had long considered the surest proof of their civilization's superiority." Notably, the image of the male fighter pilot was spared much of that crushing sense of disillusionment, and the American flyer doubly so, due to America's late entry into the war. Thus, not only did American popular culture emerge on the world stage as a beacon of hope—the "technocracy of the future"—but that future looked particularly bright for returning American flyers.[151] The merging of man and machine in the flying ace perhaps signaled the possibility of a more fulfilling and manly form of industrial work. In April 1919 the *Los Angeles Times* wrote that four million Americans had lost their jobs with the signing of the armistice. The vast majority of veterans would return to jobs with a "drab future of scratching out a living stretched drearily before them," but for the fifteen thousand trained aviators, the end of the war brought with it "the promise of a wonderful new career" in a business, "the colossal future of which" had only begun to be "unfolded before our startled eyes."[152] It was not clear, however, exactly what form that colossal future would take. After the war, a new round of jurisdictional disputes broke out over the fate of American aviation, the lines of that dispute drawn less between scientists and thrill makers than between freelance operators and corporate commercial interests. One thing became certain: in an important sense, the future of aviation would be bound up with the cinema, another American industry whose colossal future was unfolding after the war.

WING WALKER

After the war the U.S. government sold thousands of surplus airplanes at a fraction of their original cost. Across the country, former military flyers bought those cheap planes and took up the life of the barnstorming "gypsy flyer," traveling across the country giving aerial demonstrations and short passenger trips for a few dollars a head.[153] As more and more barnstormers took to the air, flyers had to differentiate themselves by adding increasingly thrilling stunts to their repertoire. One barnstormer wrote that by 1922 supply far exceeded demand, and "the firmament teemed with semi-professional flyers." As a result, "specialty stunts of the most fantastic kind became our only hope."[154] The turn to stunt flying was encouraged by the fact that government surplus planes were equipped with a host of wires and struts that could serve as handholds in a new kind of aeronautic acrobatics.[155] One postwar American stunt flyer achieved a remarkable degree of celebrity as a pioneer in that new kind of performance and in the process left a lasting impression on Hollywood filmmaking: Ormer Locklear.

Locklear, who joined the U.S. Air Service in October 1917, first performed an airplane stunt while taking a wireless test in which cadets were sent a ten-word message from the ground while flying over the airdrome. To avoid the interference caused by the wings of the plane, Locklear climbed down to the landing gear, thus becoming the first candidate to correctly receive all ten words of the radio message. By November 1918 Locklear had developed what would become his trademark performance: the midair transfer between two planes with a rope ladder. In May 1919 he performed the transfer at the Pan-American Aeronautical Convention in Atlantic City.[156] Locklear signed a contract with Lincoln Beachey's former promoter William Pickens, and soon he became a national fairground attraction. One newspaper claimed that he was "the most sensational and biggest drawing card the business has ever produced. From John Ringling down he has received congratulations as the greatest attraction in showdom."[157] During his performances over state fairgrounds and aviation fields, pilot Milton Elliott would take the controls while Locklear climbed all over the plane, balancing on his head on the wings, hanging by his knees from the wings and landing gear, and posing on the upper wing before climbing a ladder to a second plane flying above. Another surefire thriller was to have the two planes fly so closely together that their wings overlapped, and Locklear would then walk across the wings from one plane to the other.[158] A critic at *Billboard* magazine wrote that Locklear's act "defied every law of physics" and was not only "the greatest sensational 'stunt' in the history of the world" but "the limit of human adventure."[159]

At the 1919 Arizona State Fair, twenty thousand people "watched aghast" at Locklear's act, which a local paper described as follows:

"Locklear is in the air," rang out the cry of the announcer, and all eyes were turned to a machine approaching the grandstand. A little block of white marked the shirt of the acrobat, and this was seen to ascend. As the plane drew nearer Locklear was seen standing unsupported on the upper wing, his arms outstretched as though in mockery of death itself. Then rounded into view the second plane, approached from the east and flying above the plane bearing Locklear. . . . For a moment he hesitated as though about to spring, then sank to a sitting position. Locklear had failed, and the machines had to be maneuvered into place again for the second trial. "I am not afraid," Locklear signaled to the waiting throngs. He did so by hanging head down from the fuselage of his machine and flying low opposite the grandstand. If this were not enough to convince, he climbed about from tail to propeller,

FIGURE 20. Ormer Locklear in a midair walk atop the wings of a plane. Courtesy of Corbis.

standing on his head a few feet back of the whirling blades, contact with which would have meant instant death. . . . On comes the two machines again, their courses slightly angling. . . . For an instant one could have heard a pin drop. And then came a mighty sigh of relief as the tiny white speck was seen hanging by his hands from the last rung of the rope ladder dangling from the upper plane. And then as though in supreme mockery to the crowds, Locklear hung from his knees again, his body swaying against the wind, his head and arms dangling into space. This climax to Locklear's program of thrills brought the crowd to a realization for the first time that the stunt artist was really out of danger, and as one accord the crowd rose, while it let forth a mighty roar of approval.[160]

As this account illustrates, Locklear would often make several attempts before successfully completing his transfer from plane to plane. This was actually a bit of stage business choreographed by his manager, Pickens, who claimed that "the more difficult a stunt appears, the more pleased and awed the yokels will be. . . . [M]ake it too easy and they'll think they can do it themselves."[161]

We should notice a continuity from Washington Donaldson's "drop act" to Lincoln Beachey's "death drop" to Locklear's staged failure to complete his plane-to-plane transfer: all involve the fabrication of a breakdown of the performance frame in order to heighten suspense and convey the performer's virtuosic skill.[162] Recall how Goffman defined the stunt in relation to primary frameworks of the "guided doing" and the natural event. Stunts "astound" when they are pitched at exactly the boundary between those two frameworks, when an act cannot easily be defined as social doing or a natural event. The stunt performer hoping to astound an audience would thus need to craft an act so that the loss of control was, or seemed to be, a real possibility; a natural event such as a gust of wind or stalled engine must be seen as capable of overwhelming the performer's careful planning. That a stunt was most affective when pitched between Goffman's primary frameworks helps to explain the oft-noted tendency of thrill makers to perpetually escalate the apparent danger of their acts. A commentator in Lincoln Beachey's day wrote of how "circus aviators" had to "take ever greater chances" in order to produce thrills: "No sooner has he mastered one convolution than its staleness drives him to another, since nothing evaporates more quickly than public excitement over the same spectacle. Such mad progression can have no other end but death."[163] That "mad progression" resulted from the audience's ever-changing estimation of the degree of control maintained by the performer. Once an act seemed too "professional," too reliably under guided control, it might fail to astound. We might say that stunts have a short shelf life, and techniques such as the "drop act" and Locklear's near misses were useful vaccinations against an act's too rapid loss of affective power.

Though Locklear's transfers and wing walking share a family resemblance to the "drop act" and the "death drop," I cannot help but see them as an index of postwar American optimism. More than the loops and dives of the birdmen, Locklear's displays were a playful domestication of aviation technology. Here was the male performer unperturbed by the shock and speed of modernity but instead able to walk gracefully astride roaring airplanes. Moreover, this thrilling stunt was accomplished by a man whose military service cleansed him of the residual aura of the reckless birdman. If that weren't enough, Locklear had movie-star looks: "He is tall, but the army training has given him a splendid physique that is neither fat nor thin. He has clear blue eyes and a snappy little moustache and is quite the man to whom the girls would write mash notes."[164] It is not surprising, then, that in July 1919 Carl Laemmle offered Locklear a contract to make a film with Universal Pictures.

In the previous chapter we saw how Hollywood became a national center for wild animal trainers, and how the spatial convergence of film studios, zoos, wild animal farms, and circus winter quarters had important implications for both the American cinema and the thrill makers. During the same decades that film companies and circuses were moving west, Southern California also became the heart of American aviation, with consequences for both the film industry and for freelance flyers. Several factors drew aviators to California: mild weather and sunshine allowed for year-round flying; open fields provided temperamental airplanes with spaces for emergency landings; and amateur flyers were within easy reach of scenic deserts, mountains, and beaches.[165] By 1929 the *Los Angles Times* could boast that Southern California had become the country's center of aerial activity: the region contained one-third of the nation's commercial airplanes, it had more airplane factories than any European nation except France, and Los Angeles was doing more than twelve times as much air business as New York City.[166]

The growth of aviation in Southern California coincided with the growth of the area's film production. One way to gauge that parallel development is through Laemmle's Universal, which first opened a facility in Hollywood in 1912. Laemmle's West Coast operation was greatly expanded with the opening of Universal City on March 15, 1915, just one day after Lincoln Beachey plunged to his death at the San Francisco exposition. Laemmle presided over a two-day opening celebration, unlocking the gate to Universal City with a golden key and leading a procession that featured "gaily-clad Universal girls" and a "cavalcade of mounted cowboys and Indians in their war paint."[167] Festivities continued into the next day, when the featured attraction was a display of aerial stuntwork by flyer Frank Stites. A crowd of more than one thousand people, including Laemmle, watched the filming of a "spectacular war play," in which Stites was to bomb a "dummy" plane moving on a wire cable stretched between two hills. Stites ascended over the field and dropped his bombs, but the explosions caused the flyer to lose control of his machine, which crashed to the ground in front of the horrified spectators. The ceremonies were quickly brought to a close, and Universal City's celebratory flags were brought to half-mast for the dead flyer.[168] Stites's ill-fated performance shows a convergence of Hollywood and "circus flying" dating from the days of the prewar birdmen. After the war, Hollywood director Cecil B. DeMille was one of many private citizens to buy government surplus airplanes. DeMille used his planes not for his own barnstorming flights, however, but to pioneer commercial passenger aviation. The director built two airfields, and in 1919 he joined with stunt flyer Al Wilson to form the Mercury Aviation Company, which flew the first scheduled passenger and mail service between Los Angeles, Bakersfield, San Francisco, and San Diego.[169] Across the street from DeMille Field was Chaplin Aerodrome, owned by Charles Chaplin's brother Syd, who had bought government planes and opened a passenger service from Los Angeles to Catalina. Movie star Edna Purviance broke a bottle of California grape juice on one of Chaplin's planes to mark the opening of the service in July 1919.[170] That same year, Ormer Locklear came to Hollywood to make his first film for Universal. Locklear's film, which was the first to be made at DeMille Field, used planes rented from DeMille and thus relied upon an emerging infrastructure that linked Hollywood and aviation.[171] I argued in the previous chapter that the presence of the roaring lion on the MGM logo was an important index of the convergence of wild animal shows and Hollywood cinema. It is equally significant that for most of the 1920s and 1930s the Universal Pictures logo was an airplane circling the globe.

Locklear's film at Universal, *The Great Air Robbery* (1919), featured an assortment of stunts, including transfers from plane to plane and from car to plane. Locklear played Larry Cassidy, a pilot in the U.S. Air Mail service who encounters a secret band of aerial pirates called the Death's Head Squadron.[172] Perhaps the most notable aspect of the film was the way in which Universal promoted it. Ads in the *Motion Picture News* claimed that the film would seat the audience "in the clouds": "Imagine it! The audience is within 50 feet of Daredevil Locklear all the time the action goes on over One Mile High in the Air." Ad copy was accompanied by images of the cinema audience seeming to float in the air near the airplanes. Much has been written about how the cinematic close-up allowed for a more intimate view of actors than was provided by the stage, helping to spur both the star system and new kinds of film narrative. Here we find the proximity of the camera as a means to outdo an adjacent form of popular mass entertainment— not the stage but the aviation meet. Locklear's film was marketed as a remediation of fairground entertainment that had solved the problems of the aviation spectator, since customers could see all the details of Locklear's stunts without getting a sore neck.

Universal did not pick up the option to make a second Locklear film, and after a stint back on the fairground circuit Locklear signed on with the Fox Film Corporation to make *The Skywayman*. Locklear played Captain Norman Locke, a former World War I ace turned stunt flyer who has lost his memory due to shell shock. He agrees to help a beautiful Russian aristocrat to intercept stolen jewels in a plot whose primary function seems to have been the motivation of plane-to-plane and plane-to-train transfer sequences and a plane crash into a church steeple. While shooting the film's last stunt at DeMille Field, Locklear and his pilot Elliott went into a planned spin but came out of it too late, perhaps confused by the arc lights. Their plane crashed, killing them both, while four cameras filmed the action and hundreds of people, including many film stars, looked on.[173] Locklear, who was romantically involved with the screen actress Viola Dana, had become a fixture on the Hollywood social scene, and the film community was shocked by his death. Film stars and studio executives took part in the procession that led the bodies of Locklear and Elliott to the train station as planes from the Mercury and Chaplin aviation companies followed the procession dropping flowers, and when the procession passed by the film studios, all work ceased in tribute to the dead airmen.[174] Flowers were sent to Locklear's family in Texas by film stars Roscoe "Fatty" Arbuckle, Charlie Chaplin, and Tom Mix.[175] Despite the death of its star, Fox rushed the film to theaters and publicized that a percentage of profits would go to the families of the dead flyers.

Though neither of Locklear's' films was particularly successful at the box office, his short career was significant in several respects. Locklear had many imitators, and wing walking became a common fairground attraction in the early and mid-1920s.[176] As the decade went on, however, legislation to curb dangerous stunts brought the era of the gypsy flyer to an end. Locklear had been the first pilot in Los Angeles to receive a warrant for reckless flying, but in 1923 the L.A. city commissioners enacted an ordinance designed to eliminate all stunt flying.[177] The city cracked down on stunt flying even further after July 1926, when a pilot killed two young girls when he landed at Venice Beach.[178] In 1927, the Los Angeles chamber of commerce launched a "determined program of defense" against "reckless or inexperienced aviators" in order to safeguard beachgoers from such events.[179] Men who had seen a postwar career opportunity in barnstorming were increasingly directed toward the emerging commercial industry.

The same flood of cheap government surplus planes that had jump-started the careers of countless freelance flyers had also caused a postwar slump in the American airplane business, since manufacturers could not compete with the government's low prices. One business journal complained about how, by 1922, the country "swarmed with gypsy aviators without regulation," and half the capital had disappeared from the aviation industry, causing commercial interests to put pressure on the government to intervene. The government responded by forming the President's Special Aviation Board and passing regulatory legislation administered by the Bureau of Aeronautics, a unit of the Department of Commerce.[180] An important component of the government's new plan for commercial aviation was the airmail service. Locklear had claimed that his stunts had practical value for the airmail and spoke of a future in which bags of mail would be passed from one plane to another during long flights using his transfer stunt.[181] Needless to say, that future did not come to pass, and such stunts would find no place in the government's mail service.

Neither was there a place for stunt flying in the emerging commercial passenger industry. Of the aviation-minded denizens of Hollywood, it was DeMille and Chaplin, not Locklear, who were the true heralds of the future. As part of the aviation industry's campaign to revitalize itself in the 1920s, there was a concerted effort to convince the public that modern aircraft were safe and easy to operate. Companies had an economic interest in preventing accounts of reckless flyers from being published in order to reassure the public about the fledgling passenger industry.[182] Aerial stunts thus became an obstruction, not to the cause of science but to industry. In 1927 the *Los Angeles Times* complained that, although America had invented the airplane, it had been content to use it "as a toy for stunt flying." The vast economic possibilities of commercial flying, the newspaper hoped, would soon mean that "gypsy flying" was no longer the sole employment of the nation's planes.[183] That same year the pioneer aeronaut Augustus Post published an article that divided aviation history into four periods: the period of "inventors and builders," the era of "demonstrators" and "aerial jockeys," the period of the wartime ace, and a dawning era of commercial aviation, in which "the machine and the organization that made its operation possible on a large scale" would take first place in the public mind.[184]

The passing of the era of "aerial jockeys" and the rise of commercial aviation also had consequences for female pilots such as Ruth Law. The decade after World War I saw short-term gains and long-term losses for female aviators. After being denied the opportunity to fly in combat, Law returned to the fairground circuit, and in 1919 advertisements for her act declared that she was "The Girl Who Out-Aces the So-Called Aces."[185] Like other barnstorming pilots, Law had escalated the apparent danger of her act, and her newly formed Ruth Law's Flying Circus put on displays of plane-to-plane transfers and ladder stunts. These kinds of dangerous stunts led to several tragic accidents, such as the October 1921 death of a young woman auditioning for the flying circus. By some accounts, this event precipitated Law's retirement from flying, since her husband and longtime manager, Charles Oliver, became so worried for her safety that he had a nervous breakdown. Law stated, "I felt that since he had allowed me ten years of the sport, I owed it to him to give it up."[186]

Law's exit from the public stage was part of what was perceived to be a larger decline in the number of female aviators at this time. "The aviatrix seems to be a thing of the past," a female journalist wrote in 1923, concluding that women had deserted "the flying game" not because it had become too dangerous but because all of its "thrills" were being prohibited by the "sky traffic cops" who had "put up the stop sign on looping the loop, tail spins, nose dives, barrel and other stunts." The author of the article interviewed aviator Betty Scott, who complained that men had spoiled aviation by "tabooing county and state fair stunt flying" and making "traffic rules": "They have made it impossible for women to make money at flying. There were many women who flew purely for the large sums of money they could make. What with no thrill and no money—what's the use."[187] Five years later another female writer observed that "the days of spectacular flying and barnstorming appear to have ended for women pilots." As evidence that Americans had lost interest in the daredevil feats of female pilots, the author pointed to a recent German aviatrix who had abandoned her program of exhibition flights because of a lack of response.[188]

Although the number of female licensed pilots in the late 1920s and 1930s was small, consisting, by one account, of "less than one-thirtieth of all aviators," they briefly played a significant role in commercial aviation. Joseph Corn describes how, when both the "intrepid birdman" stereotype and the wartime ace came to be seen as obstacles to the development of aviation, the industry saw the female pilot as a public relations antidote. This strategy, of course, relied upon what Corn calls the "lady-flier stereotype," which assumed women to be frail, timid, unathletic, and unmechanical. If women can fly an airplane, the stereotype suggested, then it must be safe and easy. Paradoxically, the stereotype begat certain opportunities: "Because they appeared to the public as less capable than they really were, women fliers became marvelous advertisements for the ease of piloting and the safety of flying." This state of affairs opened up some opportunities in aviation sales departments, but women found it "almost impossible" to land jobs as pilots with the commercial airlines. "In no other branch of aviation, save of course for the military," Corn writes, "did discrimination and the limits of woman's place in the air show so clearly," and he notes that until the 1970s, "only one woman found a place flying with a scheduled airline, and even then discrimination cut short her tenure."[189] By the end of the 1930s the primary position open to women in commercial flying was that of the stewardess, a role in which they worked to allay public anxieties about flight as domestic workers.[190] For female flyers, then, the rise of commercial aviation meant a narrowing of opportunities to an even greater degree than for male barnstormers.

Early aviation meets had been a site of rhetorical struggle over the enunciation of aviation, with the pilot emerging in popular discourse as the site of spectacular labor in aerial displays. During the period of commercial aviation, that struggle was reignited when the public was encouraged to shift its attention from the pilot to the organizations and institutions in whose name they flew. I have compared the jurisdictional dispute over aviation to the changing perception of the site of cinematic labor, which shifted from the medium and the inventor to the production company, and then to the film player. Post's periods of aviation history suggest another comparison, this one with the history of radio technology. Radio and aviation were, after all, referred to as "twin miracles of the air."[191] As historians of broadcasting have shown, there was a flourishing culture of radio amateurs in America who were tinkering with their radio sets during the same decades that birdmen such as Lincoln Beachey were tinkering with their airships. As with aviation, the war brought about an increased role for the American military in the regulation of radio technology, which shifted from individual to institutional control.[192] Just as radio technology came to be "embedded in interlocking corporate grids" over the course of the 1920s, so aviation technology shifted from the domain of freelance operators to regimes of military management and government regulation.[193]

In short, the rise of corporate commercial aviation represented a dramatic shift in the aeronautic structure of feeling and the public image of the pilot. We can gauge that shift by a 1925 article that stated that Americans had to rid their minds of the idea that flying was "a difficult art requiring remarkable acrobatic gifts": "No different qualities are required to steer an airplane than to steer a motorcar. It takes a normal person no longer to learn to fly than to learn to ride a bicycle—and indeed the two accomplishments are somewhat alike."[194] Such sentiments were a dramatic change of tack from the coverage of either the heroic birdmen of a decade earlier, or the chivalrous wartime ace. Where Eddie Rickenbacker had been celebrated for his triumphant transformation from chauffeur to ace, flyers in the 1920s were urged to make the reverse trip, from stunters to stable, reliable chauffeurs. One former "gypsy" pilot wrote that freelance flying was "too haphazard, too adventurous, too risky" to survive: "Commercial aviation was destined from the first to become a scientific industry, highly organized, controlled to the minutest detail. Like the covered wagons, our old Canucks and Jennies belong to a by-gone period." Writing in 1929, he concluded that "in the flying business we are all executives now. There are no more gypsies."[195] For a handful of flyers there was one last domain in which stunt flying could find a place in modern American industry: Hollywood filmmaking.[196] Carl Laemmle stated that Ormer Locklear's films marked the beginning of a "regular and extensive use of airplanes by movie companies."[197] As Locklear's transfer stunts became part of the vocabulary of action films in the 1920s, a niche was created in Hollywood production for stunt flyers.

Hollywood aviators maintained a level of their "gypsy" independence in the system of film production, but this was not without its drawbacks. At the end of the 1920s the convergence of airfields, ex-military stunt flyers, and studios, as well as the public desire to reengage with the memory of the Great War, resulted in what was called an "avalanche of air films" that relied upon, and in one case took as their narrative subject, former military flyers who became stuntmen.[198] As the cycle continued, the image of the chivalrous flyer had to accommodate shifts in the social role of the aviator and a pervasive sense of postwar disillusionment, and stunt sequences would less depict flyers soaring nobly over the trenches or gracefully walking on wings than enact the violent failure of modern technology.

SPENT BULLETS

The American film industry emerged from World War I reputable and prosperous at home and newly dominant abroad due to the wartime collapse of European production.[199] Hollywood had released films to help in the war effort during the 1910s, but a cycle of films featuring a different depiction of the war came to the screen toward the end of the 1920s. These films took part in what cultural historian Modris Eksteins calls "the ritualistic commemoration of the war," which took the form of countless memorials and cemeteries erected in 1927.[200] That year also saw the transatlantic flight of Charles Lindbergh, accomplished not due to the "easterly current" that John Wise had theorized but because of the airman's plucky endurance on a long solo flight in his state-of-the-art metal aircraft, *The Spirit of St. Louis*. Lindbergh is clearly a pivotal figure in the history of aviation and modern celebrity, and he has been discussed as such elsewhere.[201] For now, suffice it to say that Lindbergh's truly unprecedented fame in the late 1920s dwarfed the renown of royalty, politicians, and film stars and showed the public's continued fascination with the heroic deeds of headstrong aviators, despite the PR efforts of the aviation industry. Also note that Lindbergh's first official act in Paris was to place flowers at the Tomb of the Unknown Soldier. In doing so the heroic flyer took part in a wave of war commemoration that included stage productions and films such as *The Big Parade* (1925) and *What Price Glory?* (1926).[202]

Aviation played an important part in narratives commemorating the war, most notably in the case of the classic Hollywood epic *Wings* (1927). Leslie Midkiff DeBauche notes that many of the most influential war narratives of this time were written by men who had served in Europe, with the result being "an accommodation of the conventions of war films to date."[203] The talents of several veteran flyers informed the production of *Wings*. The first of these was writer John Monk Saunders, who had been a Rhodes Scholar at Oxford before becoming a lieutenant in the Army Air Services during the war. After the armistice he spent time in Paris before working as a writer back in the states. When he pitched *Wings* to film producer Jesse L. Lasky, Saunders stressed the suitability of the air war for the cinema: "With the increased penetration of the motion picture camera into every realm of life, here was yet a virgin province—the kingdom of the sky. Here was the battlefield of the war flyers; here aerial combats took place and planes fell in flames and balloons were shot down. Here was action that could not be put upon the stage or imprisoned within the covers of a book. Here was a subject whose proper medium of presentation was—the screen."[204] Lasky was receptive, though concerned about the cost, but Saunders soon secured the support of the U.S. War Department to provide aid in making the picture.

Once *Wings* was on track for production, a second former World War I flyer, director William A. Wellman, joined the project. Wellman had flown in the Lafayette Flying Corps during the war, and afterward he was stationed in San Diego, where he began to spend time with an old acquaintance, the movie star Douglas Fairbanks. Wellman used to fly his Spad airplane to Beverly Hills and land in Fairbanks's backyard.[205] After a brief stint as a film actor, Wellman decided that he would rather direct, and through his connection to B. P. Schulberg at Paramount, he was hired to direct Saunders's film, largely on the basis of his experience in the military. Indeed, Wellman talked about how his military service had taught him to be "a sky-gazer" in order to take advantage of protective cloud cover during aerial combat. Directing Hollywood epics required a similar pragmatic attention to the sky because of the importance of shooting during periods of sunlight.[206]

We have seen how, from Lyman Howe and Lincoln Beachey to Ormer Locklear, the spectacle of aviation has offered compelling cinematic subject matter as well as challenges for those filmmakers who sought to remediate it. Wellman talked about the problems of "practical cinematics" posed by the air film. Airplanes in flight were, he said, "almost worthless" for screen "thrill value," since there was usually no object with which to contrast the movement of the plane: "Motion on the screen is a relative thing. A horse runs on ground, or leaps over fences or streams. We know he is going rapidly because of his relation to the immobile ground." Wellman described the three shooting options open to filmmakers: the camera could be placed on the ground pointing into the air, in a captive balloon or tower, or in another airplane. Each had its drawbacks. Cameras on the ground produced shots in which the airplanes were small and gave little sense of their speed; cameras in a balloon had limited visual range; and shooting from an adjacent airplane tended to minimize the sense of movement or velocity.[207] Wellman and his crew approached these problems through a combination of shots taken using all of these options interwoven in the editing stage, as well as careful attention to the mise-en-scène.

Following on the early experiments of aerial motion picture photography by stunt pilots such as Beachey and Frank Coffyn, *Wings* made use of the skills of professional aerial cinematographers such as Harry Perry, E. Burton Steene, and Elmer G. Dyer. Cameras were also attached to airplanes so that they pointed backward at the faces of actors Charles Rogers and Richard Arlen while in the air. In terms of the mise-en-scène, much thought was given to designs that would address the problem of the relativity of motion on the screen. In the first big aerial scene the flying field was lined with telephone poles adorned with prosthetic leaves and branches to resemble a row of French poplar trees in order to create a vertical contrast to the airplanes as they took off.[208] Wellman also waited for heavy banks of clouds to serve as a visual point of reference for aerial shots, and when shooting from plane to plane the filmmakers tried to show multiple planes crossing at different directions and altitudes in order to set off their respective movement.[209] When it came to editing, the filmmakers studied every aerial sequence in order to obtain "a maximum of contrasting movement."[210] In short, the accommodation of the stylistic conventions of the war film brought about by these veteran flyers involved the application of an aesthetic of collision and contrast akin to Soviet montage in order to convey the dynamism of aerial battle.

The filmmakers' stylistic choices in depicting aviation met with much success. The film was a box office smash, critics raved about it, and the Hollywood community signaled their approval by giving the film the first award for "outstanding motion picture production," a forerunner to the Academy Award for best picture.[211] The *Christian Science Monitor* echoed Saunders's initial pitch to Lasky, declaring that the air picture represented "the new medium of the screen in full cry, smashing its way through thick and thin like the great planes."[212] Audiences were said to be "overwhelmed by the magnificence" of the film, in part because it dramatized the airplane: "There is no object perhaps that could be linked in a more perfect way mechanically with the present."[213] During the first aerial combat scene, an enlarged screen and special soundtrack were put to use, and one critic declared that the viewer was "lifted virtually from one's seat in the theater by the massive and overwhelming double effort." It was "a sensation without parallel in the world of make-believe," and one that demolished "all rules of beauty and order in the creating of entertainment, but the results [were] nothing short of momentous."[214] The film was thus experienced as exhibiting a new degree of vivid realism, even though, as we have seen, its effects were carefully constructed at every level of film production. The result was a film that set a new standard for the synthesis of cinema and aviation and began a cycle of air pictures that lasted for a decade.

Writer John Monk Saunders was responsible for many of the films in that cycle, including *Legion of the Condemned* (1928) and *The Dawn Patrol* (1930), for which he won the Academy Award for best screenplay.[215] Saunders's films after *Wings* were increasingly cynical about the nature of wartime heroism. In this they resemble other war narratives of this era whose dark tone DeBauche interprets as an index of prevalent skepticism about the government's wartime propaganda: "The more high-toned metaphorical description of this war as the Great Crusade of Civilization against Autocracy was at odds with the soldier's experience."[216] Consider a film based on Saunders's only novel, *Single Lady* (1931). Critics dismissed the novel as a second-rate rip-off of Ernest Hemingway's *The Sun Also Rises*. In fact, Fox had even intended to make *Single Lady* under the title *The Sun Also Rises*.[217] Like Hemingway's influential novel, Saunders's novel concerned American veterans in Paris engaged in endless rounds of drinking, contained pivotal scenes at a bullfight, and featured wounded male protagonists.[218]

The film version, which was released in 1931 by First National Pictures under the title *The Last Flight,* focused on the experience of aviators. In the press kit for the film, Saunders wrote that there was "something that high-speed flying in war times does to a man that changes the course of his whole life": "His nerves are shattered. His life, far above the earth where ordinary mortals live, has been a succession of thrills. Imagine then, the effect on him, when such activity is suddenly brought to a halt, and he is thrust back into the ordinary routine of life. He cannot possibly acclimate himself to it. He cannot fit himself into the old groove, complacently sit at a desk or bench. He is still vibrant with surging nervous energy. Something in him clamors for wild action, for speed, for anything but humdrum." The film begins with a depiction of the nerve-shattering thrills of war: artillery fire flashes from opposite sides of the screen, and rapid cuts alternate between the legs of horses, advancing troops, tanks, and explosions, all from contrasting and disorienting angles and directions. We then see images of the sky and an air battle. Notably, the pace of the editing slows down during the air battle, providing a visual analog to the notion that pilots escaped some of the worst chaos of the ground war.

As was the case in many of the air pictures of the 1930s, aerial combat is represented here through the intercalation of shots made using a range of techniques. We see actors in the studio operating fabricated airplane cockpits and firing their machine guns at rear screens depicting approaching enemy planes, an illustration of the importance of rear projection technology for films of the early and mid-1930s. Rear projection shots were combined with images of actual airplanes flown by stunt pilots, seen against a background of clouds or with a number of planes moving in different directions to indicate movement. Another common technique was to show a stunt flyer enacting a tailspin toward the ground followed by a shot of a plane smashing into the ground. We see just such a juxtaposition in the opening sequence of *The Last Flight,* followed by a dissolve to a hospital chart showing a patient in critical condition. When the war ends, two injured American flyers are released from the hospital, one with a nervous tic and the other with badly burned hands. An Army major at the hospital explains to a fellow officer that the two had fallen six thousand meters to the ground. "Like dropping a fine Swiss watch on the pavement," he says, it "shattered both of them, their nervous systems are deranged, disorganized, brittle." The two flyers were "spent bullets," the major continued. "They're like projectiles, shaped for war and hurled at the enemy, they have described a beautiful high-arching trajectory, and now they've fallen back to earth, spent, cooled off, useless." In fact, the working title of *The Last Flight* had been *Spent Bullets*.[219] The rest of the film charts the flyers' painful and largely unsuccessful attempts to fit back into an "ordinary routine of life," their shattered nerves and broken bodies drawing into question the airman's perfect melding of man and machine so celebrated in wartime rhetoric.

Saunders's depiction of the aviator's shattered nerves intensified with *The Eagle and the Hawk* (1933), the story of ace fighter pilot Jerry Young (Fredric March), who becomes increasingly uneasy with his role as an official hero. "I wanted to fly, I thought there'd be some sport in it," he tells his commanding officer. "I didn't expect to be a chauffeur for a graveyard, driving men to their death day after day." Despite his reservations, awards for bravery are heaped upon Young, and he is presented as a "shining example for youngsters." At one point Jerry is asked to say a few words to some new recruits. "The first time you shoot down a man, don't let it get you," he stutters, his voice cracking. "Try to remember the cause you are fighting for is right and just," he says, his voice breaking on the last word. "They're your enemies, you're fighting for humanity, and for the . . . preservation of civilization." His lack of belief in the military platitudes he intones is made clear as he turns his back on the awestruck recruits and dejectedly hangs his head over a glass of whiskey. The dissonance between the official rhetoric of the speech and March's performance succinctly undercuts the notion of the flying ace as noble knight of the air. Indeed, Jerry's rise to fame as an ace is accompanied by a deterioration in his morale and even his sanity as he grapples with the cognitive dissonance between the brutality of his work and society's regard for it. This reaches a climax when the squadron raises a toast to celebrate that Jerry has shot down a well-known German ace. Jerry has discovered that the German flyer was just "a blonde kid," and he declares to the assembled squadron that it was by killing children that he earned all of his metals, which were thus "chunks of torn flesh and broken bones and blood, and for what?" His comrades laugh off this outburst as the result of too much liquor, but Jerry retires to his quarters and shoots himself. Only his gunner, Henry Crocker (Cary Grant), hears the shot, and he quickly conceals Jerry's death. Later that night he secretly carries Jerry's body into a plane, and, once in the air, he shoots holes in the wings to give the impression of a dogfight. He then carefully points the machine gun at Young's head and fires, giving a final salute. The camera tilts down to an image of a skeleton carrying a scythe painted on the side of plane, which then dissolves to a plaque reading, "Captain J. H. Young, who gallantly gave his life in aerial combat to save the world for democracy."

Critics were surprised by this stark, cynical ending. A *New York Times* critic wrote that it was refreshing to see "a story done as well as this, for in so many instances, the producers would have insisted upon a happy ending." The "grim surprise" of Young's suicide was "something one might read in a book, but which the picture makers dodge invariably for the sake of sending patrons away in a cheerful state of mind."[220] A writer for the *Los Angeles Times* exclaimed, "What treason this would be not so many years ago—the star disgraced in the eyes of the theater patrons at the end of the picture!" Covering up the hero's suicide through faked air combat was "a modern sardonic note not usually found in the cinema."[221] Saunders's films were thus part of a postwar accommodation of the conventions of the war film, an accommodation achieved in large part through an interrogation of the tensions between the public image and the subjective experience of wartime aviators. The growing sense of postwar disillusionment and hopelessness was vividly expressed by the preoccupation with suicide found in Saunders's films. That narrative trope took on chilling new meaning when, after a separation from his wife, the Hollywood star Fay Wray, Saunders hung himself in 1940. Saunders and William Wellman were key figures in Hollywood's air picture cycle, but the new aeronautic aesthetic found in these films also relied upon former military pilots who worked as stuntmen. Given what we have already learned about the air cycle and the veterans who helped to create it, it is fitting that these stunt flyers referred to themselves as the "Suicide Gang."[222]

THE SUICIDE GANG

The production of *Wings* crucially relied upon not only Wellman and Saunders but also the talents of stuntman Dick Grace. When he was sixteen, Grace had a fateful meeting with a barnstorming pilot at a county fair. He recalled his excitement at receiving "a word and a grin from the godlike flyer" and spent the summer working for him and learning to operate an airplane.[223] At the outbreak of the war, Grace enlisted and flew in Europe. Grace's father expected him to take up the family law practice after the war and urged him to go to college. Like one of John Monk Saunders's "spent bullets," however, Grace felt changed by the war in ways that he had difficulty describing, and he was unable to acclimate himself to college or office life. Grace wrote that he had "graduated into a life beyond what school could teach," and, despite his father's opposition, he returned to aviation as a commercial flyer.[224] Inspired by the success of Ormer Locklear, Grace began changing planes in midair, and eventually he moved to Hollywood in search of work.[225] Grace was part of a "mass migration" of former service men, expatriates, and "movie-struck youngsters" who flooded Hollywood during the 1920s. Most of these refugees became extras, a group that lacked organized labor representation and had little hope of advancement.[226] During the silent era there was a certain degree of mobility in the film industry. An extra might become a featured actor, and the ability to do stunts was one way to change one's status. The introduction of sound created a more pronounced division between actor and extra. In the cinematic version of the larger trend toward labor segmentation, producers turned to the legitimate stage rather than to the supply of hopeful extras and stuntmen in order to look for talent.[227] In Dick Grace's grim assessment, by the end of the 1920s stunt performers had "not one chance of ever reaching solid success. . . . [I]t's a torture, a misery, for a thinking man to kid himself from one year to another—to find in the end that the door is absolutely closed."[228]

Though typically seen by Hollywood producers as a special type of extra, stuntmen differed from their cohorts in the way they were paid. The studios separated stuntmen from the other extras and paid them a flat fee in order to avoid having to pay any additional benefits should a performer be injured. In some instances organized stunt performers established their pay scale. Hollywood flyers formed the organizations the Thirteen Black Cats in 1925 and the Associated Motion Picture Pilots in 1931, both of which established standard rates for stunts and sought to control who could fly for the studios. Being paid by the stunt meant that stuntmen earned more money than other extras, but it also placed the responsibility for the safe completion of the stunt solely with the performer. This arrangement lent an aura of romance

FIGURE 21. Dick Grace, Hollywood stunt flyer and
the author of *The Lost Squadron*.

and independence to stuntwork, but it also put performers at the mercy
of filmmakers, who could insist that a dangerous stunt be repeated with
no pay until they were satisfied.[229]

Consider the 1925 court case of John Montijo, a movie stunt flyer
who sued Samuel Goldwyn Inc. for damages to a plane that was
wrecked during filming. The Goldwyn company hired Montijo to operate an airplane as it passed over a speeding automobile. The stunt was
successfully completed after four attempts, but when the shots were
screened in the projection room, neither the director nor Goldwyn was
satisfied: the cameras, which had been placed in a second car, were too
far from the action. The filmmakers thus decided to retake the scene
with the cameras in the stunt car. This time, however, the wheel of Montijo's airplane hit the car, resulting in serious damage. The court ruled
that since Montijo had been acting as an "independent contractor," he
couldn't claim any damages.[230] This case illustrates both how stuntmen often had to repeat dangerous stunts to please producers and their

lack of legal protection should that repetition result in serious injury or damage to property.[231] Dick Grace gave his own account of this labor dynamic, recalling how a director asked him to perform a twenty-five-foot fall again and again. Grace noticed that the director and his staff were laughing each time he hit the ground. Fellow stuntman Bob Rose intervened, warning Grace that the director was having him repeat the stunt for his own sadistic pleasure. For Grace, this was a rude awakening to the kind of treatment a stuntman might expect: "So this was the attitude of those for whom we made thrills! As far as they were concerned, we were just a nonentity. A bunch of flesh thrown together to furnish necessary footage for pictures—and when we were worn out, or killed, they could always find more fools to take our places."[232] Freelance stunt performers could thus earn more money and attain a higher degree of professional agency than other extras, but they also faced serious risks and lacked institutional protection.

Grace found an outlet for his frustration in his 1929 memoir *The Squadron of Death,* which described his experience as a stuntman, and the novel *The Lost Squadron,* which was made into a film by RKO in 1932. RKO's film was part of the avalanche of air pictures released in the wake of *Wings,* but the focus on Hollywood stunt flyers gave it a key point of differentiation. Note that one of the promotional catch lines in the *Lost Squadron* press kit announced, "Not an air film—but a film behind the scenes when an air film is made."[233] *The Lost Squadron* could thus be marketed as both a thrilling air picture and a look "behind the Hollywood scenes."[234] As in Saunders's *The Last Flight,* the film's narrative follows World War I fighter pilots as they try to adjust to postwar life. During a montage sequence of returning troops, a politician assures a crowd that the soldiers will find things exactly as they left them. Despite this rhetoric, the three returning aviators find their lives drastically changed for the worse: Woody (Robert Armstrong) finds that he has lost his fortune; Gibby (Richard Dix) has lost the love of his sweetheart, the actress Follette Marsh (Mary Astor); and Red (Joel McCrea) has lost his job. Another montage makes clear that we are to connect the plight of these airmen to larger social events: with the patriotic song "Over There" playing on the soundtrack, we are shown a series of newspaper headlines that begins with "Nation Salutes Service Men" but then dissolves to "Service Men Ask Help," then "Congress Disputes Bonus," and finally "Service Men in Bread Line." These headlines are a stark reminder that the film was made at the height of the Great Depression, what Thomas Doherty calls the "central American trauma of the twentieth century," when the fundamental beliefs, animating myths, and cultural values of the nation were "seriously up for grabs." The headline about bonuses refers to a cash bonus for military service promised to World War I veterans, due to be paid in 1945. In June 1932, seventeen thousand vets went to Washington, D.C., to demand an early payment from Congress on their promised bonus.[235] The men of the "Bonus Army" traveled east to the nation's capital, where they were met with mounted troops and tear gas. In *The Lost Squadron*, disenchanted veterans head in the opposite direction in search of an escape from postwar malaise: vowing to stick together, two of the flyers and their mechanic (Hugh Herbert) ride the rails west to California in order to join Woody, who has become a Hollywood stuntman. "It's easy money," Woody tells them, "fifty bucks a flight." Soon all of the men are working for the sadistic director Arthur Von Furst (Erich Von Stroheim) on a new film that stars Gibby's old flame, Follette, who has since married Von Furst in order to further her career.

On one level, then, the film depicts Hollywood as the final frontier for American "gypsy" pilots and as the last preserve of authentic male adventure and camaraderie in the world of postwar corporate industry. That the film makes explicit connections to current debates about veterans' bonuses is indicative of Hollywood "social problem" films of this era and arguably provides a more politically engaged narrative than the novel. Grace's novel, however, was critical of film production in a way that the film tries to blunt. First, the film tones down the novel's critique of film stars. In the film no explicit contrast is made between the stuntman and the male actor, although in one scene Von Furst tells his male star, "For once in your life try to give me a little expression, don't stand here like a stuffed cow." The book more explicitly contrasts different types of male screen performance when the narrator, a stunt flyer named Red, complains about the "vaseline-haired, weak-minded" actor Harold Natwood and the fact that stuntmen never get screen credit: "They all believe out there that if you mentioned a flyer other than the God-almighty star it would detract from the prestige of the he-man idol. They're supposed to do all their flying, all their stunts, all their crashes. A laugh? Well, the sap public eats it up."[236] The female film star Follette comes across as much more selfish and vindictive in the novel than in the RKO film, and at one point in Grace's book Red dismisses all female Hollywood stars as "just a flock of ermine and mink and sable and paint."[237]

RKO's *Lost Squadron* also makes significant changes to the novel's depiction of the sadistic film director. First, dialog added to the film script makes it clear that the director Von Furst is an isolated case, avoiding any suggestion of more systematic mistreatment of labor in the film community. Woody tells his fellow flyers that "no on-the-level producer" would give Von Furst a job, and that "the *real* producers won't have anything to do with him." Equally notable is the change of the director's name from De Forst to Von Furst, a change that both downplays any possible reference to Cecil B. DeMille and also signals that the director is to be read as German.[238] The tensions that arise between above- and below-the-line film workers register less in terms of labor dynamics than in lingering war resentment, which is amplified by shots that frame Von Furst, played in the film by Von Stroheim, against German airplane insignia, and the director's tendency to bark orders in German at his extras in the trenches. In the novel, the disputes between stunt flyers and the director are explicitly tied to industrial labor. At one point the stunt squadron leader Gibson tells De Forst that the stuntmen aren't his slaves. "Everyone who has to work and take orders is a slave," De Forst replies. "You've got to do as I say if you're working for me. Age of industrialism."[239] In another episode found in the novel but not in the film, the narrator Red runs into engine trouble while performing a dive for the cameras and is forced to plunge into the ocean. De Forst has no interest in whether Red has survived the crash but is enthusiastic about the thrilling stunt that has been captured on film. When the director flatly refuses to give Red a bonus, the other pilots expose the film negative that contains his stunt.[240] This episode illustrates the novel's intent to compare stunt pilots to alienated workers more than to soldiers, and to reveal the stunt performer's vulnerability in the of Hollywood production system, where their health and safety was their own responsibility, and the valuable images made of their dangerous feats were out of their control.

In both the novel and the film Red discovers that the vengeful director has sabotaged a plane in order to kill a stunt pilot, and so the flyer secretly locks him in the airplane hangar with the intention of administering his own form of justice. The novel takes this opportunity to implicate the Hollywood elite in larger systems of corruption. When Gibson tries to convince Red to let the police take care of the director, Red replies, "You'll turn De Forst over to the police. Sure. And then what'll happen? He'll go to jail for a couple of days and be out on bond. . . . Epic Pictures and De Forst chip in and hand a line of golden persuasion here and there and that's all there is to it. They'll either forget to prosecute or will lay down on the job. . . . Gibson, there's no justice in courts. You can't convict a millionaire."[241] Moving into such thematic territory certainly would have thrown up red flags at the Hollywood Production Code Administration, and in the film Gibson tells Von Furst, "I'm not going to kill you, I'm going to let the state take care of you and hang you by the neck until you're dead." Nonetheless, the darker suggestion of a deeper, more systematic corruption are given haunting stylistic expression in the film, which essentially transforms from an air picture into a film noir avant la lettre during the final sequence in the hangar, in which the director is shot and killed in a struggle. These scenes are lit by a circling searchlight and permeated by an ominous howling wind on the soundtrack. Gibson decides to conceal the murder by dropping the director's body from a plane in what will look like an accident, but instead he crashes the plane as a noble act of suicide.

The film adaptation of Grace's novel, then, is careful both to index current social anxieties and to avoid any critique of Hollywood's own labor practices. The shift in register from the novel's labor tensions to the film's wartime xenophobia resembles a dynamic that Danae Clark finds in the film musical 42nd Street (1933), which shifted attention away from actor-producer conflicts in its backstage narrative in order to offer a New Deal parable.[242] RKO's The Lost Squadron downplays any systematic critique of Hollywood production practices, but it cannot fully erase the point of view of below-the-line workers in its subtle critique of film stars, the analogy that it makes between the work of film extras and trench warfare, and the depiction of a murderous conflict between stuntmen and director. The fact that these themes could fly beneath the Hollywood radar is testament to both the momentum of the air picture cycle and the cultural profile of the heroic aeronaut, both of which created a space for a critique of Hollywood mythology.

One of the ironies of The Lost Squadron was that Von Furst's obsessive and sadistic interest in filming dangerous airplane crashes was a fairly accurate portrayal of a Hollywood production practice that Dick Grace had made his specialty. Grace described how William Wellman had called him soon after being assigned to direct Wings and asked him to be in charge of the film's aerial stunts. So important were Grace's controlled airplane crashes—or "crack-ups"—that Wellman offered to let the stuntman set the shooting schedule.[243] Grace's autobiography reveals the nervous strain that accompanied these dangerous stunts, amplified by days spent waiting to shoot with the right kind of cloud cover.[244] Grace crashed a Spad in No Man's Land for the film, as well as a German Fokker into the side of a building, the latter resulting in the flyer's broken neck. Grace's crack-up can be added to the lineage of aerial stunts I have described: from Donaldson's drop act, to Beachey's death drop, to Locklear's transfers and wing walking. There is something sobering about the fact that the spectacle of the noble aeronaut "lifted above the brute creation" culminates in a performance of the ultimate failure to master technology, a violent return to earth that gives form to repressed undercurrents of technological fantasy. In the logic of remediation, this is simply another example of how film producers were able to top the popular entertainment competition. As lion tamers working in the cinema had trained their animals to attack in order to give audiences a closer look at a circus "fighting act," so stunt flyers provided the shocking conclusion that the drop act and the death drop were only meant to suggest, repackaging the fairground spectacle of the fiery wreck for mass consumption.

Grace could sustain a long career through his ability to perform controlled crack-ups in part because many other aerial stunts were increasingly achieved through other, safer and more reliable, means. I have already mentioned rear projection, which allowed for close-ups of actors in the cockpit without actually sending them into the air. Developments in miniatures also helped to reduce the need for certain kinds of stunt flying. Film companies had used models and miniatures since at least the 1910s. In 1916, the *New York Tribune* wrote that miniatures, models, and mannequins were used by filmmakers to "blow up a dam in a washtub, to sink a liner in a dishpan, to have a vicious head-on collision on the studio table," and they were inserted into films so cleverly that few people noticed. They had become, the paper claimed, the stuntman's "only fear."[245] In 1932, Universal Studios constructed its first soundstage dedicated to special effects. Though it would come to be best known for optical and makeup effects used in horror movies such as *Dracula* (1931), *Frankenstein* (1931), and *The Mummy* (1933), the effects stage also filmed miniature airplanes for air pictures. By 1934 stuntman Bob Rose could write that "miniatures and other mechanics" were replacing the "vanishing brotherhood" of stuntmen, just as new technologies had replaced skilled laborers in so many other industries.[246]

Just as studios were playing it safe by using miniatures instead of stunt flyers, the message of air films such as John Ford's *Air Mail* (1932) and Howard Hawks's *Ceiling Zero* (1936) was that a generation of aviators had to learn to play it safe and fit into a new era of commercial aviation.[247] The narrative of *Air Mail* takes pains to illustrate how pilots at Federal Transcontinental Airways received regular physical exams, and when the eyesight of pilot Mike Miller (Ralph Bellamy) is found to be weakening, an avuncular medical examiner sends a report to Washington and explains the likelihood that his license could be revoked. The dramatic tension of the film arises with the appearance of Duke Talbot (Pat O'Brien), a freelance flyer of the old school, who threatens to disrupt this safe, bureaucratic system. Talbot makes his entrance at the airport with a display of loops, upside-down flying, and a spectacular flight through an open airplane hangar, all performed by the Hollywood stunt flyer Paul Mantz. When Mike crashes and is stranded in the mountains, Duke's stunts are put to practical use when he does a loop in order to make a precarious landing and rescue Mike. The film thus offers a fantasy world where aerial acrobatics of the Locklear school could be integrated into commercial aviation. Duke, however, can only find an ambiguous and uncertain place in this new commercial world. After rescuing Mike, who parachutes to safety, Duke crashes, and though he is alive in the ambulance in the final scene, the narrative implies that there is no sustainable place for his kind of heroics at Federal Airways.[248]

A similar message is conveyed by Hawks's *Ceiling Zero*.[249] The film's opening titles make clear that, in the era of commercial aviation, the audience was encouraged to see the site of aeronautic enunciation not in the "animator" (the pilot) but in the "principal" of aviation science and industry: "Today's lighted airways, expert radio and weather service, de-icers and other safety devices enable the large passenger liners to give safe and dependable transportation which speed mail and passengers along the skyways and are a fitting memorial to the vision and courage of those pioneers who gave their lives in the early stages of this industry to complete the mastery of the air." The narrative elaborates on that message by both celebrating those aviation "pioneers" and making clear that they now stood in the way of progress. Jake Lee (Pat O'Brien) is in charge of Federal Air Lines' Newark, New Jersey, airport. He receives a visit from Al Stone (Barton MacLane) of the New York office, who warns of the arrival of Jake's old war buddy Dizzy Davis (James Cagney), whom Al sees as a menace and a liability. "We're running a business. If the wartime pilots don't fit today's standards, they're through," Al says. "Compare Dizzy to the type of youngster we're getting today. They're college men, educated for the job, technically expert. They'll never pull anything wild, and they can fly, too." Later we see Jake fire just such a "college boy" who, despite his credentials, lacks "nerve." But more than nerve was needed to navigate the government-military-industrial networks of modern aviation, and as the film's narrative develops, one has the growing feeling that Jake and Dizzy are in over their heads. Like Duke in *Air Mail,* Dizzy arrives doing stunts, but upon landing he is met by a Department of Commerce inspector, who explains that his next stunt will cost him a suspension. In one scene a slick manufacturer tries to bribe the flyers at Federal Air Lines with cigars and bourbon in order to convince them to purchase his company's mediocre products. Later, the narrative grinds to a halt as Dizzy gets a lecture from a young "college boy" on the workings of new deicer technology. Dizzy is revealed to be the lynchpin to all of the film's narrative conflicts. The New York office insists that Jake get rid of him; his presence has thrown a monkey wrench in two romantic pairings at the airline, and Jake is prepared to succumb to institutional corruption by buying mediocre planes in order to get Dizzy's license renewed. It dawns on the audience at about the same time that it dawns on Dizzy that the only solution is for him to join the "Suicide Gang." Dutifully, Dizzy goes up in bad weather and heroically performs a final test of the new deicer before crashing to his death.[250]

Robert Wohl writes that *Ceiling Zero* dramatized "the moment in the mid-1930s when the fledgling industry of aviation was beginning to emerge from the era of barnstormers, racers, and record-breaking aviators who risked their lives for celebrity, thrills and the sheer fun of flying."[251] In terms of stunt performance, we might also say that the film took part in a cycle that marked the moment when a long tradition of aeronautic thrills that had developed alongside the cinema, and whose practitioners had at times achieved a celebrity that rivaled that of film stars, became just one standardized component of Hollywood's second unit production. Only twenty years after the entertainment trade press had proclaimed the "sure and rapid" growth of the fairground air meet as an avenue of popular amusement, Hollywood film had become the almost exclusive purveyor of "aviation as entertainment."[252]

Social theorist Edgar Morin wrote that the nineteenth century bequeathed two new machines to the world that were born on almost the same date: the cinema and the airplane. The airplane had realized the "insane dream" of "soaring into the aerial beyond where only the dead, the angels, [and] the gods sojourned," but it became "the *practical* means of traveling, of commerce, and of war." By contrast, the "laboratory eye" of the cinema had originally reflected only "down to earth reality," but soon soared into the realm of dreams, "toward the infinity of the stars—of 'stars' . . . escaping the mundane world, of which it was to be, to all appearances, the savior and the mirror."[253] The enigma of the cinema, Morin concluded, was to be found in "the uncertainty of a current that zigzags between play and research, spectacle and laboratory," in the "Gordian knot of science and dream, illusion and reality."[254] Morin's comments are useful as I conclude this chapter, as they link the cinema to aviation, but they also locate the "dream" of the cinema in its star players. The case studies in this chapter reveal another braid in that Gordian knot, since the stunt pilot rode exactly the zigzag current between spectacle and laboratory, between science and dream. At one point in *Ceiling Zero,* Jake, exasperated at Dizzy's disregard for procedure, shouts, "We're running an operations office, not a circus!" Jake's words echo back through half a century of the aeronautic structure of feeling, where aviation technology and display were always pitched somewhere between scientific management and circus thrills. As was the case with so many of the nineteenth-century thrill makers, fairground flyers were, in the end, unable to compete with the type of large institutional forces that came to control aviation. It is fitting, however, that the last holdout for stunt flyers was in Hollywood, since the film studios were perhaps the American industry most successful at combining science and thrills, dreams and factory production, "down to earth reality" and "the infinity of the stars." Jake's line in *Ceiling Zero,* then, trenchantly describes the tensions inherent not only to a 1930s airdrome, but also to the Hollywood cinema, which was, of course, both an operations office and a circus.

Conclusion

Less than a year after RKO released *The Lost Squadron*, the same studio produced the film *Lucky Devils*, which begins in a bank lobby with a high, domed ceiling circled with windows. Suddenly, the barrel of a machine gun breaks through one of the high windows and a man shouts, "Don't any of you mugs move, this is a stickup!" Frightened bank customers scream as more robbers enter, their guns blazing. A bank teller sets off an alarm with his foot, and a gunfight ensues when the police arrive. During the battle a security guard falls over a railing, and a female switchboard operator is thrown down a flight of stairs. When the gunman at the ceiling window is shot, he breaks through the glass and falls, grasping at a chandelier on his way to the floor. The piercing sound of the burglar alarm abruptly stops, and a shift in perspective reveals that the bank lobby is, in fact, a movie set: we see lighting equipment, microphones, the crew operating a crane shot, and a director who yells, "All right, cut it!" A young woman who has been watching the action with her parents exclaims, "Oh, wasn't it *thrilling!*" "It simply took my breath away," agrees her mother. "I never knew they took such chances," adds her father. The excited young woman approaches the switchboard operator from the scene, who is leaning over to adjust her stockings after having fallen down the stairs. "You were just simply wonderful. I didn't know girls could do such dangerous things," says the spectator. "Will you sign my autograph book?" The performer removes a wig to reveal a somewhat world-worn and unmistakably male face.

"Sure, honey," he says, embracing her, "with love and kisses!" "You're a man!" she manages to say. "Sure," he replies, "a stuntman." Visibly astounded and impressed, the young woman runs back to tell her parents, "They aren't actors and actresses, they're *stuntmen!*"

Lucky Devils is, along with *The Lost Squadron,* one of the rare moments in pre-1940s Hollywood film in which the labor of stunt performers takes center stage. The male performer in drag who fell down the stairs was Bob Rose, a longtime Hollywood stuntman who, like Dick Grace, had written the film's script based on his years of experience doubling for Hollywood stars. Rose began his career in entertainment as a Wild West and carnival performer, performing trick riding, high dives, parachute jumps, and airplane stunts.[1] Rose's career trajectory encapsulates the ways in which the film industry repackaged the spectacle of the thrill makers, even as the modern media did much to marginalize them. *Lucky Devils* broaches the subject of stuntwork through a series of revelations, and so forms a convenient bookend with the 1916 *New York Tribune* report on the "unsung" and "anonymous heroes" of the Stunt Men's Club described in the introduction to this book. The opening scenes of *Lucky Devils* reveals some of the mechanics of film production by showing the backstage, off-camera spaces of a film shoot and instances of film labor. Indeed, exhibitors were urged to plug the film as a revelation of some of "the most closely guarded motion picture secrets" and as a chance for audiences to peek "behind the curtain."[2] But the revelations of this reflexive Hollywood film only went so far and still left much obscured. In the previous chapters I have sought to pull the camera back even farther, in time as well as in space, in order to situate stunt performance in a larger history of celebrity, popular entertainment, work, and male spectacle. In this concluding chapter I will summarize some of the key themes that have emerged over the course of that investigation, as well as point to some areas of future research.

HOLLYWOOD HETEROGLOSSIA

The opening sequence of *Lucky Devils* claims to correct a misapprehension about celebrity and performance in Hollywood cinema: the "real" stars, the scene suggests, are not the actors but the stuntmen who take "such chances." The film's use of the dramatic framework of "revelation" stands as further evidence of how stuntwork was typically kept a secret due to the industrial logic of the star system. Danae

Clark reminds us that the star system refers to an institutional hierarchy established to regulate, segregate, and control not only star players but character actors and extras as well. Clark argues that film scholars have tended to adopt the studio's own "institutional point of view" by studying star actors and neglecting other screen workers, thereby reinscribing the "inequities that exist behind the image."[3] Histories of early film performance and stardom have similarly privileged dramatic acting such that other pertinent genealogies of performance have been neglected. I hope that my historical analysis of stunt performance will help to broaden the sample of what counts as screen labor in media studies.

If the scholarship on screen performance has placed too much emphasis on star players, the subject of media spectacle has often been conflated with film technologies. Note, for example, how Tom Gunning's influential notion of the "cinema of attractions" has been more frequently associated with technologies of spectacle and special effects than with modes of screen performance.[4] Returning to Francesco Casetti's suggestive notion of cinema's "excited gaze" described in the introduction to this book, we might say that the performances of the thrill makers were just as constitutive of that gaze as were techniques of narrative and montage, or modern technologies of entertainment and scientific observation. Cinema has, as Casetti asserts, sometimes been a merry-go-round, a telescope, an experimental painting, and a self-reflexive novel; but it has also been a suspension bridge, a skyscraper, a circus big top, and a fairground. That is, cinema has also been a stage upon which thrilling stunts were performed.[5] The case studies in this book suggest that scholars need to pay as much attention to cinematic "body techniques" and "performer-oriented" histories of media spectacle as they have to the cinema's "industrial technologies." That said, the thrill makers reveal that the boundary between those categories has always been permeable: the use of prosthetic dummies, miniatures and models, and rear projection were all intricately intercalated with embodied performances. In an era of CGI motion capture, more work is needed on the interpenetration of embodied performance and media technology.

One of the goals of this book has been to encourage readers to "see double," that is, to appreciate the history and labor of the unnamed stunt double and thereby add to our understanding of the cultural meaning found in film performance. V. N. Volosinov's notion of "multiaccentuality" has helped me to theorize the multiple appeals of the thrill makers in the decades before the cinema, as well as the nature of their role within it. We have seen that the acts of the thrill makers were dense cultural signs that sustained multiple accents and interpretations in an address to a wide audience, allowing lion tamers to be seen as both biblical allegories and purveyors of plebian entertainments; human flies to enact both the skilled labor of dangerous construction work and fantasies of adventure in the corridors of white-collar business districts; birdmen to be both heroic mechanics and aristocrats of the air. The unstable but volatile mixtures concocted by the thrill makers coalesced in the cinema as one component of the hybrid figure of the film star/stunt performer.[6]

Volosinov was part of a group of early twentieth-century Russian scholars known as the Bakhtin Circle, and another way to theorize stuntwork in Hollywood is through the Bakhtin Circle's work on heteroglossia. M.M. Bakhtin used that term to describe the novel's ability to combine "a diversity of social speech types" and a multiplicity of social voices. "At any given moment of its historical existence," Bakhtin wrote, "language is heteroglot from top to bottom: it represents the co-existence of socio-ideological contradictions between the present and the past, between different socio-ideological groups in the present, between tendencies, schools, circles and so forth, all given a bodily form."[7] The collaborative nature of cinema authorship means that films are always inherently multivocal, but Hollywood's heteroglossia was literally given "bodily form" in the suturing of the thrill maker's acts to the face and voice of the star.[8] We have seen the potential for tensions and contradictions between those coexistent performances: recall the different meanings given to human interaction with wild animals in the Tarzan narratives and in stunt double Bert Nelson's vaudeville act; or Safety Last's fusion of Harold Lloyd, Bill Strothers, and Harvey Parry; or Dick Grace's crack-ups as an index of aerial spectacle that ran parallel to the cinema. There is more to be learned from careful historical research that unpacks the tensions and synergies between co-occurring screen performances in specific media texts and contexts. Bakhtin noted that some voices in the heteroglossic mix are understood to be more "authoritative" than others. In these terms, the star system was an institutionalized process by which some performing bodies were granted authority over others through the conventions of film language and the discursive work of publicity.[9]

The erasure of the stunt performer in the system of film marketing compounded the marginalization of the thrill makers in other spheres of popular entertainment: fame seekers were prevented from jumping off bridges; city ordinances removed human flies from the sides of buildings; lion tamers were pursued by progressive reformers; and barn-storming pilots were grounded by industry-friendly legislation. Stuart Hall described how dominant cultural forces struggle to "disorganize and reorganize popular culture; to enclose and confine its definitions and forms within a more inclusive range of dominant forms."[10] The thrill makers were "enclosed and confined" within second-unit film production, and there were subsumed beneath the star actor. That process of active marginalization, however, was never complete, and audiences could always shift their attention to the faceless and uncredited stunt performer and "see double." In so doing, they could catch a glimpse of a previous cultural style of male spectacle and skilled labor. Such "embodied" forms of Hollywood's heteroglossia offer a new point of entry to discussions of cinephilia that stress the semiotic richness of the cinematic image. Just as cinephiles might revel in such peripheral details as the leaves blowing in the trees or the ruffles of a dress, so the movements of marginalized screen bodies are plentiful sites of latent meaning.[11] Stunt sequences might thus provide the raw materials for another history of cinephilia yet to be written.

MASSIVE PERSONALIZATION

Though eventually "enclosed and confined" within the cinema screen, the acts of the thrill makers initially took place against the backdrop of the lived environment, and as such they constituted a response to a paradox of modern life. Raymond Williams described two "paradoxical yet deeply connected tendencies of modern urban industrial living": on the one hand is the geographic mobility made possible by modern means of transportation and communication, and on the other is an ideology of privacy made manifest in the "apparently self-sufficient family home."[12] Williams referred to this paradox as "mobile privatization" and offered it as a framework for understanding the social construction of media technologies that often worked to resolve its contradictions: cinema allowed for a mobility of vision, and broadcasting brought far-flung images of the world into the home.[13] The thrill makers embodied a response to a similar contradiction in modern life, one that I will call "massive personalization." On the one hand, there was an expansion in the scale of modern life, as in the case of gigantic public architecture, urban population growth, the rise of mass production and consumption, the establishment of global empires, and the creation of national media publics.[14] On the other hand, the experience of modernity encouraged a heightened concern with the individual, as can be seen in the emphasis on individual "personality," forms of personal address in advertising, and increasingly "intimate" and informal media representations.[15]

The sociologist Georg Simmel identified the coexistence of these contradictory tendencies in his 1903 essay "The Metropolis and Mental Life." The modern city, Simmel wrote, was part of a culture that had "outgrown every personal element": "Here in buildings and in educational institutions, in the wonders and comforts of space-conquering technique, in the formations of social life and in the concrete institutions of the State is to be found such a tremendous richness of crystallizing, depersonalized cultural accomplishments that the personality can, so to speak, scarcely maintain itself in the face of it." At the same time, Simmel argued that "individualizations" were produced and exaggerated in order "to be brought into the awareness even of the individual himself."[16] As with "mobile privatization," the modern media developed techniques that resolved the contradictions inherent in "massive personalization": think, for example, of the cinematic close-up, the focus on the private lives of celebrities, personalized advertising appeals, and the techniques used by radio announcers and popular singers to project a sense of intimacy. The thrill makers' interaction with the lived environment was another response to the contradictions of massive personalization, albeit one that ran parallel to the modern media: human flies brought imposing skyscrapers down to human scale; bridge jumpers transformed monoliths of modern engineering into vehicles for the creation of self; birdmen humanized aviation technology over the urban skyline; and lion tamers enacted metonyms for vast global empires in the "big cage." All of these were virtuosic and individualized performances that emerged from the gravitational pull of massive "vortices of behavior" in the modern cityscape, and all of these performances spoke back to what Simmel called the "atrophy of individual culture through the hypertrophy of objective culture."[17]

The thrill makers developed acts that explored the farthest limits of a performance frame established between an individual performer and a massive copresent audience, and they did so during the decades when the emerging media industries were developing their own strategies for creating and promoting stars and convening national publics. It is not surprising that the film industry and organized professional sports—both of which found ways to rationalize thrills and professionalize publicity techniques—supplanted the thrill makers as the dominant forms of popular entertainment and male celebrity in the age of "massive personalization." In the end, individual operators such as Steve Brodie, F. S. Sutherland, Jack Bonavita, Rodman Law, and Lincoln Beachey could not compete with well-staffed, well-funded corporate publicity departments and the modern media's national channels of distribution. More research needs to be done on the relationship between performance and the lived environment, and the multiple histories of celebrity culture. The case studies in this book also raise questions about performance traditions in other national contexts. What kind of public performances have accompanied the rapid modernization of China, India, or Dubai? How have those performances intersected with the media? Have performers in other historical or national contexts articulated discourses of celebrity, publicity, and gender in a manner similar to the thrill makers?

STUNT MEN'S CLUB

One of the most startling revelations in the opening sequence of RKO's *Lucky Devils* was that the ostensibly female performer who fell down the stairs was, in fact, a man. The heroism of stuntwork is thus explicitly tied to gender: despite the dress, wig, and stockings, this is to be understood as a *male* performance. I have argued that thrill makers were frequently taken to be embodiments of an "authentic" masculinity during a time that many historians have identified as a period of crisis for Western masculinity.[18] One source of the thrill makers' resonance as male ideals was their display of activities that resembled artisanal labor. T. J. Jackson Lears has argued that the bureaucratic world of turn-of-the-century white-collar labor seemed "strangely insubstantial" to many Americans who yearned for "the authentic experience of manual labor" and idealized the premodern artisan, whose work seemed to be "necessary and demanding," was "rooted in a genuine community," and was a "model of hardness and wholeness."[19] To a greater or lesser degree, all of the thrill makers registered a sense of such "genuine" work: some made heroic leaps at the waterfalls that drove the mills where they were skilled laborers; others stole the glory of the bridges under which they had toiled as newsboys; steeplejacks worked on the sides of tall buildings for large crowds; laborers who fed and trained dangerous exotic animals became celebrity entertainers; and the "mechanics" who built and operated early airships and airplanes engaged in a form of manual labor that was sublime and even mythic. Here were performances that drew upon the body memories of an artisanal culture during an era that saw the deskilling of labor. Here was a form of work that enacted manly independence in an era of labor segmentation.[20] Here was a display of concrete intelligence that seemed to be substantial and heroic, reassuring men that meaningful and traditionally masculine work could be found in the modern world. When seen as celebrity laborers, the thrill makers add nuance to a historical narrative that demarcates a shift from "idols of production" whose fame stemmed from "industry, business, and natural sciences" to "idols of consumption" associated with the sphere of entertainment and leisure.[21] The thrill makers were icons of artisanal production as well as content providers for the modern media. Film theorist Jean-Louis Comolli once asked why the cinema has so rarely filmed work.[22] Perhaps film theorists like Comolli have been looking in the wrong places. In my discussion of stuntwork as part of the system of Hollywood labor, I argued that future scholarship should explore the various types of screen *performance* as *work*. The celebrity status of heroic artisans suggests that there is also more to be done on how *work* can be framed as *performance*.[23]

The thrill makers hearkened back to the artisanal laborer, but their resonance as male ideals was also tied to the ways in which they faced death and serious injury in the most public manner. In many cultures manhood has been understood as a state that must be attained against powerful odds, and even then it must be constantly demonstrated.[24] David D. Gilmore writes that male social imperatives are frequently dangerous and highly competitive, such that many societies require a code of male conduct to help boys to overcome their inhibitions about the battlefield, the hunt, or confrontation with rivals. Gilmore writes that boys have to be trained to "accept the fact that they are expendable," and that this acceptance constitutes the basis of "the manly pose everywhere it is encountered." But simply accepting this expendability will not do: "To be socially meaningful, the decision for manhood must be characterized by enthusiasm combined with stoic resolve or perhaps 'grace.'"[25] If Gilmore is right that an acceptance of expendability often constitutes "the measure of manhood," then this helps to explain both "the constant emphasis on risk taking as evidence of manliness" and, by extension, the heroic stature of those thrill makers who made a show of their stoic resolve in the face of danger.[26] I have tried to go beyond the observation that the thrill makers performed a certain style of masculinity to describe the particular mechanics of their acts, their relation to other embodiments of manhood in circulation at the time, and some of the ways in which they were understood by audiences. Erving Goffman's notions of action, the losability of nerve, gender display, and the calibration of risk in the performance of "stunts" have helped me to uncover shades of meaning in what easily could be dismissed as simple displays of male bravado. Future research might explore the ways in which these and other thrilling performance traditions have been mobilized to create and display gender in different historical and technological contexts. How might gender display function in cultures where "action" does not traditionally belong to the "cult of masculinity"? What cultural messages about gender can be found in online "stunt" videos, or in the burgeoning culture of urban "parkours"?

Notions of ideal masculinity change over time, and the acts of scarred and limbless lion tamers, battered bridge jumpers, precariously placed human flies, and wild-eyed birdmen took on new cultural meaning after the carnage of the First World War, an adjustment that I traced in the reconfiguration of the discourses surrounding the aviator. The marginalization of the thrill makers might be seen as part of a "civilizing process" that blunted the bloodiest displays of male courage, an argument that has also been mobilized to explain the rise of professional sports, with the boxing ring and the football gridiron understood as alternatives to the battlefield.[27] It is notable, then, that film producers made use of the thrill makers' perilous acts while concealing any accidents or deaths behind studio walls and a veil of publicity. Indeed, film allowed dangerous performances to be experienced by audiences in new ways: recall, for example, how Ormer Locklear's films were promoted as offering views of aerial stunts unavailable to audiences at the fairground or aerodrome. We might also note the comments of a theater manager in 1905, who claimed that the majority of those who paid admission to see "thrill acts" never actually saw them: "They avert their faces when the act starts and look back just as it is finished. They get their money's worth by the thrills of horror they feel while waiting to discover whether or not the man still lives or is a mangled mass."[28] Much as the cinema close-up allowed for new kinds of acting, the migration of thrill acts to cinema screens allowed audiences to carefully observe feats that might have been too troubling to watch when performed "live."

Many of those in the audience who were said to have turned their heads during thrill acts were women: recall, for example, the 1904 *Atlanta Constitution* article that described "thrill makers" who made "the women in the crowd turn pale and hide their eyes."[29] Press accounts of horrified female audience members who witnessed lion tamers being mauled or aeronauts plummeting from balloons remind us that the thrill makers were on the public scene during the years when women were

increasingly entering the public sphere as spectators at public amusements.[30] The tradition of nineteenth-century thrill makers proved to
be less successful at courting this new female audience than vaudeville
houses and the cinema. Nonetheless, women played an important role
in the thrill-making traditions I have described, as performers as well
as audience members: recall my discussion of ceiling walkers such as
Aimee Austin, the human fly antics of Dorothy Devore, lion tamers such
as Claire Heliot and Adgie Costillo, and stunt pilots such as Ruth Law.
I have argued that thrill-making acts were a cultural sphere in which
male character could be demonstrated, but those acts also became significant to the extent that they established forms and traditions in which
female performers could intervene and, in the process, expose the arbi-
trary nature of gendered divisions. The discourses that constituted the
genealogies of performance in this book help us better to understand
the stunning intervention in the thrill-making tradition achieved by
the female stars of action serials made during the 1910s and 1920s,
stars such as Pearl White, Helen Holmes, Ruth Roland, and Kathlyn
Williams.[31] Ben Singer argues that the "serial queens" displayed female
power through demonstrations of "physical prowess, quick reflexes,
and coordination especially with respect to a conventionally masculine
repertory of heroic stunts."[32] This book has provided an extended pro-
logue to Singer's claim by tracing the history of that "repertory of heroic
stunts" and describing some of the discursive work by which it came to
be "conventionally masculine." It is important to recognize the achievement of these female stars, but we also need to recognize that a crucial
component of the "technology" of their stardom was the segmentation
of screen labor and the rise of the stunt double. A host of precinematic
female thrill makers awaits further study, as do Hollywood stuntwomen
such as Ione Reed, Florence "Pancho" Barnes, Kitty O'Neil, Jeannie
Epper, and Zoe Bell.

The revelation of stuntman Bob Rose's male body underneath the
female costume in *Lucky Days* is therefore not the end of the story,
nor is it the location of any ultimate truth of stunt performance. Just
as star and stunt double were coconstitutive categories, so, of course,
are masculine and feminine, and Rose's cross-dressing is best seen not
as the revelation of the essential masculinity of stunt performance but
as a sign of the multivalent and never-finished performance of gender
in the modern media.[33] The thrill makers created rich dramatic forms
that are historically significant, not as the site of an "authentic" male
identity but as a dense transfer point in a complex cultural system of

performance that was mobilized to create and display identity, to harness the modern media's ability to establish and project celebrity, and to standardize cinematic spectacle and stardom during the formative years of Hollywood filmmaking.

It is fitting to conclude this book with Hollywood's representation of the paradigmatic thrill act. The same year that film audiences saw Bob Rose fall down the stairs in *Lucky Devils,* they could also witness a dramatization of Steve Brodie's legendary 1886 leap from the Brooklyn Bridge. In 20th Century Pictures' *The Bowery* (1933), Steve Brodie (George Raft) is approached by Mr. Herman (Herman Bing), a "big brewer from uptown," who asks Brodie for help in the promotion of his product: "If you could only do something that would bring your name into prominence," he tells Brodie, something that would create headlines in the newspapers and "make people want to patronize any place that had your name over the door." By making the capitalist brewer the impetus for the jump, the film dampens the class charge that bridge jumping had carried since the days of Sam Patch and also brackets off the commercial aspects of Brodie's messy public persona, allowing him to come across as an urban folk hero. It is Brodie, nonetheless, who strikes upon the method that he will use to make headlines. His epiphany occurs during the conversation with Mr. Herman, which takes place in front of a large rear projection screen showing the Brooklyn Bridge. As Mr. Herman speaks, Brodie's eyes widen and he says, "If a guy jumped off that bridge, the whole world will know about it." As with the "animal trend" films described in chapter 3, rear projection technology presents us with two realms of screen reality: the studio close-up of the star and the second-unit location shot of the urban landscape.

The ambivalence about the motivation for the stunt depicted in the scene with Mr. Herman is part of the film's larger confusion about how to address Brodie on the level of both narrative and style. The narrative initially depicts Brodie planning to use a prosthetic dummy to fake the jump, and we see him coach his young associate Swipes (Jackie Cooper) about when to throw the dummy into the water. Brodie examines the dummy, at one point holding a mirror so that we see its reflected face, and he says, "There you are, Steve Brodie. Take a look at yourself." In the context of this book, we might see this as a moment when a representative of the faceless stunt double in Hollywood cinema is briefly seen and addressed on the screen. Brodie's plans are ruined, however, when the dummy goes missing at the last minute and he is forced to make the jump for real. The film thus tries to have it both ways: Brodie is simultaneously a wily con man and an authentic, albeit reluctant, hero. The style of the jump sequence is stunning: rapid editing, the ear-splitting whistles of boats on the river, and the cheers of the crowd, which is seen in both close-up and long shot, all lend excitement and gravity to the event and suggest the intensity of its popular appeal. The jump itself is fragmented between a shot of Raft beginning the leap from the bridge, then a shot of a body falling as seen from above, and then a final shot of a figure striking the water as seen from a distance. Unlike the witnesses at an actual performance of bridge jumping, film audiences are never provided with a view that encompasses both the full scale of the bridge and the falling body's relation to it. But, perhaps most significantly, although the film's narrative asserts that Brodie actually made the jump, it must depict it by recourse to a prosthetic dummy at the key moment. In fact, the stuntman who doubled for Harold Lloyd in *Safety Last,* Harvey Parry, was asked to double for Raft and make the jump from the Brooklyn Bridge. Parry refused, however, on the grounds that the bridge was too high, the current was too dangerous, and there was debris floating just beneath the surface of the water.[34]

In revisiting the enigma of Brodie's jump and its representation on the screen, the film thus reminds us of Hollywood's complex relationship to adjacent traditions of popular performance and celebrity, as well as the futility of searching for essential identities outside culture and history. Whether it was Brodie or a dummy that fell into the East River is less important than the cultural meaning that accrued to the act as it was refracted through the prism of the modern media. Brodie stated as much when he was interviewed in jail the morning after his jump. A *New York Herald* reporter asked Brodie about his sensational feat: "I've been dreaming about it all night," he said. "That jump was just like a dream."[35] Brodie's jump, and the other astounding feats of the thrill makers described in this book, may have faded from the cultural stage in the morning of the media age, but they nonetheless became an essential component of the collective dream of the American cinema.

Notes

INTRODUCTION

1. Bennett, F. B. "Those Who Do the 'Stunts' in the Movies," *New York Tribune,* December 31, 1916, p. D7.

2. Gaudreault, André. "The Diversity of Cinematographic Connections in the Intermedial Context of the Turn of the Twentieth Century," in Simon Popple and Vanessa Toulmin, eds., *Visual Delights: Essays on the Popular and Projected Image in the Nineteenth Century.* Trowbridge, Wiltshire, England: Flicks Books, 2000, pp. 12–14. See also Bolter, Jay David, and Richard Grusin. *Remediation: Understanding New Media.* Cambridge, Mass.: MIT Press, 2000.

3. Williams, Raymond. *Marxism and Literature.* Oxford: Oxford University Press, 1977, p. 122. See also Acland, Charles R., ed. "Introduction" to *Residual Media.* Minneapolis: University of Minnesota Press, 2007.

4. Hall, Stuart. "Notes on Deconstructing 'The Popular,'" in Raphael Samuel, ed. *People's History and Socialist Theory.* London: Routledge, pp. 227–28.

5. Volosinov, V.N. *Marxism and the Philosophy of Language.* Cambridge, Mass.: Harvard University Press, 1973, p. 23.

6. Denning, Michael. *Mechanic Accents.* London: Verso, 1987, p. 83.

7. Ibid., p. 3.

8. Rick Altman, in Jeffrey Ruoff, ed. *Virtual Voyages.* Durham, N.C.: Duke University Press, 2006, p. 61.

9. Casetti, Francesco. *Eye of the Century.* New York: Columbia University Press, 2008, p. 140.

10. Ibid., pp. 136–37.

11. On genealogies of performance, see Roach, Joseph. *Cities of the Dead: Circum-Atlantic Performance.* New York: Columbia University Press, 1996, p. 25.

12. Altick, Richard D. *The Shows of London.* Cambridge, Mass.: Harvard University Press, Belknap Press, 1978, p. 2.

13. "How Life and Limb Are Risked to Thrill Public," *Atlanta Constitution,* August 21, 1904, p. D7.

14. Bauman, Richard. *A World of Others' Words.* Oxford: Blackwell, 2004, p. 9.

15. Goffman, Erving. *Where the Action Is.* London: Penguin Press, 1969, p. 199.

16. See Branaman, Ann. "Goffman's Social Theory," in Charles Lemert and Ann Branaman, eds., *The Goffman Reader.* Oxford: Blackwell, 1997.

17. Isaac, Rhys. *The Transformation of Virginia.* Chapel Hill: University of North Carolina Press, 1982, p. 324.

18. Roach, *Cities of the Dead,* p. 28.

19. On the nineteenth- and early twentieth-century "entertainment environment," see Toulmin, Vanessa. "Curios Things in Curios Places: Temporary Exhibition Venues in the Victorian and Edwardian Entertainment Environment," *Early Popular Visual Culture* 4, no. 2 (July 2006), pp. 116–17.

20. Goffman, Erving. *Interaction Ritual.* New York: Pantheon, 1967, p. 237.

21. Baker, Thomas N. *Sentiment and Celebrity.* New York: Oxford University Press, 1999, p. 7. See also Braudy, Leo. *The Frenzy of Renown.* New York: Oxford University Press, 1986; and Gamson, Joshua. *Claims to Fame.* Berkeley: University of California Press, 1994.

22. Susman, Warren I. *Culture as History.* Washington, D.C.: Smithsonian Institution Press, 2003 (1973), pp. xx, 277.

23. DeCordova, Richard. *Picture Personalities.* Urbana: University of Illinois Press, 2001, p. 12.

24. Bederman, Gail. *Manliness and Civilization.* Chicago: University of Chicago Press, 1995, p. 7. See also Kimmel, Michael. *Manhood in America.* New York: Free Press, 1996.

25. Lemert and Branaman, *Goffman Reader,* p. 224.

26. Goffman, *Interaction Ritual,* p. 209.

27. Geertz, Clifford. *The Interpretation of Cultures.* New York: Basic Books, 1973, p. 449.

28. Kasson, John F. *Houdini, Tarzan, and the Perfect Man.* New York: Hill and Wang, 2001, p. 19.

29. See, for example, Canutt, Yakima. *Stunt Man.* Norman: University of Oklahoma Press, 1979.

30. See Everson, William K. "Stunt Men," *Films in Review* 4, no. 8 (October 1955), p. 394.

1. THE ADVENTURES OF THE BRIDGE JUMPER

1. Rosenzweig, Roy. *Eight Hours for What We Will.* Cambridge: Cambridge University Press, 1983. Gutman, Herbert G. "Work, Culture, and Society in

Industrializing America, 1815–1919," *American Historical Review* 78, no. 3, June 1974, p. 564.

2. Johnson, Paul E. *Sam Patch: The Famous Jumper.* New York: Hill and Wang, 2003, p. 48.

3. Ibid., p. 69.

4. Ibid., p. 47.

5. Ibid., p. 39. Alan Trachtenberg describes the use of metaphors that connected manufacturing and mighty rivers in the late nineteenth century, noting that "almost half the American manufacturing establishments drew power from waterwheels and turbines." Trachtenberg, Alan. *The Incorporation of America.* New York: Hill and Wang, 1982, p. 57.

6. Couvares, Francis G. *The Remaking of Pittsburgh.* Albany: State University of New York Press, 1984, p. 9. On "initial proletarianization," see Gordon, David M., Richard Edwards, and Michael Reich. *Segmented Work, Divided Workers.* Cambridge: Cambridge University Press, 1982, p. 11.

7. Johnson, *Sam Patch*, p. 39.

8. Ibid., p. 53–54.

9. On Foucault, see Dreyfus, Hubert L., and Paul Rabinow. *Michel Foucault: Beyond Structuralism and Hermeneutics.* Chicago: University of Chicago Press, 1982, pp. 238–39. On body technique, see Mauss, Marcel. *Sociology and Psychology.* London: Routledge and Kegan Paul, 1950, p. 105; and Agacinski, Sylviane. "Incorporation," in Cynthia C. Davidson, ed., *Anybody.* Cambridge, Mass.: MIT Press, 1997, p. 35.

10. Johnson, *Sam Patch*, p. 56.

11. Goffman, Erving. *Where the Action Is.* London: Penguin Press, 1969, p. 199.

12. Ibid., pp. 126–27.

13. Ibid., p. 179.

14. Johnson, *Sam Patch*, pp. 115–17.

15. Ibid., pp. 163–64.

16. See Greene, Theodore P. *America's Heroes.* New York: Oxford University Press, 1970, p. 37; and Singer, Ben. *Melodrama and Modernity.* New York: Columbia University Press, 2001, p. 30.

17. Stephens, R.N. *The Life and Adventures of Steve Brodie, B.J., of the Bowery, New York.* New York: Thomas H. Davis, 1894, p. 42.

18. Ibid., p. 44; "A Leap for Sentiment," *New York Times*, August 9, 1889, p. 2.

19. Johnson, *Sam Patch*, p. 164.

20. Schudson, Michael. *Discovering the News.* New York: Basic Books, 1978, pp. 22–23. See also Baker, Thomas N. *Sentiment and Celebrity.* New York: Oxford University Press, 1999, p. 7; and Gamson, Joshua. *Claims to Fame: Celebrity in Contemporary America.* Berkeley: University of California Press, 1994. Greene finds "revolutionary changes" during the decade from 1894 to 1903, when magazines such as *McClure's* and *Cosmopolitan* began to cover more contemporary figures in a manner that was "timely, lively, and full of human interest" (Greene, *America's Heroes*, pp. 68–69).

21. "Notoriety That Pays," *Weekly Courier-Journal* (Louisville, Ky.), March 18, 1889, p. 5.

22. Stephens, *Life and Adventures of Steve Brodie*, p. 5. Also see Harlow, Alvin F. *Old Bowery Days*. New York: D. Appleton and Company, 1931, pp. 306–7.

23. Stephens, *Life and Adventures of Steve Brodie*, p. 7. See also Harlow, *Old Bowery Days*, p. 417.

24. Nasaw, David. *Children of the City*. New York: Oxford University Press, 1986, p. 62.

25. On youth social clubs such as the Life-savers, see Peiss, Kathy. *Cheap Amusements: Working Women and Leisure in Turn-of-the-Century New York*. Philadelphia: Temple University Press, 1986, p. 59.

26. "Four Young Heroes," *New York Times*, October 1, 1878, p. 8.

27. Bishop, W. H. "Nan, the Newsboy," *St. Nicholas*, August 1879, p. 679.

28. "Notoriety That Pays," p. 5.

29. Stephens, *Life and Adventures of Steve Brodie*, p. 9.

30. Bishop, "Nan, the Newsboy," p. 682.

31. "Nan, Gil, and Ed Eat High Pie," *New York Times*, December 29, 1878, p. 7.

32. McNeill, Archibald. "An Evening with Captain Boyton," *Gentleman's Magazine* 14 (June 1875), p. 715.

33. Ibid., pp. 716–17.

34. "Capt. Paul Boyton," *Chicago Tribune*, January 9, 1879, p. 7. Boyton attended college but preferred swimming to "bothering with books." In 1863 he left college to go trading "among the Indians" with his father, who "had a sort of traveling business, and used to strike from New York up to the frontier, lodging goods at the stations as he went on, and sending them down rail by train when he'd got sufficient." After the Civil War, he briefly operated a "light fancy business in Oriental goods," and then bought a "submarine diving-dress and traveled to the Gulf of Mexico engaging in pearl diving, until he lost his diving suit in a fire. He claims to have served in the "Mexican war" and the "Franco-German War" before settling down in Atlantic City (McNeill, "An Evening with Captain Boyton," pp. 716–22).

35. "King of the Deep," *St. Louis Globe-Democrat*, January 25, 1876, p. 8. See also "A Diver's Adventures: Some of the Submarine Experiences of Paul Boyton," *Daily Evening Bulletin*, July 13, 1875, p. A.

36. A 1874 newspaper article reported, "Mr. C.S. Merriman, of New York, the patentee of the life dress, has offered five hundred dollars to Mr. Paul Boyton, the diver, to make a sea voyage in his suit, in order to demonstrate to the public its merits as a life preserver" (*Cleveland Daily Herald*, August 6, 1874, p. 4).

37. Anonymous. *A Night with Paul Boyton and Other Stories*. Akron, Ohio: Werner, 1899, p. 15.

38. Ibid., p. 22; "Capt. Boyton," *Chicago Tribune*, January 19, 1879, p. 12.

39. "Merrieman's Life-Saving Apparatus," *Freeman's Journal and Daily Commercial Advertiser* (Dublin, Ireland), October 30, 1874.

40. "Captain Boyton's Experiments," *Freeman's Journal and Daily Commercial Advertiser* [Dublin, Ireland], November 9, 1874.

41. "Novel Voyage on the Thames," *Daily News* (London), no. 8,971, January 25, 1875.

42. "Captain Boyton at Osborne," *Daily News* (London), no. 9,032, April 6, 1875.

43. "The Channel Crossed by Captain Boyton," *Penny Illustrated Paper and Illustrated Times*, June 5, 1875, p. 353.

44. "An Amphibious Animal," *Indiana Democrat*, April 6, 1876, p. 1.

45. "An Exhibition by Paul Boyton," *New York Times*, January 15, 1876, p. 7.

46. "Boat Racing on Potomac Is Twenty-Five Years Old," *Washington Post*, January 20, 1907, p. S4.

47. "Paul Boyton's Exhibition," *Brooklyn Eagle*, June 21, 1888, p. 1.

48. "Paul Boyton in the Allegheny," *New York Times*, February 7, 1879, p. 5.

49. "Boyton's Business," *Rocky Mountain News* (Denver, Colo.), June 28, 1886, p. F. "Paul Boyton: The Record of an Amusing Trip down the Arkansas," *Daily Arkansas Gazette*, January 19, 1882, p. C.

50. Later that month the association between Boyton and the Life-savers seems still to have been strong. On January 26, 1879, Nan, the Newsboy and Boyton made a "midnight journey to Stapleton, Staten Island [from Battery] in his improved swimming suit, accompanied by James Crulman, a member of the [lifesaving] corps, similarly incased in rubber" ("Boyton's Midnight Trip," *New York Times*, January 26, 1879, p. 7).

51. "Out with the Volunteers," *New York Times*, January 5, 1879, p. 12.

52. "Boyton and the Life-Savers," *New York Times*, July 17, 1879, p. 8.

53. Bishop, "Nan, the Newsboy," p. 679.

54. "Miscellaneous City News, The Life-Savers Disband," *New York Times*, July 14, 1879, p. 8.

55. "A Statement from Capt. Boyton," *New York Times*, July 16, 1879, p. 8.

56. "The Boys Go Forth Alone," *New York World*, July 17, 1879, p. 3.

57. "Boyton and the Life-Savers," p. 8; "The Boys Go Forth Alone," p. 3.

58. For more on Boyton's Barnum-esque self-promotion, see chapter 2. For example, in 1888 Boyton announced that he was going to establish an "aquatic museum" that would contain "all the wonders of the deep," including a sea serpent ("The Sea Serpent Caught," *Chicago Tribune*, December 21, 1888, p. 11). Not surprisingly, it turned out to be a fraud: the sea serpent was an alligator's head attached to a leather bag ("General Metropolitan News," *Chicago Tribune*, December 23, 1888, p. 12).

59. "Boyton Isn't Bashful," *New York Times*, April 12, 1887, p. 2. Boyton's suit also allowed him to achieve seemingly superhuman feats in the water. So, for example, we read that in 1890 five thousand people saw Boyton "walk on the water" while dressed in his "wonderful rubber suit" ("Paul Boyton at River View," *Washington Post*, May 26, 1890, p. 6). This was a description of Boyton's ability to stand upright in the water due to the buoyancy of his inflated suit: "The captain had been standing upright in the water, head and shoulders out, looking as firm as though he was upon the bottom, although I knew the river must be at least forty feet deep where we were" (Anonymous, "A Night with Paul Boyton and Other Stories," p. 23).

60. "Nan, the Newsboy," *St. Louis Globe-Democrat*, June 18, 1883, p. 7. Stephens writes that Nan was fired for drunkenness, joined a mission where he

delivered the lecture "The Evils of Drink," and later drove a truck (Stephens, *Life and Adventures of Steve Brodie*, p. 21). In 1881 the *St. Louis Globe-Democrat* wrote that Nan claimed to have been "ruined by the temptations to drink offered to every policeman, that he was tendered the freedom of every saloon on his beat, and invited to drink by every one who had a sinister purpose in dealing with the police" (*St. Louis Globe-Democrat*, February 1, 1881, p. 4. See also "City and Suburban News, 'Nan' as a Policeman," *New York Times*, July 24, 1880, p. 8). In 1902 Nan's story could be referenced as an example of the futility of charity work: "With the best of intentions . . . wealthy and wise patrons proceeded to make him over from a bohemian into a conventional hero. He stood the glare of greatness and the ordeal of prosperity a little while, and then became a drunkard and a tramp. There are a good many boys who, like Nan, won't bear making over. Nature has already marked the place they are to fill in the world, and when philanthropy pulls them out of it and insists on putting them somewhere else, it does them a positive wrong" ("Let Him Decide for Himself," *Washington Post*, November 23, 1902, p. 18).

61. "Off the Brooklyn Bridge," *Newport Daily Advocate*, July 24, 1886, p. 1; Stephens, *Life and Adventures of Steve Brodie*, p. 21.

62. Boyton tried to distance himself from bridge jumpers and Niagara Falls daredevils, saying, "A reasonable man can have but one opinion of such foolhardy performances. The men who attempt them are cranks." He admitted that he had been "confounded with these people by the public," but stated that while he had done some dangerous things, they were "with the intention of learning whether something that would prove useful could be done" ("Opinion of an Expert," *Milwaukee Daily Journal*, August 30, 1886, p. B).

63. Stephens, *Life and Adventures of Steve Brodie*, p. 33.

64. "Steve Brodie's Aquatic Feat," *Daily Inter Ocean*, May 8, 1887, p. 15.

65. "Brodie's Long Swim," *New York Times*, June 24, 1888, p. 3; "Steve Brodie Finishes His Long Swim down the Hudson," *Brooklyn Eagle*, June 30, 1888, p. 6.

66. Harlow writes that Brodie "blacked boots in front of French's Hotel, where the Brooklyn Bridge now ends" (Harlow, *Old Bowery Days*, p. 417).

67. Cadbury, Deborah. *Dreams of Iron and Steel*. New York: HarperCollins, 2003, p. 102. Also see Nye, David E. *American Technological Sublime*. Cambridge, Mass.: MIT Press, 1999, pp. 83–86.

68. Lears, T.J. Jackson. *No Place of Grace*. New York: Pantheon Books, 1981, p. 9.

69. *Syracuse Daily Standard*, May 13, 1885, p. 7.

70. "His Death Leap," *National Police Gazette*, May 30, 1885, p. 14. See also "Robert Odlum's Fatal Leap," *New York Tribune*, May 21, 1885, p. 1. According to another account he was "encouraged by Boyton," who waited for him in a boat below ("Capt. Paul Boyton," *Washington Post*, May 28, 1885, p. 4).

71. "Odlum's Leap," *Brooklyn Eagle*, May 20, 1885, p. 6.

72. "His Death Leap," p. 14.

73. "Odlum's Leap," p. 6. Odlum was born in Ogdensburg, New York, and was known as a long-distance swimmer before becoming a professional

swimming teacher in Washington, where he is said to have taught the children of Presidents Garfield and Hayes (ibid.).

74. "Fatal Leap from the East River Bridge," *Scientific American* 52, no. 22 (May 30, 1885), p. 344.

75. "Odlum's Fatal Leap," *New York Times*, June 7, 1885, p. 9.

76. Stephens, *Life and Adventures of Steve Brodie*, p. 22.

77. "He Did It," *National Police Gazette*, August 7, 1886, p. 7.

78. "A Leap from the Bridge," *New York Times*, July 24, 1886, p. 1.

79. "Off the Brooklyn Bridge," p. 1.

80. "The Bubble Reputation," *New York Tribune*, August 29, 1886, p. 4.

81. "Brodie and His Sensations," *New York Herald*, July 25, 1886, p. 11.

82. Ibid.

83. On imitators, see "Higher Than Brodie's Leap," *New York Tribune*, August 29, 1886, p. 1; and "Jumped off the Bridge," *New York Times*, August 29, 1886, p. 7, which describe Larry Donovan's jump. Also see "Trying to Imitate Brodie," *New York Daily Tribune*, July 26, 1886, p. 1; and "A Fool's Leap," *New York Evening Post*, July 23, 1886, p. 1. Larry Donovan was said to have been one of Brodie's friends, and he even passed the hat to spectators while Brodie did some of his early jumps on the wharves. Stephens writes, "One day Brodie caught Donovan shoving some of the money into the rim of his hat. As a result the boys dissolved their partnership" (Stephens, *Life and Adventures of Steve Brodie*, p. 9).

84. O'Noklast, Ik. "Picturesque People," *Peterson Magazine* 5, no. 8 (August 1895), p. 857.

85. "Bridge Jumping," *New York Times*, October 29, 1895, p. 4.

86. "Spoiled by Celebrity," *Brooklyn Eagle*, July 26, 1887, p. 2.

87. "Brodie's Unfortunate Escape," *Brooklyn Eagle*, May 21, 1889, p. 4. In 1889 the *Philadelphia Inquirer* wrote that there was "no shorter road to fame than that of the high-jumpers. It is perilous and invariably ends with a coroner's jury sitting over the shapeless remains; still we see no possible objection to such persons as have no other sphere of usefulness in this world following their calling to its legitimate conclusion. They can be easily spared and are more than welcome to their short-lived notoriety which is fame to their distorted imaginations" ("Leaping into Fame," *Philadelphia Inquirer*, August 29, 1889, p. 4).

88. "Bridge Jumping," p. 4.

89. "Brodie's Unfortunate Escape," p. 4. Greene describes the neoclassic heroic ideal as "a gentleman, conscious of his duty, moderate in all things, and displaying 'the best habits of piety.' The heroic virtues were self-restraint not self-expression, moderation not ambition, dignity not forcefulness, responsibility to one's accepted duty not making one's mark upon the world in new ways" (Greene, *America's Heroes*, p. 47).

90. Baker, *Sentiment and Celebrity*, p. 8.

91. Susman, Warren I. *Culture as History*. Washington, D.C.: Smithsonian Institution Press, 2003 (1973), p. 280.

92. Boorstin, Daniel J. *The Image: A Guide to Pseudo-Events in America*. New York: Vintage Books, 1961 (1992), p. 79.

93. Ibid., p. 13.

94. Ibid., p. 63.

95. Ibid., p. 56.

96. Graeme Turner warns that Boorstin's work resembles typical "elite critiques" of popular culture, in which "each new shift in fashion is offered as the end of civilization as we know it, with the real motivation being an elitist distaste for the demotic or populist dimension of mass cultural practices" (Turner, Graeme. *Understanding Celebrity*. London: Sage Publications, 2004, p. 5). Charles Ponce de Leon argues that "one of the most remarkable traits of the mass-circulation press was its ability to make ordinary people visible at a time when urban growth appeared to be submerging individuals into an anonymous mass" (Ponce de Leon, Charles. *Self-Exposure*. Chapel Hill: University of North Carolina Press, 2001, p. 48). For Chris Rojek, the modern notion of celebrity derives from "the rise of democratic governments and secular societies," and that "the increasing importance of the public face in everyday life" is a consequence of the rise of a public society that "cultivates personal style as the antidote to formal democratic equality" (Rojek, Chris. *Celebrity*. London: Reaktion, 2001, p. 9).

97. Marshall, P. David. *Celebrity and Power*. Minneapolis: University of Minnesota Press, 1997, pp. 5–6.

98. "Brodie's Unfortunate Escape," p. 4.

99. See Peiss, *Cheap Amusements*, p. 17; Gorn, Elliot J. *The Manly Art*. Ithaca, N.Y.: Cornell University Press, 1986, p. 133; Harlow, *Old Bowery Days*, p. 404; Rosenzweig, *Eight Hours for What We Will*, pp. 40–44. Harlow added that "in the saloon the homeless man for a nickel could get not only shelter from the storm . . . but a free lunch . . . sufficient to sustain him for the day; likewise a choice of newspapers which he could not afford to buy, and an hour or so in a warm, jovial atmosphere" (p. 404).

100. Following Raymond Williams, Rosenzweig declares workingmen's saloon culture to be an "alternative" culture (one that is "separate and distinct from dominant society"), but not an "oppositional" culture (one that is "a direct challenge to that society") (Rosenzweig, *Eight Hours for What We Will*, pp. 223, 64).

101. Peiss continues, "The public culture of workingmen was not only a potential bulwark of solidarity against the ravages of capitalism; it was also a system of male privilege in which workers' self-determination, solidarity, and mutual assistance were understood as 'manliness'" (Peiss, *Cheap Amusements*, pp. 4–5).

102. "Bowery Landmark to Go," *Suburbanite Economist*, October 30, 1908, p. 7.

103. "Steve Brodie," *Davenport Weekly Leader*, February 5, 1901, p. 2.

104. See "Bread and Coffee at Brodie's," *New York Times*, February 3, 1893, p. 2. The *Denver Evening Post* reported that Brodie had seen "a number of working girls caught in a sudden shower," and a few days later "it was known all over New York that any poor girl might borrow an umbrella at Steve Brodie's without leaving a deposit" ("The Amusement World," *Denver Evening Post*, October 28, 1896, p. 8).

105. Marshall, *Celebrity and Power*, p. 6.

106. "Notoriety That Pays," p. 5.

107. Harlow, *Old Bowery Days,* p. 418.

108. Kirshenblatt-Gimblett, Barbara. "Objects of Ethnography," in Ivan Karp and Steven D. Lavine, *Exhibiting Cultures.* Washington, D.C.: Smithsonian Institution Press, 1991, p. 410. For an example of the "museum effect" in regard to 114 Bowery, consider this 1884 press account: "Everyone who goes on the Bowery sightseeing visits Steve Brodie's and views with interest the cosmopolitan phases of life which are to be seen within its doors. The place is a curiosity shop in itself, the walls being covered with curious pictures, musical instruments, beer mugs and little statuettes of famous prizefighters" ("On the Bowery," *Philadelphia Inquirer,* August 5, 1894, p. 1).

109. Kirshenblatt-Gimblett, "Objects of Ethnography," p. 413. We might note here accounts that the commander of the Salvation Army, Frederick Booth-Tucker, had gone slumming with Brodie in Chinatown, where the two were said to have "sampled all sorts of Oriental menus, banged the sacred gongs, and investigated all the opium dens and fantan games" within reach. Booth-Tucker had disguised himself with a wig and fake beard that could soon be found prominently displayed in the show window of Brodie's saloon ("Arrest of Booth-Tucker," *New York Times,* April 29, 1896, p. 1; "Brodie Is in High Glee," *New York Times,* April 30, 1896, p. 9).

110. Dennett, Andrea Stulman. *Weird Wonderful: The Dime Museum in America.* New York: New York University Press, 1997, p. 45. Dennet observes that high-end museums sometimes featured tableaux entitled "Rulers of the World" and "People Talked About," illustrating how discourses of celebrity were part of the dime museum display (p. 48). Also note that Bunnell's museum in the Bowery had exhibits focused on "topical issues," such as wax display of "slayers of Jesse James" (p. 57).

111. Santé, Luc. *Low Life.* New York: Farrar, Straus, Giroux, 1991, p. 123. On Bowery dime museums, see Harlow, *Old Bowery Days,* pp. 378–79.

112. Stephens, *Life and Adventures of Steve Brodie,* p. 31; "Notoriety That Pays," p. 5. Stephens writes that Brodie "went to the office of Edmund E. Price, the lawyer, and signed a contract to appear under the management of Messrs. Morris and Coleman, for ten weeks, at $250 per week" (Stephens, *Life and Adventures of Steve Brodie,* p. 31). Stephens also claims that Brodie was on the stage at "the museum conducted by Morris and Coleman at Coney Island" for four weeks. "People swarmed to see him, and the other curiosities sat on their platforms neglected" (ibid., p. 29). An advertisement in the *New York Clipper* on August 21, 1886, announced that "Steve Brodie, The Newsboy Who Jumped from the Brooklyn Bridge," would appear at Morris's museum. The *New York Daily Tribune* reported that Brodie had agreed to appear at the East Side Museum at 105 Bowery, and that "the news created a sensation among the curiosities," such that Brodie would "have to keep his eyes open" if he wanted to escape "the jealousy of the fat woman, who is said to be specially vindictive" ("Hero of the Fourth Ward," *New York Daily Tribune,* July 25, 1886, p. 1). Harlow writes of Brodie's engagement at Alexander's Museum, 317 Bowery, "where he talked and danced" (Harlow, *Old Bowery Days,* p. 418).

113. "Not Allowed to Jump," *Milwaukee Sentinel,* February 24, 1887, p. 4.

114. Stephens, *Life and Adventures of Steve Brodie*, p. 32.

115. Ibid., p. 50. See also "Steve Brodie Reported Dead," *New York Tribune*, February 1, 1901, which claimed that he "first appeared on the stage as a bridge jumper in 'Money Mad' at the Standard Theatre" (p. 2).

116. Bordman, Gerald. *American Theatre: A Chronicle of Comedy and Drama, 1869–1914*. New York: Oxford University Press, 1994, p. 43.

117. Sokalski, J.A. *Pictorial Illusionism: The Theatre of Steele MacKaye*. Montreal: McGill-Queen's University Press, 2007, pp. 178–79. See also Vardac, A. Nicholas. *Stage to Screen*. Cambridge, Mass.: Harvard University Press, 1949, p. 89. Sokalski describes MacKaye's invention of the "double stage . . . two stages, stacked one on top of the other, worked like a two-floor elevator; one theatrical set was moved up or down to offer the next set to the audience as quickly as it took the stage to sink or rise to the appropriate level" (Sokalski, *Pictorial Illusionism*, p. 57).

118. Singer, *Melodrama and Modernity*, pp. 149–51.

119. Ibid., p. 158.

120. Ibid., p. 157.

121. Sokalski notes that "the strong emphasis on water effects suggested by the dominance of the water stage was a further expression of MacKaye's overriding theatrical interest in recreating natural atmospheric and weather conditions" (Sokalski, *Pictorial Illusionism*, p. 216).

122. Bordman, *American Theatre*, p. 294.

123. "With the Diving Drama," *Chicago Tribune*, July 8, 1888, p. 27. Bordman refers to MacKaye's production of this year as *An Arrant Knave* (Bordman, *American Theatre*, p. 286).

124. Roach, Joseph. *Cities of the Dead: Circum-Atlantic Performance*. New York: Columbia University Press, 1996, p. 28.

125. "With the Diving Drama," p. 27. See also "A Noble Rogue Succeeds," *New York Times*, July 4, 1888, p. 1.

126. Sensational melodrama found a receptive audience among Brodie's Bowery milieu. Santé writes that Bowery melodrama after the 1840s became increasingly spectacular, featuring "giant set-pieces that depended far more on the deployment of stage machinery than on acting or writing," and it also took part in water tank effects: "Tank dramas involved the use of a large pool of water, taking up most of the stage, on which were mobilized entire ships" (Santé, *Low Life*, p. 76).

127. Bordman, *American Theatre*, p. 367. See also "On the Bowery a Sensational Play, with Scenes in New-York," *New York Times*, September 11, 1894, p. 5.

128. See Santé, *Low Life*, p. 76. Santé writes that "in 1849 the managers of the Bowery hit on a new gimmick, one that was just as crowd-pleasing as the spectacles without costing nearly as much to produce: they engaged the well-known saloonkeeper, gang leader, and boxer Tom Hyer to appear in a play" (ibid.). Dan Streible notes that James J. Corbett, the world heavyweight boxing champion between 1892 and 1897, was crossing similar lines of celebrity. Not only popular as a professional boxer, he was also as "a stage idol, picture

personality, lecturer, fight promoter, columnist and raconteur" (Streible, Dan. *Fight Pictures.* Berkeley: University of California Press, 2008, p. 50).

129. "Amusements," *Morning Oregonian,* October 9, 1896, p. 5. According to the *Trenton Evening Times,* the production featured "uncommonly fine scenic equipment," and the "the wonderful Brooklyn Bridge scene" was "pictorial in the highest degree possible to a play of its kind" (*Trenton Evening Times,* March 18, 1896, p. 2). A Buffalo, New York, newspaper wrote that "the interior of Brodie's sporting house is one of the most perfect scenic pictures ever seen on the stage," and that "every detail of the construction of the bridge is shown in this great scene, including the most perfect illusions of great height and long perspective" ("Lyceum Theater," *Buffalo Courier,* August 26, 1894, p. 4).

130. Santé, *Low Life,* p. 125.

131. "On the Bowery a Sensational Play," p. 5.

132. *Decatur Bulletin-Sentinel,* November 2, 1895, p. 8.

133. Stephens, *Life and Adventures of Steve Brodie,* p. 55.

134. "Steve Brodie As He Is," *Morning Oregonian,* October 9, 1896, p. 5.

135. "What Brodie Says," *Buffalo Courier,* March 16, 1895, p. 6. On stage, Brodie was said to be "just himself, without any frills, and sensibly does not attempt to be dramatic" ("At the Theaters," *Buffalo Courier,* March 12, 1895, p. 6).

136. Bordman, *American Theatre,* p. 367.

137. DeCordova, Richard. *Picture Personalities.* Urbana: University of Illinois Press, 2001, pp. 87–88; Gamson, *Claims to Fame,* p. 26; King, Barry. "Articulating Stardom," *Screen* 26, no. 5 (September–October 1985), p. 30. The confusion over whether or not Brodie was "acting" or simply exhibiting himself resembles early articles about cinema that alternately define the work of film performers as "posing" for a photograph or "acting" on the stage (deCordova, *Picture Personalities,* pp. 34–35).

138. "Steve Brodie and His Bowery Play," *San Francisco Chronicle,* September 8, 1896, p. 9.

139. "Entertainments," *Hartford Courant,* April 1, 1896, p. 6.

140. Wilentz, Sean. *Chants Democratic.* New York: Oxford University Press, 2004 (1984), p. 300. For an insightful discussion of ethnic caricature in early film comedy, see King, Rob. *The Fun Factory.* Berkeley: University of California Press, 2009, pp. 80–82.

141. Gorn, Elliott J. "Good-Bye Boys, I Die a True American: Homicide, Nativism, and Working-Class Culture in Antebellum New York City," *Journal of American History* 74, no. 2 (September 1987), p. 408. Harlow writes that many of the Bowery boys were "workingmen, not a few being engaged in one way or another, in the butcher's trade. Others were mechanics, shipbuilders, carpenters, or unskilled laborers. Some . . . were saloon-keepers, gamblers, ward heelers, casual employees around barrooms and dives, or just plain loafers" (Harlow, *Old Bowery Days,* p. 195).

142. Stansell, Christine. *City of Women.* Urbana: University of Illinois Press, 1987, p. 91. On the "republic of the Bowery," see Wilentz, *Chants Democratic,* pp. 257–59.

143. Dorson, Richard M. *America in Legend.* New York: Pantheon, 1973, p. 107. See also Harlow, who writes that the first New York Mose sketch was greeted by "a yell of recognition as had never been heard in the little house before" (Harlow, *Old Bowery Days*, p. 213).

144. "On the Bowery a Sensational Play," p. 5. In 1898 Brodie took part in a vaudeville sketch entitled "One Night in Brodie's Barroom" ("Steve Brodie Is Dead," *New York Times*, April 1, 1898, p. 7).

145. "On the Bowery Draws a Big Audience to the Boston," *Boston Daily Advertiser*, August 21, 1894, p. 5.

146. "Very Happy Crowd," *Denver Evening Post*, November 6, 1896, p. 10.

147. "Steve Brodie at the Lyceum—See?" *Buffalo News*, March 12, 1895, p. 4; "On The Bowery," *Buffalo Evening News*, August 28, 1895, p. 5.

148. "The Lyceum Theater," *Buffalo Courier*, January 31, 1899, p. 7.

149. "What Brodie Says," p. 6.

150. "Steve Brodie and His Bowery Play," p. 9.

151. "Steve Brodie Makes a Hit," *Morning Oregonian*, October 9, 1896, p. 5.

152. "Can Fight As Well As Jump," *Boston Daily Globe*, February 16, 1896, p. 18.

153. "Bowery in Real Life: Two Members of Steve Brodie's Company Arrested," *Idaho Daily Statesman*, October 21, 1896, p. 4.

154. "Notoriety That Pays," p. 5.

155. Johnson, *Sam Patch*, p. 80. John Sears argues that Niagara Falls' "height and breadth, and the inexhaustible volume of water flowing over it made it an apt emblem for the resources of the new nation" (Sears, John F. *Sacred Places: American Tourist Attractions in the Nineteenth Century.* New York: Oxford University Press, 1989, p. 12).

156. Sears describes how railroad fares declined after the Civil War, bringing fewer "genteel" tourists to Niagara Falls, as well as a campaign by Frederick Law Olmsted to have the state of New York keep sideshows away from the falls, which he felt inhibited their "true enjoyment," which required "a quiet and pensive contemplation of their beauty." Sears concludes that Niagara "lent itself as much to being a thrilling spectacle, an act in a circus, as it did to being nature's masterpiece in a picturesque park, and it remained both" (Sears, *Sacred Places*, pp. 186–89).

157. Dunlap, Orrin E. "Niagara and Its Notoriety-Seekers," *Current Literature* 32, no. 3 (March 1902), pp. 333–35. Sears compares the consumption of Niagara Falls to "the public museum, the exposition, and the popular resort," all of which "offered diverse attractions under the umbrella of a unifying spectacle, functioned as instruments of the mass consumption of culture, and provided a democratic stage on which the obscure and famous could share the same experience and where, increasingly as the century progressed, members of all classes could mingle as they would also do at Coney Island" (Sears, *Sacred Places*, p. 27).

158. "Over Niagara Falls," *New York Times*, September 8, 1889, p. 3.

159. "Brodie Will Try It Again," *New York Times*, September 9, 1889, p. 8.

160. "They Make Oath to It," *Washington Post*, September 10, 1889, p. 2.

161. "Over the Falls by Affidavit," *Washington Post*, September 10, 1889, p. 4.

162. "Discrediting Steve Brodie's Jump," *Chicago Tribune*, September 10, 1889, p. 8. In 1894 the *Brooklyn Daily Eagle* reported that nobody saw Brodie make the Niagara trip, and "his friends now admit that exploit to be a 'fake'" ("His Own Advertising Bureau," *Brooklyn Eagle*, August 6, 1894, p. 4). The account in Brodie's biography held that the saloon keeper had gone to Niagara Falls to investigate the possibility of jumping over the falls, but he had given up the idea and returned to New York when "a newspaper man who had gone with him to Niagara conceived the idea of fooling the public and wrote an entirely fictitious account of a jump which he said Brodie had made over the falls. . . . Brodie is prompt to avow that he never went over Niagara Falls and that he will never attempt that performance" (Stephens, *Life and Adventures of Steve Brodie*, p. 44). According to Harlow, Brodie had been "daunted by the wild, white, icy water" at Niagara and "would not release his hold of the rope which was to give him his start, and finally screamed to be drawn out" (Harlow, *Old Bowery Days*, p. 418).

163. "It Was Not Brodie After All," *New York Times*, September 30, 1888, p. 16.

164. "Steve Brodie Badly Hurt," *Milwaukee Daily Journal*, November 9, 1888, col. D.

165. "Bowery Landmark to Go," p. 7.

166. "Brodie Fond of Publicity," *Washington Post*, February 3, 1901, p. 17. In 1930 the *Brooklyn Daily Eagle* interviewed a retired police sergeant who had befriended Brodie. The sergeant stated that he had asked Brodie in confidence if the bridge jumping had been a trick: "No, I didn't do it," Brodie replied, "and I never said I did" ("Questions Still Surface on Brodie's 'Plunge,'" *Daily Intelligencer*, July 27, 1986). Even as early as 1895 the *Brooklyn Eagle* reported on word of a scheme to drop "a dummy" from the bridge and then have an accomplice in a rowboat ready to roll into the water and be picked up by his friends: "This is an easy way to get the glory of jumping from the bridge. The hero simply gets a ducking in the river and then poses in dime museums as a man who has leaped from dizzy heights" ("Bridge Jumpers for Revenue," *Brooklyn Eagle*, May 18, 1895, p. 6).

167. See "King of the Bowery Dead," *Milwaukee Journal*, March 31, 1898, p. 7; and "Steve Brodie Dead," *Denver Evening Post*, March 31, 1898, p. G.

168. "Brodie on a Train," *Chicago Tribune*, April 1, 1898, p. 6.

169. There were also accounts that Sam Patch had faked his death. See, for example, "Domestic Varieties: Sam Patch Alive," *Ariel*, December 12, 1829, p. 130.

170. "Is Again a Bride," *Chicago Tribune*, April 2, 1898, p. 6.

171. Press reports had also circulated in the 1840s about the supposed death of lion tamer Isaac Van Amburgh, whom I will discuss in chapter 3. Van Amburgh was alive, appearing in England.

172. DeCordova, *Picture Personalities*, p. 140.

173. For a discussion "the world's first special effects shot," see Rickitt, Richard. *Special Effects: The History and Technique*. London: Virgin Publishing, 2000, p. 10.

174. Burch, Noel. *Life to Those Shadows*. Berkeley: University of California Press, 1990, p. 99.

175. Joseph Roach argues that cultural memories can be stored in the body by means of what he calls the "kinesthetic imagination," a "faculty of memory" that is "a way of thinking through movements—at once remembered and reinvented" (Roach, *Cities of the Dead*, pp. 26–27).

176. Boyton opened The Ship, a "pretentious public house" on 21st Street that quickly went out of business ("The Ship Wrecked," *Daily Nebraska State Journal*, February 2, 1886, p. 6). For information on the founding of Sea Lion Park, see Kasson, John F. *Amusing the Million*. New York: Hill & Wang, 1978, pp. 34, 57; Dennett, *Weird Wonderful*, p. 126; and Peiss, *Cheap Amusements*, p. 127.

177. See U.S. patent no. 640,439.

178. Goffman, *Where the Action Is*, p. 146.

179. Ibid., p. 200. Also note Francesco Casetti's discussion of the cinema's ability to guarantee "a vision that is protected from risk. On the screen, the most dangerous situations can be faced, without however enduring the consequences" (Casetti, Francesco. *Eye of the Century*. New York: Columbia University Press, 2008, p. 184).

180. Peiss, *Cheap Amusements*, pp. 26–27; Dennett, *Weird Wonderful*, p. 125.

181. Peiss, *Cheap Amusements*, p. 137; Hansen, Miriam. *Babel and Babylon: Spectatorship in American Silent Film*. Cambridge, Mass.: Harvard University Press, 1991, p. 62; Streible, *Fight Pictures*, p. 49.

182. Gunning, Tom. "From the Kaleidoscope to the X-Ray," *Wide Angle* 19, no. 4 (1997), p. 32. See also Hansen's comments on how the cinema "prevailed over its live competitors by virtue of its greater profit margin," and so both "absorbed and in crucial ways surpassed the appeal of other entertainments to immigrant audiences" (Hansen, *Babel and Babylon*, p. 103).

183. Sandhu, Ranjit. "Buffalo's Forgotten Theaters," July 2002, www .buffaloah.com/h/movie/sandhu/index.html. On Mitchell Mark, see Musser, Charles. *The Emergence of Cinema*. Berkeley: University of California Press, 1990, pp. 371, 425.

2. THE ADVENTURES OF THE HUMAN FLY

1. Dardis, Tom. *Harold Lloyd: The Man on the Clock*. New York: Viking Press, 1983, pp. 117–18.

2. Ibid., p. 118.

3. Ibid., p. 128. Lloyd's films were distributed by the Pathé Film Exchange. Merrill Schleier discusses Young in her chapter on Lloyd. See Schleier, Merrill. *Skyscraper Cinema: Architecture and Gender in American Film*. Minneapolis: University of Minnesota Press, 2009.

4. "Human Fly Falls 10 Stories to Death: Harry F. Young, Scaling Martinique Hotel for a Movie Film, Misses His Grip," *New York Times*, March 6, 1923, p. 1.

5. Ibid. For a recent discussion of these events, see Schleier, *Skyscraper Cinema*, pp. 26, 31.

6. Kirshenblatt-Gimblett, Barbara. "The Future of Folklore Studies in America: The Urban Frontier," *Folklore Forum* 16, no. 2 (1983), p. 195;

Harrison-Pepper, Sally. *Drawing a Circle in the Square.* Jackson: University Press of Mississippi, 1990, p. 27. Human flies offered an individual and vertical variation on nineteenth-century American parades. See Ryan, Mary. "The American Parade: Representations of the Nineteenth-Century Social Order," in Lynn Hunt, ed., *The New Cultural History.* Berkeley: University of California Press, 1989, p. 137.

7. "Leaps Off Brooklyn Bridge," *New York Times,* April 11, 1921, p. 1.

8. Jay, Ricky. *Jay's Journal of Anomalies.* New York: Quantuck Lane Press, 2003, pp. 65–66.

9. Ibid., p. 66.

10. All cited in Turner, John Martin. *Victorian Arena—The Performers,* vol. 1, *Dictionary of British Circus Biography.* Formby, England: Lingdales Press, 1995. Accessed at the National Fairground Archive, University of Sheffield Library, July 13, 2009. Harlow refers to appearances at the Bowery amphitheater by antipodean Richard Sands in the early 1850s, as well as appearances by Professor John McCormick, "The Great Philosophical Antipodean Pedestrian from Ohio, the successful inventor of the only antipodean apparatus ever completed" (Harlow, Alvin F. *Old Bowery Days.* New York: D. Appleton and Company, 1931, p. 269).

11. "The Fly Woman Falls," *Ohio Democrat,* December 10, 1885, p. 1.

12. "Scientific Phenomena: A Startling Aeronautic Feat Explained," *Daily Northwestern,* August 2, 1890, p. 6.

13. "The Human Fly," *Milwaukee Sentinel,* June 20, 1883, p. 2; "Mlle. Aimee, The Human Fly," *New York Clipper,* December 19, 1885, p. 1. On acrobatic families in the mid-nineteenth century, see Assael, Brenda. *The Circus and Victorian Society.* Charlottesville: University of Virginia Press, 2005, pp. 108–11.

14. "A Human Fly, A Young Lady Who Walks on the Ceiling," *Daily Picayune,* November 25, 1883, p. 5. The article continued by arguing that if such an act were presented in New York, "the authorities would soon step in to prevent it." Attempts had been made to stop Mademoiselle Aimee from performing in St. Louis and Milwaukee, where "a virtual prohibition of the act was given by the authorities, but the Human Fly walked the ceiling at every performance, all the same, and thousands came to see and wonder at and applaud her" (ibid.). Also see "An Exciting Incident," *Washington Critic,* February 25, 1887, p. 4.

15. Davis, Janet M. *The Circus Age.* Chapel Hill: University of North Carolina Press, 2002, p. 91. See also Assael, *Circus and Victorian Society,* pp. 115–24.

16. Assael, *Circus and Victorian Society,* pp. 108–11.

17. "Scientific Phenomena," p. 6.

18. Jay, *Jay's Journal of Anomalies,* p. 95.

19. "Adelphi Theatre," *Times* (London), February 1, 1838, p. 3.

20. Jay, *Jay's Journal of Anomalies,* p. 97.

21. "Signor Hervio Nano," *Baltimore Sun,* March 9, 1840, p. 1. In 1840 the *Baltimore Sun* wrote that "no one can possibly complain of a want of entertainment after seeing this extraordinary man, and the thorough gratification of the audience was approved in the continuous applause and laughter during the whole performance" ("The Gnome Fly," *Baltimore Sun,* March 11, 1840, p. 2). One account described Leach's "extraordinary feats of leaping," such as

"following a horse at full speed on his hands and feet, suddenly springing on his back like a monkey, or jumping ten feet in the air. His mode of fighting, too, was most original; he used to spring in the air, and at the same time deal the most terrific blows upon his unwary antagonist's head, so that he was a very formidable combatant" ("Hervio Nano, The Man Monkey and Gnome-Fly Dissected," *New Hampshire Sentinel,* June 3, 1847, p. 1).

22. See Wheatley, Henry B. *Hogarth's London.* London: Constable and Company, 1909, p. 430.

23. Larkins claimed that the Italian performer Violante had helped to rebuild St. Martin's Church and was "quite a public celebrity in his day." After completing his work on the steeple, Violante "descended from the top head foremost on a rope stretched thence across St. Martin's Lane to the Royal Mews, the feat being witnessed by a vast concourse of people" (Larkins, William. *Steeplejacks and Steeplejacking.* London: Butler and Tanner, 1925, p. 10).

24. Strutt, Joseph. *The Sports and Pastimes of the People of England.* London: Methuen & Co., 1801, p. 181.

25. Strutt describes an exhibition of rope dancing for King Edward VI in 1564: "A rope as great as the cable of a ship stretched in length from the battlements of [St.] Paul's steeple, with a great anchor at one end, fastened a little before the dean of Paul's house-gate; and, when his majesty approached near the same, there came a man . . . lying on the rope with his head forward casting his arms and legs abroad, running on his breast on the rope from the battlements to the ground, as if it had been an arrow out of a bow, and stayed on the ground." The man then kissed the king's foot and went back on the rope to perform various feats of tumbling (ibid., pp. 179–80).

26. Benes, Peter. "Itinerant Entertainers in New England and New York, 1687–1830," in Peter Benes, ed., *The Dublin Seminar for New England Folklife: Annual Proceedings 1984, Itinerancy in New England and New York.* Concord, Mass: Boston University, 1986, pp. 118–19. New England authorities forbade such performances since "they distracted people from business, and encouraged children to imitate the feats and injure themselves" (ibid., p. 119).

27. "Steeple-Jacks," *Chamber's Journal of Popular Literature, Science and Arts* 13, no. 649 (June 6, 1896), p. 365.

28. "An Author in High Places," *Saturday Review of Politics, Literature, Science and Art* 141, no. 3668 (February 1926), p. 199.

29. Larkins, *Steeplejacks and Steeplejacking,* p. 22.

30. Ibid., p. 39.

31. Ibid., pp. 42–43.

32. Ibid., p. 101.

33. Ibid., p. 155. Larkins mentions Harry Young's death: "Young made a lot of money doing mid-air stunts for the moving pictures" (ibid., p. 156). Tensions in the English steeplejack tradition between sober work and showmanship are revealed in an 1896 article that described how steeplejacks "must not only be well skilled, but full of judgment and resource. They have, as a rule, a certain force of character which distinguishes them from other workmen; and when they are prudent they do well." Nonetheless, the article went on to describe a steeplejack living in Rochdale who "combines with his chimney-climbing the

business of music-hall proprietor, and conducts a circus of varieties in the town" ("Steeple-Jacks," p. 365).

34. Miller, Donald L. *City of the Century*. New York: Simon and Schuster, 1996, p. 302. See also Fenske, Gail, and Deryck Holdsworth. "Corporate Identity and the New York Office Building: 1895–1915," in David Ward and Olivier Zunz, eds., *The Landscape of Modernity*. New York: Russell Sage, 1992, p. 129; Jones, Robert A. "Mr. Woolworth's Tower: The Skyscraper as Popular Icon," *Journal of Popular Culture* 7, no. 2 (Fall 1973), p. 414; Domosh, Mona. "The Symbolism of the Skyscraper," *Journal of Urban History* 14, no. 3 (May 1988), p. 320; Schleier, *Skyscraper Cinema*, p. ix.

35. Willis, Carol. "Form Follows Finance: The Empire State Building," in David Ward and Olivier Zunz, eds., *The Landscape of Modernity*. New York: Russell Sage, 1992, p. 160.

36. "Times Square Steeple Jack," *New York Times* April 6, 1910, p. 7.

37. Miller, *City of the Century*, p. 308.

38. "Venturesome Climbing of the 'Human Fly,'" *World-Herald* (Omaha, Neb.), September 7, 1902, p. 13; "The Man Who Perches Aloft," *Denver Evening Post*, December 27, 1898, p. 5.

39. "Human Fly's New Job," *Allton (Ill.) Weekly Telegraph*, November 12, 1901, p. 4.

40. "Human Fly to Sue Chicago," *Montgomery Advertiser*, March 16, 1902, p. 1.

41. "Human Fly in Washington," *Pawtucket Evening Times*, November 14, 1901, p. 6.

42. "He Still Talks," *Decatur Review*, April 20, 1903, p. 4.

43. "Human Fly's New Job," p. 2.

44. "High Climb," *Denver Evening Post*, December 11, 1898, p. 6.

45. "He Still Talks," p. 4.

46. "To the Top of the Chronicle's Staff," *San Francisco Chronicle*, September 1, 1899, p. 7.

47. "Human Fly Will Do Few Stunts in This City," *Albuquerque Journal*, June 27, 1909, p. 3. Sutherland had been the chief rigger at the top of the Eiffel Tower. "Of course it took Americans to do it," he was quoted as saying. "The Frenchmen are too nervous" (ibid.).

48. "The Human Fly," *Cumberland (Md.) Evening Times*, November 11, 1905, p. 1.

49. Ibid.

50. Ibid.

51. Larkins is dismissive of female steeplejacks, whom he calls "steeplejills." He writes that "during the war, when practically every industry was invaded by women, several steeplejills attempted to do the work of steeplejacks who were away fighting. Some of them made good at it; or at least they say they did, which is not quite the same thing" (Larkins, *Steeplejacks and Steeplejacking*, p. 147). He was quick to add, however, that "any properly qualified steeplejack who knows his job has much, if anything, to fear from feminine rivalry" (ibid., p. 150).

52. Harrison-Pepper, *Drawing a Circle in the Square*, p. xiii.

53. Kimmel, Michael. *Manhood in America*. New York: Free Press, 1996, p. 103; Domosh, "Symbolism of the Skyscraper," p. 340; Blumin, Stuart M. "The Hypothesis of Middle-Class Formation in Nineteenth-Century America: A Critique and Some Proposals," *American Historical Review* 90, no. 2 (April 1985), pp. 313–16.

54. Kimmel, *Manhood in America*, p. 83.

55. Bederman, Gail. *Manliness and Civilization*. Chicago: University of Chicago Press, 1995, p. 23.

56. Kasson, John F. *Houdini, Tarzan, and the Perfect Man*. New York: Hill and Wang, 2001, p. 128.

57. Cited in Hollier, Denis. *Against Architecture*. Cambridge, Mass.: MIT Press, 1993, pp. 46–47. David Nye writes that skyscrapers "were in many ways an anti-social form" (Nye, David E. *American Technological Sublime*. Cambridge, Mass.: MIT Press, 1999, p. 97).

58. Vidler, Anthony. *The Architectural Uncanny*. Cambridge, Mass.: MIT Press, 1994, p. 70.

59. Kirshenblatt-Gimblett, "Future of Folklore Studies in America," p. 186. Kirshenblatt-Gimblett adds, "Verticality is essential to the distinctive visual character of the city, summing up as it does the corporate power that determines so much of city life" (ibid.).

60. Stewart, Susan. *On Longing*. Durham, N.C.: Duke University Press, 1993, p. 71.

61. Douglas, Mary. *Purity and Danger*. London: Routledge, 1966, p. 35.

62. "45,000 See Human Fly," *Fort Wayne News*, December 4, 1916, p. 1.

63. "Daring Feats of Gardiner Thrill Vast Crowds," *Gettysburg Times*, October 22, 1920, p. 1.

64. Goffman, Erving. *Interaction Ritual*. New York: Pantheon Books, 1967, pp. 261–62.

65. "Daring Feats of Gardiner," p. 1.

66. "Watch the Human Fly Make Trip," *Middletown Times-Press*, July 9, 1917, p. 1; "Human Fly Will Surely Win Out," *Middletown Times-Press*, July 11, 1917, p. 3.

67. Bukatman, Scott. *Matters of Gravity*. Durham, N.C.: Duke University Press, 2003, p. 188.

68. "Human Fly Climbs for K. of C.," *New York Times*, August 10, 1918, p. 7.

69. Miller, *City of the Century*, p. 303; Fenske and Holdsworth, "Corporate Identity and the New York Office Building," p. 130; Jones, "Mr. Woolworth's Tower," p. 419. See also Nye, *American Technological Sublime*, pp. 88–89; Domosh, "Symbolism of the Skyscraper," p. 327; and Girouard, Mark. *Cities and People*. New Haven, Conn.: Yale University Press, 1985, pp. 319–24.

70. In her discussion of an Australian human fly from the 1980s, Meghan Morris makes use of Michel de Certeau's distinction between strategy and tactics. Flies might be understood in terms of tactics, involving, as they do, the temporary seizing of established spatial power (Morris, Meaghan. "Great Moments in Social Climbing: King Kong and the Human Fly," in Beatriz Colomina, ed., *Sexuality and Space*. Princeton, N.J.: Princeton University Press, 1992, pp. 32–33.

71. Lears, Jackson. *Fables of Abundance: A Cultural History of Advertising in America.* New York: Basic Books, 1994, pp. 41–42.

72. Ibid., p. 203.

73. "Paul Boyton: The Record of an Amusing Trip down the Arkansas," *Daily Arkansas Gazette,* January 19, 1882, col. C.

74. "Perils of the Deep," *Godey's Lady's Book and Magazine,* December 1880, p. 584.

75. *The Globe* (Atchison, Kans.), November 8, 1881, col. D.

76. "The Human Fly Barnstorms in the Summer," *New York Times,* August 21, 1927, p. SM18.

77. "Joke Performance of the Human Fly Proves Wisdom of Barnum's Philosophy," *Chillicothe (Mo.) Constitution,* August 1, 1921, p. 1.

78. "European Buildings Lure 'Human Fly,'" *New York Times,* August 13, 1926, p. 7.

79. Bernays, Edward. *Crystallizing Public Opinion.* New York: Liveright Publishing, 1923, p. 171.

80. "Rodman Law, Cheater of Death, Never Took Chances," *Literary Digest,* November 18, 1919, p. 79.

81. Law, Rodman. "Putting the Thrills in Moving Pictures," *Photoplay Magazine,* April 1914, p. 62.

82. "Climbs 9-Story Wall," *Washington Post,* May 1, 1912, p. 14; "Rodman Law, The Human Bullet: Sky-Rocketing to the Moon Is Part of His Daily Routine," *Anaconda (Mont.) Standard,* March 8, 1914, p. 4.

83. "Father of the Newsreels," *New York Times,* June 5, 1938, p. 155.

84. "By Parachute Collar He Drops Safely from Torch of Liberty," *New York World,* February 3, 1912, p. 3.

85. Law, "Putting the Thrills in Moving Pictures," pp. 62–63.

86. Fielding, Raymond. *The American Newsreel 1911–1967.* Norman: University of Oklahoma Press, 1972, p. 44. As early as 1911 the Imp Company had released a film entitled *A Few Minutes with Steeple-Jack Lindholm,* which showed "the daredevil climber swaying in the air thirty-six stories from the pavement where a false move means death." It was referred to as "one of the most exciting pictures ever released" ("Independent Film Stories," *Moving Picture World* 10, no. 4 [October 28, 1911], p. 318).

87. Smith, Albert E., and Phil A. Koury. *Two Reels and a Camera.* Garden City, N.Y.: Doubleday, 1952, pp. 222–23. For more on Coffyn, see chapter 4.

88. For more on media publics and temporalities of circulation, see Warner, Michael. *Publics and Counterpublics.* New York: Zone Books, 2002, p. 96.

89. "Climbs 9-Story Wall," p. 14.

90. "Law Jumps Off Bridge," *New York Tribune,* July 26, 1912, p. 16.

91. "Law Hurt Flying for Films," *New York Times,* October 19, 1913, p. 5. See also Law, "Putting the Thrills in Moving Pictures," p. 65.

92. Law, "Putting the Thrills in Moving Pictures," pp. 61–64.

93. "Human Fly Is Badly Burned," *Boston Daily Globe,* March 14, 1913, p. 8.

94. "Movies Responsible for New Brand, the Unkillable Actor," *Duluth News Tribune,* August 9, 1914, p. 6.

95. "Thrilling Photo-Play at Empress Really Worth While," *Fort Wayne Journal-Gazette,* May 6, 1914, p. 9.

96. "Fighting Death, Princess Offering," *Waterloo Times-Tribune,* May 24, 1914, p. 12; "Fighting Death," *Moving Picture World* 20, no. 1 (April 14, 1914), p. 78.

97. *Motion Picture News* 9, no. 15 (April 18, 1914), p. 15.

98. "Jumps from Highbridge: Moving Picture Performer Comes Up Smiling after Leap," *New York Times,* April 7, 1914, p. 1.

99. "Rodman Law, The Human Bullet," p. 4.

100. "Human Fly Kept Busy to Tell of Paramount Week," *Moving Picture World,* September 25, 1920, p. 490.

101. Advertisement in *Daily Northwestern,* September 27, 1928, p. 6.

102. "Did You See the Human Fly?" *Fort Wayne News and Sentinel,* April 23, 1918, p. 4.

103. Bean, Jennifer M. "Technologies of Early Stardom and the Extraordinary Body," *Camera Obscura* 48, vol. 16, no. 3, p. 12.

104. See Keil, Charlie. "To Here from Modernity," in Charlie Keil and Shelley Stamp, eds., *American Cinema's Transitional Era.* Berkeley: University of California Press, 2004, p. 52.

105. See Bowser, Eileen. *The Transformation of Cinema, 1907–1915.* New York: Scribner's Sons, 1990, pp. 106–13. See also Balio, Tino, ed. *The American Film Industry.* Madison: University of Wisconsin Press, 1985, pp. 113–15; Jacobs, Lewis. *The Rise of the American Film.* New York: Teachers College Press, 1939, pp. 86–89; Maland, Charles J. *Chaplin and American Culture.* Princeton, N.J.: Princeton University Press, 1989, pp. 68, 81; Bordwell, David, Janet Staiger, and Kristin Thompson. *The Classical Hollywood Cinema.* New York: Columbia University Press, 1985, p. 99.

106. Maland, *Chaplin and American Culture,* pp. 37–38; DeBauche, Leslie Midkiff. *Reel Patriotism.* Madison: University of Wisconsin Press, 1997, pp. 118–19.

107. "Nation Gives $144,000,000 to Red Cross," *New York Tribune,* May 28, 1918, p. 1. See also "Human Fly to Perform," *New York Tribune,* November 5, 1918, p. 5; "K. of C. Opens Drive Today to Swell War Fund," *New York Tribune,* August 5, 1918, p. 6; "Brooklyn, Yonkers and Newark Hold Big Liberty Loan Celebrations," *New York Tribune,* April 27, 1918, p. 7.

108. Nielsen, Mike, and Gene Mailes. *Hollywood's Other Blacklist.* London: BFI, 1995, p. 2. Murray Ross describes Los Angeles as "the citadel of the open shop in America" (Ross, Murray. *Stars and Strikes.* New York: Columbia University Press, 1941, pp. 5–6).

109. Nielsen and Mailes, *Hollywood's Other Blacklist,* p. 6.

110. Ibid., pp. 3–7. Shelley Stamp writes that "in an effort to streamline production methods and lower costs several production companies were decreasing their stock companies in the mid-1910s and relying with greater frequency on extras . . . who could be paid by the day rather than receiving a fixed salary" (Stamp, Shelley. "It's a Long Way to Filmland: Starlets, Screen Hopefuls, and Extras in Early Hollywood," in Charlie Keil and Shelley Stamp, eds., *American Cinema's Transitional Era.* Berkeley: University of California Press, 2004, p. 333).

111. Quoted in the commercial videotape *Catch a Falling Star: Hollywood's Greatest Stunts*, GRB Entertainment, 1996.

112. Brownlow, Kevin. *The Parade's Gone By*. London: Secker and Warburg, 1968, p. 27. Baxter asserts that "while the extra had been paid a standard fee of five or seven dollars a day, the stunt performer was paid 'by the gag'" (Baxter, John. *Stunt*. Garden City, N.Y.: Doubleday, 1974, p. 83).

113. Bennett, F. B. "Those Who Do the 'Stunts' in the Movies," *New York Tribune*, December 31, 1916, p. D7.

114. Canutt, Yakima. *Stunt Man*. Norman: University of Oklahoma Press, 1979, p. 91.

115. Sullivan, George, and Tim Sullivan. *Stunt People*. New York: Beaufort, 1983, p. 15.

116. Baxter, *Stunt*, p. 16.

117. French, William Fleming. "Double's Troubles," *Saturday Evening Post*, July 25, 1936, p. 16.

118. The article continued, "The public is supposed to believe that the Errol Flynns, Robert Taylors, George Rafts . . . of the screen really face death without batting an eyelash. And stunt men don't care who gets the glory so long as they get the checks" (Wilson, Elizabeth. "Hollywood Hardpans," *Liberty*, October 20, 1945, p. 31).

119. Sullivan and Sullivan, *Stunt People*, p. 16.

120. Grace, Dick. *Squadron of Death*. London: Constable, 1930, p. 188. Grace went on to say that some stars did "their stuff": "Tom Mix does and always has done most of his work. So also does Hoot Gibson, who is one of the best horsemen in the world. Ken Maynard and Buck Jones all do their own risks with horses. Buddy Rogers and Dick Arlen both flew many hours with a pilot in *Wings*. But the majority do not take their own risks nor do they pretend to" (ibid., p. 189).

121. Baxter, *Stunt*, p. 42.

122. French, "Double's Troubles," p. 16.

123. DeCordova, Richard. *Picture Personalities*. Urbana: University of Illinois Press, 2001, p. 82.

124. Ibid., p. 85.

125. Baxter, *Stunt*, pp. 50–52.

126. Grace, *Squadron of Death*, p. 163.

127. Fairbanks was doubled by Richard Talmadge, who later starred in action serials of his own and was trained as a circus acrobat. Harold Lloyd and Pearl White did many of their own stunts but were doubled by stuntmen in others. Likewise, serial queen Ruth Roland was doubled by Bob Rose. See Sullivan and Sullivan, *Stunt People*, p. 37.

128. Parry's claims about doubling for Lloyd can be found in the Harvey Parry papers at the Margaret Herrick Library. In one document Parry's stunt-work for Lloyd is referred to as "one of Hollywood's most closely guarded secrets." Parry also claims to have doubled for Lloyd in the skyscraper film *High and Dizzy* (1920) (Harvey Parry papers, box 1, folder 1, Biographical data—1950–1985). See also Parry's comments in the videotape *Catch a Falling Star*.

129. Bean, "Technologies of Early Stardom and the Extraordinary Body," p. 20.

130. Bean also describes a "remarkably skeptical stance toward visual faculties as a means of establishing believability" and a tendency in the press to emphasize documentary proof, such as recourse to witnesses to back up truth claims about stars doing their own stunts. One pragmatic reason for that would have been to address the public's quite reasonable doubts, given the circulation of knowledge about stunt doubles and other stunt performers who were media celebrities in their own right (see ibid., p. 24).

131. *Sheboygan Press-Telegram*, August 8, 1924, p. 10; *Oakland Tribune*, August 5, 1924, p. A; *Hamilton Evening Journal*, October 23, 1924, p. 11.

132. "She's Steeple-Jill," *Los Angeles Times*, April 6, 1924, p. B20.

133. Singer, Ben. *Melodrama and Modernity*. New York: Columbia University Press, 2001, p. 226.

134. Merrill Schleier reads the narrative of *Safety Last* in terms of gender, concluding that the steeplejack character provides Harold "with requisite manhood to escape from the clutches of feminine acquisitiveness and emotionalism, Semitic greed, and primitive superstition, to a redeemed masculinity that is both cerebral and physical" (Schleier, *Skyscraper Cinema*, p. 24).

135. See, for example, *Wisconsin Rapids Daily Tribune*, February 12, 1925, p. 3.

136. Davis, *Circus Age*, pp. 108–9.

137. Assael, *Circus and Victorian Society*, pp. 115, 126.

138. Some publicity for the film sought to define her climb in terms of healthy physical culture: "Miss Devore says her athletic work in 'Hold Your Breath' has put her in the pink of condition. She is a great advocate of physical training for women and children" ("Her Daily Dozen," *Los Angeles Times*, April 27, 1924, p. 34). We might compare such publicity to Rob King's work on the use of athletic imagery and a rhetoric of physical culture to legitimize titillating images of women in the Keystone Film Company's "Bathing Beauties" films (King, Rob. *The Fun Factory*. Berkeley: University of California Press, 2009, pp. 231–32).

139. Baxter, *Stunt*, pp. 40–41.

140. Issues of stunt work and cinematic continuity might also have played a part in the trope of cross-dressing in serial-queen dramas. See Singer, *Melodrama and Modernity*, pp. 231–32.

141. "City Forbids 'Human Flies' to Climb Skyscraper Walls," *New York Times*, April 11, 1923, p. 1.

142. "Human Fly Thwarted," *New York Times*, January 8, 1927, p. 15.

143. Although human flies persisted through the 1920s and '30s, and they seem to have had something of a nostalgic resurgence in the 1950s, my examination of the popular press shows a sharp decline in their number after the mid-1920s. Public opinion in some cases turned against it, as can be seen in the response to Harry Young's death. In addition to legislation, another explanation for this decline is that the performance lost its edge. Indeed, one finds flies expanding their repertoire in the later 1920s to include airplane stunts and feats on top of the buildings that they climbed, such as riding a bicycle or feats of balancing. I will return to this issue in chapter 4.

144. Luke McKernan writes that newsreels "thrived on predictability, which a regular and popular sporting calendar naturally provided." Newsreels also "thrived on personality," which sports stars could also provide (McKernan, Luke. "Sport and the Silent Cinema," *Griffithiana* 21, no. 64 (October 1998), p. 117). Warren Susman refers to the 1920s as the "Golden Age of American Sports" and accounts for the enormous appeal of spectator sports in terms of "the mechanization of life," which produced "a particular middle-class delight in what could be measured and counted. . . . Americans could delight in the data that [Babe] Ruth and other players provided" (Susman, Warren I. *Culture as History*. Washington, D.C.: Smithsonian Institution Press, 2003 [1973], p. 141).

145. Although he got his start as a stage magician and was later known as "the handcuff king," some of Harry Houdini's best-known performances overlap with the ones I have described in this and the previous chapter, for example, his bridge jumps and aerial straitjacket escapes (see Kasson, *Houdini, Tarzan, and the Perfect Man*, pp. 127, 136).

3. THE ADVENTURES OF THE LION TAMER

1. Rothfels, Nigel. *Savages and Beasts*. Baltimore, Md.: Johns Hopkins University Press, 2002, p. 6.

2. Schallert, Edwin. "Animal Trend Sweeps Films," *Los Angeles Times*, November 30, 1932, p. 7.

3. Baratay, Eric, and Elisabeth Hardouin-Fugier. *Zoo: A History of Zoological Gardens in the West*. London: Reaktion, 2002, p. 170. As a point of comparison, see Altick's discussion of the arrival of a rhinoceros in London in 1684 (Altick, Richard D. *The Shows of London*. Cambridge, Mass.: Belknap Press, 1978, p. 37); Rothfels's discussion of a rhinoceros named Clara in Europe during the 1740s and 1750s (Rothfels, *Savages and Beasts*, p. 14); and Benes's work on early New England itinerant performance (Benes, Peter. "Itinerant Entertainers in New England and New York, 1687–1830," in Peter Benes, ed., *The Dublin Seminar for New England Folklife: Annual Proceedings 1984, Itinerancy in New England and New York*. Concord, Mass.: Boston University, 1986).

4. The animals found in such menageries were often made to fight, presenting "spectacular eruptions of violence" that sometimes involved pitting domestic animals against exotic ones. See Baratay and Hardouin-Fugier, *Zoo*, p. 25. Also note that "the first lions and tigers imported into England were used for no other purpose than fighting with bulldogs" (Hallock, E.S. "The American Circus," *Century Illustrated Magazine* 70, no. 4 [August 1905], p. 570).

5. Baratay and Hardouin-Fugier, *Zoo*, p. 73.

6. Ritvo, Harriet. *The Animal Estate*. Cambridge, Mass.: Harvard University Press, 1987, p. 214.

7. Baratay and Hardouin-Fugier, *Zoo*, p. 92.

8. Hagenbeck, Carl. *Beasts and Men*. New York: Longmans, Green, and Co., 1909, p. 11.

9. Ibid., p. 11.

10. Benes, "Itinerant Entertainers in New England," p. 114.

11. Culhane, John. *The American Circus*. New York: Henry Holt and Co., 1990, p. 17. See also Bostock, E.H. *Menageries, Circuses, and Theatres*. London: Chapman and Hall, 1927; Hallock, "American Circus," p. 571; Toulmin, Vanessa. *Electric Edwardians*. London: BFI, 2006, p. 108; Flint, Richard W. "Entrepreneurial and Cultural Aspects of the Early-Nineteenth-Century Circus and Menagerie Business," in Peter Benes, ed., *The Dublin Seminar for New England Folklife: Annual Proceedings 1984, Itinerancy in New England and New York*. Concord, Mass.: Boston University, 1986, p. 132.

12. Adams-Volpe, Judith A. "Circus and Wild West Exhibition," in M. Thomas Inge and Dennis Hall, eds., *The Greenwood Guide to American Popular Culture, Volume 1*. Westport, Conn.: Greenwood Press, 2002, p. 246.

13. Flint, "Entrepreneurial and Cultural Aspects," p. 137.

14. Thayer describes several menagerie performers who entered the cage before Van Amburgh, including Henri Martin in Germany in 1819 and early American performers such as Charles Wright, Solomon Bailey, and John Sears (Thayer, Stuart. "The Keeper Will Enter the Cage: Early American Wild Animal Trainers," *Bandwagon* 26 [November–December 1982], pp. 38–39). Frank Bostock stated that the origins of the British lion tamer act could be found in circus manager George Wombwell's traveling show established in 1805. Wombwell had hired a man to care for and feed some of his expensive African lions. When it became clear that the worker had "developed a strong affection" for the lions, Wombwell realized that "not only would the exhibition of two lions and a man in the same cage be a distinct novelty, but it would be a splendid financial speculation." When he announced that he would exhibit a "lion-tamer," thousands are said to have come "from near and far to witness this wonderful sight" (Bostock, Frank C. *The Training of Wild Animals*. New York: The Century Co., 1903, pp. 28–29).

15. "Van Amburgh, the Lion Tamer," *London Weekly Chronicle*, August 23, 1838, p. 8. Another account claims that Van Amburgh was born in Kentucky, the grandson of a Tuscarora Indian ("Van Amburgh," *Monthly Chronicle of North-Country Lore and Legend* 1, no. 6 [August 1887], p. 246). Flint describes how the joint stock company the Zoological Institute represented the merger of "nine of the menagerie companies in the United States." Lewis Titus, who is cited as being a partner to Van Amburgh on his English tours, was one of the directors of the association (Flint, "Entrepreneurial and Cultural Aspects," p. 141). Thayer claims that Van Amburgh debuted in the winter of 1833–34 and was on the road with June, Titus, and Angevine until 1838, adding that his first advertised appearance was on the stage of the Bowery Theatre in New York in 1834 in a play entitled *The Lion Lord* (Thayer, "Keeper Will Enter the Cage," pp. 39–40).

16. "Van Amburg [sic], the Lion Tamer," *Defiance Democrat*, June 24, 1847, p. 1.

17. Jacob Driesbach was another early American lion tamer. Driesbach was born in Sharon, New York, in 1807, and in the early 1830s he worked winters at the New York Zoological Gardens. By one account his career as a trainer began when he crept into a tiger's cage that he had typically cleaned from the outside ("Talk with a Lion Tamer: Herr Driesbach at Home—His Remarkable

Life," *Daily Evening Bulletin* (San Francisco, Calif.), November 1, 1872, col. D). Driesbach's act is described in the *Daily Atlas* (Boston, Mass.), June 30, 1843, col. F.

18. Frost, Thomas. *Circus Life and Circus Celebrities*. London: Tinsley Brothers, reprinted in "Circus Life," *Chamber's Journal of Popular Literature, Science and Arts* 595 (May 22, 1875), p. 336.

19. Some evidence refers to Van Amburgh's brutal methods, in particular his use of a crowbar to strike the animals (Thayer, "Keeper Will Enter the Cage," p. 40).

20. Bouissac, Paul. *Circus and Culture*. Bloomington: Indiana University Press, 1976, p. 115.

21. Ibid., p. 118.

22. Ibid., p. 115.

23. Ibid., p. 121.

24. To get a sense of how the act could blur ontological categories in a manner typical of the circus, consider an 1894 article that described how lion tamers, or "cat men," grew to resemble their animals: "It is a peculiar fact that animal trainers and men associated with wild beasts in captivity gradually grow by force of their association to resemble their savage pupils in bodily and facial characteristics. . . . Prof. Darling, who is perhaps the most daring lion trainer in the world, and a man who knows as much about lions as any one, has a distinctly leonine aspect. His beard and hair are tawny, his nose is firm, his eyes fixed somewhat and stern, with a way of looking at you much like his well-trained beasts from the savage jungle. When he walks it is with a slow, cat-like tread, strangely suggestive of the lion's gait" ("Wild Beasts and Their Trainers," *Chicago Daily Tribune*, January 28, 1894, p. 27). I return to this trope in my discussion of early pilots as "birdmen" in the next chapter.

25. Nathaniel Hawthorne saw Isaac Van Amburgh perform in September 1838 and described "the spectators looking on, so attentively that a breath could not be heard. That was impressive—its effect on a thousand people, more than the thing itself" (in Lewis, Robert M., ed. *From Traveling Show to Vaudeville*. Baltimore, Md.: Johns Hopkins University Press, 2007, p. 119).

26. Ferguson, O. J. *A Brief Biographical Sketch of I.A. Van Amburgh*. New York: Samuel Booth, 1860, p. 11.

27. Ibid., p. 10.

28. Isaiah 11:6–7.

29. Thomas, Keith. *Man and the Natural World*. London: Penguin Books, 1983, pp. 17–18.

30. Genesis 9:2–3. For further discussion, see White, Lynn, Jr. "The Historical Roots of Our Ecological Crisis," in Cheryll Glotfelty and Harold Fromm, eds., *The Ecocriticism Reader*. Athens: University of Georgia Press, 1996; and Northcott, Michael S. *The Environment and Christian Ethics*. Cambridge: Cambridge University Press, 1996.

31. "The Life of Van Amburgh, the Brute-Tamer," *Examiner* 1613 (December 30, 1838), p. 820. The idea that the act was a display of human dominance was still being put forward in 1890: "The tamer's performance is certainly one of those exhibitions which give the most valuable evidence of the superiority of

man over animals. Some morose spirits have put forth the lion's claims to royalty in rivalry to the supremacy of Adam. In the menagerie the two candidates meet each other. The lion has formidable jaws and claws; the man has only a pair of boots and a whip. Yet it is the lion that obeys! The great feline's spring through a paper hoop settles the disputed question in favour of humanity. One leaves the theatre with uplifted head and heart swollen with pride" (Le Roux, Hugues, and Jules Garnier. *Acrobats and Moutebanks*. London: Chapman and Hall, 1890, pp. 133–34).

32. Ferguson, *A Brief Biographical Sketch of I.A. Van Amburgh*, p. 12.

33. "Van Amburgh's New Lion," *Newark (Ohio) Advocate*, June 15, 1839, col. F.

34. Culhane, *American Circus*, p. 17. See also Lewis, *From Traveling Show to Vaudeville*, pp. 109–10; Flint, "Entrepreneurial and Cultural Aspects," p. 145; Benes, "Itinerary Entertainers in New England," p. 113. Lewis writes that, throughout the nineteenth century, "evangelical Christians condemned the circus as an insidious and pernicious amusement that sapped the virtue of the republic's citizens. Insidious, because what appeared to be merely a novel display of skill enticed, excited, and deluded the innocent; pernicious, because it ensnared the young, the most vulnerable, into a thoughtless love of pleasure that led to vice" (Lewis, *From Traveling Show to Vaudeville*, p. 110). Richard Altick refers to a "perennial conflict between the claims of amusement and those of earnest instruction" in nineteenth-century popular entertainments (Altick, *Shows of London*, p. 3). This argument can be overstated, and Brenda Assael argues that circuses were sometimes praised for providing a cheap, sober entertainment option for working-class audiences (Assael, Brenda. *The Circus and Victorian Society*. Charlottesville: University of Virginia Press, 2005, p. 39).

35. Hallock, "American Circus," p. 573.

36. Ibid., p. 575.

37. Ferguson, *Brief Biographical Sketch of I.A. Van Amburgh*, pp. v–vi.

38. "If You Meet a Lion Just Hold a Chair in Front of Him," *Washington Post*, March 8, 1908, SM4.

39. Kasson, John F. *Houdini, Tarzan, and the Perfect Man*. New York: Hill and Wang, 2001, pp. 68, 75.

40. "Three Months With a 'Lion King,'" *Gentleman's Magazine* 10 (March 1873), p. 255.

41. "Van Amburg *[sic]*, the Lion Tamer," p. 1. In 1854 one newspaper wrote that as "noble and majestic" as the lions in his menagerie were, Van Amburgh himself was "the greatest *lion* amongst them. And although he is said to be the kindest hearted man in the world, one feels an involuntary fear in his presence, lest he should shake his mane and devour us incontinently" ("An Hour with Van Amburgh," *Daily Picayune* [New Orleans, La.], January 17, 1854, p. 1).

42. Ferguson, *Brief Biographical Sketch of I.A. Van Amburgh*, p. 12.

43. "Court and Fashionable Intelligence," *Observer*, January 27, 1839, p. 3; "Dramatic Intelligence," *Observer*, January 27, 1839, p. 2.

44. "Dramatic Intelligence," p. 2.

45. Manson, James A. *Sir Edwin Landseer*. New York: Charles Scribner's Sons, 1902, pp. 135–36. For an interesting discussion of Landseer, see

Mackenzie, John M. *The Empire of Nature*. Manchester: Manchester University Press, 1988, pp. 31–34.

46. Culhane, *American Circus*, p. 39.

47. A French lion tamer named Signor Bidel was enacting the "lamb lying down with the lion" bit in the 1870s, albeit with mixed results. In 1873 the *New York Times* described how Bidel entered a large cage containing "lionesses, bears, hyenas, and a lamb." After Bidel led the animals through various feats, the "grand feature" of his act involved the "kiss of fraternity," in which the animals methodically touched noses. To close the performance, Bidel put the lamb's head into the mouth of a lion. The *Times* described how that part of the act unfolded on this particular occasion: "No sooner had the jaws closed upon the head of the animal than it was evident by the eyes and movement of the tail of the lion that foul play was threatened, and before a word of command could be given streams of blood were running from his mouth. Children screamed and women fainted, but fortunately the panic was of short duration. Signor Bidel, with a tremendous blow on the throat of the lion and a shout of command, forced the half-wild animal to relinquish his victim." Things went from bad to worse for Bidel, for, in dealing with the lion, he had turned his back on a lioness who leaped on his back "with a howl of rage." He managed to struggle his way to safety, and when he regained his composure he was greeted by "deafening" cheers ("Terrible Scene in a Menagerie," *New York Times*, January 13, 1873, p. 8). Three years later more trouble arose for the unfortunate Bidel when he placed a sheep on the back of a lioness: "No sooner had he done this than a powerful lion sprang upon the poor sheep and buried his teeth deep into a vital part of its body. There was a large number of spectators present, and, as may be imagined, the sudden act of the lion created an instant and general panic" ("A Terrible Encounter with Wild Beasts," *New York Times*, January 26, 1876, p. 3).

48. "In the Lion's Mouth," *Washington Post*, June 3, 1894, p. 19.

49. Thayer attributes the initial emergence of lion tamers in the 1830s to an earlier revolution in cage technology: "Early cages were what are now called 'shifting dens,' boxes with bars on one side, not much bigger than the animal and wholly unsuited for anything but display. . . . [Between 1831 and 1835] the American menagerie became entirely mobile and the wheeled cages became of a size to admit both an animal and a keeper" (Thayer, "Keeper Will Enter the Cage," p. 38).

50. "In the Lion's Mouth," p. 19.

51. Lewis, *From Traveling Show to Vaudeville*, p. 129; Adams-Volpe, "Circus and Wild West Exhibition," p. 247; Coup, W.C. *Sawdust and Spangles*. Chicago: Herbert S. Stone and Company, 1901, pp. xii–xiii.

52. Assael, *Circus and Victorian Society*, p. 5.

53. Culhane, *American Circus*, p. 167. George Conklin, a lion tamer with the Barnum and Bailey Circus in the early 1890s, provides a vivid description of a big cage act in his 1921 memoirs. Conklin writes that "the big performing cage" was pushed into the ring by an elephant while the ringmaster announced the next attraction. The leopard would put her front paws on one of the bars of the cage and, as Conklin held up her hind legs, the lions jumped back and forth over her. The leopard would then lie down with a lion on either side of her, and

Conklin would lie across the three. Conklin then led the lions in a waltz around the cage, after which he put one end of a long piece of meat in his mouth, the other end in a lion's mouth, and the two played a game of tug of war (Conklin, George. *The Ways of the Circus*. New York: Harper and Bros., 1921, pp. 37–38). Conklin's act provides an illustration of how the pleasures of some animal acts had to do with blurring ontological categories: animals act like people; animals act like furniture; people act like animals.

54. Bonavita told the press that he had begun his career in show business as an acrobat, but when he became "too large and heavy" he began to train pumas in a traveling show (Bonavita, Captain Jack. "How I Became a Wild-Animal Trainer," *The Delineator* 74 [September 1909], p. 254).

55. Bostock, *Training of Wild Animals*, pp. 217–18.

56. "Bostock's Animal Show" [advertisement], *Buffalo Courier*, May 19, 1901, p. 19.

57. In one advertisement Bostock's Great Animal Arena at the 1901 exposition was billed as "an Educational Institution of the Highest Order" ("Bostock's Animal Show," p. 19).

58. "Hagenbeck's Zoological Arena," *Chicago Daily Tribune*, March 4, 1893, p. 9.

59. Thomas, *Man and the Natural World*, p. 33.

60. Turner, James. *Reckoning with the Beast*. Baltimore, Md.: Johns Hopkins University Press, 1980, p. 19. Other factors that might have shaped the changing perception of the natural world are the closing of the American frontier and the influence of transcendentalist writers such as Henry David Thoreau.

61. Ibid., pp. 61–64. For Assael, circus animal acts offered enactments of new scientific theories at a time when evolutionary biology was transforming the way people saw themselves in relation to the natural world (Assael, *Circus and Victorian Society*, p. 64). For a discussion of Thomas's argument, see Mackenzie, *Empire of Nature*, pp. 26–27, 99.

62. Ritvo, *Animal Estate*, p. 3.

63. Coleman, Sydney H. *Humane Society Leaders in America*. Albany: The American Humane Association, 1924, p. 28. Coleman's history provides evidence of the extent to which class shaped the early history of the Humane Society.

64. Ibid., p. 31.

65. Ibid., pp. 39–40.

66. The "cruelty of overloading and using unfit animals on omnibuses and street railways was so glaring an evil," wrote Coleman, "that Mr. Bergh opened a fight against it during the first year of the society" (ibid., p. 44).

67. Couvares, Francis G. *The Remaking of Pittsburgh*. Albany: State University of New York Press, 1984, pp. 40–41. Also see Wilentz, Sean. *Chants Democratic*. Oxford: Oxford University Press, 2004 (1984), p. 53.

68. Harlow, Alvin F. *Old Bowery Days*. New York: D. Appleton and Company, 1931, p. 269.

69. Coleman, *Humane Society Leaders in America*, p. 48. Elliott Gorn provides an explanation for the appeal of such violent entertainments for the urban working class, whose daily existence "encouraged callousness as one response to pain": "The working classes of nineteenth-century American cities lived in

a world filled with potential for disaster. A fighting cock's valor in the face of death, a bulldog's relentless charge into a bear's grasp, or a prizefighter's capacity to give and take punishment served them as models of how to confront a cruel life with honor. Men gloried in bloody displays because high death rates, horrible accidents, and the specter of brutish poverty were a burden that bravado helped lighten" (Gorn, Elliott J. "Good-Bye Boys, I Die a True American: Homicide, Nativism, and Working-class Culture in Antebellum New York City," *Journal of American History* 74, no. 2 [September 1987], p. 409).

70. Turner, *Reckoning with the Beast,* p. 23.

71. Kete, Kathleen, "Animals and Ideology: The Politics of Animal Protection in Europe," in Nigel Rothfels, ed., *Representing Animals.* Bloomington: Indiana University Press, 2002, p. 26. As early as 1801 Joseph Strutt could write in his history of English sports and pastimes that bull- and bearbaiting were not encouraged by "persons of rank and opulence" and were "attended only by the lowest and most despicable part of the people" (Strutt, Joseph. *The Sports and Pastimes of the People of England.* London: Methuen & Co., 1801, p. 205). Strutt wrote that the fact that people of "rank and opulence" no longer attended bull and bear baiting indicated "a general refinement of manners and prevalency of humanity among the moderns; on the contrary, this barbarous pastime was highly relished by the nobility in former ages, and countenanced by persons of the most exalted rank, without exception even of the fair sex" (ibid.).

72. Ritvo, *Animal Estate,* p. 137.

73. For more on Hagenbeck's training methods, see Rothfels, *Savages and Beasts,* p. 149.

74. Hagenbeck, *Beasts and Men,* p. 118.

75. Ibid., p. 31.

76. Hinsley, Curtis M. "The World as Marketplace," in Ivan Karp and Steven D. Lavine, *Exhibiting Cultures.* Washington, D.C.: Smithsonian Institution Press, 1991, p. 345.

77. See Culhane, *American Circus,* p. 208.

78. "Playing with Lions," *Los Angeles Times,* August 15, 1900, p. I11; "The Light That Failed," *Los Angeles Times,* May 11, 1901, p. 12.

79. "She Controls Lions by Kindness," *Chicago Daily Tribune,* November 3, 1901, p. 48.

80. "Girl Lion Tamer Astounds Europe," *Chicago Daily Tribune,* January 24, 1904, p. A1.

81. Carr, Harry. "Polar Bear Rips His Shirt Off," *Los Angeles Times,* June 22, 1911, p. III4.

82. "Claire Heliot—Most Daring of Lion Tamers," *New York Times,* October 29, 1905, p. SM1.

83. Her trust in the lions was also connected to a Hagenbeck-esque belief in man's stewardship of the natural world. She told the *Times* that "a Divine order of things has given his soul into the keeping of man. Only when man abuses his trust does the wild beast show his strength and kill" (ibid., p. SM1).

84. "Why It Is Harder to Tame a Husband Than a Lion," *Chicago Daily Tribune,* April 1, 1906, p. F4. The article also suggested that female animal trainers were glamorous figures that could serve as intriguing exceptions to traditional

female roles. "Suppose I should marry?" Heliot asked the reporter. "I would not want to work for a husband. Then I should have to give up my lions" (ibid.).

85. Ritvo, Harriet. "The Emergence of Modern Pet-Keeping," in Andrew N. Rowan, ed., *Animals and People Sharing the World*. Hanover, N.H.: University Press of New England, 1988, p. 20. Erica Fudge argues that anxieties about modernity were "offset by the bourgeois ownership of animals, creatures who came to represent everything that had been lost—cleanliness, order and rationality" (Fudge, Erica, "A Left-Handed Blow: Writing the History of Animals," in Nigel Rothfels, ed., *Representing Animals*. Bloomington: Indiana University Press, 2002, p. 10).

86. "Claire Heliot—Most Daring of Lion Tamers," p. SM1.

87. Turner, John Martin. *Victorian Arena—The Performers*, vol. 1, *Dictionary of British Circus Biography*. Formby, England: Lingdales Press, 1995. Accessed at the National Fairground Archive, University of Sheffield Library, July 13, 2009.

88. "Girl Lion Tamer Astounds Europe," p. A1.

89. "Women 'Dare Devils,'" *Washington Post*, July 21, 1907, p. MS3.

90. Ibid.

91. "Playing with Lions," p. I11. On scarred bodies in the cinema, see Lehman, Peter. *Running Scared*. Philadelphia, Penn.: Temple University Press, 1993, pp. 61–63.

92. Singer, Ben. *Melodrama and Modernity*. New York: Columbia University Press, 2001, pp. 240–41, 253.

93. Bean, Jennifer M. "Technologies of Early Stardom and the Extraordinary Body," *Camera Obscura* 16, no. 3 (2001), p. 28.

94. The *Chicago Tribune* reported on June 11, 1894, that Mlle. Beatrice, a lion tamer who was performing at Coney Island, had "a narrow escape from being killed" by a lion. Beatrice, dressed "in her gorgeous orange silk costume," had been "in the habit of concluding her performance by opening the mouth of Brutus and kissing him." On this occasion Brutus "sprang upon her" and "the infuriated beast fastened his teeth in her face" ("In the Lion's Mouth," *Chicago Daily Tribune*, June 11, 1894, p. 5). Years later, in 1902, the *Los Angeles Times* reported, "Mme. Schell, the lion tamer at the Los Angeles Chutes, was dragged out of the cage, torn and bleeding," her "dainty gown" stained with blood ("Lioness Sprang on Her Trainer," *Los Angeles Times*, February 9, 1902, p. B1).

95. The rejection of a "softer" approach to the treatment of animals could become a badge of manliness at this time. At an 1895 address to the Harvard graduating class, Oliver Wendell Holmes Jr. warned young men about the "temptations of wallowing ease," whose key symptom of "softness" was any "revolt against pain," which might take the form of socialism, sentimental literature, or societies for the prevention of cruelty to animals. See Lears, T. J. Jackson. *Rebirth of a Nation*. New York: Harper Perennial, 2009, p. 31.

96. In 1838 an English sporting magazine wrote that crowds were flocking to see Van Amburgh as a "prodigy of manly strength and courage" ("Van Amburgh the Lion-Tamer," *New Sporting Magazine* 15, no. 90 [October 1838], p. 245).

97. Ritvo, *Animal Estate*, pp. 207–8, 231.

98. Baratay and Hardouin-Fugier, *Zoo*, p. 151.

99. Assael, *Circus and Victorian Society*, p. 75.

100. Streeby, Shelley. *American Sensations*. Berkeley: University of California Press, 2002, p. 5. Thrill makers should be included in Streeby's larger "culture of sensation," which included popular literature, journalism, blackface minstrelsy, popular theater and humor, and sensational melodrama (ibid., p. 27).

101. May, Robert E. "Young Males and Filibustering in the Age of Manifest Destiny," *Journal of American History* 78, no. 3 (December 1991), p. 857.

102. Ibid., p. 863.

103. See "A Jump for Fame," *Chester (Pa.) Evening Times*, July 24, 1886, p. 1; Stephens, R.N. *The Life and Adventures of Steve Brodie*. New York: Thomas H. Davis, 1894, p. 18; and "Peaceful Filibusters," *New York Times*, March 12, 1886, p. 2.

104. See "The Return of Captain Boyton," *Washington Post*, May 6, 1881, p. 4; "Paul Boyton in Peru," *New York Times*, April 14, 1881, p. 5; "Aquatic Stunt Showman Dies," *Los Angeles Times*, April 26, 1924, p. 12.

105. Bederman, Gail. *Manliness and Civilization*. Chicago: University of Chicago Press, 1995, p. 41.

106. Ibid., p. 23. See also Rotundo, E. Anthony. *American Manhood*. New York: Basic Books, 1993, p. 248.

107. Ritvo writes that the big game hunter's spoils "powerfully evoked the conquest and domination of exotic territories." In fact, "the connection between triumphing over a dangerous animal and subduing unwilling natives was direct and obvious, and the association of the big game hunter with the march of empire was literal as well as metonymic" (Ritvo, *Animal Estate*, p. 254). For John Mackenzie, "the colonial frontier was also a hunting frontier and the animal resource contributed to the expansionist urge," such that hunting was frequently "a ritualized and occasionally spectacular display of white dominance" (Mackenzie, *Empire of Nature*, p. 7).

108. Bederman, *Manliness and Civilization*, p. 212.

109. Roosevelt, Theodore. *The Works of Theodore Roosevelt*, vol. 24, *African Game Trails*. New York: Charles Scribner's Sons, 1926, pp. 432–36.

110. Hagenbeck, *Beasts and Men*, pp. 52–53.

111. MacAdam, George. "Circus Days at the Garden Are Passing," *New York Times*, April 5, 1925, p. SM12. A common trope from blackface humor of this era was that blacks were deathly afraid of wild animals, and lions in particular. Indeed, although lion tamers often sought to present themselves as exotically "other" by taking European stage names, I have come across only a handful of accounts of black lion tamers in America, and only one of them seems to have achieved any fame. An 1884 article in the *New York Times* describes "Delmonico" as a "rather slim but well set up African." Delmonico told the reporter that he was the only "colored man" in his regiment during the "American war," after which he came to England to perform ("Delmonico, the Lion Tamer," *New York Times*, August 11, 1884, p. 3). Notably, he seems to have found success only in Europe. Lion taming in America seems to have been almost entirely a white profession, suggesting that it functioned in part as an enactment of racial superiority.

The absence of black lion tamers in the United States is made more noticeable by the presence of several in England. A partial list includes Captain Beaumont, known as "The African Lion King," active in the 1890s; and Albert Maccoma, known as "Black Albert." According to Frost, Maccoma was famous for his daring, "which has often caused the spectators to tremble for his safety, [and] was without parallel" (Frost, *Circus Life and Circus Celebrities*, p. 133). Others included Captain Marco, whom Turner calls a "West Indian black," working in the first decade of the twentieth century; Captain Rowland, a trainer with Anderton and Haslam's circus and menagerie, from the 1890s; and Sargano and Alicamousa at E. H. Bostock's Grand Star Menagerie (Bostock, *Menageries, Circuses, and Theatres*, pp. 97, 101).

A 1901 newspaper account of Frank Bostock's early career suggests how the accomplishments of black animal trainers could be marginalized in the American press. Bostock joined his family's menagerie at the age of fourteen to replace the aforementioned Alicamousa: "The lion tamer of the aggregation at that time was a negro, who was the feature of the show. One day shortly after the return of young Bostock, he got drunk and beat the lion, so the animal would not perform. The boy recognized that animals were being wrongly handled and that they would respond to kindness far better than to brutality and a club. Going to his father he asked that he be allowed to take the place of the drunken trainer. . . . [H]e succeeded in performing the act quite as well as Alicamousa" ("Lion Tamer by Nature," *Buffalo Courier*, September 1, 1901, p. SB13). Alicamousa's long and successful career is collapsed here into a narrative about primitive brutality replaced by the enlightened white trainer.

112. "Working Lions for a Living," *Literary Digest* 84 (March 28, 1925), p. 553. Clyde Beatty wrote about the first time he saw such a performance: "To me, every detail of the performance was marvelous. The way the trainer cracked his whip was in itself pure magic. The sound reverberated through the tent like the sharp report of a gun. How could any one learn to do such things? . . . And when the trainer stuck his head 'in the lion's mouth'! Lord! Shall I ever forget the first time I saw that trick? . . . At the time it seemed to me that I was witnessing a super-miracle. The man performing it was to me the greatest man in the world" (Beatty, Clyde, with Edward Anthony. *The Big Cage*. New York: Century, 1933, p. 272). Such was still the case in the 1930s: Beatty wrote that "there are hundreds of boys who want to become animal-trainers. My mail conveys this message to me daily" (p. 280).

113. Gallup Paine, Henry. "The Lion-Tamer," *Harper's Monthly* 94 (May 1897), p. 966.

114. Rotundo, *American Manhood*, pp. 120–22. See also Rothman, Ellen K. *Hands and Hearts*. Cambridge, Mass.: Harvard University Press, 1987, p. 110; White, Kevin. *The First Sexual Revolution*. New York: New York University Press, 1993, pp. 3–7; Bederman, *Manliness and Civilization*, pp. 11–12. Rotundo writes, "This stringent code developed in the early nineteenth century, when the expansion of commerce lured young men away from the traditional values and communal vigilance of small towns. The ideology of sexual repression offered an alternative to the unchecked selfishness of the marketplace; it provided a sense of personal control and a form of moral discipline at a time

when ethical chaos seemed imminent. This doctrine of self-control hardened into a public orthodoxy once the migration from country to city became a steady, permanent flow" (Rotundo, *American Manhood*, pp. 120–21). Michael Kimmel writes that "the drive for control, for order, stems from experiencing the world as *dis*ordered, as out of control. And to middle-class American men the mid-nineteenth-century world often felt like it was spinning out of control, rushing headlong towards an industrial future" (Kimmel, Michael. *Manhood in America*. New York: Free Press, 1996, pp. 44–45). Hilkey writes that during the Gilded Age, "manhood became a form of *self-discipline*, a new code of behavior enforced by stigmatization of those who failed to practice it" (Hilkey, Judy. *Character Is Capital*. Chapel Hill: University of North Carolina Press, 1997, p. 9). On the notion of the "spermatic economy," see Barker-Benfield, G. J. *The Horrors of the Half-Known Life*. New York: Harper Colophon, 1976, pp. 178–81.

115. Rotundo, *American Manhood*, p. 121.

116. Ibid., p. 229.

117. Filene, Peter G. *Him/Her/Self*. Baltimore, Md.: Johns Hopkins University Press, 1998, p. 75.

118. Ibid., p. 89.

119. "Thrilling Experiences of Trainers," *Washington Post*, July 20, 1913, p. M2. In a *New York Times* article from 1887, Signor Bidel was asked how he was able to tame the animals. He replied, "My complete self-confidence and my courage. I consider these the only means. Red-hot irons, arms, loaded whips are the implements of the charlatan or of the coward" ("Talk with a Lion-Tamer," *New York Times*, July 25, 1887, p. 6). "Nerve, that is the great secret of the lion-tamer," wrote Le Roux and Garnier in 1890, "the sole cause of his authority over his beasts" (Le Roux and Garnier, *Acrobats and Moutebanks*, p. 150).

120. "Living Pictures of Wild Animals," *Buffalo News*, July 7, 1901. See also Rothfels, *Savages and Beasts*, p. 153.

121. According to a 1909 *New York Times* article, "Although a trainer may sit down, or kneel down, or lie down with impunity among his beasts, the moment he falls down every beast becomes startled, for the time loses all fear of the master and springs to tear him to pieces" ("Trainers of Wild Animals in Fights for Life," *New York Times*, July 25, 1909, p. SM5). Heini Hediger, in a fascinating 1955 study of the psychology of captive animals, warns that a trainer of wild cats must constantly maintain the status of the leader in the eyes of the animals. Any sign of weakness or fear in the trainer, even a stumble, could be "the signal for an attack by the animals, his social rivals, since they are always aspiring to take his place in the group" (Hediger, Heini. *The Psychology and Behaviour of Animals in Zoos and Circuses*. New York: Dover, 1955, p. 127).

122. "The Romance of the Lion Tamer," *Chicago Tribune*, July 5, 1903, p. A7.

123. Collins, Clara. "The Romance of the Lion Tamer," *Boston Daily Globe*, September 21, 1913, p. SM8.

124. Goffman, Erving. *Where the Action Is*. London: Penguin Press, 1969, p. 199.

125. Ibid., pp. 177–78.

126. Crabtree, Adam. *From Mesmer to Freud*. New Haven, Conn.: Yale University Press, 1993, p. 221. Mesmer held that animal bodies exerted an influence over one another by the action of animal magnetic fluid that could be harnessed to improve mental and physical health (p. 73). See also Nadis, Fred. *Wonder Shows: Performing Science, Magic and Religion in America*. New Brunswick, N.J.: Rutgers University Press, 2005, pp. 87–89; Darnton, Robert. *Mesmerism and the End of the Enlightenment in France*. Cambridge, Mass.: Harvard University Press, 1968.

127. "Van Amburgh," p. 247; "Three Months with a 'Lion King,'" p. 255. In the 1897 *Harper's* story mentioned above, the animals seemed to be "forced through their performance almost by hypnotism, by the power of those piercing eyes" (Gallup Paine, The Lion-Tamer," p. 965). Even as late as 1925, a scientific investigation into "the mysterious power" exerted by animal trainers found that the human gaze contained an energy with a power "sufficient to make ferocious animals cringe" ("Eyes Send Forth Electric Rays," *Washington Post*, August 16, 1925, p. SM6). Lion tamers frequently disavowed their supposed hypnotic power while simultaneously playing it up in their acts. In a 1911 interview Captain Bonavita rejected the idea that trainers held a hypnotic power over their animals, but he was quick to add that things had happened to him that he could not explain: "I've had lions rush at me across the arena with every appearance of intending to eat me alive, and have been as amazed as I was relieved to have them stop short only a few inches from me" ("Secret of Taming Lions Revealed by Maimed Trainer," *Washington Post*, October 1, 1911, p. SM4). Similarly, when George Conklin was asked if there was any truth in stories told about the power of the human eye over wild beasts, he replied disdainfully, "Not the slightest." He went on, however, explaining, "Of course it is true that a man who aims to subdue wild beasts must show a fearless front, and no doubt the eye shares with the body generally the task of impressing the beast" ("Training the Tigers," *Manchester Times*, April 17, 1891).

128. "With the Carnival Shows," *Washington Post*, August 11, 1907, p. MS4.

129. Sacher-Masoch's story concerns Herma, a female lion tamer who arouses the passionate interest of Prince Maniasko, who follows her movements "with feverish agitation": "His heart beat when she placed her pretty head in the terrible lion's mouth, and he trembled, half for pleasure, half for fear, when she began to harangue the disobedient animals and kick and flog them." The bewitched prince returns to Herma's performances again and again, until one night she asks him to come, at an hour before midnight, to the "little door" of her menagerie. He arrives "in the midst of the shades of night" and soon finds "two straining arms" around his neck, and "two burning lips . . . pressed against his own." The prince's father disapproves of his trysts with Herma since he is betrothed to a society woman. Under pressure from his father, the prince stops coming to see Herma, who is heartbroken. Herma learns of his impending marriage and sends word to the prince that she wants a final meeting at their usual place and time. The prince agrees, and, as usual, Herma leads him into the "dark space" of her menagerie, where she puts her arms round his neck and kisses him "with savage tenderness." Suddenly, however, Herma disappears and the cage door is violently shut. The prince's foot touches "something living

which moved." Herma reappears in the red glow of a torch, and the prince sees that he is in the midst of her lions. "I am celebrating my marriage with you, and my lions are to be the wedding guests," Herma announces. The lions, "irritated and encouraged by Herma's cries," sprang upon the prince, who desperately defended himself while Herma, "her face leaning against the cold bars, feasted her eyes on his mortal anguish." The lions quickly finish their "terrible work," leaving the prince dead on the floor of the den, and they slink away "to lick their bloody paws" (Sacher-Masoch, Leopold von. "Herma, the Lion-Tamer," *Fresno Republican,* February 5, 1881, p. 1). This sensual and disturbing narrative presents the big cage as the "dark space" of primitive sexuality. Equally notable is this 1890 description of the lion tamer act:

> You enter a dark booth, impregnated with a strong odour of carrion. At first the eyes can scarcely distinguish the strange sphinx-like forms extended behind the iron bars of the cages, crouching in dreamy, sleepy attitudes. Suddenly the gas-burner is lighted. Two keepers enter, covered with blood like the headsman's assistants; they bear a handbarrow laden with great quarters of horseflesh; a third person accompanies them carrying a hook. "The animals are now to be fed," he cries in a showman's voice. "The supper consists of more than 600 lbs. of meat. Those persons who wish to see the food distributed are begged to stand a little to the right." You follow the hook, the barrow and the people. . . . as [the lions] pant with rage, their breath rises in clouds of smoke, scattering the sawdust of their litter. They roar and dribble with hunger. At last the meat is within their reach, and they drag the huge pieces towards their jaws, too large to pass through the bars at first, there is a moment's struggle, and then the great lumps are triumphantly drawn in. When the booty is held, before rending it, the beasts lie down upon it, with little spasmodic rattles—the expression of satisfaction after rage. . . . [A]s the growls of enjoyment slowly, gradually subside, the menagerie resumes its usual quiet aspect, and the beasts lie drowsily on their sawdust beds, lazily licking their jaws with sighs of repletion. (Le Roux and Garnier, *Acrobats and Moutebanks,* pp. 134–36)

The account adds that when the male lion enters, it is with "the dignity of the leading performer, almost openly impatient to show himself. His mate follows him. The couple must have been worth seeing in their African solitude in their wild courtship" (p. 137).

130. Theodore Greene writes that the new emphasis on "personal magnetism" at this time was in part a "rather desperate effort to cover over the widening gap between the ideology of individualism and the changing conditions of society": "The vast power of accumulated millions and of a Standard Oil had to be explained in individual terms. Therefore the successful millionaire and trustbuilder had to be endowed with vast personal powers of will and magnetism. The increasing difficulty that a white-collar employee, however earnest his character, faced in achieving independent status and entrepreneurial rewards also had to be explained in personal terms. What he lacked must be personal force, indomitable will, and that mysterious quality of magnetism." (Greene, Theodore P. *America's Heroes.* New York: Oxford University Press, 1970, pp. 112–14).

131. "Trainers of Wild Animals in Fights for Life," p. SM5.

132. See "Great Tamer Out of Game," *Los Angeles Times,* February 12, 1905, p. H14; "Crunched by Lion," *Boston Globe,* August 1, 1904, p. 8; and "Lion Trainer in Hospital," *New York Times,* September 5, 1904, p. 10.

133. Corbey, Raymond. "Ethnographic Showcases, 1870–1930," *Cultural Anthropology* 8, no. 3 (August 1993), p. 360.

134. Ibid. Bouissac points to the fact that in Western circuses performers often give themselves "foreign"-sounding names (Bouissac, *Circus and Culture*, p. 93). Bonavita's real name was John Frederick Gentner. George Conklin was a notable exception. He wrote, "It has always been a fad with most American trainers and performers to use foreign words in so far as possible in giving directions and cues to animals. The theory is that it makes a greater impression with the audience, but I never cared to do it" (Conklin, *Ways of the Circus*, p. 55).

135. Geertz famously described the Balinese cockfight as a cultural performance that spoke to its audience in "a vocabulary of sentiment." "Attending cockfights and participating in them," wrote Geertz, was a kind of "sentimental education" in Balinese culture. Geertz, Clifford. *The Interpretation of Cultures.* New York: Basic Books, 1973, p. 449.

136. See Streible, Dan. *Fight Pictures.* Berkeley: University of California Press, 2008.

137. Toulmin, *Electric Edwardians*, pp. 108–9. It is instructive to compare the lion tamer act to boxing in terms of their suitability for the cinema. Streible argues that the latter made a good match with early cinema due to its being composed of "brief, segmented units of performance" that could be structured around "the kinetoscope's formal constraints," with rows of viewing machines arranged in sequence (Streible, *Fight Pictures*, pp. 23, 30). In 1912 the *New York Times* reported on William Sterling's demonstration in London of an invention called the "chronophone." That device was said to combine "cinematograph films" and "gramophone records" so that sound and movement were "in perfect unison." The chronophone was demonstrated with two films: the first presented a rooster crowing, and the second a lion tamer act. To the *Times* reporter, the latter film was particularly remarkable because of its "mixture of sounds," "the man speaking, the crack of his whip, the thud of the iron bar falling on the floor of the cage, and the terrible snarls and growls of the lion, all so lifelike that it seemed impossible that the actual lion cage had not been somehow spirited into the room" ("Men Move and Speak in New Pictures," *New York Times*, May 11, 1912, p. 5).

This account suggests that one reason for the dearth of early lion tamer films during the silent era had to do with the importance of the sonic dimension of the act. Silent lions would not compare well to their snarling and roaring live counterparts, presumably well known to early cinema audiences. As a way to appreciate how the spectacle of the lion act was equally balanced between sound and image, consider that one of the most iconic images in the history of film is the roaring lion of the MGM trademark. Here the lion is both potent cultural icon and the quintessential test case for the linking of sound and image, the lion's roar being just as spectacular as his image.

138. The *Los Angles Times* reported in 1923 that "Southern California is fast becoming the mecca of the out-door show world," adding that twelve circuses and carnival companies had recently established their winter quarters in or near Los Angeles, including the Al. G Barnes Circus, Golden Brothers Circus, Atkinson's Circus, Henry's Dog and Pony Circus, and Morton's Indoor Circus

("Circuses to Winter Here," *Los Angeles Times,* November 4, 1923, p. I4). Al Copeland is said to have selected the area as the headquarters of his circuses in 1920 (Gebhart, Myrtle. "The Menagerie 'Goes Movie,'" *Los Angeles Times,* April 26, 1931, p. K1). See also "Circus May Make Winter Home Here," *Los Angeles Times,* February 8, 1917, p. I15.

139. Wilson, Robert H. "The New Wild Animal Center of the World," *Los Angeles Times,* January 1, 1916, p. III74.

140. As another example of a convergence of zoos and the cinema in the first decades of the twentieth century, note Carl Hagenbeck's Tierpark Zoo in Stellingen, Germany. Opened in 1907, Tierpark marked a break with previous zoos in that it presented animals in a constructed realistic mise-en-scène and it separated animals from the public with deep trenches that allowed for the removal of any bars or railings that would interfere with the visitors' view (Hagenbeck, *Beasts and Men,* p. 41). What we find here, then, is an extremely cinematic presentation of exotic animals, part of what Vanessa R. Schwartz calls "cinematic spectatorship before the apparatus" with reference to displays in the Paris morgue, wax museums, and panoramas in the last third of the nineteenth century (Charney, Leo, and Vanessa R. Schwartz, eds. *Cinema and the Invention of Modern Life.* Berkeley: University of California Press, 1995, p. 297).

141. "Motion Picture Studios of California," *Moving Picture World* 31, no. 10 (March 10, 1917), p. 1599. On Selig, see Bowser, Eileen. *The Transformation of Cinema.* Berkeley: University of California Press, 1990, p. 152.

142. Scheuer, Philip K. "Thriller Reshaped for Betty Hutton," *Los Angeles Times,* March 3, 1946, p. B1. See also Gebhardt, Myrtle. "Beasts Transplanted Here Attract Many Visitors," *Los Angles Times,* March 30, 1924, p. B9; "New Zoo Park a Wonderland," *Los Angeles Times,* June 20, 1915, p. H10.

143. Kingsley, Grace. "Los Angeles the Globe's Moving Picture Center," *Los Angeles Times,* January 1, 1915, p. V146.

144. See Babcock, Muriel. "Film Celebrity Stands Unique," *Los Angeles Times,* May 19, 1929, p. C11; "Lion Farm Used in Many Scenes," *Los Angeles Times,* May 12, 1929, p. 18; "Hard Luck Camps at Lion Farm," *Los Angeles Times,* June 4, 1927, p. A1; "Door Shut for Always, Lion Farm Owners Say," *Los Angeles Times,* October 28, 1949, p. A1.

145. See "Great Tamer Out of Game," p. H14; and "Photographing Animals," *Washington Post,* September 12, 1907, p. 6.

146. Moulton, Robert H. "Making 'Actors' of Jungle Beasts," *Sunday Oregonian,* February 22, 1914, p. 8.

147. "Forrest and the Lion Tamer," *Bangor (Maine) Daily Whig & Courier,* January 28, 1873, issue 24, col. G. Compare this to an anecdote relating how Van Amburgh had been asked by the Duke of Wellington if he was ever afraid: "The first time I am afraid, your Grace," he is said to have replied, "or that I fancy my pupils are no longer afraid of me, I shall retire from the wild beast line" (Frost, *Circus Life and Circus Celebrities,* p. 89).

148. Some of Captain Jack's films were shot at his winter quarters in Florida. Bonavita was said to be in the employ of "the World's Best Film Company" at Sulphur Springs, Florida, where they were "making wild animal pictures" in 1913 ("Lions Tear Bonavita in Wild Animal Act," *The State* [Columbia, S.C.]

March 30, 1913, p. 32). Harold M. Shaw, "a director of the Edison films," was in charge of the company, which was being assisted by Bonavita. The first film to be made, *The King of the Jungle,* was written "by the leading man of the Imp's Film Company, Mr. King Baggot" (*The State* [Columbia, S.C.], March 2, 1913, p. 29).

149. "Scene Almost Cost Man's Life," *Indiana Evening Gazette,* May 12, 1913, p. 2.

150. In a 1955 study of animal training, Heini Hediger argues that animals are much superior to humans in distinguishing between "true and false" behavior, and so "human play-acting and make-believe misfire with the animal during training." According to Hediger, "in order to obtain a satisfactory performance, the appropriate expression and the training signals directly connected with it must be genuine; these signals must really relate to the emotional content which the animals originally had. As a rule, the animal will not respond to empty gestures and shallow mimicry" (Hediger, *Psychology and Behaviour of Animals,* p. 125).

151. The problems of the acting lion tamer might be understood in terms of James Naremore's discussion of "expressive coherence" in film acting. See Naremore, James. *Acting in the Cinema.* Berkeley: University of California Press, 1988, p. 70.

152. "Capt. Jack Bonavita Killed by Bear," *Billboard,* March 31, 1917, p. 53.

153. "The Rajah's Sacrifice," *Moving Picture World* 25, no. 11 (September 11, 1915), p. 1851.

154. Luigi Pirandello's 1926 novel *Shoot! (Si Gira)* provides a wonderful commentary on some of the central issues of this chapter. The book is narrated by Serafino Gubbio, a cinematograph operator working at the Kosmograph company, which has bought a tiger from the Zoological Gardens in Rome. The film company intends to kill the animal on camera as part of a "spectacular scenario." Notably, the title of the film is to be *The Lady and the Tiger,* an almost exact match with the film for which Jack Bonavita did stuntwork, *The Woman and the Beast* (1917). Gubbio expresses his distaste for the film, saying that everything about it will be a "sham" except for the death of the tiger. The actress Varia Nesteroff replies that "when the door of the cage is opened and the animal is driven into the other, bigger cage representing a glade in a forest, with the bars hidden by branches, the hunter, even if he is a sham like the forest, will still be entitled to defend himself against it, simply because it, as you say, is not a sham animal but a real one. . . . [T]he part of the hunter will be a sham but when he is face to face with this *real* animal he will be a *real* man!" (Pirandello, Luigi. *Shoot! [Si Gira]* London: Dodo Press, 2010 [1926], p. 62). Here is a succinct expression of the functional utility of the encounter with wild animals to ratify the performance of male identity.

155. "Mutual Program," *Moving Picture World* 28, no. 7 (May 13, 1916), p. 1123.

156. *New York Tribune,* July 23, 1916, p. E7.

157. "Killed By Polar Bear," *Idaho Daily Statesman,* March 20, 1917, p. 1; "Trained Bear Kills Capt. Jack Bonavita," *New York Tribune,* March 21, 1917, p. 9. *Billboard* described how, while working on a jungle film for Universal in

Florida, an angry lion had attacked Bonavita: "Though he was being literally torn to pieces, he shouted to the camera man: 'Keep turning, get it all!' The camera man, aghast at the sight, had lost his nerve and fled. Weeks of painful suffering in a hospital followed, but Bonavita regretted only that the film was spoiled by the happening" ("Capt. Jack Bonavita Killed by Bear," p. 53).

158. "Job of Lion Tamer Pays Well, But Chances Are That He'll Die with Boots on Inside of a Cage," *Nevada State Journal*, October 13, 1934, p. 7. During World War II an article put a different spin on the trope of the stuntman's fluid identity. In an article entitled "Stunt Man Turns Yellow," we read that Harvey Parry "has turned yellow—to work in pictures in which the treacherous Jap is shown in his true colors. . . . [H]is face was a pasty greenish yellow, his eyelids dropped menacingly and his naturally curly hair was straightened and combed back from a low hairline. 'Last week I played a Nazi soldier in Errol Flynn's picture " Desperate Journey," he said . . . I'm making money out of the war—on the wrong side'" (Harvey Parry papers, box 1, folder 6, Clippings—personal).

159. See Kasson, *Houdini, Tarzan and the Perfect Man*; Bederman, *Manliness and Civilization*; Cheyfitz, Eric. *The Poetics of Imperialism*. Philadelphia: University of Pennsylvania Press, 1991; Kimmel, *Manhood in America*, p. 154. Cheyfitz reminds us that *Tarzan of the Apes* (1912) appeared at a time when "the second great wave of immigration to the United States, which began in the 1820s, was at its crest." "In such a climate, when those perceived as foreigners—appearing in a range of figures from the colonial subject to the immigrant worker to the black citizen—threaten to become America itself, it is not surprising . . . that a new American superhero . . . should be an English nobleman, epitome of the Anglo-Saxon race" (Cheyfitz, *Poetics of Imperialism*, p. 4).

160. "Mr. Van Amburgh," *Aberdeen Journal* 4989 (August 23, 1843).

161. As Cheyfitz puts it, "In this imperial romance the lower class is as much a foreign country to the upper class as Africa is to Europe" (Cheyfitz, *Poetics of Imperialism*, p. 12). The Tarzan films provided a dramatic framework for shifting attitudes about the natural world. Consider the unsettling scene in *Tarzan the Ape Man* (1932) in which Jane, her father, and their party are captured and taken to a jungle village, where they are thrown into a pit to face a surreal giant gorilla. The leering, cheering natives who gather to watch this death match closely resemble descriptions made by nineteenth-century reformers of the working-class audiences at dog and cockfights. Recall how anticruelty reformers saw the crowds at animal pits as a "dark, barbaric, primitive horde" (Turner, *Reckoning with the Beast*, p. 23). At the moment in the Tarzan narrative when we are meant to encounter the ultimate embodiment of the foreign, the savage, and the primitive, we are shown a thinly veiled representation of the urban working class.

162. Salt, Barry. *Film Style and Technology: History and Analysis*. London: Starword, 1983, pp. 269–71.

163. See, for example, A.L. Raven's "Motion Picture Screen," February 23, 1932, patent number 1846357, and W.L. Douden's "Apparatus for Making Composite Talking Motion Pictures," January 7, 1936, patent number 2027028.

164. Fear, Ralph G. "Projected Background Anematography," *American Cinematographer* 12, no. 9 (January 1932), p. 11.

165. Salt, *Film Style and Technology,* p. 271. See also Rickitt, Richard. *Special Effects: The History and Technique.* New York: Billboard Books, 2000, p. 66.

166. Corbey, "Ethnographic Showcases, 1870–1930," p. 360. Rothfels connects the decline of such "people shows" to the increasing popularity of anthropological films and popular geographical magazines, media forms that "allowed the viewer to examine the object relentlessly without ever being discomforted by looks coming back" (Rothfels, *Savages and Beasts,* p. 144).

167. Scheuer, Philip K. "A Town Called Hollywood," *Los Angeles Times,* January 22, 1933, p. A1.

168. Bradbury, Joseph T. "Bert Nelson, Wild Animal Trainer," *White Tops,* November–December 1972, p. 49. A 1927 advertisement in the *Decatur Herald* reads, "Vaudeville's Big Sensation Princess Pat. The famous movie lion. Performing in a Steel Arena Feats of almost Human Intelligence, with the servitude of a Massive Dog." Earlier that month the same newspaper had written that Princess Pat would make an appearance "on an automobile in the streets" and claimed that she had appeared in several recent films, such as *The Monkey Talks, King of Kings,* and Zane Gray's *Man of the Forest* ("Princess Pat, Movie Actress to Come Here," *Decatur Herald,* October 25, 1927, p. 15).

169. It is remarkable to see how extensively the Tarzan films remediate the pleasures of the circus. We see Tarzan, as played by swimming star Johnny Weissmuller, present a version of the acrobat and trapeze artist as he swings through the jungle; we get the visceral spectacle of human "freaks" akin to the circus sideshow when Jane and her father are captured by a tribe of dwarves; and, above all, we are shown wild animal acts, with a large proportion of the film taken up with the performances of animals trained by a circus animal trainer named George Emerson. Emerson was credited with training "the deer and the mountain lion for 'Sequoia,' the tiger and the elephant for their act in 'O'Shaughnessy's Boy,' the water buffalo for 'The Good Earth,' the elephants for 'Tarzan Escapes,' the rhinoceros for 'Tarzan and His Mate,' and the hounds for 'The Voice of Bugle Ann'" ("Movie Trainer Gentles Tigers Easily by Scratching Their Ears," *Washington Post,* December 19, 1937, p. E1).

170. Reprinted in Bradbury, "Bert Nelson, Wild Animal Trainer," p. 57.

171. Nelson, Bert. "Lion Taming's the Bunk," *Saturday Evening Post* 207 (March 30, 1935), p. 65.

172. See "Trainer Winning Battle for Life after Lion's Bite," *Chicago Tribune,* February 7, 1932, p. 12; and "Victim of Lion Bite Improves," *Los Angeles Times,* February 7, 1932, p. 5. See also "Huge Lion Saves Life of Trainer Bitten by Tiger," *Los Angeles Times,* April 26, 1930, p. 16; and Beatty, Clyde, and Edward Anthony. *Facing the Big Cats.* London: Heinemann, 1965.

173. Culhane, *American Circus,* p. 210.

174. Scott, John. "You Can't Be Nervous with Lions," *Los Angeles Times,* February 5, 1933, p. A1.

175. Price, Dave. "Clyde Beatty: Man or Myth?" *The White Tops,* July–August 1974, p. 16. Adams-Volpe argues that the circus was in decline during the 1940s and 1950s "due to competition from motion pictures and television. Also during this time, the larger circuses suffered fires, train wrecks, poor

management, union troubles, and escalating moving costs" (Adams-Volpe, "Circus and Wild West Exhibition," p. 248).

176. A 1932 article in *Physical Culture* gushed that Beatty "carries stirring inspiration as an object lesson in those qualities of heart and mind and body that signify what we call manhood!" (May, Earl Chapin. "Nerve Is Another Name for Courage," *Physical Culture*, September 1932, p. 20).

177. Beatty and Anthony, *The Big Cage*, pp. 59–60. Captain Jack Bonavita made a similar comment when interviewed at the 1901 Pan-American Exposition in Buffalo. When asked, "Which can whip the other—a tiger or a lion?" Bonavita replied that "99 out of 100 persons will ask that very questions. . . . [I]t is the national query. From boyhood men have read of the two monarchs of the jungle, the lion and the tiger, and have, perchance, read stories of combats between the two. The sight of either excites a strange awe in the ordinary person and, on seeing both, he cannot help wondering which is the more powerful" ("Lion Tamer Talks," *Buffalo Commercial Advertiser*, November 13, 1901).

178. Beatty and Anthony, *The Big Cage*, p. 4.

179. Hediger describes how animal trainers relied upon a wild animal's "flight reaction," the instinct to flee from an approaching human. That instinct becomes a basic unit of training, allowing the trainer to send the animal to any point in the ring by overstepping the flight distance of the animal, either with his or her body or with the whip. "The whip obviously signifies to the animal the extension of a human extremity; the personality of the trainer is likewise projected into the whip, and its movements are part of his gestures" (Hediger, *Psychology and Behaviour of Animals*, p. 123). Animals born in captivity grow accustomed to humans and thus have a less reliable flight reaction, making them a less dynamic raw material for training. Another resource for animal trainers is the "critical reaction" when an animal lacks an avenue of escape from an approaching human. A wild animal in that situation will attack in self-defense. The critical reaction of an animal is particularly useful for the trainer, because it is a movement that is directional, that is, aimed straight at the trainer. This allows the trainer to put pedestals or other training equipment between him or herself and the attacking animal, "thus the animal has no alternative except to make its way over the training apparatus under the influence of critical reaction" (ibid., pp. 123–24). To stop the attack, the trainer merely steps back out of the animal's critical reaction distance. Again, critical reaction is most volatile in animals "fresh from the veldt," making them easier to train and providing another explanation for Beatty's preferences.

180. Beatty and Anthony, *The Big Cage*, 1933, p. 4.

181. Couvares, *Remaking of Pittsburgh*, p. 56.

182. Though he represented an American school known for its enactment of an antagonistic struggle with the animals, Beatty himself is depicted in *The Big Cage* as embodying a caring and nurturing type of masculinity, one that must have been appealing to an audience of young boys and that also helped to insulate him from accusations of animal cruelty. At one point in the film Beatty introduces Jimmie to the rest of his "family": a cat, a small dog, and a rabbit. Indeed, Beatty's rather small stature and easygoing manner set him apart from earlier depictions of gruff and brutal lion tamers. His unspectacular physique

is noted in the film. In his first appearance onscreen Beatty subdues an escaped tiger on a pier. When a policeman recognizes him as Clyde Beatty, the famous lion tamer, he exclaims, "No one would ever take you for an animal trainer!" "That's my trick," the puckish Beatty replies. "That's how I fool the animals." Also, though Beatty is the star of the film, he has no romantic interest. In fact, Beatty's sexuality is completely transferred to his work. Recall how he introduced Jimmie to his animal "family." Similarly, when his friend Russ comes to visit him and begins to speak about his girlfriend, Beatty introduces Perry to his own "sweetheart," a snarling tiger ("Isn't she a honey?").

183. Wallace Beery was a circus elephant trainer before becoming a Hollywood actor ("Elephants Preferred to Pirates," *Los Angeles Times*, July 13, 1924, p. B27; "Circus Pals Meet Again," *Los Angeles Times*, June 7, 1935, p. 15). Press surrounding the film emphasized how Beery had done his own animal stunts, entering a cage with a tiger while "sharpshooters sat, alert eyed, within camera range, ready to pot the beast if it got too fresh with Beery" (Tince, Mae. "Beery-Cooper Team Scores in New Movie," *Chicago Tribune*, November 14, 1935, p. 19. See also Sennwald, Andre. "Drama of a Father and Son," *New York Times*, October 5, 1935, p. 18; Skolsky, Sidney. "Hollywood," *Washington Post*, July 22, 1935, p. 14). Beery's work in *O'Shaughnessy's Boy* was offered as an example of how "effete film players whose precious hides must be protected at all costs have practically passed from the Hollywood scene. It's the he-man period today, with actors and even actresses made of strong stuff and scorning the use of doubles" (Scott, John. "Stars Who Insist on Doing Own Stunts Take Heavy Chances to Insure Realism," *Los Angeles Times*, October 20, 1935, p. A1).

184. By some accounts, West's interest in lion tamers stemmed from having seen Captain Bonavita perform at Dreamland when she was a child.

185. Beatty wrote in his memoirs that such nervous collapses "constitute one of the greatest mysteries of animal-training." When it happens, "the nerves of the man afflicted are so badly shattered that it is pathetic to watch his efforts to rally his confidence and restore himself as a trainer. He may have as much courage as ever, but something has snapped and all kinds of mental hazards develop" (Beatty and Anthony, *The Big Cage*, p. 62).

186. Beatty's rapid footwork was singled out for praise by Ernest Hemingway, who called on Beatty during an engagement at Madison Square Garden in the 1930s to give him an autographed copy of *Death in the Afternoon* (Beatty and Anthony, *Facing the Big Cats*, pp. 14–15).

187. Beatty and Anthony, *The Big Cage*, pp. 134–35. "I am sick unto death of reading about the mythical animal-trainer," Beatty wrote, "who by waving a magic hand or looking an animal in the eye with a hypnotic fixity can make his four-legged charge do anything except play the piano" (pp. 37–38). Beatty claimed that newspaper photographers had often taken snapshots of his eyes. See also Beatty and Anthony, *Facing the Big Cats*, p. 215.

188. Griffiths, Alison. *Wondrous Difference*. New York: Columbia University Press, 2002, p. 199.

189. Ibid., p. 200.

190. A 1932 *New York Times* article declared that "the custom of 'doubles' for stars confronted with dangerous stunts in their pictures was reversed" when

Clyde Beatty "substituted himself for minor players when it was necessary to enter the cages of some fifty lions, tigers and leopards. As a star, Mr. Beatty's contract provides him with a double. But as he is the only person . . . who has ever been able to put forty lions and tigers in one cage and make them do tricks, he not only plays his own part but those of others when the script calls upon the various characters to enter the big cage" ("A Star Who Doubles for Minor Players," *New York Times,* December 25, 1932, p. X5).

191. Berger, John. *About Looking.* New York: Pantheon, 1980, p. 14.

192. Ibid., p. 26.

193. Hearne, Vicki. *Animal Happiness.* New York: HarperCollins, 1994, p. 167. Wittgenstein remarked, "If a lion could talk, we could not understand him." Stephen Webb glosses that remark as follows: "The lion's form of life, presumably, would be so different from our own that there would be no shared context for communication to take place. . . . We are commonly tempted to think that animals have inner processes that are obscured by their inability to speak, and thus we pretend that they could talk, if only they were physically able. Wittgenstein, however, taught that there are no private languages, and that thinking or reasoning always takes place in a public medium of language, so that if animals cannot talk, then it is difficult, if not impossible, to say whether or not they think" (Webb, Stephen H. *On God and Dogs.* New York: Oxford University Press, 1998, pp. 8–9). For Tester, Wittgenstein was making "the largely philosophical point that the world of the lion and the world of the social are totally unconnected and, therefore, communication between them is impossible" (Tester, Keith. *Animals and Society.* London: Routledge, 1991, p. 207).

194. Hearne, *Animal Happiness,* p. 169.

195. Ibid., p. 171. "Something happens in lion training that is in part possible because of the trainer's literacy, his capacity for mediated knowledge," Hearne writes, "but is nonetheless a transcendence of the noise and skepticism that are the inevitable accompaniments of mediated awareness. This is a world without symbols and shapes of days but only the day itself—a world that has gone beyond words (by means, in part, of words)" (p. 173).

196. Ibid., p. 174.

197. Ibid., p. 192.

198. Fudge, "A Left-Handed Blow," p. 11.

4. THE ADVENTURES OF THE AERONAUT

1. Balint, Michael. *Thrills and Regressions.* London: Hogarth Press, 1959, p. 25.

2. Goffman, Erving. *Frame Analysis.* Boston: Northeastern University Press, 1974, p. 30.

3. Historian T. J. Jackson Lears writes that military service seemed to offer middle-class men "a stronger, purer sense of selfhood." Lears, T. J. Jackson. *No Place of Grace.* New York: Pantheon Books, 1981, pp. 110–12. See also Filene, Peter G. *Him/Her/Self.* Baltimore, Md.: Johns Hopkins University Press, 1998, p. 103. Leo Braudy writes that the 1890s and early 1900s were rife with the belief that war would "affirm national vitality and individual honor" and "rescue the

nation from moral decay and bring men back to the basic truths from which they had wandered, resolving the conflicts between degeneration and progress, spirituality and materialism, under a new banner of purity" (Braudy, Leo. *From Chivalry to Terrorism*. New York: Vintage Books, 2005, pp. 373–74).

4. Virilio, Paul. *War and Cinema*. London: Verso, 1989, p. 17.

5. Toulmin, Vanessa. "Curios Things in Curios Places: Temporary Exhibition Venues in the Victorian and Edwardian Entertainment Environment," *Early Popular Visual Culture* 4, no. 2 (July 2006), p. 117.

6. Stewart, Susan. *On Longing*. Durham, N.C.: Duke University Press, 1993, p. 74.

7. Lears, T.J. Jackson. *Rebirth of a Nation*. New York: Harper Perennial, 2009, p. 248.

8. Carroll, Noel. *Comedy Incarnate: Buster Keaton, Physical Humor and Bodily Coping*. Oxford: Wiley-Blackwell, 2009, p. 68.

9. Ibid.

10. "Risking Their Lives," *New York Tribune*, August 14, 1904, p. B3.

11. "Up in a Balloon, Boys," *Atlanta Constitution*, August 2, 1873, p. 3.

12. "Communication," *Boston Globe*, June 5, 1873, p. 4.

13. Wise claimed that aerial navigation might aid geological, medical, geographical, and even archaeological research. See "The Ocean Balloon Voyage," *Atlanta Constitution*, July 18, 1873, p. 2; "The Balloon as an Aid to Meteorological Research," *Scientific American* 23, no. 22 (November 26, 1870), p. 341; "The Balloon and the Aeronauts," *Scientific American* 29, no. 11 (September 13, 1873), p. 159. For more on eighteenth-century American attitudes toward ballooning, see Pethers, Matthew. "Balloon Madness: Politics, Public Entertainment, The Transatlantic Science of Flight, and Late Eighteenth-Century America," *History of Science* 48, part 2, no. 160 (June 2010), pp. 181–226. For more on John Wise, see Crouch, Tom D. *The Eagle Aloft*. Washington, D.C.: Smithsonian Institution Press, 1983, pp. 183–90.

14. "Balloon as an Aid to Meteorological Research," p. 341.

15. "Washington H. Donaldson," *Daily Inter-Ocean* (Chicago, Ill.), July 27, 1875, p. 2; Raab, James W. *America's Daredevil Balloonist*. Manhattan, Kans.: Sunflower University Press, 1999.

16. Cited in Bronson, Edgar Beecher. *The Red-Blooded Heroes of the Frontier*. London: Hodder and Stoughton, 1910.

17. "Balloon Notes," *Brooklyn Daily Eagle*, July 14, 1873, p. 2; "Washington H. Donaldson," p. 2.

18. Lears, *No Place of Grace*, p. 48. Wise raved about curative benefits of ballooning, writing that it had cured him of chronic dyspepsia and "a severe affection of the lungs caused by a long continued inhalation of dust" from his first occupation, the manufacture of pianos (Wise, John. *A System of Aeronautics*. Philadelphia, Penn.: Joseph A. Speel, 1850, p. 310).

19. All of this information is from Bronson, who also claims that Donaldson was "riding a velocipede on a tight-wire from stage to gallery of a Philadelphia theatre, the first to do this performance" (Bronson, *Red-Blooded Heroes of the Frontier*, p. 49).

20. "Donaldson's Diary," *Daily Inter-Ocean* (Chicago, Ill.), August 25, 1875, p. 2.

21. "The Flying Trapeze in the Air," *(Macon) Georgia Weekly Telegraph*, September 26, 1871, p. 1.

22. In 1865 acrobat Harry Leslie made a similar ascension with the aeronaut Professor Lowe ("Aeronautic Gymnastics," *New York Times*, October 1, 1865, p. 5). The following year, Auguste Buislay, a member of a gymnastic troupe appearing at the New Bowery Theatre, gave a similar performance in New York ("Adventures of an Aeronaut," *New York Times*, July 6, 1866, p. 8),

23. "Donaldson's Diary," p. 2.

24. "A Man with Nerves of Steel," *Lowell (Mass.) Daily Citizen and News*, February 15, 1872, p. 1.

25. "Flying Trapeze in the Air," p. 1. The author questioned the morality of Donaldson's act and hoped that the authorities would prevent a repetition of the show. He felt that it was the duty of the press to "denounce such reckless and unnecessary risk of human life for the mere gratification of morbid excitement" (p. 1).

26. Ibid.

27. "Ocean Ballooning," *Cincinnati Daily Gazette*, April 24, 1873, p. 2.

28. "The Balloon Voyage," *New York Daily Tribune*, September 10, 1873, p. 4; "That Balloon," *Brooklyn Daily Eagle*, October 7, 1873, p. 2; "Aeronautic," *Little Rock (Ark.) Daily Republican*, September 17, 1873, p. 1. The article continued by stating that, for Donaldson, "it will be all the same whether the current blows east or west. In fact, he expresses the wish that the current may carry them in a westerly direction, that he may be seen of all men from here to Cincinnati. Then he has no objection if it be reversed and carry him to London, where he hopes to be properly appreciated" ("Aeronautic," p. 1).

29. "The 'Graphic' Balloon," *New York Daily Tribune*, September 11, 1873, p. 7; "Aeronautic," p. 1; "Failure of the Balloon to Europe," *Scientific American* 29, no. 13 (September 27, 1873), p. 193.

30. "Failure of the Balloon to Europe," p. 193. An article in *Scientific American* claimed that "of all newspaper dodges to attract interest and induce large sales, this 'Balloon to Europe' affair beats all" ("To Europe in a Balloon," *Scientific American* 29, no. 3 [July 19, 1873], p. 33). See also "Up in a Balloon—The Easterly Current," *Brooklyn Daily Eagle*, August 26, 1873, p. 2; "That Balloon," p. 2. For more on the *Daily Graphic* balloon, see Crouch, *Eagle Aloft*, pp. 437–49; and Rolt, L.T.C. *The Aeronauts*. New York: Walker and Company, 1966, pp. 144–45.

31. Barnum stated that if the easterly current theory was found to be true, he would find ways to utilize it for the purposes of popular amusement in his traveling show: "Scores of scientific societies would take it and guard it, I suppose, but I wouldn't part with it for thousands to be put away like the holy cross at Treves, doing no good to anybody" ("Barnum's Balloon," *Chicago Times*, September 28, 1873, p. 12). See also "The Barnum Balloon," *New York Times*, July 7, 1874, p. 8. Wise had, in fact, worked with Barnum before the *Daily Graphic* enterprise: in 1854, when Barnum was in control of the New York

Crystal Palace, he hired Wise to make an ascension from that establishment. See Lindsay, David. *Madness in the Making.* Lincoln, Neb.: iUniverse, 2005, p. 127.

32. Stewart, *On Longing,* pp. 46, 67–68.

33. "Barnum's Balloon," *Brooklyn Daily Eagle,* April 30, 1875, p. 4; "The Balloon Ascension," *Logansport (Ind.) Daily Star,* July 9, 1875, p. 1. A *Boston Globe* reporter described a balloon ascension at night: "The great city was seen spread out, appearing, however, more like the vast firmament above on a clear Winter's night than the strange collection of buildings that had been left a short time before. The lighted streets running in all directions, the long bridges, like illuminated arms, jutting out, and the . . . gas lamps in the parks, formed strange and beautiful constellations" ("Up in a Balloon," *Boston Globe,* August 10, 1874, p. 4).

34. "Steeple-Jack's Secret," *Chambers's Edinburgh Journal* 423 (February 7, 1852), p. 91.

35. For a fascinating discussion of aerial photography and early film theory, see Amad, Paula. *Counter-Archive: Film, the Everyday, and Albert Kahn's Archives de la Planete.* New York: Columbia University Press, 2010, pp. 271–78.

36. "Super-Nubilose Nuptials," *Cincinnati Daily Gazette,* October 20, 1874, p. 8. Several authors claim that the wedding was originally intended to be between Donaldson and the Barnum equestrienne Maggie Taylor. See Raab, *America's Daredevil Balloonist,* pp. 119–20; and Kunzog, John C. "Barnum Show Balloon Wedding," *Bandwagon* 8, no. 3 (May–June 1964), pp. 11–12.

37. See "The Central Park and the Balloons," *New York Times,* October 29, 1865, p. 8. In 1890, fifty thousand people saw a couple from Springfield, Illinois, taken in the air by Professor King in Cleveland, Ohio, and married "50 feet over the heads of the crowd" ("Married in a Balloon," *Chicago Tribune,* July 5, 1890, p. 2). See also "Married in a Balloon," *New York Times,* July 5, 1883, p. 2; "Bridal Tour in the Air," *Washington Post,* October 25, 1890, p. 2. For more on circus balloon ascensions and balloon weddings, see Slout, William L. "What Goes Up . . . Comes Down," *Bandwagon* 40, no. 2 (March–April 1996), pp. 22–27; Parkinson, Bob. "Circus Balloon Ascensions," *Bandwagon* 5, no. 2 (March–April 1961), pp. 3–6; Crouch, *Eagle Aloft,* pp. 419–20.

38. "Donaldson," *Brooklyn Daily Eagle,* July 21, 1875, p. 3.

39. "The Lost Aeronauts," *Daily Inter-Ocean* (Chicago, Ill.), July 19, 1875, p. 4.

40. "The Aeronauts' Fate," *Chicago Times,* July 18, 1875, p. 3.

41. See "A Report That Donaldson Is Alive and Well in Michigan—His Attempt to Disguise Himself," *Cincinnati Daily Gazette,* August 5, 1875, p. 8; "Donaldson Reported Alive," *Wheeling (W. Va.) Daily Register,* August 10, 1875, p. 3; "A Balloonatic Who Believes Himself to Be Prof. Donaldson," *Cincinnati Daily Gazette,* August 6, 1875, p. 8; "Donaldson Heard From," *New York Herald,* August 25, 1875, p. 7. Five years after his death an old bottle that was being cleaned in a liquor storehouse in Chicago was found to contain a card, "water soaked and yellow," on which was penciled a message, signed with the name "Donaldson": "A few moments and the balloon will be in the water. Tell Barnum to give the balance of my salary to Mollie." The Hippodrome's press agent, D.S. Thomas, pronounced the card genuine and explained that

Mollie was Maggie Taylor, "Barnum's highest salaried hurdle rider, to whom Donaldson was engaged" ("A Message or a Hoax," *Cincinnati Daily Gazette*, November 3, 1880, p. 3; see also "Brevities," *Atlanta Constitution*, September 26, 1875, p. 4).

42. "A Silly Hoax," *Daily State Gazette* (Trenton, N.J.), April 23, 1875, p. 2. For more on the faked death of Donaldson in Philadelphia in April 1875, see "Barnum's Advertisement," *Boston Globe*, April 22, 1875, p. 1; and "Barnum's Puff," *Boston Globe*, April 24, 1875, p. 5.

43. *Brooklyn Daily Eagle*, July 21, 1875, p. 2; "Foolhardiness," *Daily State Gazette* (Trenton, N.J.), July 31, 1875, p. 2; "Up in a Balloon," *Hartford Daily Courant*, July 21, 1875, p. 2. A Chicago paper summed up Donaldson's career: "He never noted a single scientific fact, nor made an observation of the slightest value. He had no taste for scientific inquiries, and indeed his education was too defective to permit him to appreciate the value of scientific information" ("Washington H. Donaldson," p. 2). Ironically, the *Scientific American* was more generous, stating that "though rash even to foolhardiness, he was one of the most experienced and skillful aeronauts living, and an inventor of no small genius" ("The Rumored Death of Donaldson the Aeronaut," *Scientific American* 33, no. 6 [August 7, 1875], p. 81). See also "The Death of Donaldson the Aeronaut," *Scientific American* 33, no. 10 (September 4, 1875), p. 153. In 1881 the *Boston Globe* published what it claimed was a statement made by Donaldson to "one of his most intimate friends just before he was lost in Lake Michigan." In the statement, Donaldson bluntly dismissed the existence of the easterly current, or even any science to air navigation: "A balloon is nothing more than a feather in the air. The best man in the world has no more control over it than a child has over a lion. . . . [A]eronauting is a business. We are in it to make a living. I never said there was an eastern air current. I always said I intended to see whether there was. . . . [S]o far as gaining anything of scientific value there is no likelihood of that, absolutely none. My opinion is that the air will never be navigated, in a commercial point of view, and all air navigation with gas is too expensive ever to come into common use. Flying machines or air propellers will always exist only in the minds of enthusiasts" ("A Posthumous Opinion," *Boston Globe*, September 17, 1881, p. 6).

44. Nadis, Fred. *Wonder Shows: Performing Science, Magic and Religion in America*. New Brunswick, N.J.: Rutgers University Press, 2005, p. 14. See also Schaffer, Simon. "Natural Philosophy and Public Spectacle in the Eighteenth Century," *History of Science* 21, no. 1 (March 1983), pp. 1–51. David Lindsay describes nineteenth-century America as a land of "show inventors" who presented their technological inventions to live audiences with a theatrical flair (Lindsay, *Madness in the Making*, p. 5). Iwan Rhys Morus argues for the importance of public performance in nineteenth-century British experimental science: "Exhibitionism, in some form or another, was a crucial strategy in establishing both the experimenter and his experiments" (Morus, Iwan Rhys. *Frankenstein's Children*. Princeton, N.J.: Princeton University Press, 1998, p. 155).

45. Kasson, John F. *Civilizing The Machine*. New York: Grossman Publishers, 1976, pp. 143–47. See also Marx, Leo. *The Machine in the Garden*. New York: Oxford University Press, 1964.

46. "The Disasters of Science," *Brooklyn Daily Eagle*, October 5, 1879, p. 2.

47. "Dangers of Ballooning," *Brooklyn Daily Eagle*, October 20, 1881, p. 2.

48. "Accidents to Aeronauts," *Chicago Tribune*, September 9, 1900, p. 50.

49. Raymond Williams defined "structure of feeling" as a historically distinct quality of social experience that gave a sense of a particular generation or period. The "feeling" part of the equation concerned "meanings and values as they are actively lived and felt," a "practical consciousness of a present kind, in a living and interrelating community." "Structure" implied that this "practical consciousness" might be understood as "a set, with specific internal relations, at once interlocking and in tension" (Williams, Raymond. *Marxism and Literature*. Oxford: Oxford University Press, 1977, pp. 131–32).

50. "Sails High above City," *Boston Globe*, June 7, 1907, p. 1; "Wreck in Mid Air," *Washington Post*, June 26, 1907, p. 1; "Airship Makes Flight," *Washington Post*, July 7, 1907, p. E1.

51. "Airship Makes Long Flight," *San Francisco Chronicle*, September 27, 1905, p. 3.

52. "Inquirer Airship Will Sail over City," *Philadelphia Inquirer*, October 2, 1908, p. 1.

53. See Corn, Joseph J. *The Winged Gospel*. New York: Oxford University Press, 1983, pp. 3–8.

54. Clover, Samuel Travers. "First Meet of the Man-Birds in America," *Outing Magazine* 55, no. 6 (March 1910), p. 754.

55. Oliver, Grey. "What One Sees Trying to See the Birdmen," *Los Angeles Times*, January 22, 1912, p. II13.

56. "Thousands and Tens of Thousands Thrilled by Spectacular Flights," *Colorado Springs Gazette*, August 3, 1911, p. 1; "35,000 Necks Craned to Watch Stunts in Air," *Boston Journal*, September 8, 1910, p. 6.

57. "Open Air Amusements in America," *Billboard*, March 18, 1911, p. 11.

58. Tuttle, T.T. "Aviation as a Form of Amusement," *Billboard*, March 18, 1911, p. 18; Moisant, Alfred J. "Aviation in Its Relation to Amusements," *Billboard*, March 19, 1911, p. 19.

59. Miles, Ben L. "Aviation This Season," *Billboard*, March 23, 1912, p. 28. At the end of the decade, *Billboard* was still enthusiastic about the airplane as a form of fairground entertainment, explaining that "the flights of an airplane provide a forceful form of publicity and at the same time form the source of a direct revenue, during the holding of the fair, from passenger-carrying. For the week prior to the fair the same machine can be employed for aerial distribution of advertising literature over the radius of many miles embraced in the area from which the patronage of the fair is drawn. . . . [N]o State fair or similar gathering is complete without the addition of this modern form of enterprise and entertainment" ("Aviation and the Showman," *Billboard*, August 9, 1919, p. 47).

60. By "jurisdictional dispute," I refer to Rick Altman's discussion of "crisis historiography" of new media technologies. Altman describes how new media technologies tend to be recognized initially as several "different phenomena, each overlapping with an already existing medium." Such ambiguity leads to "conflicting definitions" of the artifact, as various social forces struggle to gain control over it. Eventually, new technologies take on stable features as the result

of culturally overdetermined factors (Altman, Rick. *Silent Film Sound*. New York: Columbia University Press, 2004, pp. 19–22).

61. For an insightful discussion of the Aero Club and its relation to entertainment flying, see Pisano, Dominick A. "The Greatest Show Not on Earth: The Confrontation between Utility and Entertainment in Aviation," in Dominick A. Pisano, ed., *The Airplane in American Culture*. Ann Arbor: University of Michigan Press, 2003, pp. 44–47.

62. Birdman, "Reign of Folly in Aviation Blow to Science and Sport," *Philadelphia Inquirer*, January 8, 1911, p. 4.

63. "Chairman Leavitt Decides Not to Hold Contests of Skill under Sanction of Any Club," *Oakland (Calif.) Tribune*, February 11, 1912, p. 1. Members of the Aero Club who "make flights while rocking in their chairs in the club rooms" were asked to "step aside in favor of the progressive element who wish to demonstrate real, up-to-date aerial stunts" (p. 1).

64. "Lincoln Beachey Is Star Performer at Ascot Meet," *Albuquerque Morning Journal*, November 29, 1912, p. 5. As indications of the range of responses that air stunts could inspire, consider two press accounts of Beachey's appearances. First, the *Washington Post* wrote that Beachey's "sensational spirals, glides, darts, quick rises, and sudden drops were designed to send chills through the spinal column rather than inspire the confidence of serious-minded men who believe that aeroplanes and dirigibles will some day be of real service to humanity as a means of transportation." For this writer, aeronautics was in danger of becoming "merely a hippodrome feature like the loop-the-loop or the somersaulting automobile familiar to spectators at the circus. It robs the business of aeronautics of its standing as a science. It destroys public confidence in the future of aeronautics. It places a premium upon recklessness and discourages invention and sane experiments" ("Beachey's Decision," *Washington Post*, May 20, 1913, p. 6). On the other hand, the *Oakland (Calif.) Tribune* wrote that, although "the average person" would hardly call Beachey a scientist, every time he executed "a single or double somersault in the mid-air science has gained something" ("Beachey to Study War," *Oakland [Calif.] Tribune*, November 13, 1914, p. 1).

65. Goffman, Erving. *Forms of Talk*. Philadelphia: University of Pennsylvania Press, 1981, pp. 144–45.

66. DeCordova, Richard. *Picture Personalities*. Urbana: University of Illinois Press, 2001, p. 112.

67. Morus, *Frankenstein's Children*, p. xi.

68. Tom D. Crouch writes that "fully one-quarter of the first 400 members" of the Aero Club of St. Louis, organized in January 1907, claimed to be millionaires: "There were railroad presidents, bank and trust company executives, merchant princes, leading physicians, surgeons, and lawyers, as well as one Catholic priest" (Crouch, *Eagle Aloft*, p. 537). Pisano writes that, with the 1905 formation of the Aero Club of America, "for the first time in American history, aeronautics had an elite social group of advocates who banded together institutionally to promote it" (Pisano, "The Greatest Show Not on Earth," pp. 44–45).

69. "Beachey in Biplane Skims Niagara River," *New York Times*, June 28, 1911, p. 1.

70. Woodhouse, Henry. "Safety and Stability of the Aeroplane Today," *The Independent,* October 23, 1913, p. 168.

71. "An Aviation Expert's View of Pégoud's Air Flights Upside Down," *Current Opinion* 55, no. 6 (December 1913), p. 417.

72. "Beachey Veritable Dr. Jekyll-Hyde," *Hartford Courant,* June 9, 1914, p. 18.

73. Beachey, Lincoln. "Looping the Loop over Exposition," *San Francisco Chronicle,* March 21, 1915, p. 5.

74. Beachey, Lincoln. "The Pacemaker for Death Quits," *Washington Post,* August 31, 1913, p. MT1.

75. "Lincoln Beachey Adds Some Thrills to Exhibitions," *Dallas Morning News,* October 30, 1914, p. 1.

76. Dare, Helen. "Daring Work of the Birdmen Thrills Many Thousands," *San Francisco Chronicle,* January 8, 1911, p. 82.

77. Ibid.

78. "Air Feats Bar Beachey," *Washington Post,* October 19, 1912, p. 5.

79. "Flying Men of America," *Current Literature* 49, no. 6 (December 1910), pp. 615, 620.

80. "Nature's Latest Creation," *Springfield Sunday Republican,* July 3, 1910, p. 12. The article explained how "the eye is a feature intimately connected" with flights carried on "in the altitudes where all other senses are in abeyance and guidance is by vision alone. It is natural that concentration upon this one sense should give the birds of the air a special, ever-peering look. Just as the seaman acquires an equally distinct way of gazing" (p. 12).

81. "How MenBirds Keep Their Balance," *Lexington (Ky.) Herald,* October 31, 1909, p. 7. See also Cockerell, S. P. "Aerodrome Reflections," *The Living Age* 274 (September 28, 1912), pp. 801–2.

82. "Air Feats Bar Beachey," p. 5. Balint argues that "the performance of an acrobat is valued more highly if he does *not* use his hands; if he hangs from the trapeze by his feet or his teeth, lets go of the handlebars of the bicycle, drops the reins of his horse when standing on his back, enters the lion's cage without a whip." What is impressive "is that the individual is on his own, away from every support, relying on his own resources" (Balint, *Thrills and Regressions,* p. 28).

83. Lebow, Eileen. *Before Amelia: Women Pilots in the Early Days of Aviation.* Washington D.C.: Bassley's, 2002, p. 4.

84. Ibid.

85. Corn, *Winged Gospel,* p. 73.

86. Lebow, *Before Amelia,* p. 52.

87. On Quimby's death, see "Miss Quimby Dies in Airship Fall," *New York Times,* July 2, 1912, p. 1; Philpott, A. J. "Fall from Aeroplane," *Boston Globe,* July 2, 1912, p. 1.

88. For discussion of Ruth and Rodman Law, see "Ruth Law Ends Flight," *Baltimore Sun,* November 21, 1916, p. 1; and Meade, Norah. "Looping the Loop," *Fort Wayne (Ind.) Journal-Gazette,* June 18, 1916, p. 53.

89. Lebow, *Before Amelia,* p. 202.

90. Lebow claims that her first exhibition performance was in Providence with Lincoln Beachey (ibid., p. 203).

91. See, for example, "Down for Lack of Fuel," *New York Times,* November 20, 1916, p. 1.

92. Advertisement in *Chicago Tribune,* November 26, 1916, p. D3. See also "Many Seek Wealth in Ruth Law's Fame," *New York Times,* November 24, 1916, p. 24.

93. "Ruth Law Ends Flight," p. 1.

94. "Ruth Law Lands Here from Chicago in Record Flight," *New York Times,* November 21, 1916, p. 1.

95. Law, Ruth. "Touring by Airplane," *Outlook,* April 25, 1917, p. 738.

96. "Ruth Law Lands Here from Chicago in Record Flight," p. 1.

97. Law, Ruth. "Miss Law Tells of Her Record Flight," *New York Times,* November 20, 1916, p. 1.

98. "Ruth Law the Idol of Boys and Girls," *New York Times,* November 26, 1916, p. 14.

99. "Signal by the President Bathes Liberty Statue in Flood of Light," *New York Times,* December 3, 1916, p. 1. See also "Lights Miss Liberty," *Washington Post,* December 3, 1916, p. 1.

100. "Ruth Law Denies Tale That She Is a Spy," *New York Times,* June 8, 1918, p. 11. Also note that Law was reportedly the only woman to ever make her way into the strictly male dining room at the restaurant Maylies in New Orleans. One reporter described "Law, the aviatrix, whose boyish appearance and leather trousers, army cap and puttees got her past the lynx-eyed door-keeper" (Dunn, Harry H. "Maylie's Is No More," *New York Times,* June 13, 1920, p. 66).

101. "Aviator Says Voyages Safer Than Marriage," *Boston Journal,* May 29, 1914, p. 3.

102. "Beachey Flighty," *Oakland (Calif.) Tribune,* June 25, 1912, p. 12.

103. "How It Feels to Fly Graphically Told by an Aviator," *New York Times,* August 13, 1911, p. SM14.

104. "The Aviator on the Stage," *New York Times,* August 30, 1910, p. 7; "Astor Theatre," *New York Tribune,* December 9, 1910, p. 7; "The Aviator Is Wholesome Farce," *San Francisco Chronicle,* April 25, 1911, p. 5. In September 1910, "The Aviator" opened to a crowded house in Boston, with two boxes full of "hope-to-die" aviators ("Tremont Opens with a Birdman Play," *Boston Globe,* September 6, 1910, p. 17). See also Hamilton, Clayton. "Plays, Home-Made and Imported," *The Bookman* 32, no. 6 (February 1911), p. 594.

105. "Keith's Vaudeville," *Boston Daily Globe,* September 20, 1910, p. 11. See also "Big Airship Shown on Keith's Stage," *Boston Journal,* September 20, 1910, p. 2.

106. "Atwood in Vaudeville," *Billboard,* September 9, 1911, p. 13.

107. The *Philadelphia Inquirer* wrote that the Beachey "aerographs" provided "a wild journey through the clouds that is enough to make the spectator hold his breath for fear of falling" ("Aero Flight Film Thriller at Lyric," *Philadelphia Inquirer,* August 1, 1911, p. 4).

108. "Do You Want to Ride with Lincoln Beachey? Here's Your Opportunity," *Muscatine (Iowa) Journal,* October 24, 1911, p. 3. Howe combined Beachey's thrilling images with characteristic sounds of the "vibrations of the

engines," a combination that afforded "a delight so keen, so unadulterated and so mysterious, that it defies analysis" ("Lyman Howe's Travel Pictures," *Daily Courier* (Connellsville, Pa.), November 14, 1911, p. 3).

109. "Lyman H. Howe Gives Demonstration of the Airship Motion Pictures," *Wilkes-Barre (Pa.) Times-Leader,* September 13, 1911, p. 11. See also Wright, Wilbur. "Flying As a Sport—Its Possibilities," *Scientific American* 98, no. 9 (February 29, 1908), p. 139.

110. Musser, Charles. *High-Class Moving Pictures.* Princeton, N.J.: Princeton University Press, 1991, p. 213. Howe had previously shown films of an air race from New York to Philadelphia that featured Beachey; a dirigible balloon in 1910; and films of the Wright brothers' aeroplane. See "Howe Shows Views of Aero Contest," *Philadelphia Inquirer,* August 8, 1911, p. 4; "Howe's Pictures Please Audience," *Duluth News Tribune,* May 16, 1910, p. 12.

111. "Eugene Ely, Birdman, Death Dip Macon Fair, Lyric Picture Today," *Macon (Ga.) Daily Telegraph,* November 8, 1911, p. 6.

112. "Pictures in the Air," *Billboard,* December 16, 1911, p. 14.

113. "Olympia Aviation Film Shows Up Great," *Olympia (Wash.) Daily Recorder,* May 25, 1911, p. 1.

114. "Goes Up in Choppy Wind," *New York Tribune,* February 17, 1912, p. 7; "Coffyn in Aerial Tricks," *New York Times,* February 18, 1912, p. 7; "Vast Crowd Sees Coffyn Fly Again," *New York Times,* February 8, 1912, p. 3; "Aeroplaning for Motion Pictures 'Twixt Heaven and Earth," *Fort Worth (Tex.) Star-Telegram,* April 20, 1913, p. 18. This is the film mentioned in my discussion of thrill makers and newsreel production in chapter 2.

115. "Through the Air," *Moving Picture News* 4, no. 35 (September 2, 1911), p. 19.

116. "The Higher the Fewer," *Moving Picture World* 10, no. 5 (November 4, 1911), p. 388. In October 1911, Powers Pictures' *First Mail by Aeroplane* showed the first letter carried in an airship ("First Mail by Aeroplane," *Moving Picture News* 4, no. 41 [October 14, 1911], p. 33). Airships and airplanes were also used for film promotion. The *Moving Picture News* printed an advertisement for a Cincinnati, Ohio, company that specialized in "aerial publicity novelties" for five-cent theaters. An illustration showed the "circular distributing airship" in action, dropping a trail of circulars on the city and sporting the slogan "Star Theater, Above Them All," written across the balloon (*Moving Picture News* 4, no. 39 [September 30, 1911], p. 15). Rob King describes how the Keystone company was using a Wright model airplane in comedies in 1915 (King, Rob. *The Fun Factory.* Berkeley: University of California Press, 2009, p. 183).

117. "Beachey Takes Another Chance; This One Is with Vaudeville," *Chicago Tribune,* June 29, 1913, p. B3; "Vaudeville," *New York Times,* August 31, 1913, p. X6; "Week's Bill in Theatres," *New York Times,* September 3, 1913, p. 9.

118. Beachey, "The Pacemaker for Death Quits," p. MT1.

119. "Lincoln Beachey Falls to His Death," *San Francisco Chronicle,* March 15, 1915, p. 1. On his skywriting, see *Sky Writing Corporation of America v. Phillips Petroleum Co.; Savage v. Same,* Nos. 6411, 6412, United States Court of Appeals for the Seventh Circuit, 97 F.2d 218; 1938 U.S. App. LEXIS 3744, May 28, 1938.

120. Beachey, "The Pacemaker for Death Quits," p. MT1. See also "Beachey Will Fly No More," *New York Times,* May 13, 1913, p. 6.

121. Birdman, "Deaths Appall World; But Conquest of Air Is Future Certainty," *Philadelphia Inquirer,* July 7, 1912, p. 9.

122. Kinkade, Walter. "Birdmen Soar in Dark and Destroy the Fort," *Los Angeles Times,* January 26, 1912, p. III3; "Airmen Score in First Aerial Battle," *San Francisco Chronicle,* January 26, 1912, p. 1.

123. Like Donaldson, who performed aerial gymnastics on a portable balloon, birdmen such as Beachey were able to convert the "total space of the city" into performance space. In New York, thirty thousand people saw Beachey do his loops at Brighton Beach, with many spectators sitting on "housetops, in trees and on special stands erected by enterprising owners of abutting properties" ("Housetop Throngs Watch Beachey Flirt with Death," *New York Tribune,* May 25, 1914, p. 16). See also "Like a Big Bird over Capitol," *Boston Globe,* September 29, 1914, p. 16; "Beachey Thrills City," *Washington Post,* September 29, 1914, p. 14.

124. "Wilson Sees Beachey Fly," *New York Times,* September 29, 1914, p. 10.

125. Paris, Michael. *Winged Warfare.* Manchester: Manchester University Press, 1992, p. 124.

126. Fritzsche, Peter. *A Nation of Fliers.* Cambridge, Mass.: Harvard University Press, 1992, p. 3. For one example of permeable borders between showmanship and aeronautics, see the life of Samuel Franklin Cody, a pioneer English aeronaut as well as a stage performer known as "Captain Cody, King of the Cowboys." See Lee, Arthur Gould. *The Flying Cathedral.* London: Methuen & Co., 1965.

127. "The adventure of flying, the conquest of speed and space, the loneliness of the pilot, had all the makings of myth, and the conquest of the sky, where the gods lived and from which they descended to earth, had always held a vital place in human mythology" (Mosse, George L. *Fallen Soldiers.* Oxford: Oxford University Press, 1990, p. 119). See also Kern, Stephen. *The Culture of Time and Space, 1880–1918.* London: Weidenfeld and Nicolson, 1983, p. 242; and Goldstein, Laurence. *The Flying Machine and Modern Literature.* Bloomington: Indiana University Press, 1986, pp. 3–5.

128. Fritzsche, *Nation of Fliers,* p. 86. Virilio, *War and Cinema,* p. 70. Kennett argues that aviation's role in the Great War was, in fact, "not a major one" when compared to the exploding artillery shell, a "supreme killing device" that "blew its shards of steel across the battlefield like a deadly hail" and inflicted three wounds out of four (Kennett, Lee. *The First Air War, 1914–1918.* New York: Free Press, 1991, p. 220).

129. See Kennett, *First Air War, 1914–1918,* p. 148.

130. Virilio, *War and Cinema,* p. 70.

131. See Fritzsche, *Nation of Fliers,* p. 70; Kennett, *First Air War, 1914–1918,* pp. 72–73; Paris, *Winged Warfare,* p. 8. Contrary to popular belief, wartime flying did not place a premium on the ability to do tricky or complicated stunts. Aces like Boelcke and Richthofen disdained solo acrobatics and taught their pilots to "duck in and out of cloud fringe, to maintain the advantage of height in order to dive at the opponent, and to attack flying away from the sun

so that the sun's glare obstructed the enemy's view. Once these techniques were learned, it was not so important to be an especially skillful pilot" (Fritzsche, *Nation of Fliers*, p. 92).

132. Fritzsche, *Nation of Fliers*, p. 85. Several authors note how, of all soldiers, "pilots had the fewest mental breakdowns," a fact that some attributed to "their active sense of control over their fate" (Kern, *Culture of Time and Space, 1880–1918*, p. 297). See also Adas, Michael. *Machines as the Measure of Men*. Ithaca, N.Y.: Cornell University Press, 1989, p. 378.

133. Morrow, John H., Jr. *The Great War in the Air*. Washington, D.C.: Smithsonian Institution Press, 1993, p. 366. Morrow argues that "aerial heroes provided a much-needed, though misleading, affirmation of the importance of the individual and of youth in the slaughter of both." Morrow, John H., Jr. "Knights of the Sky," in Frans Coatzee and Marilyn Shevin-Coatzee, eds., *Authority, Identity and the Social History of the Great War*. Providence, R.I.: Berghahn Books, 1995, p. 321; Eksteins, Modris. *Rites of Spring: The Great War and the Birth of the Modern Age*. London: Bantam Press, 1989, p. 265.

134. Braudy, *From Chivalry to Terrorism*, pp. 384–85.

135. Paris, *Winged Warfare*, p. 217. See also Morrow, "Knights of the Sky," p. 315; Fritzsche, *Nation of Fliers*, p. 63; and Robertson, Linda R. *The Dream of Civilized Warfare*. Minneapolis: University of Minnesota Press, 2003, p. 276.

136. Lears, *No Place of Grace*, p. 100. See also Mosse, *Fallen Soldiers*, p. 121; Kennett, *The First Air War, 1914–1918*, p. 156; Eksteins, *Rites of Spring*, p. 265.

137. Mosse, *Fallen Soldiers*, p. 121.

138. Filene, *Him/Her/Self*, p. 148.

139. Fritzsche, *Nation of Fliers*, p. 67, Morrow, *Great War in the Air*, p. 366.

140. See Fritzsche, *Nation of Fliers*, p. 96.

141. Dyer, Richard. *Stars*. London: BFI, 1998, pp. 26, 34.

142. Morrow, "Knights of the Sky," 1995, p. 314; Kennett, *The First Air War, 1914–1918*, p. 154; Fritzsche, *Nation of Fliers*, p. 76.

143. Kennett, *The First Air War, 1914–1918*, p. 153; Fritzsche, *Nation of Fliers*, p. 66.

144. Robertson, *Dream of Civilized Warfare*, pp. 101, 112.

145. "To Wed Famous Air Ace," *Los Angeles Times*, October 25, 1918, p. II1; "Noted Ace to Wed in New York," *Los Angeles Times*, September 3, 1922, p. I10; "Capt. Eddie Rickenbacker," *Washington Post*, March 30, 1919, p. S9. Since Rickenbacker's home state was California, he was even feted by Hollywood royalty such as Roscoe "Fatty" Arbuckle and Ben Turpin at a reception at the Shrine Auditorium ("Diamond Ring Is Given Ace," *Los Angeles Times*, June 24, 1919, p. II3).

146. DeCordova, *Picture Personalities*, p. 98.

147. Law, Ruth. "If the President Said to Me, 'Go Get the Kaiser,'" *Atlanta Constitution*, July 22, 1917, p. 18. Law observed that "people generally look upon a woman as an irresolute creature, unable to kill enemies," but she concluded that this was due to culture, not biology: "Woman's training has not been along the lines of warfare. If it had been, she could react to danger with a man's decision and promptness" (p. 18).

148. "Bars Up to Miss Law," *Washington Post*, December 15, 1917, p. 11.

149. See Law's comments in "Bars Up to Miss Law," p. 11. In 1942 a female writer noted that "the first World War grounded most of the early women flyers, but as soon as it was ended they were 'up and at it' again" (Kerr, Adelaide. "Women Pilots Make Mark," *Baltimore Sun*, October 18, 1942, p. SM8).

150. Fritzsche, *Nation of Fliers*, p. 86.

151. Adas, *Machines as the Measure of Men*, pp. 369, 408. For Adas, Lindbergh rekindled "faith in the potential inherent in the combination of men and the most advanced machines—if the men were skillful and firmly in control" (p. 381). Eksteins writes that Lindbergh "seemed to satisfy two worlds," one a world of values and decorum revolving around family, religion, nature, and a moral life, and another the emerging modern age (Eksteins, *Rites of Spring*, p. 251). See also Braudy, Leo. *The Frenzy of Renown*. New York: Oxford University Press, 1986, p. 19.

152. Henry, William M. "Airplanes' Commercial Future," *Los Angeles Times*, December 1, 1918, p. VI1.

153. "Commercial fliers" were frequently referred to with monikers such as "pioneers of a new vocation" and "the true pioneers of civil flying" ("Modern Gypsies Ply Their Trade Up above the Clouds," *New York Times*, August 3, 1924, p. XX9; Flier, A. Gypsy. "Barnstorming and Making Money," *Aviation*, April 24, 1924, pp. 397–98). We might compare the "gypsy flyers" to the 1910s culture of automobile "gypsies" (see Belasco, Warren James. *Americans on the Road*. Cambridge, Mass.: MIT Press, 1979). Charles Lindbergh described his time as a barnstorming pilot in his memoir (Lindbergh, Charles. *We*. New York: Knickerbocker Press, 1928).

154. Underhill, Elliot. "In Aviation's Gypsy Days," *Atlanta Constitution*, November 24, 1929, p. J8.

155. Pendo, Stephen. *Aviation in the Cinema*. Metuchen, N.J.: Scarecrow Press, 1985, p. 43; Baxter, John. *Stunt*. Garden City, N.Y.: Doubleday, 1974, p. 120. Stuntman Dick Grace wrote that "the sudden flooding of the market with cheap war left-overs" meant that "no more were people attracted by the mere sight of a ship; indeed they hardly noticed the loops, barrel rolls, and tailspins of those more theatrically inclined. Thus we passed into another period, that of jumping from airplane to airplane" (Grace, Dick. *Squadron of Death: The True Adventures of a Movie Plane-Crasher*. Garden City, N.Y.: Doubleday, Doran and Co., 1929, p. 217).

156. "Catches Rope Ladder Dangling from Plane," *Los Angeles Times*, May 25, 1919, p. IV16.

157. "Locklear Will Flirt with Death at Dallas Fair," *Fort Worth Star-Telegram*, October 13, 1919, p. 4.

158. See, for example, "Air Devil Thrills 'Em," *Los Angeles Times*, February 2, 1920, p. H1.

159. Mars, J.C. (Bud). "Aeronautical Attractions," *Billboard*, June 28, 1919, p. 52.

160. "Huge Crowd Watches Locklear in Death-Defying Feats in Mid-Air over State Fairgrounds," *Tuscan Citizen*, November 4, 1919, p. 2.

161. Ronnie, Art. *Locklear: The Man Who Walked on Wings.* South Brunswick, N.J.: A.S. Barnes and Company, 1973, p. 146. David Lindsay notes that P.T. Barnum had a similar rule of thumb about his technological exhibitions: "They should not be perfect. Something should be slightly amiss about them, on the premise that a noisy automaton made for a noisier crowd" (Lindsay, *Madness in the Making,* p. 85).

162. I've used Dell Hymes's concept of the "breakthrough into performance" as a way to think about moments that suggest the reverse move in order to provide a sense of authenticity. See Smith, Jacob. *Vocal Tracks: Performance and Sound Media.* Berkeley: University of California Press, 2008, p. 74.

163. "Lincoln Beachey's Death," *New York Tribune,* March 16, 1915, p. 6. A Minnesota newspaper complained in 1910 that it was no longer enough to see the birdmen soar in the heavens, but audiences were demanding "a reckless risk of life" ("Flying with Death," *Duluth News Tribune,* November 25, 1910, p. 8.) A similar discourse can be found surrounding other thrill-making acts. Note, for example, that lion tamer Clyde Beatty told the press in 1937 that "you've got to keep on taking bigger and bigger risks and no matter what you did last time, you've got to do more next time. It's like a drug." Cited in Joys, Joanne Carol. "Clyde Beatty and the New York Press," *Bandwagon* 34, no. 1 (January–February 1990), p. 42.

164. "Playing Tag with Airplanes," *Kansas City Star,* June 22, 1919, p. C26.

165. See Wynne, H. Hugh. *The Motion Picture Stunt Pilots and Hollywood's Classic Aviation Movies.* Missoula, Mont.: Pictorial Histories, 1987, pp. 2–3; "Whole Aviation World Now Looking to Los Angeles," *Los Angeles Times,* September 10, 1911, p. II1; Henry, William M. "Southern California Soon to See Commercial Aircraft," *Los Angeles Times,* April 20, 1919, p. VI3. For an insightful analysis of Hollywood and aviation, see Wohl, Robert. *The Spectacle of Flight.* New Haven, Conn.: Yale University Press, 2005.

166. Henry, William M. "The New Air Capital," *Los Angles Times,* January 2, 1929, p. D26.

167. Kingsley, Grace. "Universal City Opens," *Los Angeles Times,* March 16, 1915, p. III4.

168. "Dash to Earth Ends Life and Its Hope," *Los Angeles Times,* March 17, 1915, p. II1. For a remarkable description of the opening of Universal City, including the death of Stites, see Koszarski, Richard. *An Evening's Entertainment.* Berkeley: University of California Press, 1990, pp. 6–7.

169. See "Will Fly South Today," *Los Angeles Times,* September 9, 1920, p. II5; Ronnie, *Locklear,* p. 101; "Five Air Liners Coming," *Los Angeles Times,* July 16, 1920, p. II1; "Dollar a Mile for Air Trip," *Los Angeles Times,* May 12, 1919, p. II1. Al Wilson was said to have gained fame by being "the first man to change planes in the air without employing the use of a rope ladder" ("Daring Aviator Star of Picture," *Los Angeles Times,* August 10, 1924, p. B30).

170. "Sky-Bus to Fly Today," *Los Angeles Times,* July 12, 1919, p. II8; "Whole Flock of Airplanes His," *Los Angeles Times,* June 11, 1919, p. II10.

171. Ronnie, *Locklear,* p. 131.

172. For a full plot synopsis, see ibid., pp. 126–30.

173. "Locklear and Elliott Plunge to Death While Making Night Movie," *Fort Worth Star-Telegram*, August 3, 1920, p. 1; "Dare-Devil Locklear Killed," *Los Angeles Times*, August 3, 1920, p. I1; Wynne, *Motion Picture Stunt Pilots and Hollywood's Classic Aviation Movies*, pp. 24–25.

174. "Carry Airmen Side by Side," *Los Angeles Times*, August 5, 1920, p. I18.

175. "Last Tribute Paid to Flyer Locklear," *Los Angeles Times*, August 9, 1920, p. I4.

176. The Gates Flying Circus, which appeared across the country during the 1920s, featured "Diavalo" Krantz, who would transfer between speeding planes, and Flight Commander Clyde E. "Upside Down" Pangborn, who would do loops and fly upside down ("Flying Circus Coming Back to Provide More Thrills," *Syracuse Herald*, August 12, 1926, p. 3).

177. "Law Will Curb Stunt Flyers," *Los Angeles Times*, July 21, 1923, p. H16. Locklear was among the first flyers to be issued a complaint for disturbing the peace. See "First Warrant for Reckless Flyer Issued," *San Francisco Chronicle*, April 8, 1920, p. 3.

178. "Plane Kills Two Girls," *Los Angeles Times*, July 22, 1926, p. 1. See also *The People v. Carrol B. Crossan*, Crim. No. 1492, Court of Appeal of California, Second Appellate District, Division One, 87 Cal. App. 5; 261 P. 531; 1927 Cal. App. LEXIS 42, November 17, 1927, Decided.

179. "Low Flyers under Attack," *Los Angeles Times*, March 3, 1972, p. A13. In 1920 the *Philadelphia Inquirer* wrote that "dangerous stunts by harebrained aviators flying over crowds in and near Philadelphia have stirred the resentment of citizens," leading to calls for a "municipal ordinance punishing with a fine and imprisonment anyone flying over any part of the city lower than a certain height" (Beamish, Richard J. "Seek to Restrain Stunts by Fliers over City Throngs," *Philadelphia Inquirer*, October 29, 1920, p. 1).

180. Harrington, John Walker. "Aviation's Financial Future," *Bankers* 118, no. 2 (February 1929), pp. 171–72.

181. "Locklear's Stunts Will Be Adapted to Commercial Use," *Fort Worth Star-Telegram*, October 17, 1920, p. 8.

182. Corn, *Winged Gospel*, p. 75. Pisano writes that the National Aeronautic Association (NAA), formed in 1922, led a "crusade for government regulation that culminated in the 1926 Air Commerce Act," which "spelled the end of the barnstorming era of aviation" (Pisano, "The Greatest Show Not on Earth," pp. 52–56). In 1928, the assistant secretary of the Navy told a meeting of aeronautic engineers that the best way to overcome public fear of passenger service was "to give constant evidence of safety. The people lump all this flying business together. They do not differentiate between the never-failing reliable means of air travel and the class that includes reckless and unlicensed persons flying in old and obsolete planes. When a stunt flyer . . . has a wreck—too many persons just mark it up against all air travel" ("Education of Public on Safety of Air Travel Urged by Warner," *Los Angeles Times*, September 12, 1928, p. A3). See also Driggs, Laurence. "Can Air Be Too Free?" *The Independent*, December 11, 1920, p. 357.

183. "Gypsy Flying," *Los Angeles Times*, September 12, 1927, p. A4; "Aviation Industry Rapidly Becomes Commercial Giant," *Christian Science Monitor*,

January 2, 1930, p. 20; MacCulloch, Campbell. "Taxis of the Air," *McClure's* 51, no. 6 (June 1919), p. 27.

184. Post, Augustus. "Columbus of the Air," *North American Review* 224, no. 836 (September–October 1927), pp. 357–58.

185. Ads in *Billboard*, June 7, 1919, p. 51, and June 14, 1919, p. 49.

186. Hoffman, Ellen. "Ruth Law Oliver Dies at 85, Aviatrix in the Early Days," *Washington Post*, December 4, 1970, p. B18. According to Lebow, Law read the news of her retirement in the newspaper after her husband had given the announcement without consulting her (Lebow, *Before Amelia*, p. 223).

187. Scarberry, Alma Sioux. "They've Taken the Thrill From Flying!" *Atlanta Constitution*, May 6, 1923, p. G15.

188. Gee, Henrietta. "Mistresses of the Sky," *Baltimore Sun*, October 14, 1928, p. SM13. There was, the author concluded, a disconnect between the prominence of "handsome leather flying suits" in exclusive Fifth Avenue show windows and photographs of "adventurous looking young women in flying helmets" seen in newspapers, on the one hand, and the "cold, impersonal statistics" that showed that the Department of Commerce had only licensed eighteen female pilots, on the other. "These chic flying suits remind experts of the fancy suits of bathing beauties who only lounge upon the beach, and the firm-looking girls pictured in flying helmets suggest diving girls who pose on the spring board without ever making a real plunge" (p. SM13).

189. Corn, *Winged Gospel*, pp. 72–80.

190. Ibid., p. 89. On stewardesses, see also Kolm, Suzanne. "Who Says It's a Man's World? Women's Work and Travel in the First Decades of Flight," in Dominick A. Pisano, ed., *The Airplane in American Culture*. Ann Arbor: University of Michigan Press, 2003, pp. 147–64.

191. Sandifer, Thaddeus Nelson. "Twin Miracles: Radio and Aviation," *Outlook* 134, no. 9 (July 18, 1923), p. 418.

192. Douglas, Susan J. *Inventing American Broadcasting*. Baltimore, Md.: Johns Hopkins University Press, 1987, p. 240.

193. Ibid., p. 290.

194. Hillman, W. "Flying Today and Tomorrow," *Living Age* 327 (December 19, 1925), p. 630. See also Hambridge, Gove. "How Safe Is Flying?" *Forum and Century* 84, no. 3 (September 1930), p. 171; Mingos, Howard. "Making Flying Safe," *North American Review* 230, no. 4 (October 1930), p. 470; and Smith, Willard Hart. "Putting the Aeroplane to Work," *Forum* 61, no. 3 (March 1919), p. 321.

195. Underhill, "In Aviation's Gypsy Days," p. J8. See also Andrews, Marshall. "Showmen of the Early Flying Days," *Washington Post*, November 17, 1929, p. SM1.

196. The *Los Angeles Times* wrote that Hollywood stunt pilots had to make an application to the United States Department of Commerce for a permit to do certain stunts (Delapp, Terrel. "Aviation," *Los Angeles Times*, August 18, 1929, p. E6). On Venice Beach flyers and newsreels, see Wynne, *Motion Picture Stunt Pilots and Hollywood's Classic Aviation Movies*, p. 17; Baxter, *Stunt*, p. 121.

197. Ronnie, *Locklear*, p. 13.

198. "Straight from the Studios," *Washington Post*, December 29, 1935, p. M2.

199. DeBauche, Leslie Midkiff. *Reel Patriotism*. Madison: University of Wisconsin Press, 1997, p. 158. See also Sklar, Robert. *Film: An International History*. New York: Harry N. Abrams, 1993, p. 75; and Bordwell, David, and Kristin Thompson. *Film History*. Boston: McGraw-Hill, 2003, pp. 56–57.

200. Eksteins, *Rites of Spring*, p. 262.

201. See, for example, Ponce De Leon, Charles L. "The Man Nobody Knows: Charles A. Lindbergh and the Culture of Celebrity," in Dominick A. Pisano, ed., *The Airplane in American Culture*. Ann Arbor: University of Michigan Press, 2003.

202. See Eksteins, *Rites of Spring*, p. 261. See also DeBauche, *Reel Patriotism*, p. 178.

203. DeBauche, *Reel Patriotism*, p. 173.

204. Saunders, John Monk. "The War-in-the-Air," *New York Times*, July 31, 1927, p. X3. For more on Saunders and the making of *Wings*, see Wohl, *Spectacle of Flight*, pp. 121–22.

205. Wellman, William, Jr. *The Man and His Wings*. Westport, Conn.: Praeger, 2006, pp. 25, 61; Brownlow, Kevin. *The Parade's Gone By*. London: Secker and Warburg, 1968, pp. 169–70; "The Spectacular Career of a Director of Spectacles," *Washington Post*, August 12, 1928, p. A2; Wellman, William A. *A Short Time for Insanity*. New York: Hawthorn Books, 1974, p. 29; Schickel, Richard. *The Men Who Made the Movies*. London: Elm Tree Books, 1977, pp. 195–99.

206. Wellman, *A Short Time for Insanity*, p. 171.

207. "Some Difficulties of a Producer," *New York Times*, July 10, 1927, p. X3.

208. A sense of motion was also created by shooting the American planes taking off in the late afternoon, which gave the cameras "full benefit of long shadows from the trees," and by adding a line of marching troops and cars driving on the road at the side of the flying field ("Poet Puts Rhythm into Film Epic," *New York Times*, November 20, 1927, p. X6).

209. "Some Difficulties of a Producer," p. X3.

210. "Poet Puts Rhythm into Film Epic," p. X6. See also "Salient Facts Pertaining to Airplane Epic," *Washington Post*, January 27, 1929, p. F2.

211. On the first Academy of Motion Picture Arts and Sciences Merit Awards, see Koszarski, *An Evening's Entertainment*, pp. 316–17.

212. Flint, Ralph. "Wings, Epic New Paramount Picture," *Christian Science Monitor*, October 4, 1927, p. 10.

213. Schallert, Edwin. "Air Spectacle Thrills Throng," *Los Angeles Times*, January 17, 1928, p. A11; Tinee, Mae. "Wings Is Brilliant, Poignant, and in Spots 'Most Too Real," *Chicago Tribune*, November 1, 1927, p. 37.

214. Schallert, "Air Spectacle Thrills Throng," p. A11.

215. Several reviews noted how *Dawn Patrol* broke with tradition by focusing entirely on men: "There is no 'Paris leave' when war weary aviators make merry in gay cabarets to relieve the strain of their duty. No gay companions to help them forget. There isn't a woman in the picture, not even the usual

motherly French inn-keeper" ("Dawn Patrol, Picture of War Flyers," *Hartford Courant*, August 2, 1930, p. 18; "Dawn Patrol Remains at the Strand," *Hartford Courant*, August 10, 1930, p. D2).

216. DeBauche, *Reel Patriotism*, p. 174.

217. Goff, Jill Jividen. "Singling Out John Monk Saunders: Hemingway's Thoughts on an Imitator," *Hemingway Review* 28, no. 1 (Fall 2008), p. 139. Saunders might be seen as part of "a group of writers associated with the youth culture of the 1920s" who "advocated styles of manliness that were heavily influenced by the underworld styles of masculinity that they openly admired," with Hemingway being the best example (White, Kevin. *The First Sexual Revolution*. New York: New York University Press, 1993, p. 51). A review of the play based on Saunders's novel noted "the superficial and not too faint resemblance of Mr. Saunders's triple-play post-war epic to the style of Ernest Hemingway. . . . [T]he resemblance stops short with a great deal of disconnected dialogue, a surfeit of nervous drinking, some two acts and fifteen scenes that wander from Paris to Portugal and cry on their sleeves as they go." Summing up, the reviewer wrote that the play was mostly "noise and dullness, suggesting that if the sun also rises, it also sets, and, in this case, not gently" ("Nikki Reappears, with Music," *New York Times*, September 30, 1931, p. 34).

218. See Messent, Peter. *Ernest Hemingway*. London: Macmillan Press, 1992, p. 97.

219. "Spectacular Crash Will Be Shown in Film," *Los Angeles Times*, May 24, 1931, p. 24. In Klaus Theweleit's famous study of the German Freikorps, the soldiers had expressed fantasies of a bulletlike "eruption outward" in the moment of attack: "Ultimately, they themselves become the shots spreading outward, bullets hurtling from the military machine toward their body-targets. At these moments, they anticipate the most intense possible sensation" (Theweleit, Klaus. *Male Fantasies, Volume II*. Cambridge: Polity Press, 1989, p. 181).

220. Hall, Mordaunt. "Fredric March, Jack Oakie and Sir Guy Standing in a Drama of World War Air-Fighting," *New York Times*, May 13, 1933, p. 16.

221. Scott, John. "Screen Continues Air War," *Los Angeles Times*, May 19, 1933, p. A7.

222. Scott, John. "Suicide Gang Inspires Film," *Los Angeles Times*, April 17, 1932, p. B15.

223. Grace, *Squadron of Death*, p. 12.

224. Ibid., pp. 2, 40. We might notice a lineage here, from Washington Donaldson and his photographer father to Dick Grace and even to Charles Lindbergh, whose father was a farm owner and congressman, and who in college "turned his imagination against the culture of literacy he identified with his father and the whole nineteenth century" (Goldstein, *Flying Machine and Modern Literature*, p. 101).

225. Grace, *Squadron of Death*, p. 46.

226. Ross, Murray. *Stars and Strikes*. New York: Columbia University Press, 1941, p. 65.

227. Ibid., pp. 86–87. Clark writes that by the mid-1920s the studios maintained an open shop policy, but they had begun to negotiate with craft unions

and make concessions "in the hopes of appeasing the demands of talent groups while forestalling their unionization" (Clark, Danae. *Negotiating Hollywood*. Minneapolis: University of Minnesota Press, 1995, p. 32). On labor segmentation, see Gordon, David M., Richard Edwards, and Michael Reich. *Segmented Work, Divided Workers*. Cambridge: Cambridge University Press, 1982, p. 215.

228. Grace, *Squadron of Death*, p. 178.

229. Pendo, *Aviation in the Cinema*, pp. 44–46; Wynne, *Motion Picture Stunt Pilots and Hollywood's Classic Aviation Movies*, p. 38; Farmer, James H. *Celluloid Wings: The Impact of Movies on Aviation*. Blue Ridge Summit, Penn.: Tab Books, 1984, p. 55; Kelly, Shawna. *Aviators in Early Hollywood*. Charleston, S.C.: Arcadia Publishing, 2008, pp. 8–9; Hylan, Dick. "Risking Life and Limb," *Photoplay*, November 1927, p. 125; Baxter, *Stunt*, p. 85.

230. *John G. Montijo v. Samuel Goldwyn, Inc. of California*, Civ. No. 356, Court of Appeal of California, Fourth Appellate District, 113 Cal. App. 57; 297 P. 949; 1931 Cal. App. LEXIS 777, March 28, 1931, Decided; "Stunt Flyer Decision Upheld," *Los Angeles Times*, March 29, 1931, p. 8.

231. As one author put it in 1945, "Hollywood stunt men are a law unto themselves. With no union and no agents, they have no union dues or agents' fees to pay." They "are called directly by the company needing them, not—like extras—by Central Casting" (Wilson, Elizabeth. "Hollywood Hardpans," *Liberty*, October 20, 1945, p. 30).

232. Grace, *Squadron of Death*, pp. 175–76.

233. *Lost Squadron* press kit, from Cinema Pressbooks of the Major Hollywood Studios, Primary Source Microfilm, p. 13.

234. "Behind Scenes Story Told at Orpheum Screen," *Los Angeles Times*, April 20, 1932, p. 7. See also Scott, "Suicide Gang Inspires Film," p. B15.

235. Doherty, Thomas. *Pre-Code Hollywood*. New York: Columbia University Press, 1999, pp. 16, 41–43. See also Balio, Tino. *Grand Design*. Berkeley: University of California Press, 1993, p. 13.

236. Grace, Dick. *The Lost Squadron*. New York: Grosset & Dunlap, 1931, p. 51. A similar narrative trope can be found in several early slapstick comedies. In Mack Sennett's *The Daredevil* (1923) Ben Turpin plays a stunt double for an effete actor. At one point Turpin says, "I take the risks, he takes the credit." In the Larry Semon comedy *The Stunt Man* (1927), we see the stunt performer doubling for a female star in drag, as well as witness tensions with an overbearing director named Seesal Sawmille. Part of Grace's critique of stars had to do with questions of the actor's masculinity: "I noticed a number of men who got in wore ridiculous make-ups. They had rouge on their lips and black around the eyes. The majority had their faces covered with a rather dark pink grease paint. I had none of this paraphernalia" (p. 56).

237. Ibid., p. 45.

238. Nonetheless, when we see Von Furst's insignia on the planes, they closely resemble the logos that DeMille put on all of his planes and that were often used in Hollywood air pictures.

239. Grace, *Lost Squadron*, pp. 53–54.

240. Ibid., pp. 95–97.

241. Ibid., p. 179. See also Grace's anecdote on pp. 190–91.

242. Clark, Danae. *Negotiating Hollywood*. Minneapolis: University of Minnesota Press, 1995, pp. 91–101.

243. Grace, *Squadron of Death*, pp. 197–98. In an article on the film, *Popular Mechanics* wrote that "never before had such crash scenes been attempted; even the producers were doubtful whether they could be consummated successfully" (Jamieson, Leland S. "Crashes Made to Order," *Popular Mechanics*, November 1928, p. 805). On sound in *Wings*, see Crafton, Donald. *The Talkies*. Berkeley: University of California Press, 1999, pp. 134–35; and Farmer, *Celluloid Wings*, p. 40. Shawna Kelly claims *Lost Squadron* makes reference to the unresolved death of stunt flyer B.H. "Daredevil" DeLay (Kelly, *Aviators in Early Hollywood*, pp. 117–19).

244. Grace, *Squadron of Death*, p. 221. The provisions of Grace's RKO contract for *Lost Squadron* included "compensation while he is incapacitated and full hospital attention during that time. Also he is provided with a rescue crew of eight . . . [to] extricate Grace from his wrecked and burning ship within thirty seconds" (*Lost Squadron* press kit, p. 11).

245. Bennett, F. B. "Those Who Do The 'Stunts' in the Movies," *New York Tribune*, December 31, 1916, p. D7.

246. Rose, Bob. "Walking with Death for a Living," *Los Angeles Times*, September 30, 1934, p. 18. Grace complained that the public thought that "all thrills are faked or double-printed." "They're certainly getting clever now! Wasn't that a beautiful fake?" The audience had just witnessed a net fall which broke the pelvic bone of a stunt man" (Grace, *Squadron of Death*, pp. 190, 80). On Universal, see Rickitt, Richard. *Special Effects: The History and Technique*. New York: Billboard Books, 2000, pp. 21, 212. See also Farmer, *Celluloid Wings*, pp. 78–79; Jamieson, "Crashes Made to Order," p. 809.

247. Both of these films were written by former military flyer Frank Wead, who also wrote the screenplays for the Hollywood air pictures *Dirigible* (1931) and *Test Pilot* (1938). See "Good Flying Weather," *Wall Street Journal*, April 13, 1935, p. 9; "Mr. Wead Comes Out of the Clouds," *New York Times*, May 5, 1935, p. X5. It is also worth noting that director Howard Hawks's brother Kenneth died during an airplane crash off Redondo Beach while shooting an air picture for Fox Studios. Kenneth Hawks had been a flyer in the Army during the war ("Ten Air Deaths Criticized," *Los Angeles Times*, January 9, 1930, p. A1; "Death Directs Filming of Episode above Ocean," *Los Angeles Times*, January 3, 1930, p. 2).

248. The promotion of these films demonstrates the extent to which synergies had developed between movie theaters, commercial airports, and government airmail. Press kits suggested putting on an "Air Week" with the cooperation of local airlines, airports, and political officials. Commercial airlines would plug the film, audiences would be bused for special tours of the airport, and the post office could be urged to start a "special drive for the air mail." The space of the movie theater was to be decked in the accoutrements of the airport, with "wind-socks" from the local airport flying over the theater, a searchlight from the local landing field or Army post set up on the marquee, and the lobby decorated with airplane models, barometers, visibility charts, and beacon lights (*Ceiling Zero* press

kit, from Cinema Pressbooks of the Major Hollywood Studios, Primary Source Microfilm, pp. 6, 7, 27). Similar promotional advice can be found in the press kit for First National's *Central Airport* (1933), directed by Wellman. RKO urged theaters showing *Air Mail* to hire well-known aviators to attend screenings and give talks on flying, as well as to organize model plane contests to appeal to the kids who were "the backbone of the support of air magazines today" ("Thrills and Love Interest Make 'Air Mail' One to Draw Crowds to Your B.O.," *RKO Now*, November 12, 1932, p. 5). Joseph Corn describes how model airplanes became a national craze for American youth between the late 1920s and the Second World War, when model-building clubs such as the Junior Birdmen of America spread "airmindedness" (Corn, *Winged Gospel*, pp. 114–16).

249. Hawks was also a flyer in World War I. See Schickel, *Men Who Made the Movies*, p. 104. For a fascinating discussion of the Production Code Administration's concerns about the film, see Pisano, "The Greatest Show Not on Earth," pp. 60–63.

250. The suicide trope can be found in a Hollywood film from this era depicting a female aviator. Dorothy Arzner's *Christopher Strong* (1933) features Katharine Hepburn as Lady Cynthia Darrington, an aristocratic aviatrix. As an index of cultural assumptions that aviation was not compatible with femininity, we quickly learn that Darrington's love of flying has meant that she has never fulfilled heterosexual female roles: she has never been married and never had a love affair, choosing instead the "lonely life" of the aviator. She falls in love with Sir Christopher Strong (Colin Clive), even though he is happily married to his wife, Lady Elaine (Billie Burke). The two nonetheless have an affair, with Strong meeting her as she completes a flight around the world. Her flight is depicted in a stunning montage of press coverage and aerial views that echoes the Barnum balloon's combination of publicity and views from the sky. When she learns that she is pregnant, Darrington sees no way out, and in another stunning montage we see her airplane climb as she breaks an altitude record, intercalated with flashbacks to her affair with Strong. She removes her oxygen mask and passes out as the plane plummets to the earth. When we compare *Christopher Strong* to a film like *The Eagle and the Hawk*, we might say that a similar kind of critique is being leveled through the aviator, not of hollow wartime rhetoric, but of the restrictions of normative heterosexual romance and marriage. Furthermore, if Dizzy's suicide in *Ceiling Zero* conceded that there was no place for the barnstorming birdman in the era of commercial aviation, so Cynthia Darrington's concedes to a similar inability to find a place for the female aviatrix in the future of aviation.

251. Wohl, *Spectacle of Flight*, p. 140.

252. Pisano, "The Greatest Show Not on Earth," p. 59.

253. Morin, Edgar. *The Cinema, or the Imaginary Man*. Minneapolis: University of Minnesota Press, 2005 (1956), pp. 5–7.

254. Ibid., p. 11.

CONCLUSION

1. Rose, Bob. "Walking with Death For a Living," *Los Angeles Times*, September 30, 1934, p. 18.

2. "Shoot for Big Box Office with 'Lucky Devils,'" *RKO Now,* January 15, 1933, pp. 4–5.

3. Clark, Danae. *Negotiating Hollywood.* Minneapolis: University of Minnesota Press, 1995, pp. 4–5.

4. Gunning, Tom. "Now You See It, Now You Don't: The Temporality of the Cinema of Attractions," *Velvet Light Trap* 32 (Fall 1993), pp. 3–12; Gunning, Tom. "The Cinema of Attractions: Early Film, Its Spectator and the Avant-garde," in Thomas Elsaesser, ed., *Early Cinema: Space, Frame, Narrative.* London: BFI, 1990, pp. 56–62. The investigation of "attractions" has taken performance as its focus in work on the comedic gag, a form with close connections to early stunt performance. See Gunning, Tom. "Crazy Machines in the Garden of Forking Paths: Mischief Gags and the Origins of Film Comedy," in Kristina Karnick and Henry Jenkins, eds., *Classical Hollywood Comedy.* New York: Routledge, 1995; Jenkins, Henry. *What Made Pistachio Nuts?* New York: Columbia University Press, 1992; and Smith, Jacob. "Seeing Double: Stunt Performance and Masculinity," *Journal of Film and Video* 56, no. 3 (Fall 2004), pp. 35–53.

5. Casetti, Francesco. *Eye of the Century.* New York: Columbia University Press, 2008, pp. 137, 140.

6. Hansen writes that the cinema's "voracious intertextuality," its dependence upon popular entertainments and "the fragments of bourgeois culture," and its "indiscriminate appeal to as yet untapped audiences" produced an "unstable mixture" of old and new cultural practices, as well as the conditions for an "alternative public sphere." The "alternative potential" of the first decades of the Hollywood cinema was, for Hansen, an "accidental effect of overlapping types of public sphere, of 'nonsynchronous' layers of cultural organization" (Hansen, Miriam. *Babel and Babylon: Spectatorship in American Silent Film.* Cambridge, Mass.: Harvard University Press, 1991, pp. 92–93).

7. Bakhtin, M.M. *The Dialogic Imagination.* Austin: University of Texas Press, 1981, pp. 262–63, 291.

8. King, Rob. *The Fun Factory.* Berkeley: University of California Press, 2009.

9. See Bauman, Richard. *A World of Others' Words.* Oxford: Blackwell, 2004, pp. 150–51.

10. Hall, Stuart. "Notes on Deconstructing 'The Popular,'" in Raphael Samuel, ed., *People's History and Socialist Theory.* London: Routledge, 1981.

11. Keathley, Christian. *Cinephilia and History, or The Wind in the Trees.* Bloomington: Indiana University Press, 2006.

12. Williams, Raymond. *Television: Technology and Cultural Form.* Hanover, N.H.: Wesleyan University Press, 1992 (1974), p. 20.

13. Spigel, Lynn. "Introduction," in Raymond Williams, *Television: Technology and Cultural Form.* Hanover, N.H.: Wesleyan University Press, 1992 (1974), pp. xxi–xxii.

14. See Singer, Ben. *Melodrama and Modernity.* New York: Columbia University Press, 2001, p. 21.

15. See ibid., pp. 30–32. See also Susman, Warren. *Culture as History.* New York: Pantheon, 1984; and Marchand, Roland. *Advertising the American Dream.* Berkeley: University of California Press, 1985, p. 357.

16. Simmel, Georg. *On Individuality and Social Forms.* Chicago: University of Chicago Press, 1971, pp. 337–38.

17. Ibid., p. 338. Simmel writes that "individuality in being and action generally increases to the degree that the social circle encompassing the individual expands" (p. 252).

18. See Kimmel, Michael. *Manhood in America.* New York: Free Press, 1996, p. 5.

19. Lears, T.J. Jackson. *No Place of Grace.* New York: Pantheon Books, 1981, p. 60.

20. Roach, Joseph. *Cities of the Dead: Circum-Atlantic Performance.* New York: Columbia University Press, 1996, pp. 25–26.

21. Lowenthal, Leo. *Literature, Popular Culture, and Society.* Palo Alto, Calif.: Pacific Books, 1961, p. 115.

22. Comolli, Jean-Louis (trans. Annette Michelson). "Mechanical Bodies, Ever More Heavenly," *October* 83 (Winter 1998), p. 19. One of Comolli's answers has to do with the fact that cinema, as machine, has tended to be fascinated with other machines.

23. On folklife festivals and "restored" behavior, see Bauman, Richard, Patricia Sawin, and Inta Gale Carpenter, *Reflections on the Folklife Festival.* Bloomington: Folklore Institute, Indiana University, 1992, p. 28; Schechner, Richard. "Restoration of Behavior," *Studies in Visual Communication* 7, no. 3 (1981), pp. 2–45.

24. Kimmel, *Manhood in America,* pp. 119–20. See also Gilmore, David. *Manhood in the Making.* New Haven, Conn.: Yale University Press, 1990, p. 11.

25. Gilmore, *Manhood in the Making.* pp. 223–24.

26. Ibid., p. 121.

27. See Nash, Roderick. "Sports Heroes of the 1920s," in Steven A. Riess, ed., *Major Problems in American Sports History.* Boston: Houghton Mifflin, 1997, p. 324.

28. "100 Ways of Breaking Your Neck," *Chicago Tribune,* April 16, 1905, p. H3.

29. "How Life and Limb Are Risked to Thrill Public," *Atlanta Constitution,* August 21, 1904, p. D7.

30. See Rabinovitz, Lauren. *For the Love of Pleasure.* New Brunswick, N.J.: Rutgers University Press, 1998; Rosenzweig, Roy. *Eight Hours for What We Will.* Cambridge: Cambridge University Press, 1983, p. 212; Hansen, *Babel and Babylon,* p. 62.

31. Bean, Jennifer M. "Technologies of Early Stardom and the Extraordinary Body," *Camera Obscura* 16, no. 3 (2001).

32. Singer, *Melodrama and Modernity,* p. 226.

33. Indeed, Goffman includes actors and live entertainers in his list of persons who voluntarily took practical gambles (Goffman, Erving. *Interaction Ritual.* New York: Pantheon Books, 1967, p. 173).

34. Harvey Parry papers, box 1, folder 1, Biographical data—1950–1985. See also, Flaherty, Vincent. "Risks—For a Big Payoff," *Los Angeles Herald-Examiner,* June 13, 1971, pp. 22–24.

35. "Brodie and His Sensations," *New York Herald,* July 25, 1886, p. 11.

Further Reading

CELEBRITY CULTURE

Baker, Thomas N. *Sentiment and Celebrity*. New York: Oxford University Press, 1999.

Bean, Jennifer M. "Technologies of Early Stardom and the Extraordinary Body." *Camera Obscura* 16, no. 3 (2001).

Becker, Christine. *It's the Pictures That Got Small*. Middletown, Conn.: Wesleyan University Press, 2009.

Braudy, Leo. *The Frenzy of Renown*. New York: Oxford University Press, 1986.

deCordova, Richard. *Picture Personalities*. Urbana: University of Illinois Press, 2001.

Dyer, Richard. *Stars*. London: BFI, 1998.

Gamson, Joshua. *Claims to Fame: Celebrity in Contemporary America*. Berkeley: University of California Press, 1994.

Greene, Theodore P. *America's Heroes*. New York: Oxford University Press, 1970.

Marshall, P. David. *Celebrity and Power*. Minneapolis: University of Minnesota Press, 1997.

Ponce de Leon, Charles. *Self-Exposure*. Chapel Hill: University of North Carolina Press, 2001.

Rojek, Chris. *Celebrity*. London: Reaktion, 2001.

Stacey, Jackie. *Star Gazing: Hollywood Cinema and Female Spectatorship*. London: Routledge, 1994.

Susman, Warren I. *Culture as History.* Washington, D.C.: Smithsonian Institution Press, 2003 (1973).

Turner, Graeme. *Understanding Celebrity.* London: Sage Publications, 2004.

MEDIA AND PERFORMANCE

Baron, Cynthia, and Sharon Marie Carnicke. *Reframing Screen Performance.* Ann Arbor: University of Michigan Press, 2008.

Bauman, Richard. *A World of Others' Words.* Oxford: Blackwell, 2004.

Baxter, John. *Stunt.* Garden City, N.Y.: Doubleday, 1974.

Bouissac, Paul. *Circus and Culture.* Bloomington: Indiana University Press, 1976.

Canutt, Yakima. *Stunt Man.* Norman: University of Oklahoma Press, 1979.

Goffman, Erving. *Interaction Ritual.* New York: Pantheon, 1967.

Harrison-Pepper, Sally. *Drawing a Circle in the Square.* Jackson: University Press of Mississippi, 1990.

Kirshenblatt-Gimblett, Barbara. "Objects of Ethnography." In *Exhibiting Cultures,* ed. Ivan Karp and Steven D. Lavine. Washington, D.C.: Smithsonian Institution Press, 1991.

Naremore, James. *Acting in the Cinema.* Berkeley: University of California Press, 1988.

Roach, Joseph. *Cities of the Dead: Circum-Atlantic Performance.* New York: Columbia University Press, 1996.

Schechner, Richard. *Performance Theory.* London: Routledge, 1988.

Smith, Jacob. *Vocal Tracks: Performance and Sound Media.* Berkeley: University of California Press, 2008.

Volosinov, V.N. *Marxism and the Philosophy of Language.* Cambridge, Mass.: Harvard University Press, 1973.

MASCULINITY

Barker-Benfield, G.J. *The Horrors of the Half-Known Life.* New York: Harper Colophon, 1976.

Bederman, Gail. *Manliness and Civilization.* Chicago; University of Chicago Press, 1995.

Braudy, Leo. *From Chivalry to Terrorism.* New York: Vintage Books, 2005.

Filene, Peter G. *Him/Her/Self.* Baltimore, Md.: Johns Hopkins University Press, 1998.

Gilmore, David. *Manhood in the Making.* New Haven, Conn.: Yale University Press, 1990.

Hilkey, Judy. *Character Is Capital.* Chapel Hill: University of North Carolina Press, 1997.

Kasson, John F. *Houdini, Tarzan, and the Perfect Man.* New York: Hill and Wang, 2001.

Kimmel, Michael. *Manhood in America.* New York: Free Press, 1996.

Mosse, George L. *Fallen Soldiers.* Oxford: Oxford University Press, 1990.

Rotundo, E. Anthony. *American Manhood.* New York: Basic Books, 1993.

Streible, Dan. *Fight Pictures*. Berkeley: University of California Press, 2008.

White, Kevin. *The First Sexual Revolution*. New York: New York University Press, 1993.

HISTORY OF AMERICAN POPULAR CULTURE

Assael, Brenda. *The Circus and Victorian Society*. Charlottesville: University of Virginia Press, 2005.

Bowser, Eileen. *The Transformation of Cinema*. Berkeley: University of California Press, 1994.

Clark, Danae. *Negotiating Hollywood*. Minneapolis: University of Minnesota Press, 1995.

Culhane, John. *The American Circus*. New York: Henry Holt and Co., 1990.

Davis, Janet M. *The Circus Age*. Chapel Hill: University of North Carolina Press, 2002.

DeBauche, Leslie Midkiff. *Reel Patriotism*. Madison: University of Wisconsin Press, 1997.

Dennett, Andrea Stulman. *Weird Wonderful: The Dime Museum in America*. New York: New York University Press, 1997.

Denning, Michael. *Mechanic Accents*. London: Verso, 1987.

Gorn, Elliot J. *The Manly Art*. Ithaca, N.Y.: Cornell University Press, 1986.

Hansen, Miriam. *Babel and Babylon: Spectatorship in American Silent Film*. Cambridge, Mass.: Harvard University Press, 1991.

Johnson, Paul E. *Sam Patch: The Famous Jumper*. New York: Hill and Wang, 2003.

Lears, T. J. Jackson *No Place of Grace*. New York: Pantheon Books, 1981.

Musser, Charles. *The Emergence of Cinema*. Berkeley: University of California Press, 1994.

Nadis, Fred. *Wonder Shows: Performing Science, Magic, and Religion in America*. New Brunswick, N.J.: Rutgers University Press, 2005.

Peiss, Kathy. *Cheap Amusements: Working Women and Leisure in Turn-of-the-Century New York*. Philadelphia: Temple University Press, 1986.

Rosenzweig, Roy. *Eight Hours for What We Will*. Cambridge: Cambridge University Press, 1983.

Singer, Ben. *Melodrama and Modernity*. New York: Columbia University Press, 2001.

Wilentz, Sean. *Chants Democratic*. Oxford: Oxford University Press, 2004 (1984).

Index

TEXT
10/13 Sabon Open Type

DISPLAY
Sabon Open Type

COMPOSITOR
BookComp, Inc.

PRINTER AND BINDER
IBT Global

CPSIA information can be obtained
at www.ICGtesting.com
Printed in the USA
FSOW01n0041041115
12929FS